Boardsailing

Oregon

Boardsailing

Oregon

A Guide to the

Best Windsurfing

in Oregon

Featuring the Columbia River Gorge

John R. LaRiviere

Menasha Ridge Press

Birmingham, Alabama

Printed in the United States of America
Published by Menasha Ridge Press
First edition, first printing

Library of Congress Cataloging-in-Publication Data
LaRiviere, John R.
    Boardsailing Oregon : a guide to the best windsurfing in Oregon : featuring the
columbia River Gorge / By John LaRiviere.
        p.   cm.
    Includes bibliographical references.
    ISBN 0-89732-088-3
    1. Windsurfing – Oregon – Guide-books. 2. Windsurfing – Columbia River Gorge
(Or. and Wash.) – Guide-books. 3. Columbia River Gorge (Or. and Wash.) – Description and Travel – Guide-books. 4. Oregon – Description and travel – 1981 – Guide-
books. I. Title. II. Title: Guide to the best windsurfing in Oregon.
GV811.63.W56L37 1990
797.3'3'0970954-dc20   89-37748
                                                                              CIP

Menasha Ridge Press
Post Office Box 59257
Birmingham, Alabama, 35259-9257

To Michael

Table of Contents

List of Maps   xi
List of Illustrations   xv
Acknowledgments   xvii
Introduction   xix
General Location Map   xxii-xxiii

Region One: The Columbia River and "the Gorge"   1

Jones Beach   11
Rooster Rock State Park   15
Dalton Point   19
Cascade Locks Marine Park   21
Stevenson, Washington   25
Home Valley Park, Washington   29
Drano Lake, Washington   33
"Swell City," Washington   35
The Hatchery, Washington   37
Hood Vista Sailpark, Washington   39
Hood River   41
Koberg Beach   47
Bingen Marina, Washington   49
Mosier Beach   53
Mayer State Park, East Rowena   55
Doug's Beach, Washington   59
Boat Basin Beach, The Dalles   61
Horsethief Lake, Washington   65
Avery Park, Washington   67
Celilo Park   69
Maryhill State Park, Washington   73
Giles French Park, Rufus   77

Snell Park, Arlington   79
Roosevelt Park, Washington   81
Three Mile Canyon   83
Boardman Marine Park   85
Crow Butte State Park, Washington   87
Irrigon   91
Plymouth Park, Washington   93
Marine Park, Umatilla   95
McNary Beach, Umatilla   99

Region Two: The Oregon Coast   103

Fort Stevens State Park   111
Youngs Bay   115
Seaside Beach   117
Tolovana Beach   121
Manzanita Beach   123
Nehalem Bay State Park   127
Tillamook Bay   131
Oceanside Beach   135
Netarts Bay   137
Tierra Del Mar   141
Pacific City   143
Devil's Lake   147
D-River Wayside   149
Siletz Bay   151
Beverly Beach   155
Agate Beach   157
Yaquina Bay   159
South Beach   163
Alsea Bay   167
Neptune Beach State Park   169
Heceta Beach   173
Siuslaw Bay   175
South Jetty, Siuslaw Bay   179

Woahink Lake   181
Siltcoos Lake   185
Empire, Coos Bay   187
Whiskey Run Beach, Seven Devils Wayside   191
Coquille Bay   195
Face Rock Wayside   197
Floras Lake   199
Paradise Point   203
Port Orford   205
Cape Sebastian   207
Pistol River   211

Region Three: Interstate 5 Corridor   213

Foster Reservoir   217
Fern Ridge Lake   221
Dorena Lake   223
Cottage Grove Lake   227
Lost Creek Reservoir   229
Emigrant Lake   233
Howard Prairie Reservoir   235

Region Four: The Cascade Lakes   239

Lost Lake   243
Clear Lake   247
Timothy Lake   249
Detroit Lake   253
Suttle Lake   255
Elk Lake   259
Cultus Lake   261
Wickiup Reservoir   265
Waldo Lake   269
Odell Lake   271
Crescent Lake   275
Diamond Lake   277

Region Five: The Desert Lakes and Points East   281

Haystack Reservoir   285
Ochoco Reservoir   289
Agency Lake   291
Upper Klamath Lake   295

Appendix A: Boardsailing Shops   301
Appendix B: "Sailboarding Oregon Safely," Advice
             from the Oregon State Marine Board   306
Appendix C: Travel Information   310

Bibliography   317

Maps

General Location Map   xxii-xxiii

Region One: The Columbia River and the Gorge

Jones Beach	12
Rooster Rock State Park	14
Dalton Point	20
Cascade Locks Marine Park	22
Stevenson, Washington	26
Home Valley Park, Washington	28
Drano Lake, Washington	32
"Swell City," Washington	36
The Hatchery, Washington	38
Hood Vista Sailpark, Washington	40
Hood River	42
Koberg Beach	46
Bingen Marina, Washington	48
Mosier Beach	52
Mayer State Park, East Rowena	56
Doug's Beach, Washington	58
Boat Basin Beach, The Dalles	62
Horsethief Lake, Washington	64
Avery Park, Washington	68
Celilo Park	70
Maryhill State Park, Washington	72
Giles French Park, Rufus	76
Snell Park, Arlington	80
Roosevelt Park, Washington	82
Three Mile Canyon	84
Boardman Marine Park	86

Crow Butte State Park, Washington	88
Irrigon	90
Plymouth Park, Washington	92
Marine Park, Umatilla	96
McNary Beach, Umatilla	98

Region Two: The Oregon Coast

Fort Stevens State Park	112
Youngs Bay	116
Seaside Beach	118
Tolovana Beach	120
Manzanita Beach	124
Nehalem Bay State Park	128
Tillamook Bay	130
Oceanside Beach	134
Netarts Bay	138
Tierra Del Mar	142
Pacific City	144
Devil's Lake	146
D-River Wayside	150
Siletz Bay	152
Beverly Beach	154
Agate Beach	158
Yaquina Bay	160
South Beach	164
Alsea Bay	166
Neptune Beach State Park	170
Heceta Beach	172
Siuslaw Bay	176
South Jetty, Siuslaw Bay	178
Woahink Lake	182
Siltcoos Lake	184
Empire, Coos Bay	188
Whiskey Run Beach, Seven Devils Wayside	192
Coquille Bay	194

Face Rock Wayside   198
Floras Lake   200
Paradise Point   202
Port Orford   204
Cape Sebastion   208
Pistol River   210

Region Three: Interstate 5 Corridor

Foster Reservoir   218
Fern Ridge Lake   220
Dorena Lake   224
Cottage Grove Lake   226
Lost Creek Reservoir   230
Emigrant Lake   232
Howard Prairie Reservoir   236

Region Four: The Cascade Lakes

Lost Lake   244
Clear Lake   246
Timothy Lake   250
Detroit Lake   252
Suttle Lake   256
Elk Lake   258
Cultus Lake   262
Wickiup Reservoir   266
Waldo Lake   268
Odell Lake   272
Crescent Lake   274
Diamond Lake   278

Region Five: The Desert Lakes and Points East

Haystack Reservoir   286
Ochoco Reservoir   288
Agency Lake   292
Upper Klamath Lake   294

Windsurfing, as any boardhead knows, is the quintessence of sailing. Nothing comes between the sailor and the environment. Indeed, the sailor is an integral part of the sailing machine. Furthermore, the sport can be practiced almost anywhere there is water and a modicum of wind. Perhaps this is the reason windsurfing, as a sport, has gained such worldwide popularity. Or maybe it is the portability of windsurfing equipment. Conventional sailing craft are usually limited to homewaters unless their owners undertake a lengthy passage or unless they can be trailered overland to new locations. Sailboards on the other hand, can be lashed to the car and the sailor can be on the road in a matter of minutes. As a boardsailor grows in skill and confidence, it is only natural he or she would seek out more demanding wind and water conditions.

This explains how windsurfing as a sport, along with the equipment and technology, has evolved so quickly, to the point of gaining Olympic status. It also explains why the Columbia River Gorge has become to windsurfing what Aspen, Sun Valley and St. Moritz are to alpine skiing. It has become the premier location in the continental United States and one of the two best locations in the world for the sport. The strong, consistent wind blowing daily through this natural wind funnel draws boardsailors of all skill levels from around the globe for fun, lessons and world class competition.

No one who has been there will deny that the Gorge is "awesome" for windsurfing, and at times it is downright intimidating. Even experienced Gorge sailors may be reluctant to venture out into winds in excess of 45 MPH and mast-high swells. The wind here has been so strong at times that even barges have been flipped out of the water. But despite all the stories of "nuclear winds," there are actually days when the wind doesn't blow at all in the Gorge. And at other times the winds can be extremely variable with 4.2 winds at Doug's Beach, near the center of the Gorge, and 6.0 conditions at Home Valley, 30 miles to the west. Winds can also vary considerably throughout the day at any given location.

Dave Gladstein's van was one of the more outrageous "gorge cruisers."

So contrary to all the hype, it is possible for intermediate and even first-time sailors, with proper instruction, to enjoy themselves in the Gorge.

When the wind doesn't blow, boardsailors, unlike sailors of conventional sailing craft, can always pack up and move to a locations where conditions are better. Judging by the number of boards strapped to the top of cars, it almost seems that boardsailors spend as much time looking for wind and sailing sites as they do sailing. In Oregon, there are over 1600 lakes covering more than a half-million surface acres, with major rivers like the Columbia and more than 300 miles of coastline, this search can be very challenging. The guidebook which follows was written in an attempt to halt this senseless waste of time and energy, and help to alleviate the congestion on our highways.

The sites included in this book were chosen primarily because they offer excellent sailing conditions. Even though some may be off the beaten path, every site should be worth the trip and most offer breathtaking scenery and excellent facilities to make the experience even more enjoyable. This guide was not intended to be all-inclusive. Because of the number of potential sailing sites there are many excellent locations, particularly in the east, which have not yet been explored. Also, many sites which may be popular with local sailors are excluded because they are simply "average."

The state was divided into five regions based on similarities in physical or climatological conditions. Region one includes the Gorge and lower Columbia River; region two covers the coast; region three includes the interior valleys between the Cascade and Coastal mountains; region four covers the high lakes in the Cascade Range; and region five covers the desert lakes of Central Oregon and points east.

Since the Gorge is the center of windsurfing activity in Oregon, most sailors traveling through the state are either heading to or returning from there. Because of this, the location descriptions for each site are given in relation to the major traffic corridors leading to the Gorge. These include I-84 and U.S. Hwy. 30, the major east-west routes, as well as U.S. Highways 101 and 97 and I-5, heading north and south. Individual site information was gained from interviews with local boardsailors and windsurfing shop proprietors throughout the state, and from actual site visits. Locals shared their knowledge of sailing conditions, access points, hazards, food, lodging and other attractions in the immediate area.

Sailing conditions: This section describes the best months of the year and times of day for sailing. Prevailing wind direction and wave conditions are also included. The sites have been defined as either "short board" or "long board" sailing areas. In order to be rated as a short board area the site must have side shore winds of sufficient velocity to permit water starts. An area rated as a short board site doesn't necessarily exclude long board sailing. On the other hand, short board sailing is generally not possible at sites rated for long boards because of unfavorable wind direction or velocity.

Access: Recommended launching sites, wind and wave direction, beach conditions, and shoreside amenities are described under this section. Alternative launch sites are also mentioned as are any periods of the day or year when the site may be closed.

Hazards: This section includes any known hazards that could endanger boardsailors or their equipment, either on land or in the water. The general hazards in a region are discussed in the specific descriptions for each site and also in the chapter introductions. Readers are cautioned to make their own hazard surveys before sailing in unfamiliar waters. It is possible that some hazards have been overlooked, or that conditions have changed, creating new hazards which did not exist when this book was written.

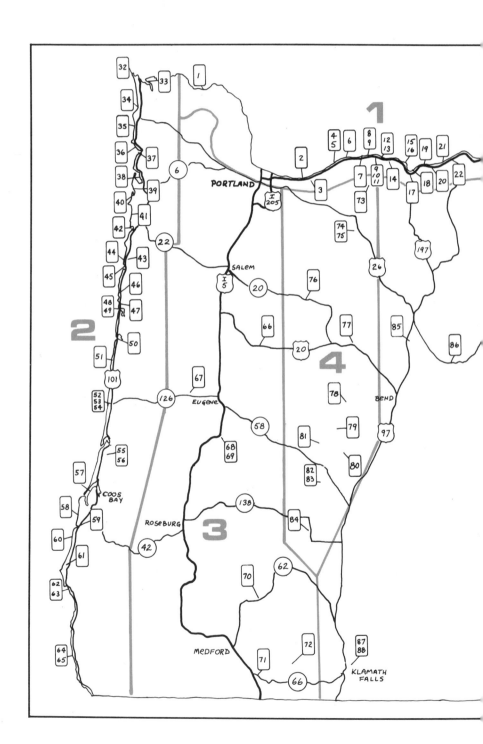

Boardsailing lessons using a dryland simulator enable the beginner to get out on the water in a matter of hours with a minimum of frustration.

Helmets are becoming more popular with boardsailors in the Gorge. Wearers say they improve their sailing enjoyment by giving them the confidence to go all out.

Board and may be repealed before this book goes to print. Out-of-state boardsailors are advised to check with local sailors and obey the rules to avoid a citation and fine.)

Helmets like the ones used by kayakers are becoming more popular with boardsailors especially in crowded areas like the Gorge. Collisions with other sailors or aerial bailouts can be dangerous. The use of helmets actually improves performance by enabling sailors to go to the limit without fear of serious injuries.

Windsurfing, like any high-speed sport, involves a certain amount of risk. The following safety rules should be followed at all times regardless of sailing area or individual skill level:

1) Never sail alone.
2) Always let someone know where you plan to sail and when you will return.
3) Make sure your equipment is in good repair, including your wet or dry suit.
4) Wear an approved personal flotation device.
5) Carry waterproof pocket flares.
6) Know your limits and quit before becoming exhausted.

Appendix B, "Sailboarding Oregon Safely," was produced by

Never sail alone, particularly in the ocean. It is also a good idea to carry pocket flares when sailing offshore.

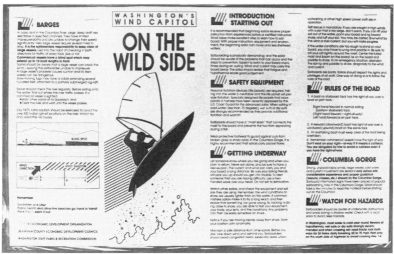

Signs like this one, providing rules and advice for boardsailors, are located at the more popular sites in the Gorge. A few minutes spent reading this information (which is also contained in Appendix B) may help avoid an accident.

the State Marine Board and reprinted with their kind permission. In it, the Oregon boating regulations that affect boardsailors are explained in more detail, along with tips for preventing accidents.

The author hopes this guide is helpful and that it serves to increase the popularity and enjoyment of windsurfing in Oregon. Readers' comments and suggestions are welcomed and encouraged for possible inclusion in future editions.

Region One: _____

_____The Columbia River

_____and the Gorge

The Columbia River
and the Gorge

For generations, since the first settlers discovered the Columbia River, the ceaseless winds that blew through the Gorge were accepted as just one more of life's annoyances. It wasn't until Hoyle Schweitzer developed the "windsurfer" that God's true plan for the Gorge became known. Windsurfers discovered the area in the late seventies and since then have been flocking, in ever-increasing numbers, from all corners of the globe to test their skills against the Gorge "wind machine."

The Gorge is now recognized as one of the two top windsurfing locations in the world, a boardsailor's paradise. All the major equipment manufacturers have located test centers here and many production plants have opened in the area. Each year competitive events such as the Gorge City Blowout and the Columbia Gorge Pro-Am Slalom, which is rated as one of the top ten international events, attract world class boardsailors to compete for cash and prizes.

But what is it about the Gorge that makes it so special? The Columbia is the third largest river in North America. It drains an area of almost 260,000 square miles. More than 180 million acre feet* of water flow into the Pacific Ocean from the Columbia each year. Over the eons, as it made its way to the Pacific, the river cut through the Cascade Mountain range, creating the Columbia Gorge. These mountains act as a barrier to the moist marine air coming off the Pacific Ocean and create a rain shadow in the high desert area to the east. It is this difference in climate, between the west and east sides of the Cascades, that powers the Gorge wind machine.

---

* An acre foot is the volume of water that would cover an acre of land one foot deep. It is a common term in the west, especially for measuring stored water or water used for irrigation. The equivalent in gallons is 58.7×10^{12} or 58.7 trillion gallons.

Windsurfing is big business in Hood River, with almost every major manufacturer represented. The old fruit canneries now house sail lofts and custom board shops.

As the sun heats the eastern side of the mountains the air rises in thermals, creating a pressure differential between east and west. Cooler air from the western side of the mountains rushes through the Gorge to equalize the pressure difference. As this air passes through the natural wind funnel of the Gorge, the speed intensifies. Winds of up to 30 to 35 MPH are common. The greater the temperature difference between east and west, the harder the wind blows. When it is overcast in Portland and sunny in Bend, you can bet the sailing is hot in Hood River. This same phenomena occurs to some extent in all the Cascade mountain passes and in the Clatskanie area where the Columbia River cuts through the coastal mountains.

The second feature that makes the Gorge so special is the strong current (up to five knots) of the Columbia River. When the downstream current meets the opposing wind, large "radioactive" swells are created. These two forces cancel each other out, so windsurfers never have to sail upwind to return to their starting points on shore. Sailing the swells of the Gorge is the windsurfing equivalent of skiing on moguls. It adds a new dimension in thrills but, like skiing, it is not something for the novice to attempt. Even experienced sailors are advised to take lessons in high wind techniques before sailing the Gorge for the first time. Fortunately, there are several windsurfing schools located in the Gorge offering lessons daily throughout the summer.

The Gorge sailing season begins with the first warm weather of spring, usually in early March, and continues through September. July and August are usually the best months, with strong winds, warm water (70° F) and air temperatures between 80 and 90 degrees. Even with the warm weather, wet or dry suits are still recommended to prevent hypothermia.

Visitors to the Gorge can expect at least 20 days per month of good sailing winds. But the wind can be unpredictable, blowing like stink in one place and barely 5 MPH just a few miles away. Gorge sailors must be prepared to travel in search of the right conditions. Occasionally the temperatures on the west side of the Cascades will reach the upper 90's and the Gorge wind machine stops. This doesn't happen often and usually doesn't last more than a few days. When it does happen, real fanatics head to the coast for their daily wind fix.

The starting line for a major event like the "Blowout" can be very crowded and recalling 250 boardsailorsis not practical. A "rabbit" start is used and anyone over early is disqualified.

Winters in the Gorge can be severe. Some hearty souls sail all year round but most local sailors either seek warmer waters or hang up their boards and head for the nearby slopes of Mt. Hood, which offer excellent skiing in both winter and summer months.

Strong winds and large swells are not the only challenges the Columbia has to offer. The river is a major commercial thorough-fare. Tug boats maneuver large barges and rafts of logs through the Gorge from as far upstream as Lewiston, Idaho to Astoria at the mouth. In the lower river, oceangoing freighters and fishing boats come as far upstream as the Willamette River and the city of Portland. These deep draft vessels are confined to the main chan-

Range markers are use to locate the navigation channel. Just like a range finder on a camera, when the vertical stripes are aligned one above the other the viewer is in the center of the channel.

nel and cannot alter speed or direction to avoid collisions. Range markers are used by river pilots to locate the navigation channel. These are large, brightly-colored diamond or rectangle shapes with a contrasting vertical line down the center. There are always two, one usually near the water and the second above on the hillside. When the two vertical lines appear one above the other, the viewer is in the center of the channel.

Boardsailors should use range markers to get a general idea of where the channel lies so this area can be avoided when large vessels are nearby. Barges and freighters move much faster than you think and may require more than a mile or two in order to stop. They also block the wind, creating wind shadows on their leeward sides. This, combined with limited visibility from the pilot house, can mean big trouble for any hapless sailor who gets too close. The propeller suction can easily pull a downed sailor underwater, board and all, and the bow and stern wakes can be equally dangerous. Stay at least 50 feet away.

In many Gorge sailing areas, flags are hoisted to warn of approaching barges. This warning flag is bright yellow with a red X from corner to corner. Since not all areas use the warning flags, the best advice is to keep a constant watch for commercial boat traffic; warn other sailors when traffic is spotted; and retire from the river until the commercial vessel passes. If you're down and having troubles when a barge is approaching, ditch your rig and paddle your board to safety. This will save your board and your butt. The rig can always be recovered or replaced later. Barges and windsurfers can peacefully co-exist if this advice is followed. Remember, in any confrontation on the water the barge will always win, and anyone caught obstructing commercial traffic can be fined up to $250.

Other sailing hazards along the Columbia include:

Slow-moving tug boats are usually towing rafts of logs. These rafts are connected by cable and may stretch for almost a mile behind the tug. They ride low in the water and may be impossible to see until it is too late. Hitting one of these obstacles at 30 MPH or more is guaranteed to ruin your day.

Gill nets are stretched across the current, usually near shore, by Indians to catch migrating salmon. These nets can be spotted by their floats, usually plastic bottles or old inner tubes. Windsurfers should avoid sailing in these areas. If carried into a gill net by the

Barges have the right-of-way and only a fool would argue the point. Clear the river when a barge approaches. This allows the pilot to concentrate on any sailors who may be in trouble.

current, keep your body and rigging up on the board to avoid becoming entangled.

The Indian fishing grounds extend from Bonneville to McNary Dams and nets may be in the water in February, March, and June through September. The largest salmon runs occur during August and September and the nets will be more numerous then. A limited amount of gill net fishing is done in the lower river from Bonneville Dam to Astoria, but it does not pose a danger for windsurfers. The nets are not left unattended and most of the fishing is done at night.

Trains travel both sides of the river close to the water and windsurfers are often obliged to cross the tracks in order to reach launch sites. As many as 24 trains a day may pass a given site and approaching trains are difficult to hear. People have died because of carelessness at these railroad crossings. Always be careful when crossing. Never leave vehicles or equipment close to the tracks.

Wing dams, long rows of closely-spaced pilings perpendicular to the shoreline, are used to control the current and help keep the

Wing dams, like this one near Rooster Rock State Park, can be found all along the Columbia River. The current is very strong on the upstream side and could easily trap a boardsailor against the pilings.

river channel free of sediment and debris. When the water is high these pilings can be difficult to spot; at times they are completely submerged. A sailor caught on the up-current side of a wing dam will have trouble getting free and may damage board, sail and rigging.

Poison oak is found all along the Columbia River, particularly at less developed launching sites. A low shrub or vine with three leaves resembling true oak, its oils can cause a rash or swelling on the exposed skin of sensitive people.

Rattlesnakes are found in the arid regions of Oregon, east of the Cascades. They are often found near water, although rarely in populated areas. Sailors who find themselves on an isolated shore, particularly at the eastern end of the Gorge, should walk cautiously. Snakes for the most part will avoid contact with people unless surprised or cornered.

Rocks line most of the banks along the Columbia to help prevent erosion. It is advisable to wear protective footwear to prevent cuts and stubbed toes.

Almost any place in the Gorge where you can get to the water should be a great place to sail. The sites listed in this section are the more popular sites. Although this is primarily a guide to Oregon, windsurfing sites on the Washington side of the Columbia are also included. However, one site, often visited by first-time Gorge sailors, has not been included. Aptly named Bozo Beach, it is located on the Washington side across from the Hood River Sailpark. This is where the current takes those who are not yet proficient at high wind sailing. If you wind up at Bozo Beach, about the only way to return is by car. Just hope that one of your friends will remember to come for you.

Jones Beach

Locals refer to Jones Beach as "The Other Gorge." It is fast becoming another sailboarding hot spot. Located near Clatskanie, this area is about the same distance from Portland as the Gorge, but still uncrowded. This site is in the wind funnel created where the Columbia River cuts through the Coast range, with wind conditions similar to the Gorge. It is especially popular in late summer when the Gorge "wind machine" can shut down. Many Seattle sailors prefer Jones Beach to the Gorge because it is two hours closer to home.

Skill rating: Novice through expert

Location: The fastest route from Portland is I-5 north toward Seattle. Take the first Longview exit and follow the signs to Oregon. After crossing the Columbia River head west on Hwy. 30 past Clatskanie. Turn right on Midland Dist. Road (4 miles), Marshland Road (4.5 miles) or Woodson Road (5 miles), any one of which will take you to Riverfront Road and Jones Beach.

Sailing conditions: (Short Board) The best sailing is from June through September when the winds average 25 to 30 MPH. If the weather is hot in Portland and overcast on the coast the sailing should be great at Jones Beach. The wind starts picking up around 2:00 PM and increases 4 to 5 MPH every half hour.

Beginners can sail Jones Beach from early morning until mid-afternoon June through September or almost all day the rest of the year. Anyone who cannot water start should sail between the beach and Wallace Island, staying out of the main channel where the current is very strong.

Access: This would definitely be a three-star site if the access was better. The beach is privately owned and currently undeveloped – chemical toilets are the only facilities at this time. There is

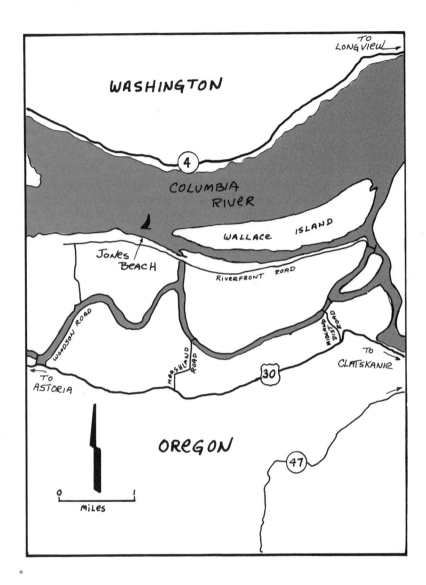

plenty of room for parking and lots of room on the beach for rigging. The area is also a popular fishing spot. Anglers and windsurfers have learned to co-exist by keeping to their own ends of the beach. Respect their rights and stay clear of fishing lines. After all, they were here first. Also heed parking and no trespassing signs, and haul your trash out, so windsurfers will continue to be welcome here in the future.

Hazards: Watch out for barges and freighters. The current here is very strong, especially on out going tides. Stay out of the main channel if you can't water start. Avoid sailing near the wing dam on the Washington shore. The strong current can pull you against the pilings and a wind shadow in that area makes water starts difficult.

Wind and water reports: 728-2847 – Sporty's, Clatskanie • 728-2626 – Hump's Restaurant, Clatskanie • (503) 386-4646.

Food and lodging: Clatskanie has several good restaurants and motels. The area is still pristine compared to towns in the Gorge, so prices are reasonable.

Hump's Conestoga Restaurant in Clatskanie caters to boardsailors with breakfast, lunch, dinner and takeout box lunches.

The Bear Tavern is the watering hole closest to Jones Beach, at least for now.

Mr. Fultano's Pizza Parlor in Clatskanie delivers. Unfortunately there's no phone on the beach.

Other attractions: There is an old-fashioned Fourth of July celebration in Clatskanie.

A helicopter shuttle to the Gorge is one of the services planned by Sporty's in Clatskanie. Contact them at (503)728-2712 to check on schedules and rates.

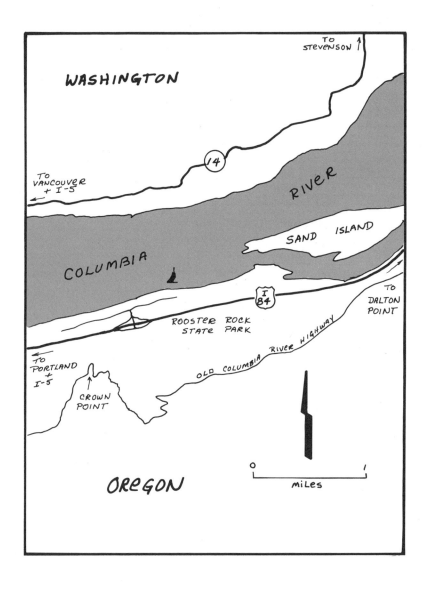

Rooster Rock State Park

Rooster Rock is a great east wind location. From fall through early spring the wind really cranks. Fifty mile per hour winds are not uncommon, but in the summer when the wind is from the west, this is a nice, casual place to sail. Sailors who desire or appreciate a great all-over tan will love this site – swimsuits are optional.

Skill rating: Intermediate to expert

Location: Rooster Rock is approximately 20 miles east of downtown Portland on I-84 at exit 28. The entrance is well marked.

Sailing conditions: (Short Board, Long Board in west winds) The best sailing is in the fall and early spring when the east wind blows. Locals here talk about "liquid smoke" conditions when 3.5 sails or smaller are required. Since the wind and current are going in the same direction, the waves are smaller than at west wind sailing sites in the Gorge.

Access: An excellent state park is located at Rooster Rock, with plenty of paved parking near the beach, rest rooms, a food concession, large grass areas for rigging, and sandy beaches for easy launching.

Hazards: Barges pass close to the Oregon side. The area is also popular with recreational boaters. There are large rocks close to shore that may be completely submerged when the river is high. There are also two wing dams in the area. Wing dams are rows of pilings, running perpendicular to the beach, which are used to control the current. These structures can be completely submerged in early spring. Being accidentally swept onto a wing dam may result in personal injury or damage to your equipment.

> ATTENTION
> YOU ARE LEAVING THE NUDE
> SUNBATHING AREA. ALL VISITORS
> MUST BE ADEQUATELY CLOTHED
> BEYOND THIS POINT.

For anyone who has wanted to try boardsailing in the buff, Rooster Rock is the place. Unfortunately the best winds here are in the winter when the sun rarely shines. This is still a good alternative on a hot summer day when the Gorge winds aren't cooperating.

Wind and water reports: (503) 695-2220 – Rooster Rock State Park.

Food and lodging: *The Royal Chinook Inn* has relaxed family dining with a view of the river. Take exit 22 off I-84.

Ainsworth State Park has 45 sites with full hookups. It is open only during the summer. Take exit 35 off I-84.

Additional gas, food, and lodging can be found at Troutdale to the west or at Cascade Locks heading east.

Other attractions: Rooster Rock State Park is the site in this guide closest to Portland, the "Rose City." It would be a grave oversight if the annual *Portland Rose Festival* were not mentioned. This event in early June, runs for almost three weeks and includes a Grand Floral Parade that rivals the Pasadena Rose Parade. The festivities also include world-champion auto racing, carnivals, naval ships, ski races on Mount Hood, and much more.

Rooster Rock State Park is a hot east wind sailing site. Hearty souls sail here in the winter and early spring when the strong east winds turn the river to "liquid smoke."

Crown Point, near Corbett, offers a panoramic view of the Columbia River Gorge.

Multnomah Falls, at exit 31, and other waterfalls along the Old Columbia River Highway shouldn't be missed.

The Mt. Hood Festival of Jazz, held each August in nearby Gresham, has grown into a major event attracting the country's best known musicians.

Hiking, hang gliding, and rock climbing are other popular sports in the Rooster Rock area.

Multnomah Falls, one of many throughout the Gorge, is the second highest waterfall in the U.S. A hike to the top of the 620-foot falls is a challenge, but rewarding.

Dalton Point

Dalton Point is an east wind sailing site, similar to Rooster Rock State Park. There are fewer amenities here and it is harder to reach, but it won't be as crowded.

Skill rating: Intermediate through expert

Location: Dalton Point, approximately 3 miles east of Rooster Rock State Park, can only be reached from westbound I-84 at exit 28. There is no eastbound exit. Ainsworth State Park, exit 35, is the nearest place to turn around.

Sailing conditions: (Short Board) The best sailing is in the fall or early spring when east winds are strongest. Waves tend to be smaller here than at Rooster Rock, and since the wind and current are moving together, large swells will not develop.

Access: There is plenty of paved parking and a small grass rigging area, which is sheltered from the wind. Pit privies are the only amenities. The beach is rocky with a shallow entry. The area to the west of the boat ramp is the best.

Hazards: There are some old pilings offshore to the west of the boat ramp and some large rocks close to the beach which may be submerged in high water. Beware of barges and recreational boaters.

Wind and water reports: (503) 695-2220 – Rooster Rock State Park

Food and lodging: *Multnomah Falls Lodge,* at exit 31, offers both casual dining and a snack bar with great views of the falls.
See Rooster Rock State Park

Other attractions: See Rooster Rock State Park

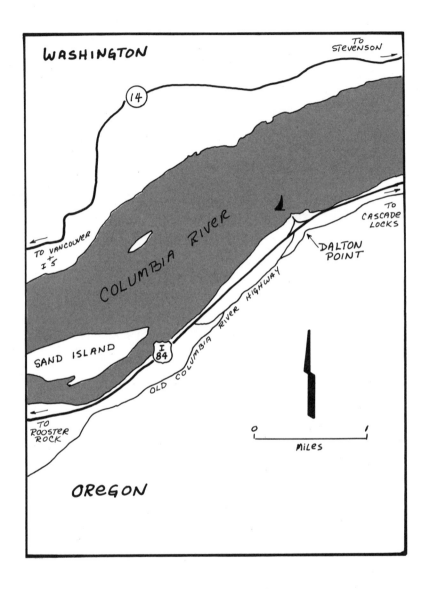

Cascade Locks

Marine Park

Good high-wind sailing. Cascade Locks is the starting point for the Gorge City Blowout, a 20-mile downwind race to the town of Hood River, held each year in late July or early August.

Skill rating: Intermediate through expert

Location: Forty-five miles east of Portland and 17 miles west of Hood River via I-84. Both exit 44, heading east, or westbound exit 47 lead into town. The entrance to the park is marked with an official Oregon windsurfing sign. Turn right after crossing under the railroad tracks and follow the signs to the far east end of the park. Amtrak serves the town of Cascade Locks and the station is less than a quarter mile from the beach.

Sailing conditions: (Short Board) Wind and currents are generally moderate compared to other Gorge sites. The best sailing is in west winds from mid-April to September.

Access: The launch site at the east end of the park has a small gravel parking area. Additional parking is available west of the boat basin. The gravel beach is small and sheltered from the west wind by the marina breakwater. With east winds, the waves are right on shore. Grass has been planted near the beach for rigging. The nearest rest rooms are located at the visitor's center.

Only a small part of the park is developed for windsurfing now, but many improvements are planned for the near future, including a better beach and a larger, more convenient parking area.

Hazards: Strong currents in the early spring can make it difficult to return to the launch site.

21

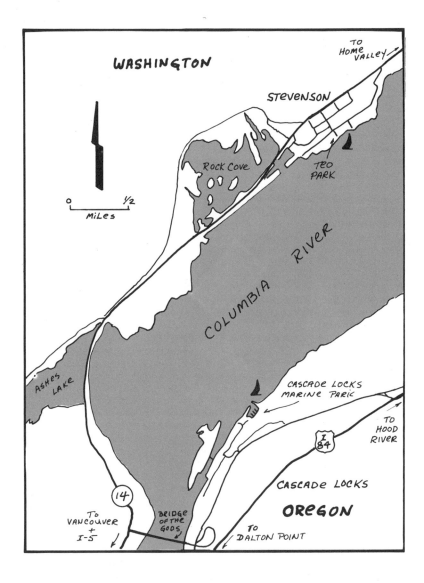

Wind and water reports: (503) 374-8619 – Port of Cascade Locks, 8:00 AM to 7:00 PM (8:00 AM to 5:00 PM, October through March)

Food and lodging: Gas, food, and lodging are available within walking distance of the Marine Park. There is also a campground

Major racing events like the Gorge City Blowout, a 20-mile downwind race from Cascade Locks to Hood River, attract the world's top professionals to compete for more than $30,000 in prize money.

Highway signs like these mark the route to many windsurfing sites in Oregon (left) and Washington (right). To qualify, a site must have adequate parking, safe water access, and restroom facilities. Many popular sites do not meet these minimum requirements and are not marked.

The Sternwheeler Columbia Gorge is a popular attraction during the summer as it sails between its berth at Cascade Locks, Stevenson, Washington, and Bonneville Dam.

in the park itself, with tent and RV sites. Additional camping is available at *Eagle Creek Park*, west on I-84 at exit 41.

Other attractions: *The Sternwheeler Columbia Gorge* operates from the Marine Park between mid-June and September, with excursions to Stevenson, Washington, and Bonneville Dam ((503) 374-8427.)

Bonneville Dam and Fish Hatchery, located at I-84 exit 40, is open to the public and features a visitor's center with underwater viewing of migrating salmon climbing the fish ladder.

Bridge of the Gods Trail, part of the Pacific Crest Trail, begins at the south end of the bridge and climbs to the top of the Gorge, providing an eagle's eye view of the river below.

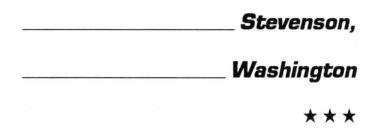

_____ *Stevenson,*

_____ *Washington*

★ ★ ★

This site is located just across the river from Cascade Locks and has similar sailing conditions. Facilities are limited as compared to other sites in the Gorge, but many improvements are planned as this area is becoming more well known.

Skill rating: Intermediate through expert

Location: The site is approximately two miles east of Cascade Locks on the Washington side. From I-84, cross at the Bridge of the Gods (50-cent toll) and take Hwy. 14 east to Stevenson. A new park is being built on the west end of town by the Port of Skamania County. An official Washington windsurfing area sign * marks the turnoff.

Sailing conditions: (Short Board) A good location in both easterly and westerly winds. Sailing is possible from early March into October but the best winds are found in the summer when the westerly winds reach speeds of 25 to 35 MPH.

Access: Teo Park on the waterfront is small with limited parking, but there is a lot of grass and shelter from the wind. The park also has picnic tables, a barbeque pit and chemical toilets during the summer. There is a steep bank down to a small gravel and cobble beach.

The Port of Skamania County is improving the beach west of the tour boat dock for windsurfers. Additional improvements, including parking for 25 cars, better water access and chemical toilets, are being developed east of Teo Park on Cascade Avenue, just

* See p. 23 for photographs of official windsurfing signs.

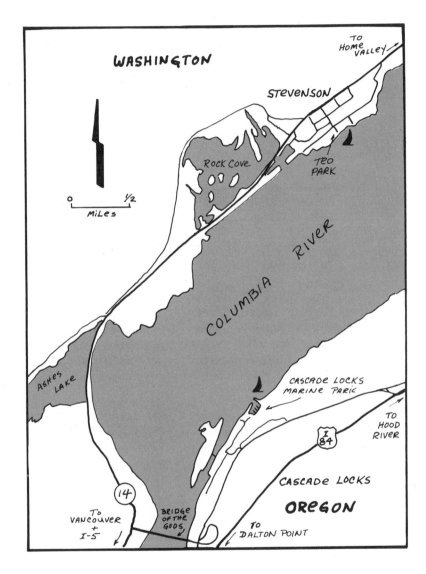

past the Willamette Industries Mill. This work is scheduled for completion in 1989.

Hazards: There are pilings on either side of the beach and a large pier at the park. Many gill nets in the area may make it difficult to get offshore. The barge channel is located in the center of the river.

Wind and water reports: (509) 427-5484 – Port of Skamania County, 8:00 AM to 5:00 PM, Monday through Friday.

Food and lodging: Gas, food, and lodging are available in Stevenson. Additional services are available across the river in Cascade Locks.

Hidden Cove Camp Ground, one mile east of Stevenson on Hwy. 14, has water access.

Other attractions: _The Sternwheeler "Columbia Gorge"_ stops at Stevenson twice daily between mid-June and September; call (503)374-8427.

The Columbia Gorge Bluegrass Festival is held each year in July at Stevenson.

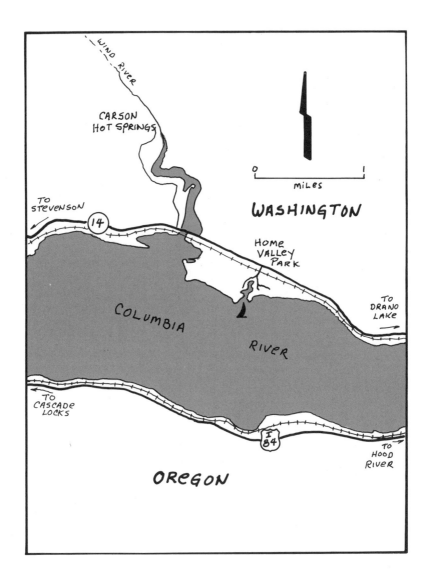

Home Valley Park, Washington

Home Valley is one of the best places — and sometimes the only place — in the Gorge to sail in east winds. It is also good when the west winds are too strong at Swell City or the Hatchery. Locals call this Afterburner Beach because of the frequent wind gusts. The park here has had many improvements in recent years and is less crowded than many other Gorge sites.

Skill rating: Intermediate to expert

Location: Home Valley is on Hwy. 14 approximately 7 miles east of Stevenson and 14 miles west of White Salmon, Washington. From I-84 on the Oregon side the nearest bridge is in Cascade Locks. The turnoff from Hwy. 14 is just east of milepost 50 and is marked with an official Washington windsurfing area sign.

Sailing conditions: (Short Board) Here there are high wind and big waves with slow currents compared to other Gorge areas. Waves are onshore with east winds.

Access: There is plenty of parking close to the water; a good rigging area; a sand and gravel beach with easy water access; and chemical toilets and rest rooms (closed in winter). Ball diamonds, a picnic area with covered shelters, barbeque grills and a separate swimming beach are some of the other amenities.

Hazards: There are large rocks along shore. Also watch out for barges and gill nets.

Wind and water reports: (509) 427-5484 — Port of Skamania County, 8:00 AM to 5:00 PM, Monday through Friday (nearest gauge — Stevenson, WA)

A visit to Carson Hot Springs near Home Valley, Washington, is a trip back in time. For more than a century people have come to enjoy the mineral baths and stay at the St. Martin Hotel. This is the perfect place to end a day of nuclear sailing.

Food and lodging: A grocery store and gas station are located on Hwy. 14 near the park entrance and free camping is available within the park itself.

Carson Hot Springs Resort, approximately 2.5 miles west on Hot Springs Avenue, has hotel rooms, cabins, and RV and tent camping at unbelievably low prices. There is also a fine restaurant with good, old-fashioned home cooking.

Other attractions: The main feature of *Carson Hot Springs Resort* is the mineral baths. Followed by a Swedish massage, there is no better way to work out the kinks after a hard day's sailing.

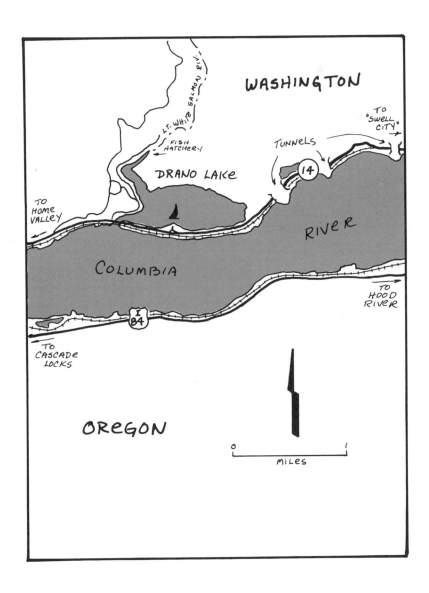

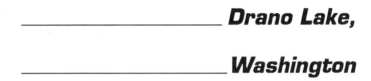# *Drano Lake,*

Washington

★

This is an ideal place to practice high-wind sailing in sheltered waters before heading out on the Columbia. Located at the confluence of the Columbia and Little White Salmon rivers, Drano Lake is separated from the strong Columbia River currents – but not from the wind – by Hwy. 14. It is possible to reach the Columbia by sailing under the highway bridge, through probably not practical.

Skill rating: Novice through intermediate

Location: The lake is approximately 9 miles west of the Hood River bridge on Washington Hwy. 14. Heading west, Drano Lake is at the end of a series of five tunnels. The entrance to the park is difficult to spot, at the west end of the bridge over the Little White Salmon River. Additional parking and water access are available at the historical marker located east of the bridge.

Sailing conditions: (Long Board) This is a good place for long-board sailing in east winds, which are generally not as strong here as at sites further to the west.

Access: Chemical toilets during the summer months are the only facilities at Drano Lake. There is very little parking in the park but there is some area for rigging. More parking is available at the historical marker site. A small boat ramp makes water entrance easier but there is no grass for rigging, nor any other amenities.

Hazards: There are many "deadheads" (sunken logs with one end at or near the water surface) and rocks along the north shore. Lake water levels may fluctuate quickly, without warning.

Wind and water reports: (509) 386-4646 (nearest gauge – Swell City)

Food and lodging: The gas, food and lodgings nearest to Drano Lake are located in White Salmon or Bingen, Washington.
    See Hood Vista Sailpark and Bingen Marina.

Other attractions: *The Willard National Fish Hatchery* is located at Drano lake and is open to the public.
    Broughton Flume, high on the mountain above Drano Lake, has been using water power to carry saw logs to the Burlington Northern railhead since the 1920s.

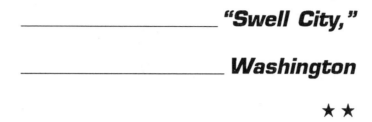

"Swell City," Washington

★ ★

A popular place, winds here are typically 5 to 10 MPH stronger than at Hood River Marina. The waves here are large and well-developed – that's how this site got its name. This is also a good place for spectators.

Skill rating: Expert

Location: Approximately 4 miles west of the Hood River bridge on Hwy. 14, this site is not much more than a wide spot in the road and may be hard to spot if you are the first one there. If you reach the tunnels heading west, you've gone too far.

Sailing conditions: (Short Board) This is often the only place in the Gorge with wind. The beach is protected, with flat water near shore. Out in the river the current is strong and the waves are excellent for jumping and jibing.

Access: Parking is limited and there is a $2.00 fee. The beach is small and rocky. The only other amenities are chemical toilets and a food concession during the summer months.

Hazards: Large rocks are just below the surface near shore. Watch out for barges and gill nets.

Wind and water reports: (509) 386-4646

Food and lodging: The nearest gas, food and lodging are in White Salmon or Bingen, Washington. However, most people sailing here stay in Hood River.

Other attractions: See Hood River or Bingen Marina.

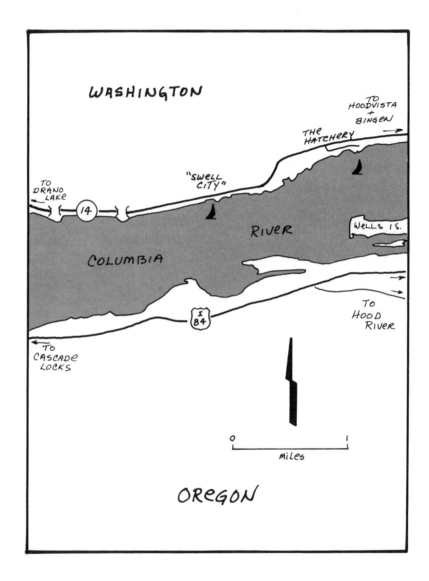

The Hatchery,
Washington

★

Another experts-only site with strong currents, 6- to 8-foot swells and high winds. Launching and landing are difficult and facilities are limited, otherwise this would be a two star site.

Skill rating: Expert

Location: The Hatchery is located approximately 3.5 miles west of Hood River on the Washington side. Cross the bridge at Hood River and head west on Hwy. 14. Turn left on the Spring Creek Fish Hatchery access road.

Sailing conditions: (Short Board) The waves are large and the wind is sometimes stronger than at Swell City. Sailing is best here in west winds from mid-April through September.

Access: Access to this site is courtesy of the U.S. Fish and Wildlife Service, with the understanding that boardsailors and spectators will not interfere with operations at the fish hatchery. This means do not block the access road and remove all garbage. A small gravel parking lot and rigging area have been provided along with chemical toilets. Additional parking is found outside the hatchery grounds along Hwy. 14. There is a nice grass rigging area but water entry is difficult, with a steep rock bank facing directly into the wind and waves. Once in the water, the bottom drops off quickly.

Hazards: Landing on the rocks is difficult. The local shops make a nice piece of change repairing boards damaged here. Watch out for barges and gill nets.

Wind and water reports: 386-4646 (nearest gauges – Swell City and Hood River)

37

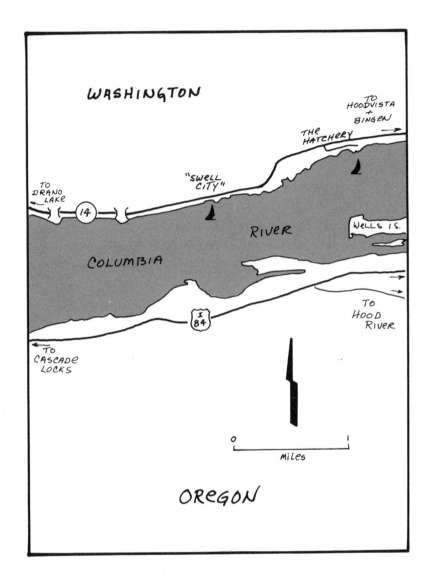

Food and lodging: The nearest gas, food, and lodging are in White Salmon or Bingen, Washington. However, most people stay in Hood River.

Other attractions: *Spring River Fish Hatchery* is open to the public.

See also Hood River or Bingen Marina.

Hood Vista Sailpark, Washington

★ ★ ★

This park is a fairly new site, with five riverfront acres privately developed specifically for sailboarding. An access fee is charged for day use of park facilities.

Skill rating: Intermediate through expert

Location: Entrance to the park is just across the bridge from Hood River. Head west on Hwy. 14 for approximately one-quarter mile, then turn left across the railroad tracks. An official Washington windsurfing area sign marks the turnoff.

Sailing conditions: (Short Board) Conditions are similar to those at Columbia Gorge Sailpark. There are big waves and strong winds in mid-river, stronger than near shore. Sailors are cautioned not to sail beyond the reef until proficient at water starts.

Access: Parking for 40 cars, shaded lawns for rigging, and a nice sandy beach with a large shallow area for practicing water starts are some of the amenities here. Chemical toilets, water and camping facilities are also available. Food concessions should be operating here in the near future. In the meantime, there is a barbeque pit and a volleyball court for entertainment while waiting for the wind to build.

Hazards: A shallow reef is located approximately 100 yards offshore. The bottom is rocky and there are a number of old pilings and other junk in the water. Buoys mark some, but not all, of the hazards. Depths can vary hourly so the safest route back to the beach may change. Watch out for barges and gill nets.

Wind and water reports: 386-4646 · 976-WIND · 387-WIND

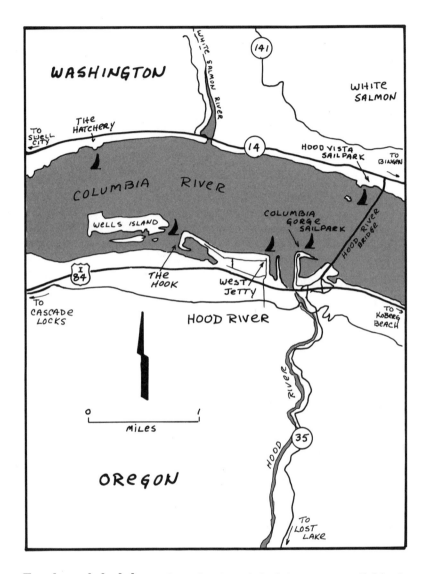

Food and lodging: Gas, food and lodging are available in White Salmon and Bingen, Washington; and across the river in Hood River. Camping is available in the park, but there are no hookups for RV's.

Other attractions: See Hood River or Bingen Marina.

Hood River

★ ★ ★

If the Gorge is the windsurfing center of the country, then Hood River is its capital. According to the Oregon State Parks Division, Hood River is the number one place for boardsailing in the state. There are three great launch sites. The Columbia Gorge Sailpark is probably the busiest site in the Gorge. All the local shops – and there are many – use this beach for teaching water starts and jibes. Because of its popularity, the Sailpark has become very crowded, especially when one of the many boardsailing events is being held here. The Hook and West Jetty launch areas are not as well-developed as the Sailpark and, therefore, are not as crowded.

Skill rating: Intermediate through expert (Novice long board sailing is possible in sheltered areas.)

Location: Hood River is located 62 miles east of Portland on I-84. The city of Hood River is served by Amtrak and Greyhound in addition to limousine service from Portland International Airport. To reach the Sailpark, take exit 64 and head north, turn left just before the Hood River bridge and follow the signs to the launch area.

The Hook and West Jetty sites are located approximately 1 mile west of the Sailpark. The easiest way to get there is by the freeway. Take exit 63 and head north on Second Street. West Jetty is at the end of Second Street. To get to the Hook, turn west on Portway Avenue, go past the warehouses and the wastewater treatment plant and follow the gravel road to the end.

Sailing conditions: (Short Board) *Sailpark:* Great west wind sailing is possible from April to September. Winds here, as a rule, are not as strong as at Swell City or the Hatchery further to the west, but at times they may be stronger. The water close to shore is

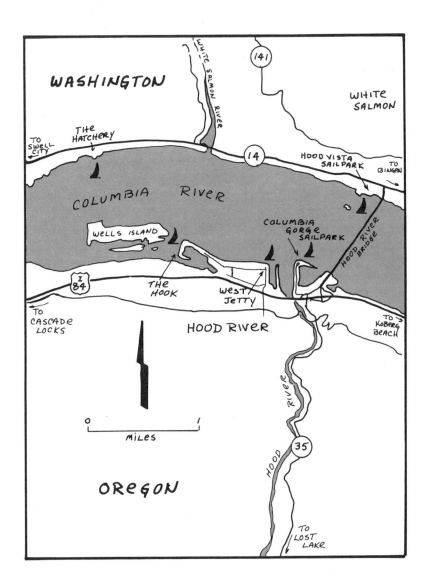

more protected than in midriver making it a good place to practice water starts and high wind jibes.

West Jetty: Conditions are the same as at the Sailpark.

The Hook: Excellent west wind sailing is possible from April through September. The winds are often stronger and more consistent here than at the Sailpark just one mile to the east. The wind shadow from Wells Island makes it tricky to reach the main channel but, once outside, the conditions are similar to those at the Hatchery, with smaller waves.

Access: _Sailpark:_ There is excellent access with plenty of parking, grass areas for rigging, and easy shallow-water entry. Other amenities include rest rooms with showers, and food concessions. Also, there is water near the beach for washing boards and other equipment. Loading zones are provided near the beach. Parking regulations are strictly enforced. This site is also popular with spectators and is always crowded. Kodak Point at the west end of the beach was so named because of the number of photographers who gather there.

West Jetty: There is a large gravel parking lot on top of the jetty with a boat ramp for easier access to the water. The jetties protect the area from waves and reduce the wind somewhat, making it a good launch site for first-time gorge sailors. There are no toilets or other facilities here yet.

The Hook: There is a large parking lot with chemical toilets. A food concession is provided during the season. The Hook is covered with rocks and gravel; there is no good place for rigging. Many sailors use carpeting to save wear and tear on their equipment. Ramps lead down to the water on either side of the Hook and there is a small sand beach at the west end. Because the beach is somewhat sheltered from the west wind by Wells Island, it is a good place for first time sailors to learn Gorge sailing skills. The water is shallow on the south shore and many local instructors use this area for teaching water starts. While the shore facilities are not the best, the Port of Hood River has plans to improve this site in the near future.

Hazards: _Sailpark and West Jetty:_ Barges are not a big problem at this site since the channel is near the Washington shore. A sandbar at the mouth of the Hood River can be very shallow at times. The strong current of the Columbia, combined with the flow from the Hood River, can make it difficult to return to the Oregon side. This is particularly true in the spring. If trouble occurs in mid-channel, head for Bozo Beach on the Washington side. The area is so named because nearly all first-time Gorge sailors end up here.

The Hook: The main channel is approximately mid-river but barges and tugs must maneuver close to the Oregon shore to reach the dock facilities at the Port of Hood River.

Wind and water reports: 386-4646 · 976-WIND · 387-WIND

Food and lodging: The town of Hood River goes out of its way to make windsurfers welcome. There are food and lodging facilities to suit every taste and price range. During the season advance reservations are recommended. Additional facilities can be found across the river in White Salmon or Bingen.

Bette's Place in Oak Mall, 416 Oak Street, is a popular breakfast spot for boardsailors.

Columbia Gorge Hotel, a National Historic Landmark, offers the classic elegance of the Roaring Twenties with a great view of the river. It is rated as one of America's finest country inns. Take exit 62 from I-84.

The Inn at the Gorge, located right on the river, provides complete boardsailing vacation packages, including rental equipment and instruction.

Gorge View Bed and Breakfast is run by boardsailors for boardsailors.

Viento State Park, 8 miles west of Hood River, is the nearest state park campground. It has tent and RV sites with water and electric hookups, rest rooms and showers. Even though there is no river access, most of the campers are boardsailors.

Other attractions: Boardsailing is not the only important industry in Hood River. The area is also one of the most productive fruit-growing regions in the country. Each year in late April, Hood River hosts the *Blossom Festival* to celebrate this fact, with an arts and crafts fair, wine tours, barbeque and carnival.

Three Rivers Winery, across from Columbia Gorge Hotel, offers tours, picnic area and wine-tasting.

Timberline Lodge at Mt. Hood, with year-round skiing, is only 45 miles from Hood River via Hwy. 35.

Take the *Fruit Blossom Special* for a rail excursion through the scenic Hood River Valley. Trains run Wednesday through Sunday from June to October and on weekends during April and May.

The historic Columbia Gorge Hotel in Hood River is rated as one of the finest country inns in America. During the Roaring Twenties this was a favorite getaway for the rich and famous.

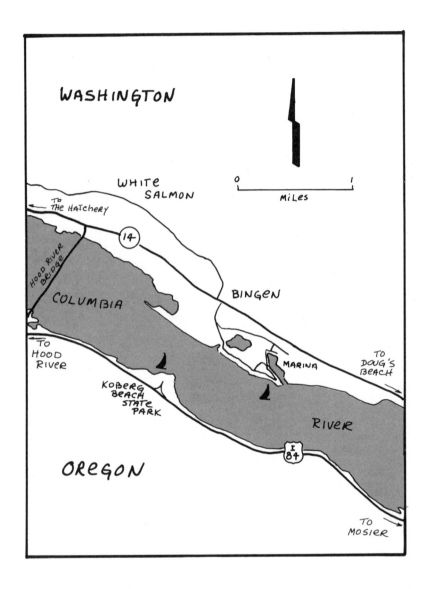

Koberg Beach

Koberg Beach State Park is a good place to learn Gorge sailing techniques. This site has been used in the past for teaching high wind sailing. Port tack jumps are possible here on "nuclear" days.

Skill rating: Intermediate through expert

Location: The beach is approximately one mile east of Hood River and directly across the Columbia from Bingen Marina. The only access is from I-84 westbound at exit 76. Eastbound traffic must go to the Mosier exit, two miles east, to turn around.

Sailing conditions: (Short Board) There are good high-wind sailing conditions with westerly winds, mid-April through September. Winds here are often stronger than at Hood River.

Access: Usually uncrowded, Koberg Beach State Park has a large gravel beach almost 300 feet in length, good parking, and rest rooms. It's a short walk from the paved parking area to the beach. Unauthorized vehicle use has cut new trails to the beach but their use is not recommended without four-wheel drive.

Hazards: A large rock outcropping makes approaching barge traffic particularly hard to see from the beach. Currents can be very strong in this area.

Wind and water reports: 386-4646 (nearest gauge – Hood River) · 976-WIND · 387-WIND

Food and lodging: The nearest gas, food and lodging are in Hood River.

See also Hood River

Other attractions: See Hood River

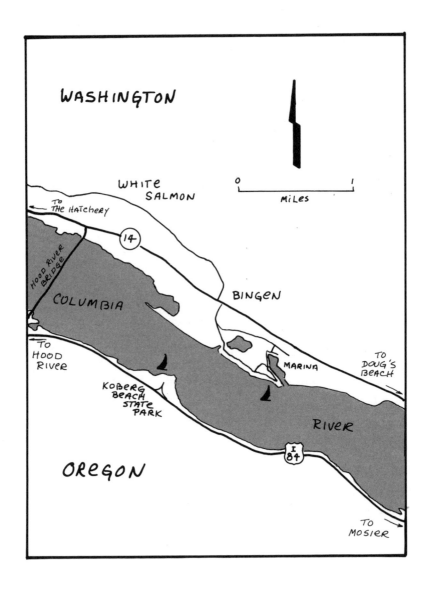

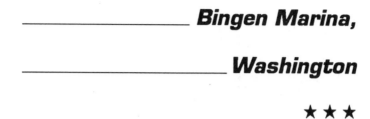

Bingen Marina,

Washington

★ ★ ★

This is the site of Bingen Winds, which is being developed as a major windsurfing resort. The first phase includes improved rigging and launch areas. Eventually this site will feature a hotel, restaurants and anything else a boardsailor's heart could desire.

Skill rating: Intermediate through expert

Location: The marina is approximately 2 miles upstream from Hood River and almost directly across from Koberg Beach. From I-84, cross the bridge at Hood River and head east on Hwy. 14. The turnoff to the marina is at the Shell gas station. An official Washington windsurfing area sign is on the corner. Follow the signs past the log yard. The windsurfing area is out on the dike at the southeast end of the boat basin.

Bingen is served by Amtrak. The station is located about a mile west of the marina.

Sailing conditions: (Short Board) Conditions are similar to those at Koberg Beach across the river. The wind fills in right up to the beach for easy launching. Well-formed swells develop in mid river. Inside the marina the water is smooth and flat – great for speed trials and practicing water starts and jibes.

Access: Parking is more than adequate and there is an acre and a half of grass for rigging with large poplar trees to block the wind. The long sand beach has wide ramps leading down from the dike for easy access. Chemical toilets are provided during the summer and rest rooms are available at the marina.

Improved facilities, like these access ramps at Bingen Marina, are being developed by communities throughout the Gorge in hopes of attracting more boardsailors to their area.

Hazards: Log loading areas are located to the east and west of the beach, and barges and tugs pass within 50 yards of shore. Offshore, there are pilings and a large rock outcropping parallel to the beach. Watch out for gill nets.

Wind and water reports: 386-4646 (nearest gauge – Hood River) · (509)493-3340 – North Shore Windsurfing, Bingen, Washington

Food and lodging: Bingen offers a full range of services.

The Bingen Bakery has become a legend with windsurfers.

The White House Restaurant caters to windsurfers with fine family dining.

Guido's Italian Cuisine is small but inviting.

The Grand Old House Bed and Breakfast features gourmet cuisine in its three dining rooms. The inn also has a cozy lounge and an acre of grounds, featuring a hot tub surrounded by a Japanese garden.

The Inn of the White Salmon has twenty rooms, each with a

spectacular view. It offers a world-famous country inn breakfast and an outdoor hot tub.

Wind Ranch, overlooking the Bingen Marina, caters to board sailors with tent and RV camping, rest rooms, showers and barbeques. The ranch also has a dormitory, a workshop and facilities for board storage.

The Bingen School Inn offers economical lodging with hostel beds starting at $10.00 per night and private rooms, which sleep 6 to 10 people, from $45.00. A lounge, kitchen, lockers and gymnasium are included in the price.

Other attractions: The *Mont Elise Winery* in Bingen produces an award-winning Gewurtztraminer. Visitors are welcome from noon to 5:00 PM.

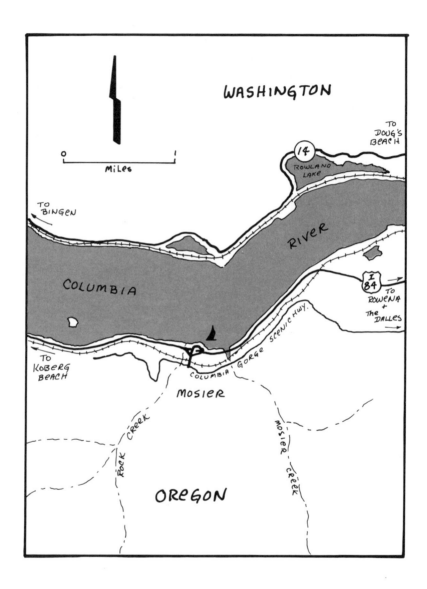

Mosier Beach

This beach is a good alternative when the sailing conditions at Doug's Beach or Hood River are too severe. Unfortunately, getting to the water is an ordeal. Despite the poor access, this site gets a fair amount of use.

Skill rating: Intermediate through expert

Location: Mosier is approximately 12 miles east of Hood River on I-84 at exit 69. The beach is visible from the freeway but the only way to reach it is by trekking under the freeway overpasses for Mosier and Rock creeks. Finding a place to park near these overpasses may be challenging.

Sailing conditions: (Short Board) Expect good winds from mid-April through September. Because Mosier Beach is located at a river bend, the west winds are generally not as strong as at other sites. The waves here tend to have a slight cross-chop.

Access: Access to Mosier Beach is almost impossible without a four-wheel drive vehicle, but improvements are planned for the near future. Boardheads determined to sail here must follow the creek channels under the freeway. This is quite a distance to carry equipment. The beach is a long sandspit jutting out into the river. This location will be excellent for practicing water starts when the improvements are completed. For the time being, however, there are no good places for rigging and no rest room facilities or other amenities.

Hazards: Watch out for barges, stumps and gill nets.

Wind and water reports: Q104 FM Radio, The Dalles, Wind reports daily at 8:00, 9:00 and 10:00 AM with an update at 3:00 PM · 386-4646 (nearest gauges – Hood River and Doug's Beach) · 976-WIND · 387-WIND

53

Food and lodging: There is a limited selection of gas, food and lodging facilities in Mosier. More are expected to open in the future as the launch facilites here are improved.

The Wind Haven Cafe and Lodging in Mosier serves breakfast, lunch and dinner with a special Saturday barbeque. Lodgings include studio and one and two bedroom units with fully furnished kitchens. Reservations are recommended: (503)478-WIND.

See also Hood River.

Other attractions: *The Columbia Gorge Scenic Highway* to Rowena passes through the center of Mosier.

See also Hood River.

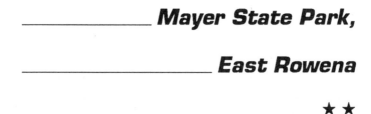

Mayer State Park,

East Rowena

★ ★

A 1986 study by the Oregon State Parks and Recreation Division determined this area to have the greatest potential for becoming a high-performance windsurfing park. In the past, the best launch sites were either privately owned or in the undeveloped portions of the park where there was no safe access. The recent completion of a new river access point at East Rowena (made possible by the cooperative efforts of the Columbia Boardsailing Association; federal, state, and local governments; and the Union Pacific Railroad) has changed all of this.

Skill rating: Expert

Location: This park is approximately ten miles west of The Dalles and twelve miles east of Hood River on I-84 near the town of Rowena. Exit 76 leads to the East Rowena site to the north, and to Mayer State Park on the south side of the freeway.

Sailing conditions: (Short Board) East Rowena is located across the river from Doug's Beach. Environmental conditions here are excellent. Good sailing winds occur from mid-April through September but the most consistent winds are from May to July. Waves are often flat at the west end of East Rowena, and become larger to the east. Not all boardsailors agree with the quality of sailing at East Rowena but everyone welcomes this new alternative to the crowds at Hood River.

Access: The East Rowena site is located at the east end of East Rowena River Road. This site has parking for 90 cars, a gravel beach, vault toilets and picnic tables. There are a few trees now for shade and additional vegetation will be planted for wind breaks. This is a day-use only area; overnight camping is not allowed.

55

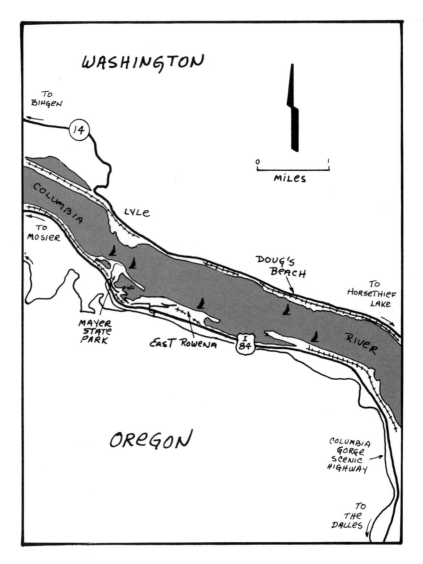

There are two other launch sites in the western section of Mayer State Park, at the end of Lyle-Rowena Ferry Road. These sites are usable, but will probably not be developed in the near future. The windsurfing conditions are only fair and river currents are dangerous. Also, it is difficult to spot approaching barges in this area. There are no nearby facilities. Pit privies are located in the park.

Hazards: Approaching barge traffic is difficult to spot at the west end of the park. Watch out for poison oak in the undeveloped areas.

Wind and water reports: 386-4646 (nearest gauge – Doug's Beach) · Q104 Radio FM – wind reports daily at 8:00, 9:00, and 10:00 AM with an update at 3:10 PM.

Food and lodging: The nearest gas or food is in The Dalles. Camping is available at Memaloose State Park four miles east of Mayer State Park. There is no eastbound access from I-84.

Other attractions: The scenic _Old Columbia Gorge Highway_ between Rowena and Hood River climbs to the top of the Gorge. There are spectacular views from Rowena Crest.

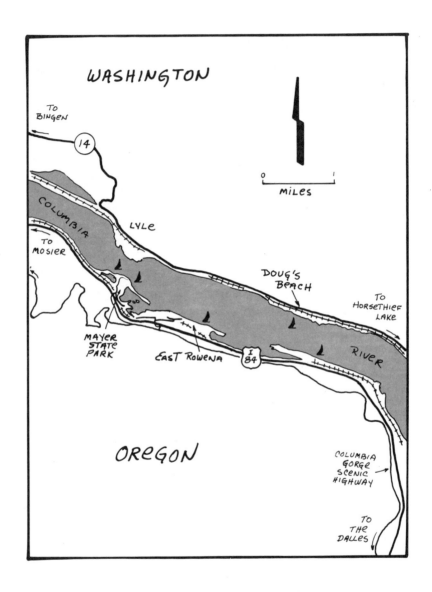

Doug's Beach,

Washington

This site is named for Doug Campbell, owner of Hood River Windsurfing and organizer of all the major sailing events in the Gorge, who discovered the site. Doug's Beach is located at the eastern end of a long straight stretch of river. The swells here easily reach 6 to 8 feet. This is no place for the beginning or even intermediate sailor. Doug's Beach is undeveloped at this time. With better access and facilities, it would definitely be a three-star site. The state of Washington hopes to develop a day-use park at this site and the legislature has appropriated $50,000 toward the project.

Skill rating: Expert only

Location: Doug's Beach is located between Hood River and The Dalles on the Washington side. From I-84, cross the river at either of these towns and take Hwy. 14. The site is approximately 2.5 miles east of the town of Lyle. Look for the line of cars parked along the highway near milepost 79.

Sailing conditions: (Short Board) There is consistently good wind from April to September; however, the best sailing is from May to July. There are huge waves for jumping and surfing.

Access: Access is poor. The only parking is alongside the highway. Follow the path across the railroad tracks and through the field to the beach. At present there are no rest rooms or other facilities available. The beach is sand with a shallow entry. There are plenty of sheltered grassy areas for rigging. Despite its limitations, Doug's Beach gets very crowded, especially on those "radioactive" days when the wind really cranks.

59

Hazards: Loading and unloading boards and equipment along-side the highway is dangerous. Be sure to exit your car on the passenger's side. Watch out when crossing the railroad tracks. Don't leave boards and equipment where they could be damaged by passing trains.

Approaching barges come from behind a point, and they pass very close to shore, making them difficult to see. There is also a sandbar on the Oregon shore which may be a hazard when the water is low.

Wind and water reports: 386-4646 · Q104 Radio FM – 8:00, 9:00, and 10:00 AM and 3:00 PM daily.

Food and lodging: The nearest gas, food and lodging are in Bingen or Lyle, Washington, or in The Dalles. Most sailors prefer to stay in Hood River and commute to Doug's Beach.

Other attractions: None. See Hood River.

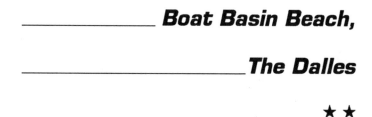

Boat Basin Beach, The Dalles

★ ★

The Gorge is generally thought of as being limited to intermediates and experts only. But many people do learn to sail here and The Dalles Boat Basin is one of the best places for beginners. This is an excellent place to practice water starts and jibes before trying some of the more "radioactive" Gorge sites.

Skill rating: Novice through expert

Location: The Dalles is 83 miles east of Portland on I-84. Take exit 85 and turn left – you can't miss it. Amtrak also serves The Dalles.

Sailing conditions: (Short and Long Board) This is a good place for long board sailing, but the ability to water start is required. Conditions at the Boat Basin can be inconsistent, but generally there are good side-shore and on-shore winds to push struggling sailors back to the beach. Advanced short board sailors may be disappointed.

Access: Access is excellent with plenty of paved parking, a nice sand beach, and acres of grass for rigging, spectating and picnicking. Rest rooms and food concessions have been added. A group of islands shelter this area from strong currents, waves and barge traffic. There's even a sand beach downwind to catch you if you get in trouble. The park facilities open Memorial Day weekend. Prior to that you can launch at the west end of the park near the boat ramp.

Hazards: There are no hazards here as long as you stay inside the island barrier.

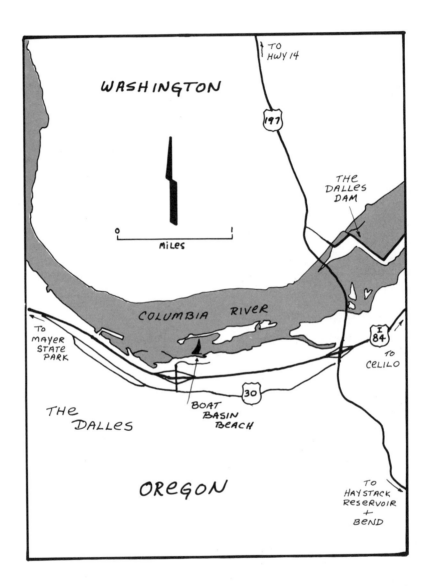

Wind and water reports: Q104 Radio FM – daily wind reports at 8:00, 9:00, and 10:00 AM with a 3:00 PM update • 386-4646

Food and lodging: There is a good selection of gas, food and lodging facilities available in The Dalles.

The historic *Williams House Inn* features breakfast served in the

secluded gazebo. Special windsurfing packages are available; call
(503)296-2889.

Deschutes River State Park, 17 miles east of The Dalles, has 34
sites for tent and RV camping.

Other attractions: *The Deschutes River Recreation Area* is about
18 miles east of The Dalles with world-famous fishing and white
water rafting.

Take the tour train from the downtown visitors center to *The
Dalles Lock and Dam.*

The Dalles Natatorium near the west end of town has an outdoor swimming pool and tennis courts which are open to the public.

In early April, The Dalles is the scene of *The Northwest Cherry
Blossom Festival. Fort Dalles Days and Rodeo* are held in mid-July.

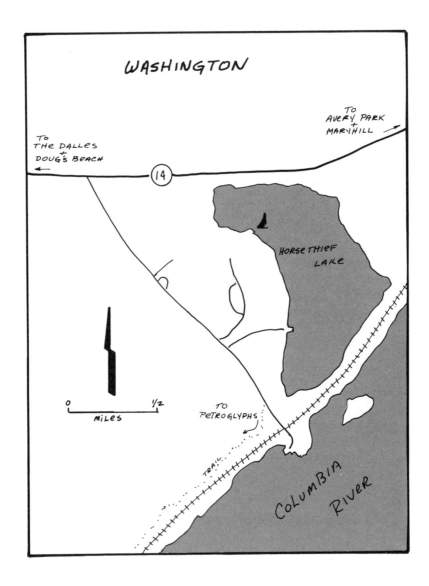

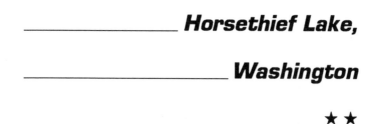

Horsethief Lake, Washington

★ ★

Separated from the river by railroad tracks, the lake has warm, sheltered water, strong winds and no current. Access to the Columbia is possible but the wind is offshore, making this an undesirable launch site.

Skill rating: Novice through intermediate

Location: The lake can be reached approximately 6 miles east of The Dalles bridge on Hwy 14.

Sailing conditions: (Long Board) Flat-water long board sailing is good from May through September. During July the wind blows strong and steady day and night, down the canyon toward the lake. On the east arm of the lake the wind is side-offshore; making short board sailing possible sometimes.

Access: This is a nice park with plenty of grass and parking areas, picnic tables and barbeque grills, a good beach and rest rooms. The park is closed in the winter but open from April first through November thirtieth. The day-use area is open from 8:00 AM to 5:00 PM.

Hazards: The winds are fluky on the west arm of the lake. On the east arm the wind is strong and steady. Novice sailors can become stranded on the far shore; it is a long walk back over sharp rocks.

Wind and water reports: (509)767-1159, park manager, 6:30 AM to dusk.

Food and lodging: The nearest gas and food are in The Dalles. Camping is available in the park with 12 tent and RV sites (no hookups). The park has rest rooms but no showers, and an RV dump station.

Other attractions: This was once the site of the Wishram Indian village of Nixluidix. Indian petroglyphs can still be seen by hiking west on the trail from the lower parking lot. In 1972 Horsethief Lake State Park was added to the National Historic Register.

See also Boat Basin Beach, The Dalles.

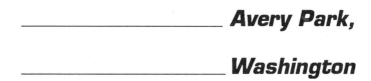

Avery Park,

Washington

This is a great sailing spot but facilities are limited. Located at the downwind end of a long, straight stretch of river, Avery Park has clean winds and well-shaped waves.

Skill rating: Intermediate to expert

Location: The entrance to the park is approximately 12 miles east of The Dalles bridge along Washington Hwy. 14.

Sailing conditions: (Short Board) Avery Park is a good high-wind sailing area, often gusty. It is best from April through September. The current is slower here, so the waves are not as high as at other sites.

Access: The park is undeveloped but it is open year round. A boat ramp is located downwind of a breakwater, making launching easier. The beach is sand and gravel with shallow water entry. There is grass nearby for rigging but parking is limited and the only other facilities are pit privies.

Hazards: Barges pass between shore and Brown's Island in mid-river. Also watch out for gill nets and trains.

Wind and water reports: 386-4646 (nearest gauges – The Dalles and Maryhill) • Q104 Radio FM – daily wind reports at 8:00, 9:00, and 10:00 AM with a 3:00 PM update.

Food and lodging: A gas station, motel and mini-mart are located approximately one mile east on Hwy. 14. Otherwise, the nearest gas, food and lodging are in The Dalles or Biggs Junction. Overnight camping is allowed at the park, but the five available

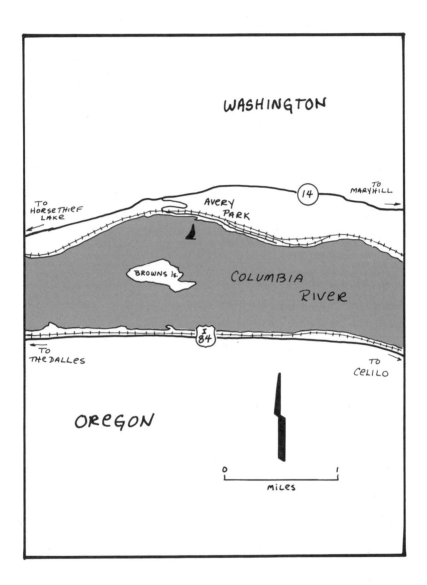

sites are primitive. Better camping can be found at Maryhill State Park or Horsethief Lake.

Other attractions: See Boat Basin Beach, The Dalles or Maryhill State Park.

Celilo Park

Celilo Park has excellent facilities, good wind – and it's rarely crowded! These factors alone should be enough to draw a crowd in the Gorge. The conditions here are often better than at Hood River or The Dalles, especially in May and June.

Skill rating: Intermediate to expert

Location: The park is 12 miles east of The Dalles on I-84 at exit 97.

Sailing conditions: (Short Board) Strong currents and high, gusty winds occur from mid-April through September. The waves are choppy, but excellent for starboard tack jumping. Side-onshore winds make this a good place to learn water starts.

Access: A large parking area is situated close to the river with plenty of grass for rigging. There is no beach and water entry is very rocky but not steep. Launching can be tricky because of the onshore waves. The park has rest rooms and a nice, sheltered area for spectators.

Hazards: The channel is very close to the Oregon shore at this location and barges approach from around a corner, making them difficult to spot. Celilo is the location of ancient Indian fishing grounds, so gill nets are apt to be numerous in this stretch of river.*

Wind and water reports: 386-4646 (nearest gauges – The Dalles or Maryhill) · Q104 Radio FM – daily wind reports at 8:00, 9:00, 10:00 AM with a 3:00 PM update.

* The Indian tribes Nez Perce, Umatilla, Warm Springs and Yakima currently fish these waters.

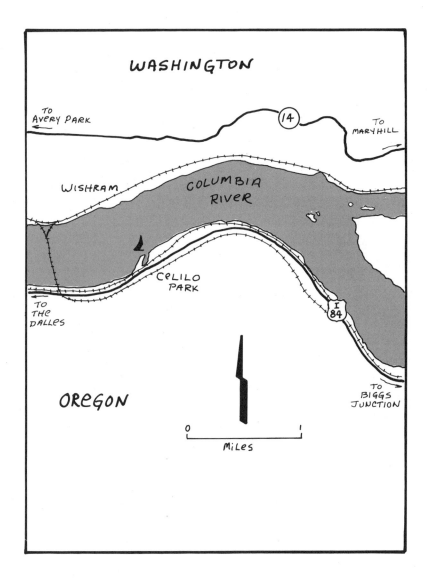

Food and lodging: The nearest gas, food and lodging are in The Dalles or Biggs Junction. Camping is available at the *Deschutes River Recreation Area*, six miles east on I-84.

Other attractions: See Boat Basin Beach, The Dalles or Maryhill State Park.

The navigation channel is very close to the Oregon shore at Celilo Park. The bend in the river makes it difficult to see barges approaching from the east.

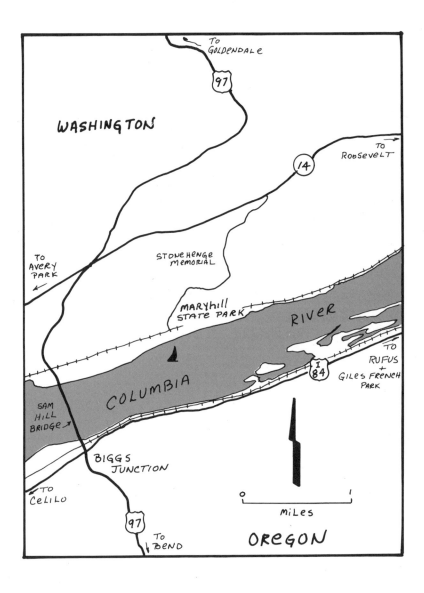

Maryhill State Park, Washington

★★

Maryhill is one of the finest high-wind, wave-sailing spots in the Gorge with excellent facilities. Some sailors gave it a four-star rating. Sailing is best early in the season when this is one of the windiest places in the Gorge. Being toward the east end of the Gorge, it also gets warmer sooner than sites farther downriver.

Skill rating: Expert

Location: Maryhill is located at the junction of Washington Hwy. 14 and U.S. Hwy. 97. From the Oregon side take I-5 east for approximately 20 miles past The Dalles. Cross the river at the U.S. Hwy. 97 bridge at Biggs Junction and follow the signs east to the state park.

Sailing conditions: (Short Board) Consistently strong west winds blow from early March through July. There may be no wind at all here in August. Temperatures are generally higher than at sites farther west.

Access: The state park has plenty of paved parking, large grass areas for rigging with rows of poplar trees blocking the wind, a pea gravel launch area (no stubbed toes), and dressing rooms with hot showers. What more could you ask for?

Hazards: The river is only four-tenths of a mile wide at this point so the current is strong. If you get in trouble, you'll end up a long ways downstream. The barges travel close to shore even though the channel is right down the middle of the river. The wind can reach 60 MPH here and has actually flipped campers on the Sam Hill Bridge, U.S. 97.

Wind and water reports: 386-4646

Food and lodging: Maryhill State Park has an excellent camp-ground. There are 50 sites with full hookups. Reservations are rec-ommended; call (509)773-5007.

Peach Beach, located next to Maryhill State Park, also has river-side campsites with plenty of grass and trees. This private camp-ground, owned by Gunkel Orchards, is the site of the annual Celilo Cup Race.

Gas, food and lodging are also available in Biggs Junction just across the Sam Hill Bridge on U.S. 97.

Other attractions: *Stonehenge*, a full-scale replica of the origi-nal stone-age monument on the Salisbury Plain in England, is set high on the hill just west of Maryhill State Park. It was built by Sam Hill, a wealthy and eccentric pioneer, as a monument to the men of Klickitat County who died in World War I.

Sam Hill's "Castle on the Columbia," now the *Maryhill Art Museum*, features the country's finest collection of works by the French sculptor Rodin. The museum is open from March 15 to November 15, 9:00 AM to 5:00 PM.

Sam Hill's "Castle on the Columbia" looks very out of place on the barren hills above the river. It now houses the Maryhill Museum of Art.

This replica of Stonehenge, high on the bluffs near Maryhill State Park, was built by the eccentric millionaire Sam Hill as a memorial to those who lost their lives in World War I.

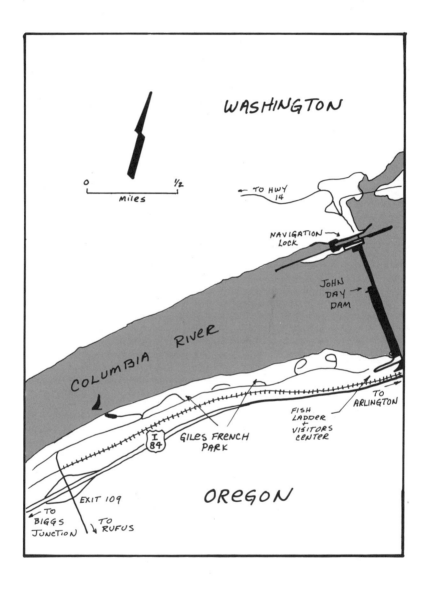

Giles French Park,

Rufus

★ ★

A good high-wind area for experienced sailors, this park has conditions similar to those at Maryhill State Park, which is along the same stretch of river on the Washington side. This area became a hot spot almost overnight, much to the dismay of the boardsailors who discovered it.

Skill rating: Expert

Location: Giles French Park is located just below the John Day Dam, 5 miles east of Biggs Junction near the town of Rufus. Take I-84, exit 109.

Sailing conditions: (Short Board) Good sailing can be found here from early March through July with strong current, high winds and enormous waves. The east end of the Gorge warms up sooner in the spring than at sites farther west, making early season sailing possible.

Access: The park stretches for several miles along the river. The beach is steep and rocky but good water access is available at the boat ramp at the west end of the park. A jetty provides shelter from the waves. There is a dock for easier entry. The park has plenty of grass for rigging, and also has pit privies.

Hazards: The channel is very narrow with strong currents. Water released from the John Day Dam can cause sudden changes in river levels. Barge traffic entering or leaving the John Day Locks travels along the Washington shore. A series of low islands and gravel bars separates the barge channel from the Oregon shore.

Wind and water reports: 386-4646 (nearest gauge – Maryhill, 4 miles west)

Food and lodging: Gas, food and lodging are available in Rufus and in Biggs Junction. There is no camping at Giles French Park but excellent facilities are available at Maryhill State Park, across the river from Biggs Junction.

Other attractions: The *John Day Dam* visitor's center is open daily to the public with tours of the facilities.

See also Maryhill State Park.

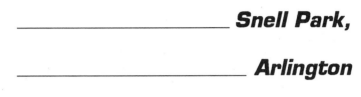

Snell Park,

Arlington

Snell Park is becoming more popular with Gorge sailors as sites farther west become overcrowded. The Port of Arlington is making many improvements to the park for the benefit of boardsailors; a wind gauge has been installed and a new beach with better river access is planned. When completed, this site will rate two or even three stars.

Skill rating: Expert

Location: Arlington is 53 miles east of The Dalles and across the river from Roosevelt Park. Take I-84 to exit 137 and head north toward the grain elevators.

Sailing conditions: (Short Board) This is another early season site, with sailing from March through August. The winds are strong and the waves are large and well-formed. Experienced Gorge sailors rate the sailing here as "fantastic."

Access: The park here is nice with plenty of parking, a marina, rest rooms, swimming areas and lots of grass and trees for rigging, all of which are sheltered from the sun and wind. Water entry is down a steep, rocky bank. The Port of Arlington plans to improve access by installing steps down to the water at the west end of the parking lot near the grain elevators. In the meantime, boardsailors have been launching in the marina and swimming their boards out into the river.

Hazards: The river is very wide at this point and the winds can be overpowering. Watch out for barges and gill nets.

Wind and water reports: 386-4646

79

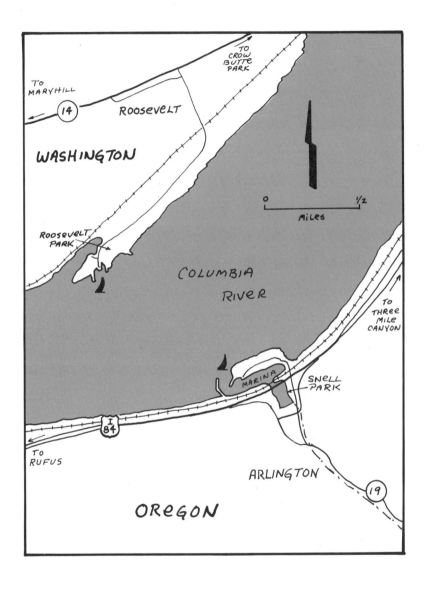

Food and lodging: Gas, food and lodging are available in Arlington.

Other attractions: None

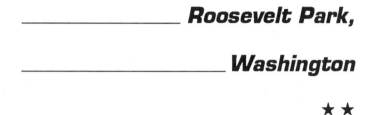

Roosevelt Park, Washington

★ ★

Sailing here is excellent, with "radioactive" winds and great waves. Sometimes the winds can be too strong. Once, a barge was overturned by the wind along this stretch of river.

Skill rating: Expert

Location: Thirty-three miles east of Maryhill on Hwy. 14, this site is just across the river from Snell Park, Arlington. From I-84, cross the US Hwy. 97 bridge at Biggs Junction and head east.

Sailing conditions: (Short Board) Sometimes Roosevelt Park is the only place in the Gorge with decent wind. Conditions here are often good when Hood River and Maryhill are flat. The sailing is best early in the season. March winds can reach 30 MPH by 10:00 AM, but by August there may be no wind at all. The river is a mile wide at this point; the best conditions are close to the Oregon shore. The current is slow but, because this site is located at the east end of a long, straight stretch, it has some of the best-formed jumping waves in the Gorge.

Access: Roosevelt Park is open year-round. There is a nice sand beach at the west end, with shallow water entry sheltered from the waves by a rock jetty. The rest rooms in the day use section of the park are closed in the winter, and their summer use depends on the availability of volunteer park attendants. There are also pit privies near the boat ramp at the west end.

Hazards: The width of the river can be a real hazard if trouble develops. Winds can become overpowering. Watch out for gill nets and barges – the channel is in mid-river.

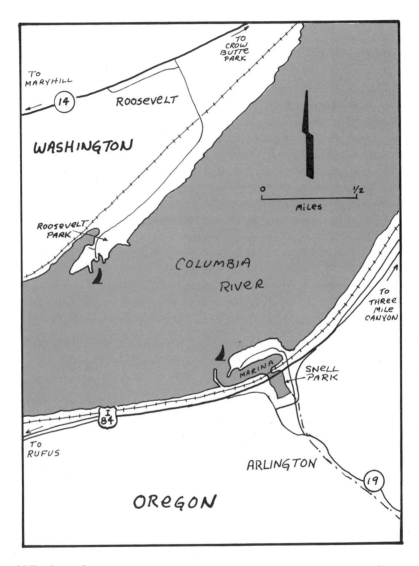

Wind and water reports: 386-4646 (nearest gauge – Arlington)

Food and lodging: There are no gas, food or lodging establishments in Roosevelt. Two cafes are located on Hwy. 14 approximately one mile east. Both are closed in the winter.

Other attractions: *Mercer Ranch Winery* is located near Aldervale approximately 15 miles east on Hwy. 14.

Three Mile Canyon

★

This site is unique in that it is separated from the river by a stone breakwater almost a mile long. This stops the waves and current but not the strong winds, creating an excellent place for practicing downwind slalom technique. There are openings in the breakwater for access to the main river.

Skill rating: Intermediate to expert

Location: Three Mile Canyon is located between Arlington and Boardman on I-84 at exit 151.

Sailing conditions: (Short Board) Inside the breakwater expect flat-water, high-wind sailing from early March through August. Outside the breakwater the river is very wide with long rolling waves and strong, consistent winds.

Access: There is a primitive park here, with plenty of parking and pit privies, but not much grass for rigging. Water entry is rocky and there is no beach. The best launch site is at the boat ramp near the west end of the parking area.

Hazards: There are no hazards inside the breakwater.

Wind and water reports: 386-4646 (nearest gauge – Arlington, 14 miles east)

Food and lodging: The nearest gas, food or lodgings are in Arlington or Boardman.

Other attractions: None

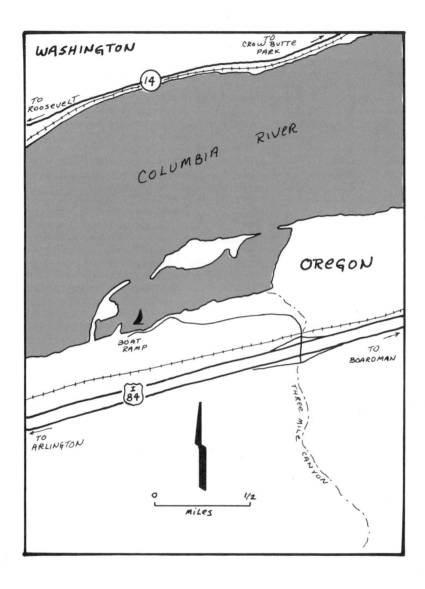

Boardman Marine Park

Boardman is located near the east end of Lake Umatilla, the 76-mile-long backwater created by the John Day Dam. The current is not strong but the winds are, and the waves can be quite large. The weather here is hot and dry with summertime temperatures often exceeding 100° F.

Skill rating: Expert

Location: Boardman is 80 miles east of The Dalles on I-84 at exit 159. Head north from the freeway, past the high school, and follow the signs to the marine park, which is located at the foot of Main Street.

Sailing conditions: (Short Board) The strongest winds are predominantly in the spring and summer from early March through August. The river is wide at this point, so there is not much current.

Access: Boardman Marine Park has rest rooms and plenty of parking. The only launch site is in the campground. Water access is down a steep, rocky bank and there is not much beach. The park is open year-round but facilities like the rest rooms and campground are closed from mid-December to mid-March.

Hazards: Watch out for barges and gill nets.

Wind and water reports: 481-7217 – park ranger, 7:00 AM to 6:00 PM daily, March 15 through December 15

Food and lodging: There is a campground at the park. Gas, food and lodgings are available in Boardman.

The C & D Drive-in, home of the "Bozo Burger," also has a bakery that makes excellent cinnamon rolls.

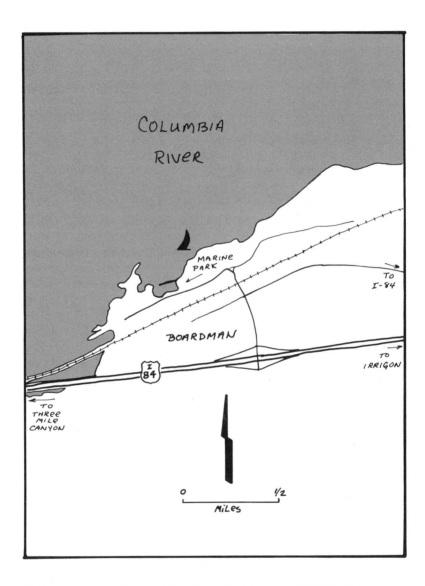

Other attractions: The *Umatilla National Wildlife Refuge* was established to restore wildlife habitat lost by the construction of the John Day Dam. Hundreds of thousands of waterfowl stop over here on their annual migrations.

Crow Butte State Park,

Washington

★ ★

Strong winds, flat water and excellent facilities make this a great windsurfing site. The distance from Hood River prevents Crow Butte from becoming crowded like the more popular sites farther west. The weather at this end of the Gorge is hot and dry with summer temperatures often exceeding 100° F.

Skill rating: Novice to intermediate

Location: Crow Butte is located off Hwy. 14 at milepost 155. From I-84, cross the bridge at Umatilla and head west approximately 25 miles. The park is on an island in the Columbia that is accessed by a causeway.

Sailing conditions: (Short board) From early March through August the wind is strong and the water relatively flat and sheltered. There is no current and the west wind is slightly onshore, making this a good place for beginners to practice water starts. The channel is narrow and not very challenging for the experienced Gorge sailor.

Access: Crow Butte State Park has plenty of parking, lots of grass for rigging, rest rooms, swimming, and picnic and camping areas. There is a small sand beach at the launch site between the boat ramp and swimming area. The waves are directly onshore when the wind is out of the west, making launching tricky. An alternate launch site east of the marina is more sheltered from the wind and waves. From November to March the park is only open on weekends and holidays.

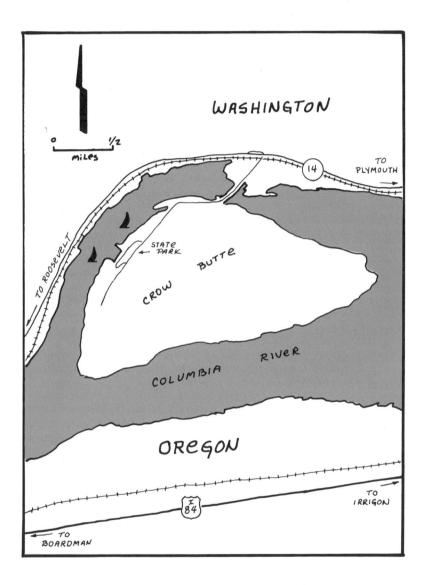

Hazards: Mooring buoys are located just offshore at the east end of the marina.

Wind and water reports: (509)875-2644 – park manager, 6:30 AM to dusk

Food and lodging: There is no gas or food nearby. The camping facilities at Crow Butte are very nice with 50 tent and RV sites, some with full hookups.

Other attractions: Crow Butte Island is at the west end of the *Umatilla National Wildlife Refuge*. A hiking trail leads to the top of Crow Butte, affording a nice view of the river and surrounding countryside.

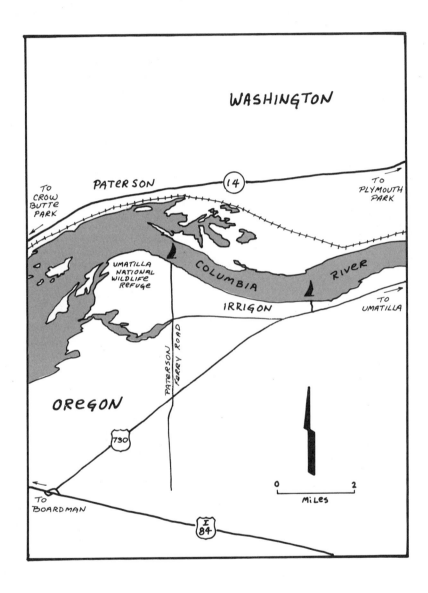

Irrigon is located just east of a large bend in the river. As a result the wind and waves at this site are not as strong or as large as at sites farther to the east or west. Irrigon is a good bet when sailing conditions are too severe at Arlington, Boardman or Umatilla. Summertime temperatures here are hot!

Skill rating: Intermediate to expert

Location: Irrigon is 9 miles west of Umatilla on U.S. Hwy. 730. Coming from the west, take exit 168 from I-84 and head east for 7 miles. The launch site is located at the end of First Street near the boat ramp.

Sailing conditions: (Short Board) The wind and waves here are moderate. Sailing is best from early March through August.

Access: At the First Street launch site there is a small dirt parking area and a sand beach with shallow water entry. No other facilities are available. An alternate site is located just west of the fish hatchery at the end of Patterson Ferry Road. More parking is available at this site. The bank is steep but a boat ramp makes water access possible. There are no facilities here, either, but public rest rooms are located at the Umatilla National Wildlife Refuge information booth, two miles south on Patterson Ferry Road.

Hazards: The channel is narrow and eastbound barges are difficult to see because of the bend in the river. Large rocks close to shore may also present a hazard. This is a popular bank fishing site, so respect anglers' rights.

Wind and water reports: 922-3939 – Umatilla Marine Park (9 miles east)

Food and lodging: Gas, food and lodging are available in Irrigon, Boardman and Umatilla.

Other attractions: See Umatilla Marine Park.

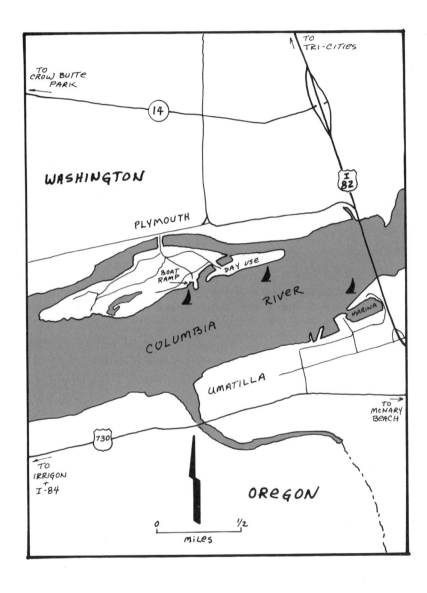

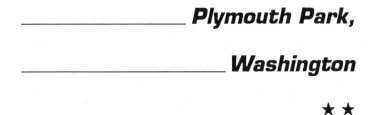

Plymouth Park, Washington

★ ★

Another early season site, Plymouth has strong winds and enormous waves. This site is generally not crowded because of the distance from the more popular sites near Hood River. The summer weather is hot and dry, and temperatures frequently exceed 100° F.

Skill rating: Expert

Location: Plymouth is just across the river from Umatilla, Oregon. From I-84, cross the bridge at Umatilla and head west on Hwy. 14 approximately 1 mile to the Plymouth turnoff. Once at the park, follow the signs to the boat ramp and day-use areas, which are located on a small island across from the campground.

Sailing conditions: (Short Board) The winds are strong and the waves large, especially on the Oregon side of the river. There is a sheltered lagoon in the day use area, where long board sailing is possible. Access to the main channel is possible on the north side of the island. The best winds occur from early March through May. Winds can be inconsistent so it is best to call ahead.

Access: The park has plenty of paved parking, rest rooms, picnic shelters and a lot of grass in the day use area. A nice gravel beach at the east end makes water access easier. The day use area and campground are open from Memorial Day through Labor Day. For the off-season, an alternate launch site is located at the west end of the island beyond the boat ramp. An unimproved gravel road leads to a small beach in the cove formed by the boat basin jetty. The bank is steep and rocky. The only amenity is a chemical toilet near the parking lot.

Hazards: Watch out for barges and gill nets.

Wind and water reports: 922-3939 – Umatilla Marine Park

Food and lodging: There is a grocery store, a cafe and a tavern in the town of Plymouth. Camping is permitted in the park during the summer. Additional gas, food and lodging can be found across the river in Umatilla.

Other attractions: See Umatilla Marine Park

Marine Park,

Umatilla

★ ★

Located across the river from Plymouth Park, this is another early-season site with huge waves and strong winds.

Skill rating: Expert

Location: Umatilla is 20 miles east of Boardman. From I-84 take exit 168 and head east on U.S. Hwy. 730, approximately 16 miles. The Marine Park is one-half mile west of the Umatilla bridge; the entrance is well marked.

Sailing conditions: (Short Board) Conditions here are similar to those at Plymouth Park, but the waves are much larger on this side of the river. The best winds occur from early March through May. Winds can be inconsistent at this end of the Gorge, so it is best to call ahead.

Access: Umatilla Marine Park has nice facilities with plenty of parking, grass, rest rooms, and swimming and picnic areas. Water access is difficult in the developed portion of the park. The best launch site is off the jetty at the east end of the marina. A gravel road behind the fenced boat storage yard leads out to the jetty, where limited parking is available. There are no facilities here but the large sand beach makes water entry easy.

Hazards: The launch site is just downstream from the bridge, and barge traffic is close to shore. The beach is also a popular bank-fishing area, so respect the angler's rights. Watch out for the wing dam at the west end of the jetty.

Wind and water reports: 922-3939 – park operator

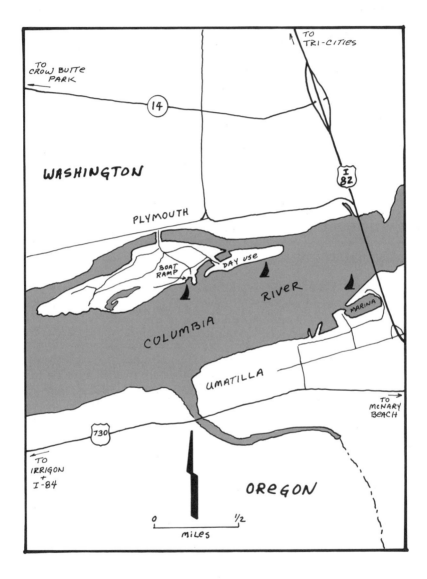

Food and lodging: Umatilla offers a selection of gas, food and lodging establishments. There is an RV campground with full hookups located in the Marine Park.

Other attractions: Umatilla is the melon capital of Oregon. Roadside watermelon stands are plentiful during the season.

The *Umatilla National Wildlife Refuge* headquarters are located in Umatilla, providing visitor information to refuge attractions.

McNary Dam Visitor Center is open 7 days a week from mid-April through September offering guided tours of the dam and lock facilities.

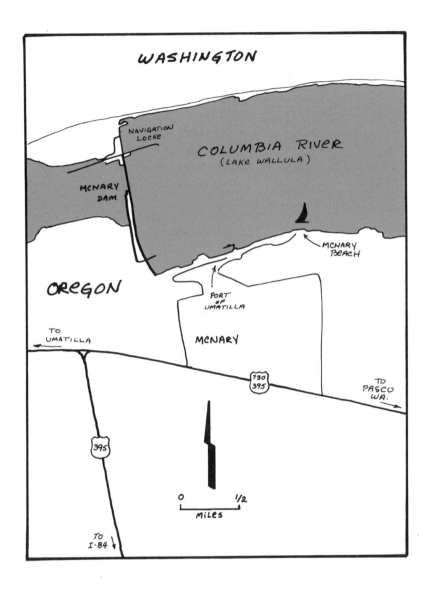

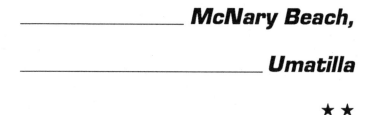

McNary Beach, Umatilla

★ ★

McNary Beach is located on Lake Wallula, the back- waters of McNary Dam. The winds are strong here and the river is more than a mile wide. There is not much current. The waves are much smaller than at the Plymouth Park and Umatilla sites below the dam. Expect hot, dry weather in the summer, with temperatures approaching 100° F.

Skill rating: Intermediate to expert

Location: McNary Beach is four miles east of Umatilla on U.S. Hwy. 730. The beach access road is located about one-quarter mile past the road to the Port of Umatilla Industrial Park, on the left hand side. The turnoff is well marked.

Sailing conditions: (Long and Short Board) This is a good spot for long or short board sailing with strong winds and relatively small waves. It may even be possible to uphaul sails under moderate wind conditions. The best sailing winds occur from early March through May. Winds are inconsistent here so it is best to call ahead.

Access: There is a nice park with plenty of paved parking, rest rooms, a lot of grass and trees, and swimming and picnic areas. Water entry is difficult in most of the park because of the steep, rocky bank. The best launch site is at the far east end of the park where there is a small sand beach. The park is open year-round but the rest rooms are only open from April through mid-October.

Hazards: McNary Dam is just downstream a short distance. The navigation channel and locks are on the Washington side but barges approach the Oregon side to reach the docks at the Port of Umatilla Industrial Park.

Wind and water reports: 922-3214 – control room at McNary Dam, 24 hours a day

Food and lodging: There is no overnight camping at McNary Beach, but there is a private campground at Hat Rock State Park, 5 miles east on U.S. Hwy. 730. The nearest gas, food or lodgings are in Umatilla.

Other attractions: See Umatilla Marine Park.

Region Two: _____

_____The Oregon Coast

The Oregon Coast

Next to the Gorge, the most exciting and challenging boardsailing in Oregon is found along U.S. Hwy. 101, the Coast Highway. Sailing in the open ocean is the essence of "windsurfing," jumping waves on the offshore reach, and surfing on the return. It is not something for the novice, and intermediate sailors are cautioned to avoid extreme high wind and surf conditions. If you cannot make a water start in waves of at least three feet, you have no business going out in the ocean. This should not stop beginners from visiting the coast. There are plenty of sheltered waters to be found in the coastal lakes and bays, having almost the same strong consistent winds found on the ocean beaches. These are ideal places to perfect sailing skills, before gradually making the transition to ocean wave sailing.

Oregon's ocean beaches are public domain up to the line of vegetation, and the state has one of the finest networks of parks and waysides in the nation. Beach access points are never more than a mile or two apart. Boardsailing is relatively new to the Oregon coast, so for the time being, at least, there is plenty of space on shore and in the water. You will not encounter the crowded conditions that have become commonplace in the Gorge.

The locations listed in this chapter are favorites with local sailors or are otherwise popular because of their proximity to Portland and the Willamette Valley. Since there are not many local sailors along the coast, many potentially excellent areas have never been sailed. So, if you come upon a promising site that is not listed in this book, go for it! And if you feel generous, tell a friend.

As the weather along the Oregon coast is mild, never too hot in the summer or too cold in the winter, it is possible to sail here year-round. The water is always cold, no matter what the season, and wet or dry suits are required. Ocean sailing is usually best in the months of May through September, when the prevailing wind is from the northwest and the surf averages 3 to 6 feet. In the winter months the wind shifts to the southwest. Severe storms and rough surf conditions between November and March can make

Sailing in the open ocean is the essence of "windsurfing."

sailing in the ocean extremely dangerous. There are a few places where ocean sailing is possible in the winter, but most local sailors prefer the bays and coastal lakes at this time of year.

The northwesterly summer winds are most consistent in the months of June and July, blowing 30 to 35 MPH almost daily. The onshore breezes usually begin around noon as the air from the cooler ocean rushes in to replace the warmer air rising over land.

Dave Bender from Wichita Kansas has the right prescription for midwest windsurfing blues. A quick ambulance ride to the Oregon coast.

Generally speaking, the further south along the coast you go, the stronger the winds blow. On the other hand, the waves and surf decrease as you head south. If conditions are not to your liking where you are, you should be able to find the right combination of wind and surf somewhere else along the coast.

The best locations for ocean wave sailing are usually to the south of headlands. When the summer winds encounter these land masses, the air is deflected around the obstacle. In doing so, the speed increases much the same way air speed increases when it passes over the wings of an airplane or on the windward side of a sail. This increase may be as much as twice the prevailing wind speed. Large offshore rocks and even the jetties at river mouths can create this same phenomena. By projecting a line from the tip of the headland in a southeasterly direction toward shore, the line of optimum wind can be located. To the north of this line the wind will be fluky because of the eddies formed behind the obstacle. Farther south the wind speed diminishes.

The second ingredient for a hot wave-sailing location is a

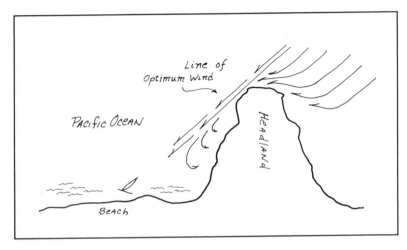

gentle, evenly sloping sand beach. At these locations the waves
will generally run parallel to the beach regardless of the angle from
which they originated. On gently sloping beaches the surf will
break in a peeling wave which, as surfers know, makes for the
longest ride. During the winter storms the sand is piled higher on
the beach, which makes the slope much steeper and creates plunging rather than peeling waves. Sailing in this type of surf is very
rough and unpleasant, one reason why most ocean wave sailing is
done during the summer months.

Getting the most enjoyment from ocean wave sailing requires
the right equipment. Wave boards are generally shorter, for jumping, with smaller sails to handle the stronger winds. Equipment
designed for use in the Gorge is ideal for the coast as well. Most
production boards, however, may not be strong enough for serious
wave jumping. Without stringers to provide extra strength, they
may be broken easily in heavy surf. Many wave riders prefer to
use asymmetrical boards, especially in big, fast waves. These are
custom boards with a portion of the tail cut away on one side to
make bottom turning easier. If you don't have the right equipment
for ocean wave sailing, you can usually rent what you need from
one of the local shops.

Sailing in coastal waters can be dangerous for the unexperi-
enced. If you have never sailed in tidewaters, it is a good idea to
go with someone familiar with local conditions. The following are
some potential hazards that must be taken into account:

Tides: Along the Oregon coast the tides rise and fall twice each day. Tidal changes occur approximately every 6 hours and 15 minutes. Prior to each turn of the tide there is a period of slack water when things are relatively calm. Outgoing tides can be extremely dangerous, particularly near the mouth of a shallow estuary. Here the outrushing water meets the opposing force of the ocean swells, creating an area of very rough water called a "bar." The height of the tide is a good measure of the potential current strength. The higher the tide, the stronger the current. An unwary boardsailor could easily be swept over the bar and out to sea by the force of a strong outgoing tide.

Incoming tides can also be dangerous. Logs on the beach are easily moved in the rising water. Every year in Oregon someone is injured or killed by logs rolled by sneaker waves. People can also become trapped by the incoming tide. Headlands, rocks and tide pools that are easily accessible during low tides may be completely surrounded or submerged by water when the high tide returns. Tide tables, which predict the times and heights of the tides, should be consulted before venturing out in coastal waters. These tables can be found almost anywhere along the coast – just ask.

Fog: Some areas along the coast experience a perpetual fog bank during the summer months. The fog moves offshore as the land heats up during the day and the sea breeze begins to blow. Normally fog is not a problem for boardsailors. If there is enough wind for sailing, any fog will be quickly dissipated. However, in the evening, as the land cools once more, the fog can move onshore rapidly. A boardsailor caught in fog may become disoriented. This is certainly no state in which to be if you get in trouble.

Fog occurs in pockets along the coast. If you arrive at a planned launch site and find it fogbound, try another location. Often, moving a mile or two north or south is all it takes.

Rip Currents: These are strong offshore currents created where the surf runs back out to sea. Once waves break on the beach, the water tends to move in a direction parallel to the shoreline until it can escape through the incoming surf. This is the location of a rip current. Usually they occur where the water is deeper or where there is a break in an offshore barrier or reef.

(See figure 2.) Rip currents can sometimes be spotted by the muddy color of the water, caused by the sand stirred up by the pounding surf. Boardsailors downed in a rip current will find themselves being swept out to sea. If caught in this situation, don't panic. Stay with your board and ride the current out past the breakerline, where the current will die out. Another solution is to paddle your board across the current until free.

Sharks: Shark attacks are generally not common along the Oregon coast, partly because the water is so cold. However, "man eaters," such as the great white shark, are found in the area and at least three accounts of surfers being attacked by sharks have been reported in recent years. One attack occurred near Haystack Rock off Cannon Beach and another near Cape Kiwanda at Pacific City. Sharks feed on sea lions, which are quite common on the large offshore rocks during the summer months. It is easy to understand how a hungry shark might mistake a surfer for a sea lion. It is hard to say if the same would be true for a downed boardsailor. Certainly the behavior and appearance of a boardsailor in the water is quite different from that of surfers, who lie on their boards waiting for the "right wave." Nevertheless, if sea lions are in the water you should assume that sharks may be there also and take the necessary precautions. Leave the water at the first sight of a tell-tale dorsal fin.

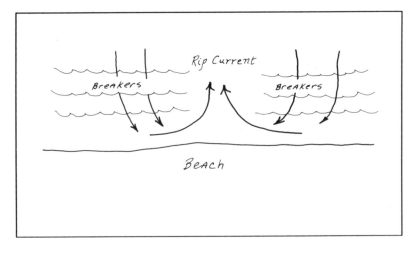

Reefs: Many Oregon beaches have reefs or rocks offshore that may be completely submerged during high tides. Where these are known to exist, they have been listed under hazards in the individual site descriptions. But it is possible that some have been overlooked. Likewise, if you are sailing in an area that is not listed in this guide, you should be on the lookout for these hazards. Submerged rocks or reefs offshore can sometimes be spotted by the occurence of white water beyond the normal line of breakers. If the obstacle occurs within the breaker zone, the pattern of waves will be different in that area. Take a moment to scan the surf for possible hazards before heading offshore.

Sailing in coastal waters can be dangerous, but the risks can be minimized if you obey the rules discussed in the introductory chapter and in Appendix B. In addition to these safety rules, there are certain rules of etiquette that apply to wave riding, regardless of where you are sailing:

1) Always give the right of way to downed boardsailors, surfers or swimmers.
2) The first sailor on a wave has rights to that wave over all other sailors.
3) If two sailors catch the same wave at the same time, the upwind sailor has the right of way.
4) Sailors changing course or jibing have no rights over other sailors.
5) Sailors making water starts must wait until they have a clear path before going.

Great boardsailing is only part of the fun on the Oregon coast. There are numerous other sites and activities to ensure a memorable trip. The scenery is some of the finest in the world with lush green forests, rocky headlands jutting out into the ocean, long stretches of white sand with hidden treasures for the beachcomber, and fantastic sunsets. Twice each year, in the early spring and again in the fall, herds of gray whales make their annual migration between the Arctic and their breeding grounds off the Baja Peninsula. They can be seen from elevated headlands such as Neah-kah-nie Mountain near Manzanita. For a closer look, guided boat tours are available. Many of these opportunities are mentioned in the individual site descriptions.

For the sportsman, the beaches, bays and rivers offer a veritable smorgasbord. Crabs, clams, mussels, shrimp, salmon and deep sea fish can easily be caught, or purchased fresh at local markets, for that perfect beach party after a great day of sailing. If you prefer to dine out, the coast offers a wide choice from small diners featuring home-style cooking to four-star gourmet restaurants. Towns along the coast vary from sleepy little communities that haven't changed in 30 years to lively tourist meccas with all the amenities. No matter what their size, almost every community has some sort of festival celebrating coastal life. During the summer months you can count on finding one or more of these events almost every weekend. So be sure to save a little time to sample the local color.

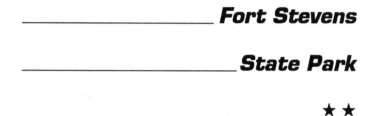

Fort Stevens

State Park

★ ★

Fort Stevens State Park has something for everyone regardless of equipment or skill level. There are three launch points within a mile, each with different sailing conditions. Jetty Lagoon offers great flat water sailing year-round, with conditions similar to "The Ponds" in southern California. This is an excellent place for flat out speed sailing. The beach at South Jetty provides easy access for open ocean wave sailing. If the surf is too rough or the wind is out of the east, the Columbia River offers a third alternative.

Skill rating: Novice through expert

Location: Fort Stevens State Park is located 7 miles west of Astoria and 13 miles north of Seaside. The turnoff from U.S. Hwy. 101 is well marked. Follow the signs to the day use area. Jetty Lagoon is located across the road from Parking Area B. An old railroad trestle at the north end marks the spot. South Jetty access is located at parking area C and access to the Columbia River is located at parking area D.

Sailing conditions: (Long and Short Board) *Jetty Lagoon:* Shallow, with flat water, this is a good place for beginners to practice water starts. These sheltered waters permit both summer and winter sailing.

South Jetty: Excellent open ocean wave sailing is possible from June through August, when winds are from the northwest and the waves are small. Afternoons are typically the best time of day. The jetty provides shelter from the wind and waves, making launching easier.

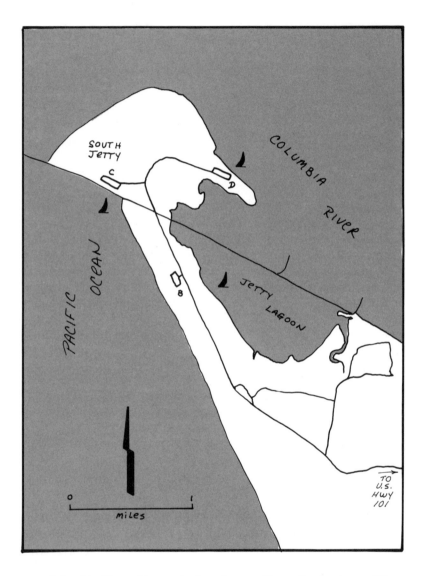

Columbia River: Fantastic for river sailing, the best conditions exist during the months of April through September when the northwest winds can reach 30 to 50 MPH. Although the river is almost two miles wide at this point it is still affected by the ocean swells and tides. This is a good place to get a feel for offshore sailing before venturing out in the open ocean.

Flat water speed sailing is the main attraction of the coastal lakes and estuaries.

Access: *Jetty Lagoon:* Getting to the water requires a short hike across a tidal marsh. The ground is usually firm and the marsh grass provides a good setup area. There are no rest rooms or other facilities in the immediate area although they are located elsewhere in the park.

South Jetty: To reach the water you must climb down over the jetty, which is constructed of large rocks. At low tides there is a narrow sand beach. At high tides the surf may come right up to the jetty, making water access difficult, if not dangerous. An observation tower at this site is useful for determining surf conditions and for taking photographs. There is no grass for rigging. Privies in the parking lot are the only amenities.

Columbia River: A narrow, gently sloping sand beach makes rigging and launching very easy. Privies are located at the southeast end of the parking area.

Hazards: *Jetty Lagoon:* none

South Jetty: Strong rip currents and undertows can occur, particularly after exceptionally high tides. Avoid sailing north of the jetty; currents at the mouth of the Columbia can be extremely hazardous. Sailing in southwest winds is not recommended.

Columbia River: Strong outgoing currents following high tides can sweep an unwary sailor out to sea. Remember, the Columbia River is a major commercial waterway. Try to avoid the main channel and watch out for freighters, barges and large fishing boats.

Wind and water reports: (206)642-3565 – U.S. Coast Guard, Ilwaco, Washington · 738-7888 – Cleanline Surf Co., Seaside

Food and lodging: Gas, food and lodging can be found in Astoria and Seaside.

Fort Stevens State Park has over 500 camp sites with 213 full hookups, 130 electrical hookups and 262 tent sites.

Other attractions: *Fort Stevens State Park* has a number of attractions including an old Civil War fort with historical interpretive museum; Fort Clatsop, site of Lewis and Clark's settlement during the winter of 1805-06; and the wreck of the *Peter Iredale*, a four-masted British sailing ship that ran aground on Clatsop Spit in 1906.

The Union Baths, 285 W. Marine Drive in Astoria, offer public steam baths, hot tubs and tanning booths.

The Astoria Tower, built in 1926, is 125 feet high with murals by renowned artist Attilio Pusteria depicting historical events of the area. The view from the top of the tower is breathtaking, especially at sunset.

The Columbia River Maritime Museum, in Astoria, features exhibits depicting the history of marine commerce on the Columbia River.

Youngs Bay

Youngs Bay is the point where the Youngs River enters the Columbia River Estuary. The bay is oriented toward the northwest so it receives perfect side shore winds and the waves are clean. The U.S. Hwy. 101 causeway crosses the north end of the bay, eliminating most commercial boat traffic. This spot is not very popular yet, but it will be.

Skill rating: Novice through intermediate

Location: Youngs Bay is located southwest of Astoria. Take U.S. Hwy. 101 south from town. At Hwy. 202 head east approximately one-half mile, toward the town of Jewel.

Access: The best access is just west of the Dairy Queen. There is parking along both sides of the road, but little shelter or room for rigging. A low riprapped bank leads to the water. There are no public rest rooms or other amenities.

Sailing conditions: (Long and Short Board) The best sailing conditions are in the spring and summer months, May through September, when the wind is out of the northwest. The causeway dampens the impact of the ocean swells, making this a good flat water sailing site.

Hazards: A row of old pilings about 50 yards offshore may be submerged during high tide. There are also rocks extending 5 to 10 feet from shore which can easily damage a skeg. Gillnetters fish Youngs Bay in late summer and fall.

Wind and water reports: (206)642-3565 – U.S. Coast Guard, Ilwaco, Washington · 738-7888 – Cleanline Surf Co., Seaside

Food and lodging: In addition to the Dairy Queen, the Bay View Motel is located right across the highway from this site.

115

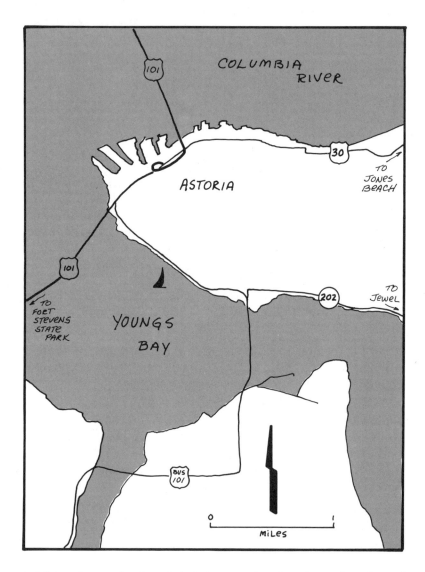

Additional gas, food and lodging can be found in Astoria and Seaside.

Other attractions: Fishing is very important to the local economy and *The Great Astoria Crab and Seafood Festival* is held each year in late March to help celebrate this fact.

See also Fort Stevens State Park.

Seaside Beach

Seaside Beach is included partly because of its boardsailing conditions, which are generally good, but also because of its other attractions. Seaside is Oregon's equivalent of Coney Island or Venice, California. Broadway and The Prom, along the beachfront, have the atmosphere of a carnival midway, although they have become somewhat more sophisticated in recent years. In typical Oregon fashion, many attractions are indoors so that inclement weather won't spoil the fun.

Skill rating: Expert

Location: Seaside is located on U.S. Hwy. 101 approximately 16 miles south of Astoria and 75 miles west of Portland via U.S. Hwy. 26, the Sunset Highway.

Sailing conditions: (Short Board) This site offers good open ocean wave sailing May through September, when northwest winds can range between 30 and 50 MPH.

Access: Seaside Beach is several miles long; however, it is against city ordinance to launch sailboards along The Prom. Launching is permitted north of Twelfth Avenue or south of Avenue U. A small parking area located at the end of Twelfth Avenue is only a short walk from the water. The beach is sand at this point, which is easier for rigging, but there are no rest rooms or other amenities.

A better launch site is located at the end of Avenue U on the south end of town. There is a small parking area, picnic tables and barbeque grills. The beach is rocky, making rigging more difficult, but the bottom is sandy once you're in the water. There is food, lodging and even a small market within a block or two of the parking lot.

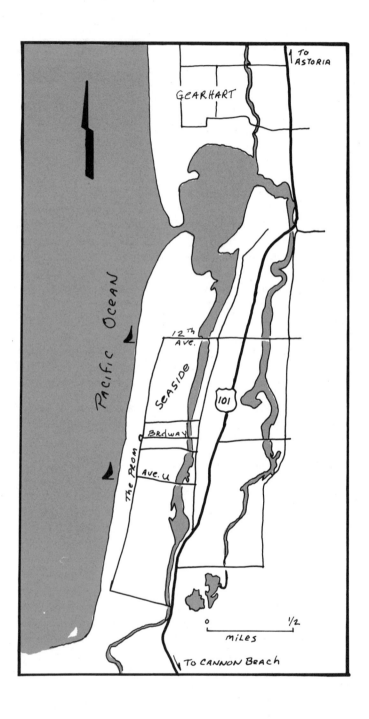

Hazards: In addition to the normal hazards of ocean wave sailing, like tides and rip currents, beware of low-flying kites and Frisbies, tourists on mopeds, skateboarders and rollerskaters.

Wind and water reports: 738-7888 – Cleanline Surf Co., Seaside · (206)642-3565 – U.S. Coast Guard, Ilwaco, Washington

Food and lodging: A wide selection of gas, food and lodging accommodations is available in Seaside. Motel and bed and breakfast rates increase with proximity to the beach.

The Shilo Inn, at the end of Broadway on The Prom, has an excellent dining room and a lounge where drinks are served in fish bowls for real "party animals." The lodging accommodations include oceanfront rooms with fireplaces and an indoor pool. The Shilo is the center of nightlife in downtown Seaside.

Gearhart-by-the-Sea, just north of Seaside, has luxury condominiums on the beach, assuming money is no object.

A number of private campgrounds are located north and south of Seaside along U.S. Hwy. 101. _Venice RV Park_, on 24th Avenue, is a modern park with full hookups, TV, rest rooms and laundry facilities. The park even offers an adults-only section.

See also Tolovana Park and Fort Stevens State Park.

Other attractions: Broadway – the _Million Dollar Walk_, as the Chamber of Commerce likes to call it – has more than 50 unique shops, restaurants and arcade attractions along a five block stretch from U.S. Hwy. 101 to the beach promenade.

The Lewis and Clark Salt Cairn, on Lewis and Clark Avenue at Beach Drive, is the end of the Lewis and Clark Trail. The intrepid explorers built and operated the cairn between 1805 and 1806 to make salt by boiling sea water. The salt was used for preserving meat and for trading with the natives.

A visit to the _Seaside Aquarium_ on The Prom, is like a visit to the ocean bottom. Sea creatures of every description are on display, but the stars of the show are the harbor seals.

See also Tolovana Park and Fort Stevens State Park.

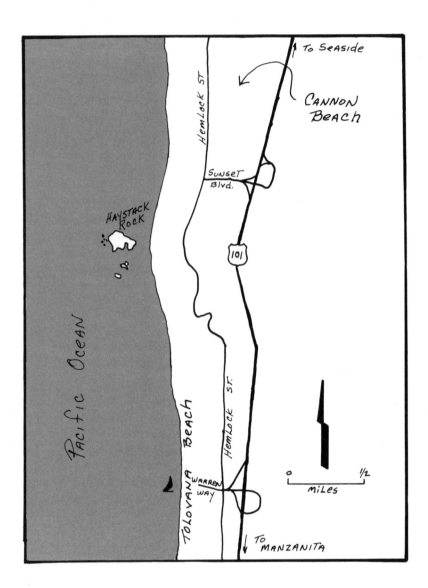

Tolovana Beach

Tolovana Beach is located midway between Tillamook Head on the north and Cape Falcon on the south, making it one of the few places on the north coast where ocean wave sailing is possible year-round.

Skill rating: Expert

Location: Tolovana Beach is approximately 27 miles south of Astoria on U.S. Hwy. 101 and 80 miles west of Portland via U.S. Hwy. 26. The turnoff is well-marked, just south of the city of Cannon Beach.

Sailing conditions: (Short Board) Ocean sailing here is good to excellent. Many locals come here in the winter, September through March, when the wind and surf are too high for wave sailing at other north coast beaches. Summer winds may be fluky because of large offshore rocks at the north end of the beach.

Access: Tolovana Beach Wayside has plenty of parking, public rest rooms, grass areas for rigging and a great sand beach for easy water entry.

Hazards: Shallow reefs located one-quarter to one-half mile off-shore may be submerged and difficult to see during high tides. Warning flags for surf conditions are posted during the summer months. Red means danger, yellow caution, and yellow and blue means swimming is allowed. A lifeguard is available by phone (436-2345).

Wind and water reports: 738-7888 – Cleanline Surf Co., Seaside · 322-3531 – U.S. Coast Guard, Garibaldi

Food and lodging: An excellent selection of food and lodging facilities are available at Tolovana Beach and in Cannon Beach, a mile or so to the north. This is an upscale resort area, so prices are apt to be high.

Tolovana Inn, across from the beach, has studio, one- and two-bedroom units with fireplaces, kitchens and private balconies. The Inn also has an indoor pool, sauna, jacuzzi and recreation room.

The *RV Park at Cannon Beach* is located on U.S. Hwy. 101 at the north entrance to Cannon Beach. The nearest state park with camping facilities is Oswald West, about 8 miles south of Tolovana Beach on U.S. Hwy. 101. The campsites are primitive. Campers must hike in about one-quarter mile from the parking area. Despite this, the 36 sites fill rapidly and are often full on summer weekends and holidays. The beach at Oswald West is a favorite with surfers and may be fun to try with a sailboard. Leave your rig on the rack; the beach is too sheltered for sailing.

See also Seaside, Manzanita Beach and Nehalem Bay.

Other attractions: Cannon Beach is home to a large colony of artists and craftspeople, with many excellent shops and galleries displaying their wares. The community is also home to *Haystack Program in the Arts*. This is a summer-long program for adults with short courses in writing, visual arts and music offered through Portland State University.

Each year since 1964 the community has held *Sandcastle Day*, a sand sculpture contest that has become world-famous, attracting tens of thousands of participants and viewers. The date of the event is controlled by the tides so it changes every year, but it usually happens in late May or early June.

The *Coaster Theatre* in Cannon Beach, is rated as one of the finest community theaters in the northwest. Check with the Chamber of Commerce concerning the current schedule of attractions.

See also Seaside, Manzanita Beach and Nehalem Bay.

Manzanita Beach

This area offers some of the best wind and weather conditions on the north coast. Sheltered on the north by Neah-kah-nie Mountain, Manzanita usually enjoys sunshine when adjacent coastal areas are fogbound. When the thermometer tops 85 degrees in Portland and the Gorge is becalmed, the windsurfing should be hot in Manzanita.

Skill rating: Intermediate to expert

Location: Manzanita is located about halfway between Seaside and Tillamook on U.S. Hwy. 101. From Portland, take U.S. Hwy. 26 west to U.S. Hwy. 101 then head south, approximately 22 miles from the Seaside Junction. The Neah-kah-nie Beach, Manzanita or Nehalem Bay State Park exits all lead to the beach at Manzanita.

Sailing conditions: (Short Board) The strong, clean winds, intensified by Neah-kah-nie Mountain to the north, make wave sailing at Manzanita Beach awesome. Like most offshore areas along the coast, the best sailing months are May through September, and sometimes October. The wind is usually calm until afternoon, then it blows steady until sunset, with side-shore breezes averaging 30 to 35 MPH.

Access: Manzanita Beach stretches for 7 miles from the foot of Neah-kah-nie Mountain to the mouth of Nehalem Bay. The beach is gently sloping sand, making for easy setup and launching. Public access is available at many points. Look for the "beach access" signs.

Most sailors prefer to rig and launch at the end of Treasure Cove Road. This is in a residential area with limited parking and no facilities. The increasing numbers of boardsailors, parking problems and incidents of trespassing have caused some local residents to complain to the city. Access to the beach at this area may be restricted in the future.

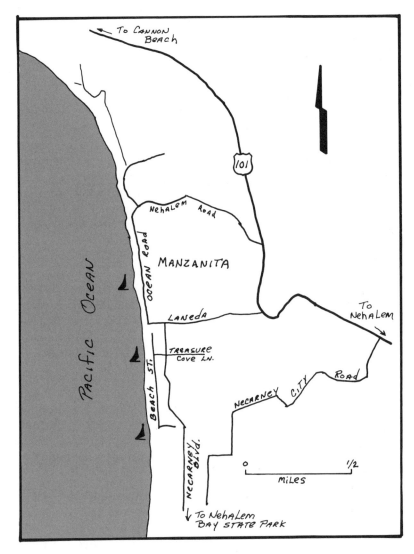

Better access can be found along Ocean Avenue in Manzanita. Roadside parking is plentiful and public rest rooms are located in town on Laneda Avenue. Beach access is also available at Nehalem Bay State Park south of town. The park day use area has plenty of parking and rest rooms. The main drawback here is the hike over the dunes to reach the water.

The beach at Manzanita has some of the best jumping waves on the north coast.

Hazards: Strong rip currents and undertows can occur, particularly following unusually high tides.

Wind and water reports: 842-7525 – Tillamook Chamber of Commerce · 738-7888 – Cleanline Surf Co., Seaside

Food and lodging: Gas, food and limited lodgings are available in Manzanita and the nearby towns of Nehalem and Wheeler. Motel rates run from moderate to expensive.

The Inn at Manzanita features a wet bar and fireside hot tub in every room, in addition to breakfast in bed.

Nehalem Bay State Park offers year-round camping with 291 sites available, all with electrical hookups. Group camping sites can be arranged and there are special facilities for equestrians, cyclists and pilots. Reservations are recommended during summer months – (503)368-5164.

There are several excellent restaurants in Manzanita and Nehalem, with prices moderate to expensive. _Nina's Italian Restaurant_, the _Uptown Supper Club_ and the _Blue Sky Cafe_ are all recommended.

Sailboards are not the only craft attracted by the strong coastal winds. The broad flat beach at Manzanita is great for landsailing; speeds of 40 to 50 MPH are not uncommon.

Other attractions: The hard, flat sands of Manzanita beach are ideal for speedsailing. This is done on a modified skate board equipped with a sailboard rig. Speeds of 40 to 50 MPH are not uncommon. Sailcarts are also popular here.

The old fashioned *Fourth of July* celebration in Manzanita is the beach party of the year. The festivities begin with a funky parade at which it's hard to distinguish the participants from the spectators. The party ends with a spectacular fireworks display on the beach at dusk.

The Northwind Music Festival, held each Labor Day weekend in Manzanita, is one of the northwest's best-kept secrets. With all the atmosphere of a church picnic, guest artists and local talent serve up a mixture of jazz, bluegrass and baroque music. Audience participation is welcome and it's free!

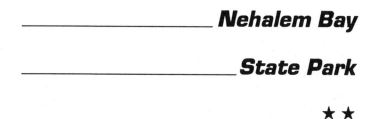

Nehalem Bay

State Park

★ ★

The sailing experience at Nehalem Bay changes with the seasons. In the summer, the sheltered bay waters provide an alternative to wave sailing at nearby Manzanita Beach. In the winter, when the wind comes from the southwest, the conditions are very similar to those at the Gorge, with strong winds and opposing currents. That's why the area is known as "The Little Gorge." The best winter conditions are usually immediately preceding or following a storm front.

Skill rating: Novice to expert (depending on time of year)

Location: Nehalem Bay State Park is located just south of Manzanita Beach. Follow the directions to Manzanita, but stay on U.S. Hwy. 101. Turn at the Texaco station, approximately three-quarters of a mile past the Manzanita junction, and follow the signs to the park.

Sailing conditions: (Long and Short Board) Summer winds out of the northwest can range from 25 to 35 MPH creating a 2- to 3-foot chop on incoming tides. Between November and April, the winds blow straight up the Bay from the southwest, reaching 40 to 60 MPH when storm fronts approach. Heavy stream runoff in the Nehalem River during the winter creates a strong opposing current on the outgoing tide.

Access: The best access to Nehalem Bay is at the boat ramp located in the state park. Just follow the signs south from the park entrance. Sandy beaches north and south of the boat ramp are excellent for setup and water entry. This is a good place to learn water starts. There is a large sandbar off Fishers Point, directly

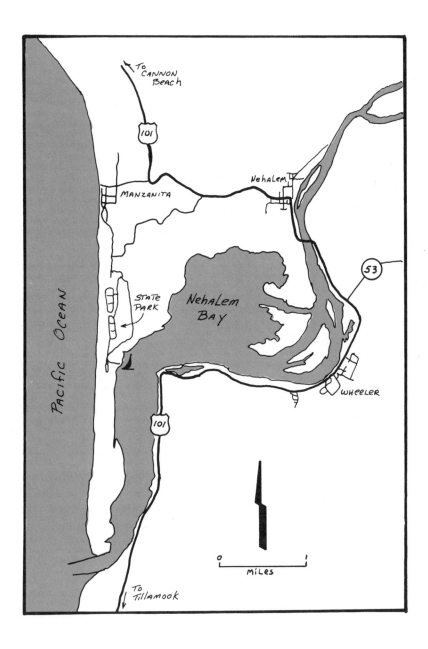

across from the boat ramp, which is ideal for land jibes. Driftwood piles along the beach provide shelter from the wind and privacy for changing, picnics or what-have-you! Privies are located near the boat ramp parking lot and rest rooms are available in the nearby day use area.

Hazards: Boardsailors should be wary of sandbars, sunken logs, crab buoys and pleasure boaters at all times. In the winter following heavy rains, be on the lookout for floating logs and debris.

Wind and water reports: 842-7525 – Cleanline Surf Co., Seaside

Food and lodging: Moderate to expensive motel accommodations are available in Manzanita. Additional lodging can be found south on U.S. Hwy. 101 in Bayside Gardens and Wheeler.

Nehalem Bay State Park offers year-round camping with 291 sites available, all with electrical hookups. Group camping sites can be arranged. Reservations are recommended during summer months, call (503)368-5164.

Other attractions: The town of Nehalem, like many other coastal communities, has several festivals throughout the year. _Nehalem Duck Days_, in February, welcomes the return of the Nehalem Navy and features "Sasquack," a sort of Neanderthal duck-ape, as master of ceremonies. In March the _Nehalem Bay Canoe Races_ are held, attracting amateur and professional racers from around the northwest. July is the time for the _Nehalem Arts Fair_, one of the oldest and largest on the north coast.

See also Manzanita Beach.

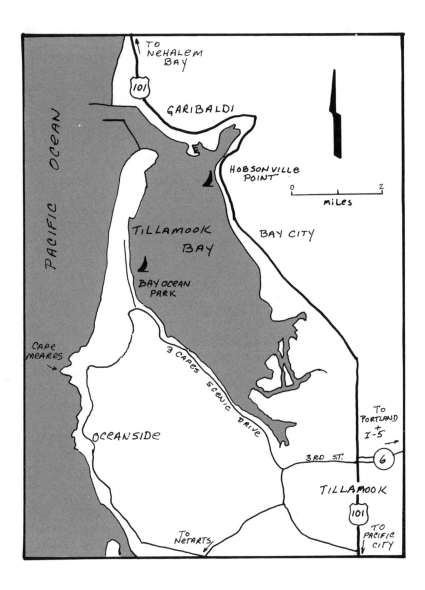

Tillamook Bay

★

Tillamook Bay has the potential of being a great boardsailing location. It has more than 8,000 surface acres separated from the Pacific Ocean breezes by only a low sand spit. The water is relatively shallow so it is warmer than most bays on the Oregon Coast; however, wet or dry suits are still required. This site was given a one-star rating primarily because the access is poor. An increase in use by boardsailors might result in improved facilities in the future.

Skill rating: Novice through expert

Location: Tillamook Bay is located on U.S. Hwy. 101 approximately 80 miles west of Portland. Take the Sunset Highway (Hwy. 26) west from Portland to the Wilson River Highway (Hwy. 6), approximately 20 miles. Follow Hwy. 6 to the junction of U.S. Hwy. 101 and head north approximately 7 miles to Tillamook Bay.

Sailing conditions: (Long and Short Board) Tillamook Bay offers year-round sailing. Wind conditions vary so it is a good idea to call ahead. The best sailing is on a high, outgoing tide with west to northwesterly winds, when fast reaches up to 3 miles long are possible.

The Bay is a popular fishing spot during the fall salmon runs, in late August through November. Several hundred fishing boats may be concentrated in a very small area when the fishing is hot. Fortunately, the winds are generally not good for boardsailing at this time of year.

Access: The only access points for Tillamook Bay are found along U.S. Hwy. 101 at Hobsonville Point, near mile post 58, or across the bay at the City of Bay Ocean Park* near Cape Meares.

* There was once a city named Bay Ocean at the site of the park. During a winter storm, the city was washed away, and the park commemorates that event.

When the wind is out of the west the best sailing can be found just south of Hobsonville Point in an area called "The Ghost Hole." There is a paved parking area off the highway at this location but water entry is over the bank, which is riprapped with large rocks. There is no beach, so rigging must be done in the parking area with little shelter from the wind. The ability to water start is necessary to sail from this location.

Better access can be found at Hobsonville Point, about a mile to the north. A short trail from the parking area leads down to a narrow gravel beach, which is usable in all but extremely high tides. The point provides shelter for rigging in both summer and winter winds. Once in the water you can sail south to find better wind and still return to the launch site by reaching across the Bay, providing the tide is with you. On the beach are the remnants of an old pier. The cement foundation makes an excellent fire pit. There are no rest rooms or other amenities at this site.

When the wind is out of the extreme northwest, there may be a wind shadow at both Hobsonville Point and The Ghost Hole, making launching difficult and returns almost impossible. At these times, head across the Bay to Bay Ocean spit. Take Third Street west out of Tillamook and follow the Three Capes Scenic Drive towards Cape Meares. The turnoff to City of Bay Ocean Park is in approximately 7 miles on the right. A large parking area with chemical toilets is located at the end of the dirt road.

Hazards: There are a number of sandbars due west of Hobsonville Point. The main channel goes right past Hobsonville Point, with strong currents on the ebb tide. Both problems can be avoided if you sail on the incoming tides. Sunken logs and snags are also a danger, particularly on the tide flats. A number of commercial oyster beds are located on the far side of the bay and up the mouth of the Tillamook River. Oyster shells are rough on bare feet; foot protection is recommended. The oystermen are not keen on people being in this area, particularly if they disturb the oysters. There are also several submerged pilings in this area, as well as large steel tubs used for harvesting oysters. These hazards can be easily avoided by staying in the northern half of the Bay. Be sure to watch the water level on outgoing tides. If you run out of water it can be a long walk back across the mudflats.

Wind and water reports: 322-3234 – U.S. Coast Guard, Garibaldi • 842-7525 – Tillamook Chamber of Commerce

Food and lodging: Gas, food and lodging are available in Garibaldi, just north of Hobsonville Point, and in Bay City and Tillamook to the south.

Miller's Bayside Restaurant, at the mooring basin in Garibaldi, has excellent seafood, fresh daily.

Lupe's Mexican Cafe, in Bay City, has some of the best food this side of Mexico City.

Downies Cafe, also in Bay City on C Street, offers down-home cooking. This is where the local people go for breakfast.

Several private RV parks are located around Tillamook Bay on U.S. Hwy. 101. The nearest state parks with camping facilities are at Cape Lookout and at Nehalem Bay. A county park, located at Barview Jetty, north of Hobsonville Point near the mouth of Tillamook Bay, has tent and RV camping. The campsites are primitive by state park standards but the park has rest rooms with running water and hot showers. Some RV sites have full hookups.

See also Oceanside Beach and Netarts Bay.

Other attractions: The *Tillamook Cheese Factory*, on U.S. Hwy. 101 just north of the city of Tillamook, welcomes hundreds of thousands of travelers annually. Visitors stop to watch the making of world-famous Tillamook Cheddar and to sample the delicious Tillamook Ice Cream. Look for the schooner *Morning Star II*, symbol of Tillamook Cheese products, on the front lawn.

The *Tillamook County Pioneer Museum* in Tillamook contains artifacts from the pioneer people, red and white, who first settled the area. The museum also contains one of the finest natural history exhibits in the state.

At the *Mid-Winter Swiss Festival* in early March, Tillamook residents celebrate their Swiss heritage. The *Tillamook Dairy Festival and Rodeo* are both held on the same weekend in late June.

Deep sea angling for salmon or bottom-fish, clam digging and crabbing are other year-round attractions of Tillamook Bay.

See also Oceanside Beach and Netarts Bay.

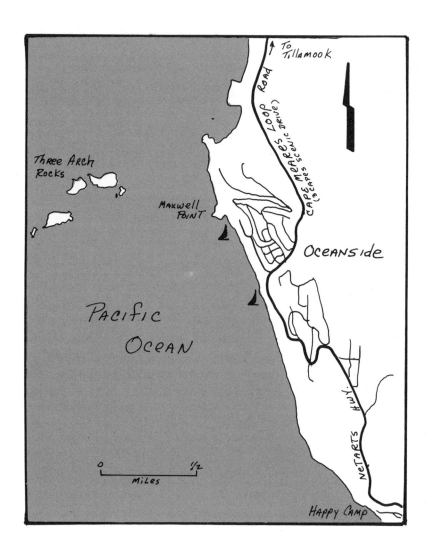

Oceanside Beach

Oceanside has to be one of the most picturesque towns on the Oregon Coast. It is reminiscent of a Mediterranean village, with the houses sitting high on the terraced hillside overlooking the ocean and Three Arch Rocks. This formation is so named because each of the offshore monoliths has an arch through the middle, carved out over the eons by the relentless surf. No one to my knowledge has done it yet, but at least one local windsurfer I talked with is determined to sail his board through the arches.

Skill rating: Intermediate through expert

Location: Oceanside is located approximately 10 miles west of Tillamook. Follow the Three Capes Scenic Route (Netarts Hwy.) west from U.S. Hwy 101. The road makes a loop so you can go either to the right along the Bay to Cape Meares or left toward Netarts and Cape Lookout State Park. The distance is about the same either way.

Sailing conditions: (Short Board) The wave sailing is good to excellent from June through August, and the scenery is some of the best on the north coast. Afternoons, when the ocean wind blows side-onshore, are best.

Access: The best wind is found just south of town but the access is difficult, down a steep bank approximately 30 feet to the beach below. There is parking alongside the road across from the waste water treatment plant. No rest rooms or other amenities are available at this location, but there is plenty of room for rigging once you reach the beach.

A better launch site is found at Oceanside Beach Wayside, right in town. This location has plenty of parking, public restrooms and a short, easy trail to the beach. The rocks offshore and Maxwell Point may cause fluky winds so you will have to walk or paddle your board south to find clean air.

Hazards: Wherever there are offshore rocks, seals and sharks may be present, particularly in late summer when the water is relatively warm. Great white sharks have been spotted at Oceanside.

The wind between the offshore rocks and Maxwell Point can be strange. In the lee of the point, the wind actually blows offshore. Strong currents and riptides can also be a problem in this area. It is best to stay south of the rocks where the wind is clear.

Wind and water reports: 842-7525 – Tillamook Chamber of Commerce

Food and lodging: Gas, food and lodging are available in Netarts and Oceanside at all price ranges. Additional facilities are available in Tillamook approximately 10 miles east.

Try *Roseanna's Cafe* or The *Anchor Tavern* in Oceanside for excellent food and ocean views.

The House on the Hill Motel, on top of Maxwell Point, has an unsurpassed view of Three Arch Rocks, Netarts Bay and Cape Lookout.

The nearest state park with camping is *Cape Lookout*, approximately 14 miles south on Whiskey Creek Road. The park, which is open year-round, has 250 tent and RV sites with full hookups, rest rooms and hot showers. Reservations are recommended in summer months. (Write: 13000 Whiskey Creek Road W., Tillamook, OR 97141.) There are also a number of privately operated RV parks in Netarts.

See Netarts Bay and Tillamook Bay.

Other attractions: *Three Capes Scenic Drive* winds along the coast for 20 miles offering the traveler spectacular ocean vistas from Cape Meares, Cape Lookout and Cape Kiwanda.

Cape Meares State Park, on the Three Capes Scenic Drive, has a lighthouse built in 1890 which is open to the public. The crystal lens for this light was hand ground in France and hoisted 200 feet up the cliff by a hand-operated crane. The Octopus Tree is also found here. Legend has it that this unique Sitka Spruce contains the spirits of departed Indian chiefs.

Cape Lookout Trail, also on the Three Capes Scenic Drive, goes out to the tip of the Cape, almost 2.5 miles offshore. From there the hiker has an excellent view of seabirds and of gray whales during their spring and fall migrations.

See also Netarts Bay and Tillamook Bay.

Netarts Bay

Netarts Bay is a favorite with locals because it has something for everyone. Near the mouth there are strong winds and ocean swells to challenge any expert. Further up the bay the swells and winds lessen, so you can pick your launch site to suit your skill level. The bay has a number of shallow sandbars which are excellent places to practice water starts.

Skill rating: Novice to expert (depending on location)

Location: Netarts Bay is approximately 7 miles west of the city of Tillamook. Follow the Three Capes Scenic Route (Netarts Hwy.) west from U.S. Hwy. 101 to the town of Netarts.

Sailing conditions: (Long and Short Board) Netarts Bay offers good sailing year round but the best conditions are found in the months of April through August, when the northwest winds average a consistent 20 MPH. Afternoons are generally best. The swells are largest near the mouth and decrease inland to flat water. For wave sailing, high outgoing tides are best.

Access: Experts will want to sail near the mouth of the bay. The best place to launch is at Happy Camp Resort. This site is located just inside the bar. There is adequate parking, a nice sand beach for rigging and rest rooms nearby. Stay on Netarts Hwy. past the town of Netarts to the Happy Camp Resort turnoff. Take this road to the end and park in front of Bay Haven Court. The surf breaks on the bar approximately 200 yards offshore from this point, with relatively quiet water toward shore. This makes water starts much easier and gives wave jumpers the opportunity to pick up speed before hitting the surf.

Intermediate sailors may want to launch near the Schooner Lounge. The turnoff is just before you enter the town of Netarts; look for the Schooner signs. There is limited parking along the

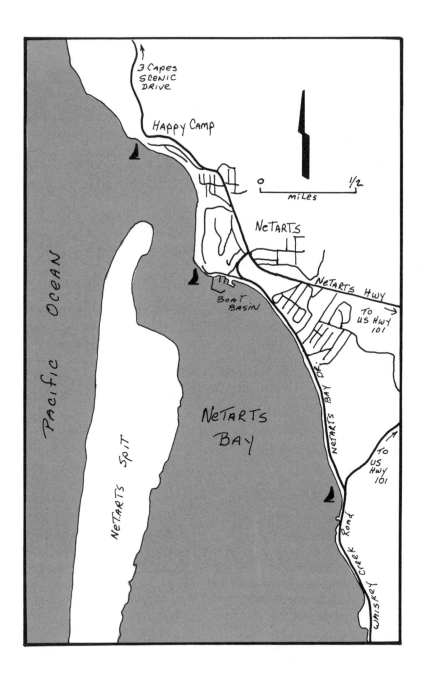

Boardsailing on the sheltered waters of Oregon's coastal bays and lakes is becoming more popular. Here a lone sailor enjoys the strong winds on Netarts Bay.

road to the west of the Schooner and a narrow sand beach for launching. Additional parking and rest rooms are found at the county boat basin nearby.

The best launch place for beginners is further up the Bay, approximately 2 miles south of Netarts at the junction of Netarts Bay Drive and Whiskey Creek Road. Follow the road signs toward Cape Lookout State Park. This site has off-road parking and a grassy setup area. The beach is rocky but the water is shallow and the bottom sandy. A small, sheltered lagoon makes uphauling easier. There are no rest rooms or other amenities here.

Hazards: Strong rip currents near the mouth of the Bay make water starts extremely difficult. At least one local sailor has lost his board over the bar here when he developed rigging trouble. This area is strictly for experts.

The area south of the county boat basin is popular for crabbing, so look out for the buoys. The shallow sandbars can also be a hazard if you don't watch the tides. It can be painful as well as embarrassing to be unexpectedly catapulted from your board into 6 inches of water.

Wind and water reports: 322-3234 – U.S. Coast Guard Station, Garibaldi · 842-7525 – Tillamook Chamber of Commerce

Food and lodging: Gas, food and lodging are available in Netarts and nearby Oceanside, as well as in Tillamook, approximately 10 miles east.

The _Schooner Lounge_ and the _Tides Inn Cafe_ both have good home cooking.

The _Terrimore Motel_ in Netarts has new units overlooking the bay and ocean.

RV camping is available at _Happy Camp Resort_, at _Big Spruce Trailer Park_ in Netarts, and at _Bay Shore RV Park_ on Whiskey Creek Road. All have full hookups and rest rooms with hot showers. The nearest state park with camping is Cape Lookout.

See also Oceanside Beach.

Other attractions: Netarts Bay, one of the cleanest and most pristine estuaries in Oregon, has excellent fishing, crabbing and clam digging. With a little effort, the ingredients of a great barbeque or clam bake can be had. Boats and equipment are available for rent at Happy Camp Resort and at Bay Shore RV Park.

See also Oceanside Beach and Tillamook Bay.

Tierra Del Mar

Although there hasn't been much action here yet, Tierra Del Mar should be a great wave-sailing beach. It is located on the south side of Cape Lookout with a gently sloping sand beach – all the right conditions for creating strong winds and spilling waves.

Skill rating: Intermediate to expert

Location: Tierra Del Mar is located approximately 2 miles south of Sandlake on Sandlake Road. The turnoff from U.S. Hwy. 101 is approximately twelve miles south of Tillamook. Heading north from Pacific City, take the Three Capes Scenic Drive. Tierra Del Mar is approximately 2 miles past Cape Kiwanda.

Sailing conditions: (Short Board) Wave sailing should be best during the summer months from May or June through August or September.

Access: There is limited parking along the roadside and it's only a short walk to the beach. Cliffs to the south provide some shelter from the wind for rigging and changing. There are no rest rooms or other amenities. The nearest public rest rooms are at Cape Kiwanda, 2 miles south.

Hazards: All the general hazards of ocean sailing apply to this area. Tierra Del Mar is fairly isolated, so a boardsailor in trouble may go unnoticed. Sailing alone is not recommended here or at any other ocean beach.

Wind and water reports: 965-6412 – Dorymen Fish Company, Pacific City • 842-7525 – Tillamook Chamber of Commerce • 322-3234 – U.S. Coast Guard Station, Garibaldi

Food and lodging: Gas, food and lodgings are available in Pacific City approximately 2 miles south. The motels are few and reservations are recommended during the summer months. Food is also available at Cape Kiwanda along with public and privately

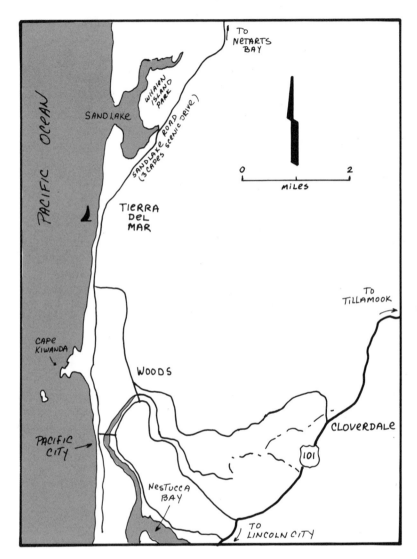

operated campgrounds. A large *Thousand Trails Campground in Woods** is open to members only. Additional camping is available at Whalen Island Park, Sandlake and Cape Lookout State Park to the north.

Other attractions: See Pacific City, Netarts Bay and Oceanside Beach.

---

* *Thousand Trails* is the name of a chain of RV campgrounds.

Pacific City

The Pacific City area is referred to as "The Chambers" by local surfers and boardsailors. The beach here is wide with a flat, gentle slope into the ocean. This causes the surf to break in long symmetrical patterns, making it a hot place for wave-riding. Pacific City is the home of the Dory Fleet. Fishermen launch their flat-bottomed dories right off the beach and head out through the surf to the fishing grounds beyond Haystack Rock.

Skill rating: Intermediate to expert

Location: Pacific City is approximately 24 miles south of Tillamook and 20 miles north of Lincoln City. The turnoff from U.S. Hwy. 101 is well marked. From I-5 take Hwy. 22 out of Salem to the Little Nestucca River Road and turn left. This road joins U.S. Hwy. 101 approximately 2 miles south of the Pacific City junction.

For a more scenic drive, try taking the Three Capes Scenic Route from Tillamook. Pacific City is just south of the last cape, Cape Kiwanda. This route passes several other good boardsailing sites at Oceanside Beach, Netarts Bay and Tierra Del Mar.

Sailing conditions: (Short Board) The locals say the wind is always great here. The best sailing is during the summer northwesterlies, June through August or September. It may be possible to sail here in the winter months as well, since the surf does not seem to be as rough as at other areas.

Wave riding is the main attraction. The wind and surf combine to give long smooth runs. For the ultimate ride at The Chambers, an asymmetrical custom board is the ticket.

Access: The best access is located behind the Turnaround Motel. Once you reach Pacific City, turn at the blinking red light and head west on Pacific Avenue. Cross over the bridge and go straight, past the stop sign, to the beach. Some parking is available

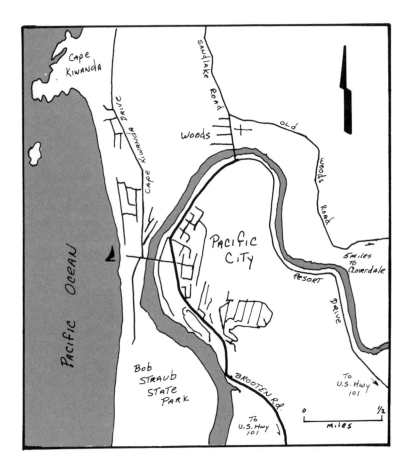

behind the motel. Vehicles are allowed on the beach at this point, but don't try it without four-wheel drive. The beach is sand with plenty of room for rigging. The dunes are slightly higher to the north of the parking area, giving some shelter from the wind. There are no rest rooms or other amenities at this location; however, public rest rooms can be found at Bob Straub State Park approximately one-half mile to the south.

Hazards: All the general hazards associated with open ocean sailing discussed in the introduction apply to this area. Haystack Rock, off Cape Kiwanda to the north, may attract seals and therefore sharks to the area.

Wind and water reports: 965-6412 – Dorymen Fish Company, Pacific City · 322-3234 – U.S. Coast Guard Station, Garibaldi · 842-7525 – Tillamook Chamber of Commerce

Food and lodging: Gas, food and lodging are available in Pacific City and at nearby Cape Kiwanda. Motels are limited but there are a number of beach houses for rent by the day, week or month.

Cape Kiwanda RV Park has 130 sites with full hookups, rest rooms with hot showers and laundry facilities.

For a quick meal try *Fat Freddy's* on Pacific Avenue, or for gourmet food in a casual setting with a view of the Nestucca River, try *The Riverhouse* on Brooten Road.

Other attractions: Cape Kiwanda, near Pacific City, is one of the few places along the Oregon Coast where fishermen launch their dory boats off the beach. Each year in mid-July the community sponsors the *Dory Festival*, with events for all ages both on and off the water. Try a dory boat charter trip for some excellent salmon and bottom fishing off Haystack Rock.

See also Netarts Bay and Oceanside Beach.

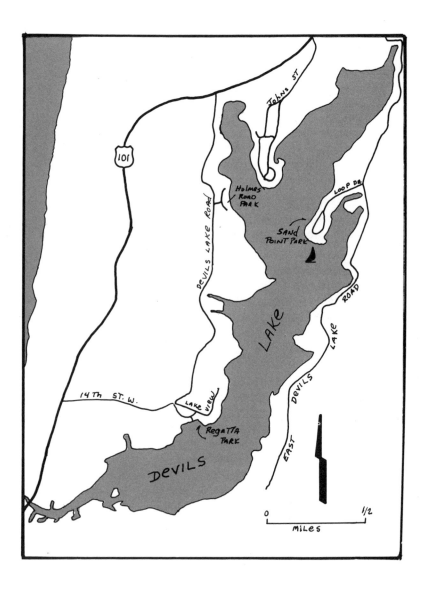

Devil's Lake combines flat water lake sailing with strong onshore coastal winds. It is a great place for novices to improve skills and gain confidence. The powerful winds and warm, sheltered waters are excellent for perfecting those water starts before heading out into the Pacific.

Skill rating: Novice through intermediate

Location: Devil's Lake is located at the north end of Lincoln City, just east of U.S. Hwy 101. From I-5, take Hwy. 22 west from Salem, then Hwy. 18 to Lincoln City. The turnoff from U.S. Hwy. 101 is well-marked.

Sailing conditions: (Long Board) The winds are generally good to excellent except during the months of August and September. In the summer the winds should be best in the afternoon. During the winter the best sailing will be just before or following a storm front.

Access: There are several state and local parks with access to Devil's Lake. The locals recommend Sandpoint Park on the northeast shore. This park has plenty of parking, rest rooms and picnic areas with lots of grass for rigging. It is located on a point at the junction of the two arms of the lake. This means that the wind will always be side-onshore regardless of direction. To reach the park, follow East Devil's Lake Road from U.S. Hwy. 101 to Loop Drive, then head west to the park.

Hazards: Aquatic vegetation in the lake can be a problem, especially for long boards with deep daggerboards. The weeds can get tangled on the daggerboard, causing drag and making sailing difficult.

Wind and water reports: 765-2123 – U.S. Coast Guard Station, Depoe Bay

Food and lodging: Lincoln City and the surrounding area, known as "The Twenty Miracle Miles," has more food and lodging facilities than anywhere on the Oregon Coast. Gas, food and lodging can also be found in Neskowin, 12 miles north, or in Depoe Bay 12 miles south of Lincoln City.

The Shilo Inn has excellent accommodations in addition to a fine dining room and lounge.

Mo's Restaurant, located on Siletz Bay in the historic Taft area of Lincoln City, is world famous for its clam chowder.

Eleanor's Undertow Take Out, located across from Mo's, features fresh baked muffins, quarter-pound chocolate chip cookies and pies baked by Eleanor's mother. In addition, they serve great hamburgers and old-fashioned ice cream and fountain treats.

The nearest state park with camping is West Devil's Lake State Park. Some sites have full hookups and the rest rooms have hot showers.

See also Siletz Bay.

Other attractions: The annual *Grass Carp Festival*, held in September, celebrates the introduction of these worthy fish to Devil's Lake to eat the masses of weeds. So far the fish haven't made much of a dent in the weed problem, but it's still a good excuse for a party.

The *Driftwood Derby*, in October, features horse racing on the beach, the only event of its kind on the Oregon Coast.

Cascade Head, approximately 10 miles north of Lincoln City, has a number of trails leading to the point of the cape with scenic vistas. This is a great place for watching migrating whales from March to May, or sunsets any time of year.

See also Siletz Bay.

D-River Wayside

This is another good wave sailing location. D-River Wayside is a popular tourist area with lots of activity. If you like to show off for the people on the beach, this is the place to go.

Skill rating: Expert

Location: D-River Wayside is at the north end of Lincoln City on U.S. Hwy. 101. Look for the huge kites that are always flying at this site.

Sailing conditions: (Short Board) The best sailing conditions are from May through August, when the northwesterly wind blows side-onshore. Winds will be strongest in the afternoon, usually dying out at sunset.

Access: The D-River Wayside has plenty of parking, rest rooms, and easy beach access. There is a small grass area for rigging and drying sails and equipment. This is a popular spot and can be very crowded, especially on summer weekends.

Hazards: Beware of strong currents and riptides.

Wind and water reports: 765-2123 – U.S. Coast Guard Station, Depoe Bay

Food and lodging: There is an excellent choice of gas, food and lodging available in Lincoln City. A kiosk, located at the north end of the D-River Wayside, contains important information on local establishments, courtesy of the Oregon State Highway Division.
See also Devil's Lake and Siletz Bay.

Other attractions: See Devil's Lake and Siletz Bay.

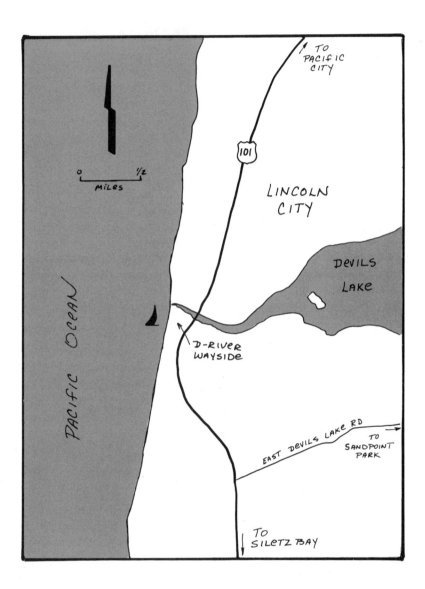

Siletz Bay offers great flat-water speed sailing. The Bay is separated from the ocean by a low, narrow sand spit that stops the surf but not the wind. Because it is very shallow (2 foot average depth) it's a good place for novices to master the water start.

Skill rating: Novice to expert

Location: Siletz Bay is located just south of Lincoln City on U.S. Hwy. 101. From I-5, take Hwy. 22 west from Salem, then Hwy. 18 to Lincoln City.

Sailing conditions: (Long and Short Board) Like most Oregon bays, it is possible to sail in Siletz Bay year-round. The most consistent winds occur between May and July, averaging 25 to 30 MPH. During August and September there is very little wind. In October, the wind pattern shifts from the northwest to the southwest and the winter storms begin. At this time of year the best winds occur a day or two before or after a storm.

Access: The locals launch near the Bay House Restaurant. Parking is limited along U.S. Hwy. 101 at this point. A narrow rocky beach lies just over the low bank. There is not much area for rigging but launching is easy in the shallow water. The remainder of the bay, for the most part, is sand bottomed.

An alternative launch site is Siletz Bay Park, approximately one-quarter mile north of the Bay House Restaurant, on the banks of Schooner Creek. It has limited parking off the highway but an adequate area for rigging and launching.

Hazards: The Bay is scattered with large stumps and logs from bygone storms, many laying just under the surface at high tide. While these obstacles make the sailing interesting, they can also be dangerous if you are not alert. Watch the water level on outgoing

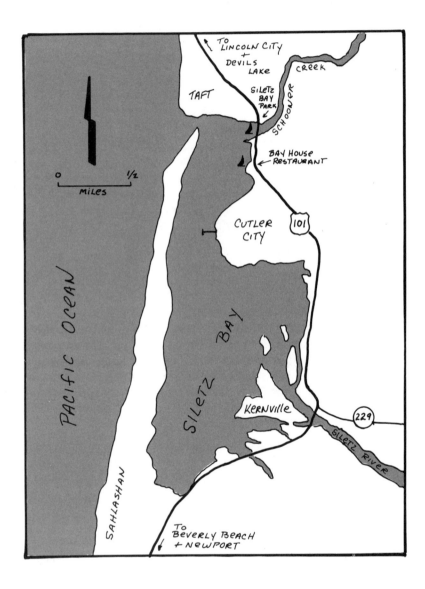

tides. Running aground on a sandbar can be painful as well as embarrassing.

Wind and water reports: 765-2123 – U.S. Coast Guard Station, Depoe Bay

Food and lodging: Lincoln City and the area to the south is known as "The Twenty Miracle Miles" because it has more food and lodging facilities and beach access than anywhere else on the Oregon Coast.

Sahlashan Resort, located at the south end of Siletz Bay, is the premier destination resort on the Oregon Coast. If money is no object, this is an excellent base of operations for your coastal boardsailing safari. The resort offers all the amenities, including an airport, 18-hole golf course, indoor tennis courts, swimming pools, fine dining and entertainment.

The Channel House Bed and Breakfast, overlooking the channel into Depoe Bay, has oceanfront suites with private whirlpool tubs.

Chez Jeannette, on Old Highway 101 in Gleneden Beach, 2 miles south of Siletz Bay, features intimate dining and excellent food.

See also Devil's Lake and D-River Wayside.

Other attractions: The Siletz River is renowned for Chinook salmon, steelhead and trout fishing. Siletz Bay itself is great for ocean perch, crab and flounder. The beaches in the Lincoln City area have some of the best tidepools on the coast. For anyone exploring tidepools for the first time, be prepared to spend several hours in this captivating pastime but don't become trapped on the rocks by incoming tides.

Depoe Bay, to the south on U.S. Hwy. 101, is one of the smallest and busiest harbors on the west coast. Charter and commercial boats negotiate the narrow channel under the highway to reach the rich fishing grounds just offshore. Whale watching and scenic coastal cruises are popular as well, with boats leaving every hour.

The *Honeywood and Oak Knoll Wineries* both have outlets with tasting rooms in Lincoln City. Watch for the signs along U.S. Hwy. 101.

See also Devil's Lake and D-River Wayside.

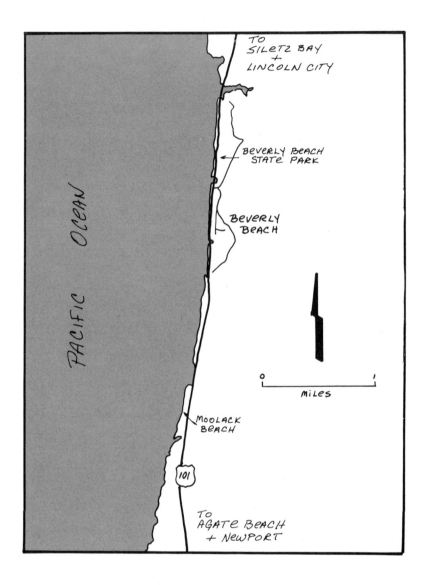

Beverly Beach

Beverly Beach is another good wave sailing location with a long flat sand beach and nice breaking waves. Access is difficult but the area is not as congested as other nearby sites with similar conditions, like the D-River Wayside.

Skill rating: Expert

Location: Beverly Beach is approximately 7 miles north of Newport on U.S. Hwy. 101 between mile-posts 134 and 136. Several parking areas are located on both sides of the highway. Additional parking is available at nearby Beverly Beach State Park.

Sailing conditions: (Short Board) Open ocean wave sailing is good between May and August when the northwest winds are side-onshore. Yaquina Head, to the south, makes winter sailing in southwest winds possible when the surf is not too rough.

Access: Local boardsailors prefer to park alongside U.S. Hwy. 101 where several steep trails lead down to the beach. The parking is limited and hauling gear to the beach is difficult, particularly on the return trip. Although farther from the beach, the access is probably easier from Beverly Beach State Park which also has rest rooms, camping, picnicking and plenty of grassy areas for rigging and drying sails. The beach, once you reach it, is broad and flat. Sail in front of the creek mouth.

Hazards: A low rock reef parallels the beach approximately one-half mile offshore. Some of these rocks are difficult to see, particularly when the surf is high.

Wind and water reports: 265-7334 – Newport Surf Designs, Newport · 265-5511 – U.S. Coast Guard Station, Newport

Food and lodging: Gas, food and lodging are available in Newport as well as at several locations both north and south of

Beverly Beach. *Beverly Beach State Park* has tent and RV camping with more than 200 sites, some with full hookups. The park also has rest rooms with hot showers and is open year-round. Reservations are recommended in the summer months. (Write: Star Route North, Box 684, Newport, OR 97365)

The Inn at Otter Crest, just north on U.S. Hwy. 101 at Otter Rock, is perched on a secluded cliff top along one of the west's most romantic coastlines. The inn features tennis, mini golf, a sauna, jacuzzi and pool. There are also an elevated tram and the State Marine Gardens. *The Flying Dutchman* at Otter Crest serves excellent food in an elegant yet casual environment.

See also Agate Beach, Yaquina Bay and Siletz Bay.

Other attractions: *Yaquina Bay Lighthouse* on Yaquina Head is open to the public 7 days a week between Memorial and Labor Days, weekends only the remainder of the year.

See also Agate Beach, Yaquina Bay and Siletz Bay.

Agate Beach

Located approximately one-half mile south of Yaquina Head, Agate Beach lies on the line of optimum wind where speeds consistently reach 10 to 15 MPH higher than at other nearby beaches.

Skill rating: Expert

Location: Agate Beach is just a mile or so north of Newport off U.S. Hwy. 101. Follow the signs from the highway to Ocean View Drive and the Agate Beach Wayside.

Sailing conditions: (Short Board) The wave sailing is best during the months of May through July, and sometimes into August. Winds are side-offshore in the spring and side-onshore during the summer months. The surf here breaks best on a high tide and tends to be "holey" on low tides.

Access: There is limited parking alongside the road at Agate Beach. Additional parking is available at the small Agate Beach Wayside. It's a short walk down to the beach, which is a broad, flat expanse of sand providing easy water entry. Grass areas for rigging and drying sails, picnic tables and rest rooms are also available at the wayside.

Hazards: Beware of strong currents and riptides.

Wind and water reports: 265-7334 – Newport Surf Designs, Newport · 265-5511 – U.S. Coast Guard Station, Newport

Food and lodging: There is a wide selection of gas, food and lodging facilities in and around Newport, with something to fit every budget.

The Hotel Newport located just across from Agate Beach, has excellent food and lodging facilities with reasonable rates for oceanfront accommodations.

The Agate Beach Tavern, just north of town off U.S. Hwy. 101 at Lucky Gap Road, serves a great steak sandwich.

157

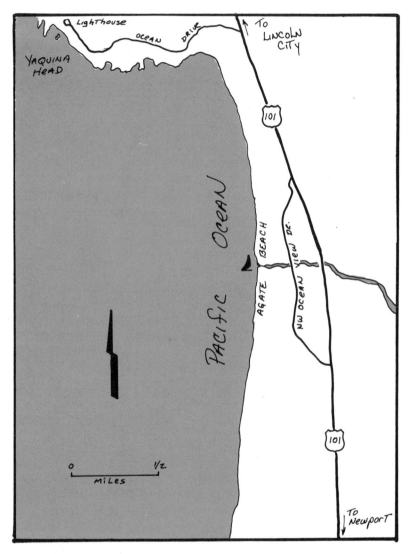

Agate Beach RV Park, located about a mile north of the turnoff to Agate Beach Wayside, has 32 paved spaces with lawns, full hookups, cable TV, rest rooms with hot showers and laundry facilities.

See also Beverly Beach and Yaquina Bay.

Other attractions: See Beverly Beach and Yaquina Bay.

Yaquina Bay

★

Yaquina Bay, like most bays on the Oregon Coast, can be sailed year-round. It offers excellent flat-water sailing in the winter months, but it is also a good alternative in the summer when the surf is too high for ocean sailing.

Skill rating: Novice through intermediate

Location: Yaquina Bay is located at the south end of the city of Newport on U.S. Hwy. 101. From I-5 and the Willamette Valley, take U.S. Hwy. 20 due east from Albany or Corvallis, approximately 70 miles.

Sailing conditions: (Long Board) Yaquina Bay is shaped like an inverted "V." In summer, May through August, the northwesterly wind is side-shore on the eastern half of the Bay. In the winter, the southwesterly wind is side-shore on the western half. For either wind direction, outgoing tides will generally produce the best swells.

Access: The best launch site is on the south shore at the Hatfield Marine Science Center. There is a small embayment with a narrow sand beach located to the north of the parking lot, between the piers for the Center's research vessels. Referred to by the locals as "The Playpen," this is a good place for the beginner. The beach area is small, the nearest rest rooms are in the Marine Science Center, and parking may be at a premium during summer months. More experienced sailors use this as a launch site and sail to other areas of the Bay.

Intermediate sailors might try sailing under the U.S. Hwy. 101 bridge. An alternative launch site is along South Jetty Road just west of the bridge. A sand spit at this site makes water entry and launching easy, parking is limited and there are no other amenities.

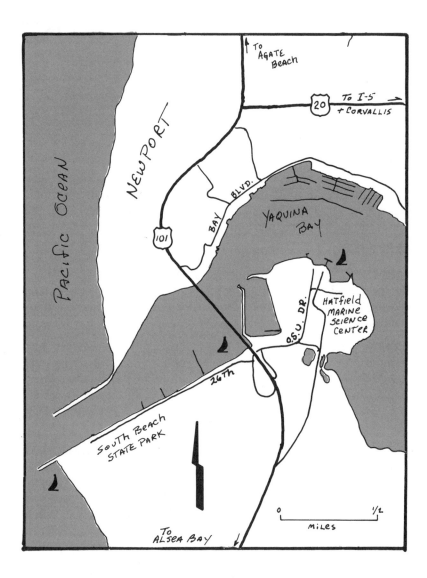

Hazards: When sailing under the bridge or near the jetties, watch out for strong currents on the outgoing tides as well as boat traffic. Also, on low or outgoing tides, look out for the mudflats southeast of The Playpen.

Wind and water reports: 265-7334 – Newport Surf Designs, Newport · 265-5511 – U.S. Coast Guard Station, Newport

Food and lodging: The selection of gas, food and lodging establishments in and around Newport is excellent.

The Embarcadero, on the north shore, offers luxury one- and two-bedroom suites overlooking the bayfront, an indoor pool, saunas, and a jacuzzi, sport fishing charters, and a fine restaurant and lounge. Even the marina here would make a good site for launching a long board.

At the other end of the price scale is the *Newport Hostel*, featuring low cost, European-style accommodations. For less than ten dollars a night hostelers get a clean bed, hot shower, a place to prepare meals and an opportunity to meet people and make new friends.

If you love seafood try the original *Mo's* on Bay Boulevard in Old Town Newport. The clam chowder here is world-famous; people line up on the street waiting for a table. *Mo's Annex*, right across the street, has the same fine food with a view of the waterfront and somewhat shorter lines.

The Canyon Way Restaurant and Bookstore, just west of Bay Boulevard on Canyon Way, also has excellent food. If there's a waiting line you can always browse in the unique bookstore.

The Rip Tide Restaurant and Lounge, at the west end of Bay Boulevard in Old Town, is open 24 hours daily with seafood fresh off the boat and the finest live entertainment on the coast, 7 days a week.

Sportsman's Trailer Park, on Marine Science Drive just across from the launch site, has 40 RV sites with full hookups, hot showers and cable TV.

Harbor Village RV Park, on S.E. Bay Boulevard in Newport, has 140 sites with full hookups, hot showers and laundry facilities.

See Agate Beach and South Beach)

Other attractions: *The O.S.U. Hatfield Marine Science Center* should not be missed. In addition to being a major institute for marine research, the Center also has outstanding exhibits and an aquarium which are open to the public.

Old Town Newport, on the historic waterfront, is still a working fishing port. Visitors can watch the catch of the day being unloaded on the docks or sample it in one of the nearby restaurants.

Other attractions along the wharf include *The Wax Works, Ripley's Believe It or Not*, and *The Undersea Gardens*.

The Newport Loyalty Days and Sea Fair Festival is held in early May, featuring a parade, barbeque and regatta.

See also Agate Beach and South Beach.

South Beach

Surfers named this site "Orange Beach" because of the oranges that wash up here from time to time.* This has always been a popular place for surfing, but more and more boardsailors are coming here for the hot waves.

Skill rating: Expert (possibly intermediate when the surf is low)

Location: South Beach is located across the Yaquina Bay Bridge from the city of Newport. Follow the signs from U.S. Hwy. 101 toward the Hatfield Marine Science Center. Turn left on 26th Street and stay on the dirt road to the end of the jetty.

Sailing conditions: (Short Board) Excellent open ocean wave sailing any time the wind is from the west to northwest. The largest swells occur in May and June but the winds can be fluky. July and August have more consistent winds but the waves are usually smaller. The jetty provides shelter for launching, making this a good place to try open ocean sailing for the first time. This site is not recommended in the winter, when the wind is out of the southwest.

Access: South Beach is a broad expanse of flat sand south of the jetty at the mouth of Yaquina Bay. There is plenty of parking on the jetty and lots of room on the beach for rigging. There are no rest rooms or other amenities nearby.

Hazards: Beware of strong currents and riptides. Yaquina Bay is a busy fishing and lumber port, so watch out for boat traffic near the jetty.

Wind and water reports: 265-7334 – Newport Surf Designs, Newport • 265-5511 – U.S. Coast Guard Station, Newport

* No one seems to know where the oranges come from -- probably from a fishing boat.

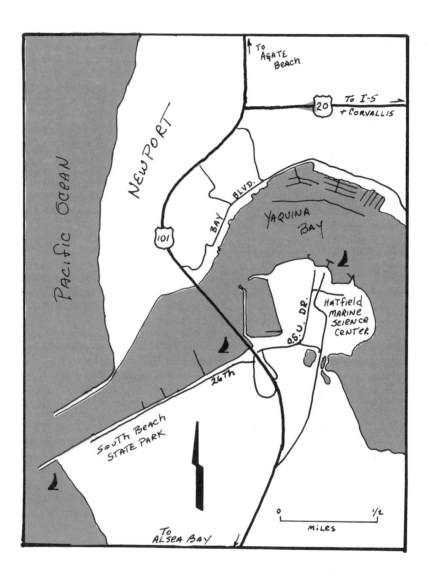

Food and lodging: Gas, food and lodging are available in and around Newport.

South Beach State Park, 2 miles south of Newport on U.S. Hwy. 101, has more than 250 tent and RV sites with electrical hookups, rest rooms and hot showers.

Whaler's Rest Resort at Lost Creek, just south of Newport on U.S. Hwy. 101, has over 100 RV and tent sites with full hookups, showers, laundry facilities, indoor pool, recreation room, tennis courts, garden golf, and jogging/fitness trails.

See also Yaquina Bay and Alsea Bay.

Other attractions: See Yaquina Bay and Alsea Bay.

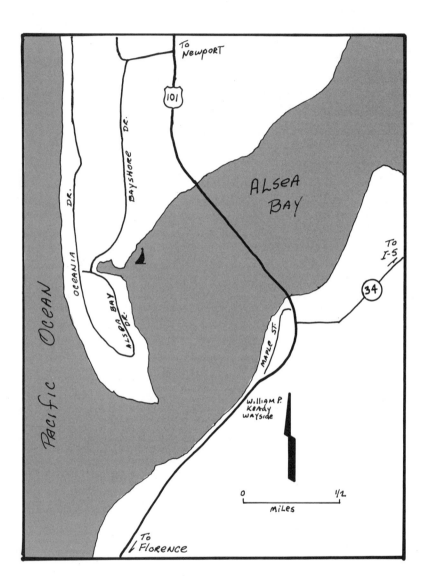

Alsea Bay

Alsea Bay is a good spot all year, but the locals say it is best in the winter. Experts will find great conditions for wave sailing in the river mouth. This is a good alternative when the ocean surf is too rough.

Skill rating: Novice to expert (depending on time of year)

Location: Alsea Bay is located in the town of Waldport on the central Oregon coast. Waldport is 35 miles north of Florence and 15 miles south of Newport on U.S. Hwy. 101.

Sailing conditions: (Long and Short Board) Alsea Bay can be sailed in any wind direction but you must pick the right tides. In summer northerly winds, there is a wind shadow near shore and you have to work yourself out to the middle of the bay to get clean air. Flood tides are recommended at this time of year. The best sailing is in the winter when the wind is out of the southwest. The wind is side-shore with swells at the river mouth averaging 3 feet on the ebb tide. Swells of 5 to 6 feet are not uncommon.

Access: The best access is at the north end of the Bay near the Bayshore Motel. Take Bayshore Drive, the first street to the left after crossing the U.S. Hwy. 101 bridge, and go approximately one mile. The launch site is an old boat ramp. There is plenty of parking, a grass rigging area and a nice sand beach. From here it's only 20 yards to the water. There are no rest rooms or other amenities.

Hazards: A large sandbar stretches from the south shore to the middle of the Bay under the U.S. Hwy. 101 bridge. Beware of outgoing tides; the current is very strong at the mouth and if you get in trouble you may be swept out over the bar. This has happened to several boardsailors and being washed up on the beach through the surf is not a pleasant experience if you are unprepared. During winter high tides, floating logs and driftwood can be a problem.

Wind and water reports: 265-7334 – Newport Surf Designs, Newport · 265-5511 – U.S. Coast Guard Station, Newport

Food and lodging: Waldport has a wide selection of gas, food and lodging establishments.

4J's Restaurant, at the foot of the Alsea Bay Bridge, has a lounge and good, home-style cooking.

Or try the *Flounder Inn Tavern* for suds and a "Flounder Half Pounder."

The Experience, 3 miles east of Waldport on Hwy. 34, specializes in seafood dinners exclusively. Reservations are required: (503)563-4555.

The Blackberry Inn Bed and Breakfast in Seal Rock, 3 miles north of Waldport, has a private entrance, separate baths and a hot tub for the enjoyment of their guests. This inn is for adults only, and reservations are recommended; call (503)563-2259.

Tent and RV camping is available at Beachside State Park, 4 miles south of Waldport on U.S. Hwy. 101. The park has electrical hookups and rest rooms with running water and hot showers. In addition, there are several private campgrounds in and around Waldport.

See also Neptune Beach, South Beach and Yaquina Bay.

Other attractions: Alsea Bay is an outstanding place for catching dungeness crab, salmon, steelhead and bluebacks (sea-run cutthroat trout), or clams. The annual Waldport Salmon Derby is held on the Alsea River in early fall.

The annual *Beachcomber Days Festival* is held each June. This three-day event has something for everyone, from the sandcastle contest to world-champion slug races.

See also Neptune Beach, South Beach and Yaquina Bay.

Neptune Beach
State Park

★ ★

Located on the south side of Cape Perpetua along the line of optimum wind, this site quickly became a hot spot. It's great for open ocean wave-sailing.

Skill rating: Expert

Location: Neptune Beach State Park is located 15 miles south of Waldport on U.S. Hwy. 101. The turnoff is not well marked. Look for the Cummins Creek trailhead sign just past the bridge over Cummins Creek. Heading north on U.S. Hwy. 101, it is about 25 miles from Florence and just a few miles past the Stonefield Beach Wayside.

Sailing conditions: (Short Board) Ocean wave sailing is good in northwest winds, May through September. The beach is located in a small cove with well-formed swells.

Access: Neptune Beach State Park has a large paved parking lot, rest rooms, plenty of grass for rigging and an easy trail down to the small sand beach. The water access is easy with nice shore breaking waves. Tide pools to the north and south of the beach provide an interesting diversion if the wind dies out.

Hazards: Beware of the killer sandbars, especially during low or outgoing tides.

Wind and water reports: 265-7334 – Newport Surf Designs, Newport • 997-2457 – Waterfront Sailboards, Florence

Food and lodging: The nearest gas, food and lodging are in Yachats, about 4 miles north on U.S. Hwy. 101. Yachats, pro-

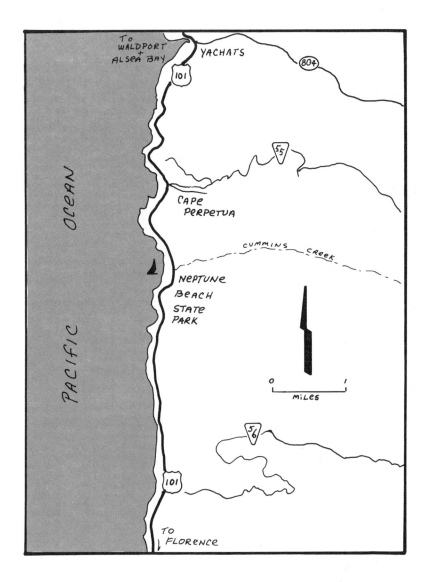

nounced "Yah-hots," has accommodations for any need and eight restaurants serving everything from fast food to gourmet cuisine.

The Oregon House, a few miles south of Neptune Beach, has unique lodgings on the sea cliffs with a trail down to a private beach. The resort offers studio units, suites or adult bed and breakfast accommodations in the main house. They also have a two-story, glassed-in tower for watching the fantastic sunsets or migrating whales. (Call (503)547-3329 for reservations.)

Camping is available at several U.S. Forest Service campgrounds in the surrounding Siuslaw National Forest. Tent and RV camping is also available at *Carl G. Washburn State Park*, 10 miles south. The park has 64 sites, 58 with full hookups, and rest rooms with hot showers.

See also Alsea Bay and Heceta Beach.

Other attractions: *Cape Perpetua*, the highest point on the Oregon coast, is located just a few miles north of Neptune Beach. A scenic route climbs from U.S. Hwy. 101 to the U.S. Forest Service visitor's center and campground on top of the Cape, 800 feet above the surf. The youthful and energetic may choose to take the hiking trail to the top. Once at the summit, the view is one of the best on the coast.

The annual community *Smelt Fry* in Yachats attracts visitors from all over the west. This is one of the few places in the world where sea-run smelt come into shore.

See also Alsea Bay and Heceta Beach.

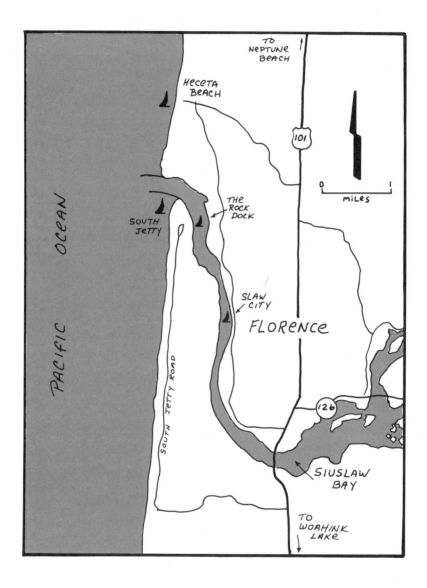

Heceta Beach

Heceta Beach is one more of the many great wave-sailing sites along the Oregon coast. The major attraction here is the location, next to the Driftwood Shores Resort. This makes Heceta Beach one of the few windsurfing destination resorts on the coast. Although lessons and rental equipment are not yet available, all the other shoreside amenities are here for a great windsurfing holiday.

Skill rating: Expert

Location: Heceta Beach is located approximately 4 miles north of Florence via Heceta Beach Road. This site can be reached from Florence on Rhododendron Drive, the first stoplight north of the Siuslaw Bay Bridge on U.S. Hwy. 101. Go past "Slaw City" to Heceta Beach Road, approximately 5.5 miles. Heceta Beach Road also joins U.S. Hwy. 101 approximately 2 miles south of the Darlingtonia Botanical Wayside.

Sailing conditions: (Short Board) Ocean wave sailing is good, with side-shore winds, May through September. Afternoon winds are best.

Access: The access point for Heceta Beach is a small park operated by Lane County. The park has paved parking for eight or ten cars, vault toilets and garbage cans. It offers easy access to the long, flat sand beach where there is plenty of room for rigging, sunbathing and what-have-you.

Hazards: Beware of strong tides and rip currents.

Wind and water reports: 997-2457 – Waterfront Sailboards, Florence · 997-2486 – U.S. Coast Guard Station, Florence

Food and lodging: *Driftwood Shores Resort*, located next to Heceta Beach Park, has a restaurant and lounge, swimming pool and AAA-approved lodgings.

More than 2000 campsites are available in and around Florence. Check with the Florence Chamber of Commerce for complete information.

See also Siuslaw Bay, Siltcoos Lake and Woahink Lake

Other attractions: *Darlingtonia Botanical Wayside*, on U.S. Hwy. 101 just north of Heceta Beach Road, was established to preserve the carnivorous cobra lily plants. Nature trails allow visitors to view these rare plants in their natural environment.

Heceta Head and Lighthouse, 10 miles north of Heceta Beach is the most photographed spot on the central Oregon coast. Legend has it that the light tender's house is haunted. This is an excellent place to view migrating gray whales from November to May.

See also Siuslaw Bay, Siltcoos Lake and Woahink Lake

Siuslaw Bay

Siuslaw Bay is the short board sailing location nearest to Eugene. While it is possible to sail Siuslaw Bay year-round, summers are best. There are two good launch sites, depending on your skill and preference. The Rockdock is good for learning water starts and practicing jibes. Slaw City is the local equivalent of Swell City in the Gorge.

Skill rating: Intermediate to expert

Location: Siuslaw Bay is on the central coast, just west of the town of Florence. It is 50 miles south of Newport and 48 miles north of Coos Bay on U.S. Hwy. 101. From I-5 and Eugene, it's 60 miles west, via Hwy. 126.

Sailing conditions: (Short Board) Siuslaw Bay is oriented toward the northwest for great summertime sailing, May through September. You can sail the Rockdock on medium through high tides. With strong winds and an ebb tide, the Rockdock is a great place for wave jumping.

Slaw City is an excellent place for flat-water speed sailing on incoming and high slack tides. On ebb tides, three-foot swells are not uncommon. The water at both these spots is too shallow for sailing on low tides.

Access: The Rockdock, named for the rock fishing pier at this location, is at the end of South Jetty Road on the west side of the Bay. This is the windiest spot on the Bay, with the northwest wind blowing side-offshore. There is a large paved parking area and vault toilets nearby. To reach the water, you must climb down over the rocks, but there is a nice sand beach for rigging and launching. This is a good spot for learning water starts, with a sand beach on the opposite shore for land jibes.

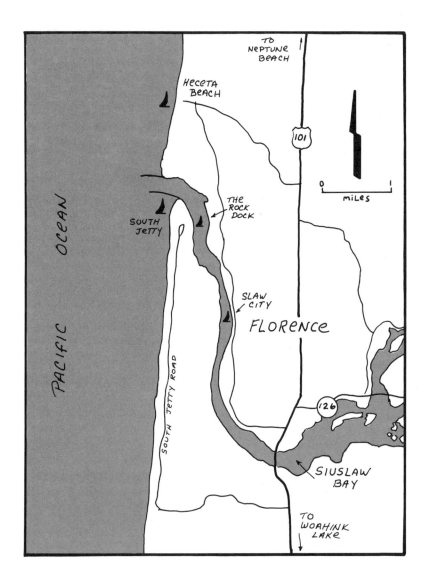

Slaw City, the other launch site, is located across the Bay and south of the Rockdock. To reach this area, cross the Bay on U.S. Hwy. 101 and turn left at the first stoplight, onto Rhododendron Drive. It is approximately 2 miles to the launch site, just past the Greentrees Mobile Home Park, near the road to the city landfill.

Four dolphins offshore mark the spot near a wide area on the side of the road for parking. There are no facilities here, and it's a steep climb down a rock bank to the water. Once at the bottom there is a small sand beach. The water is shallow for easy entry and water starts. There is another nice sand beach on the opposite shore for land jibes. The summer northwesterlies blow side-shore at Slaw City.

Hazards: Beware of tides, winds and submerged rocks at the Rockdock. If you get in trouble on an ebb tide, you may be carried out over the bar.

Wind and water reports: 997-2457 – Waterfront Sailboards, Florence · 997-2486 – U.S. Coast Guard Station, Florence

Food and lodging: The town of Florence has a wide selection of gas, food and lodging facilities. For excellent accommodations and fine dining, try the _Pier Point Inn Resort_ on U.S. Hwy. 101, just south of the Siuslaw Bay bridge.

Another excellent motel is _Le Chateau,_ located on U.S. Hwy. 101 just north of the Hwy. 126 junction.

South Jetty Resort on South Jetty Road has RV camping, groceries and access to the dunes.

See also Siltcoos Lake, Woahink Lake, and Heceta Beach.

Other attractions: Off-road vehicle access to the _Oregon Dunes National Recreation Area_ is possible at several points along South Jetty Road. Several concessionaires in and around Florence rent all-terrain vehicles for use on the dunes.

The third week in May is the time for the _Rhododendron Festival_ in Florence. A recent addition to this annual event is the _Boardsports Bonsai Expression Session,_ a fun event for amateur as well as professional windsurfers.

See also Siltcoos Lake, Woahink Lake, and Heceta Beach.

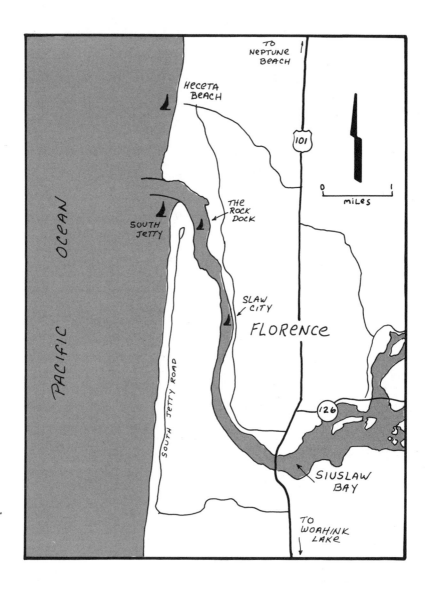

South Jetty, Siuslaw Bay

★ ★

"The best surf sailing on the Oregon Coast," say the locals. The winds here are strong and steady, with the chop blocked by the jetty. You can sail in the rolling surf south of the jetty or, if you prefer swells, inside the river mouth.

Skill rating: Expert

Location: On the central coast just west of the town of Florence, Siuslaw Bay is 50 miles south of Newport and 48 miles north of Coos Bay on U.S. Hwy 101. This area can also be reached from I-5 and Eugene, 60 miles east, via Hwy. 126.

Sailing conditions: (Short Board) Wave sailing is great May through September when the wind is from the northwest. If you sail inside the jetty, watch the tides. On north winds it's best to sail on the incoming tide, while the ebb tide is better on south wind days.

Access: South Jetty is located at the end of South Jetty Road, just beyond the Rockdock. There is parking at the end of the road and a vault toilet nearby. From here, it's a long trek over the dunes and down to the water. You can drive out on the jetty to shorten the walk and vehicles are allowed on the beach from October through April. During the rest of the year, limited parking is available along the roadside. Once on the beach, there is plenty of sand for rigging and sunbathing. There are no other facilities at this site.

Hazards: Beware of strong currents and riptides. If you get in trouble sailing inside the jetty on an ebb tide, you may be carried out over the bar.

179

Wind and water reports: 997-2457 – Waterfront Sailboards, Florence • 997-2486 – U.S. Coast Guard Station, Florence

Food and lodging: See Siuslaw Bay, Siltcoos Lake and Woah-ink Lake.

Other attractions: See Siuslaw Bay, Siltcoos Lake and Woah-ink Lake.

Woahink Lake

Woahink is a beautiful lake, fast becoming a popular year-round windsurfing spot. It is oriented to take particular advantage of the southwesterly winter winds. Winters along the coast are usually mild, with daytime temperatures into the fifties. When snow and ice shut down the rest of Oregon, this lake is sometimes the only sailing opportunity, short of Baja or Hawaii.

Skill rating: Novice to intermediate in summer, expert in winter

Location: Woahink is on the central coast, five miles south of Florence, just east of U.S. Hwy. 101.

Sailing conditions: (Long Board) The best sailing is from October through May. At this time of year the southwesterly wind blows side-onshore and it is possible to sail on a reach for the full length of the lake, almost two miles. The strongest winds are usually associated with storm fronts.

In the summer the gusty winds are offshore, making it difficult to return to the launch site. Siltcoos Lake is a good alternative at this time of year.

Access: The best winter access is the east Woahink picnic area at Honeyman State Park, on the north shore of the lake. The park has plenty of paved parking and lots of grass, right up to the water's edge, for rigging and launching. There are also picnic shelters with water, electricity, barbeques, rest rooms, a boat ramp and docking area.

Outside of Honeyman State Park, the remainder of the lake shore is in private ownership. The only possible launch site in the summer with side-offshore winds is where the southwest corner of the lake meets U.S. Hwy. 101. There is a small turnout for parking but little area for rigging and no facilities. Water entry is also difficult.

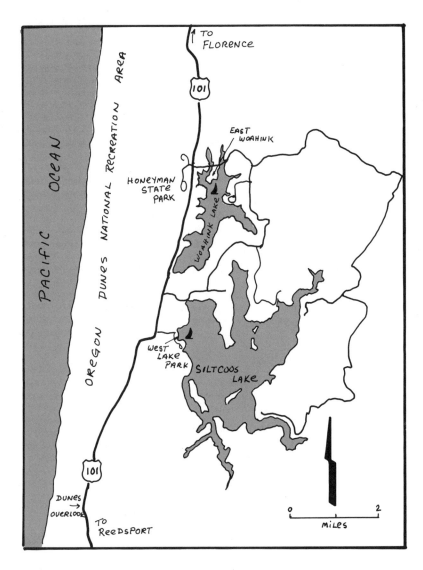

Hazards: This is a popular lake for waterskiing.

Wind and water reports: 997-2457 – Waterfront Sailboards, Florence · 997-2486 – U.S. Coast Guard Station, Florence

Food and lodging: The campground at *Honeyman State Park* is located just across the highway from Woahink Lake. This is one of the nicest state parks along the coast, with 66 full hookups, 75 electrical and 241 tent sites. The rest rooms have running water and hot showers. Reservations are recommended during the summer. (Call (503)238-7488 or, within Oregon, 1-800-452-5687, for more information.)

Gas, food and lodgings are also available in nearby Florence.

Other attractions: See Siltcoos Lake and Siuslaw Bay.

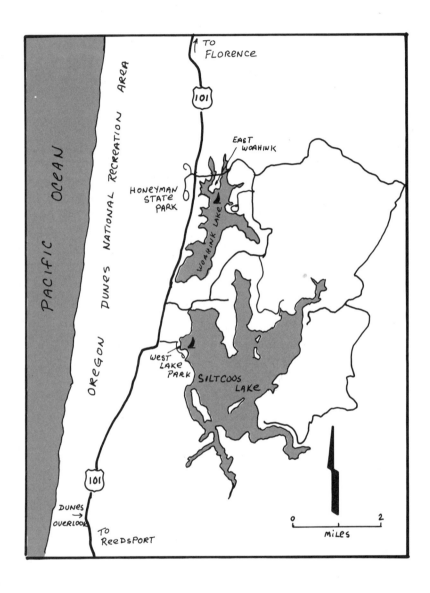

Siltcoos Lake

Siltcoos is the largest lake on the Oregon coast with a surface area of more than 3,100 acres. It is also very shallow, with an average depth of eleven feet. This makes the lake very choppy, but the water is usually quite warm by late summer and well into the fall. Wet suits are still recommended.

Skill rating: Novice to intermediate in the summer, expert in the winter

Location: Siltcoos Lake is on the central coast just east of U.S. Hwy. 101, seven miles south of Florence, and 41 miles north of Coos Bay. The lake area can easily be reached from I-5 and Eugene, 68 miles east, via Hwy. 126.

Sailing conditions: (Long Board) Sailing is best during the summer months when the northwest wind prevails. There is a wind shadow near shore because of the trees, but the wind strengthens in the center of the lake. During the winter, when the wind is from the south, the north end of the lake is the best place to sail but nearby Woahink Lake is a better alternative.

Access: There are a number of launch sites surrounding the lake but the public boat launch at West Lake County Park is the local favorite. The park has a grass area for rigging and a small sand beach. Although the shoreline is weedy, a small dock makes launching easier. The wind shadow makes getting in and out of this launching area tricky. To reach this site turn east from U.S. Hwy. 101 at Dunes City.

Hazards: An extensive growth of aquatic weeds near shore makes water entry and sailing difficult. This lake is also popular for fishing so watch out for trolling boats and lines. A heavy chop can develop on the lake when the wind pipes up; fishing boats are often swamped by the large swells. This should be no problem for intermediate boardsailors but beginners should know their limitations.

Wind and water reports: 997-2457 – Waterfront Sailboards, Florence • 997-2486 – U.S. Coast Guard Station, Florence

Food and lodging: Six private resorts surround the lake in addition to U.S. Forest Service campgrounds and the camping area at West Lake County Park.

Westlake Resort is located just south of the County boat ramp. The Resort has housekeeping cabins, a market, and a marina with a nice dock for launching sailboards.

Siltcoos Lake Resort, at Westlake Junction, has 15 RV sites with water and electric and TV hookups. They also have a marina and a motel with kitchen units.

Darling's Resort, at North Beach, has RV camping, gas groceries and a tavern. There is also a nice launch area here, winds permitting, with grass for rigging and a dock for easy water entry.

The Forest Service campgrounds near the lake are primitive, with water and vault toilets but no hookups. *Jessie M. Honeyman State Park*, 3 miles south of Florence off U.S. Hwy. 101, has almost 400 camping spaces, 66 with full RV hookups, and rest rooms with hot showers.

Additional gas, food and lodging can be found in Dunes City and in Florence, 7 miles north on U.S. Hwy. 101.

Other attractions: *Sea Lion Caves*, twelve miles south of Florence on U.S. Hwy. 101, is the only known natural year-round home and rookery on the American mainland for wild Steller Sea Lions. An elevator takes visitors 208 feet down into one of the largest sea caves in the world, where these animals can be viewed in their natural habitat.

The *Oregon Dunes Recreation Area* extends south from Florence to Coos Bay. An overlook, located off U.S. Hwy. 101 just south of Siltcoos Lake, features interpretive displays highlighting sand dune formation from an excellent vantage point above the dunes and ocean.

See also Woahink Lake and Siuslaw Bay.

Empire, Coos Bay

Coos Bay is shaped like an inverted horseshoe, the western arm of which parallels the ocean, separated only by a ridge of low sand dunes. There is nothing to block the wind from the ocean, creating excellent conditions for boardsailing on the protected bay waters.

Skill rating: Novice to expert

Location: Coos Bay is approximatly 115 miles north of the California border and 48 miles south of Florence on U.S. Hwy. 101. State Hwy. 42 connects Coos Bay with I-5 in Roseburg, 85 miles to the east. From U.S. Hwy. 101, follow the signs to "Charleston Harbor and Ocean Beaches." Newmark Street, also called the Cape Arago Highway, is the main thoroughfare from U.S. Hwy. 101 to Charleston and the ocean beaches to the south. The highway turns south upon reaching the western arm of the Bay in Empire. At this point continue straight, down the hill past the Coast Guard Maintenance Station.

Sailing conditions: (Long and Short Board) Sailing is possible here year-round. In the summer the northwest wind is onshore, making it possible to sail up and down the bay on a reach. During the winter the southerly winds will be side-onshore. At this time of year, sail the outgoing tides for the best swells.

Access: Despite an extensive shoreline, access to Coos Bay is limited. The best site is Empire on the west arm of the Bay. Launch near the U.S. Coast Guard Maintenance Station at the end of Newmark Street. There is adequate parking and a nice sandy beach but no other amenities.

Hazards: Coos Bay is a major lumber port, so deep draft vessels have the right-of-way.

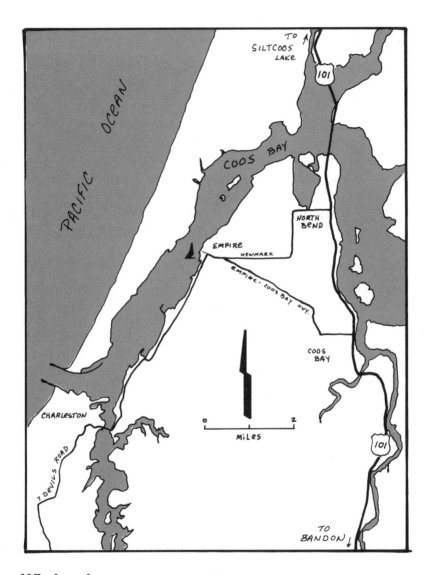

Wind and water reports: 888-3266 – U.S. Coast Guard Station, Charleston

Food and lodging: The Coos Bay-North Bend area is the largest population center along the south coast. A wide selection of food and lodging facilities can be found here in every price range.

Mo's Restaurant, on South Broadway in Coos Bay, is world-famous for their clam chowder.

The Portside Restaurant and Lounge, located at the boat basin in Charleston, features fresh caught seafood daily, in addition to French cuisine. Try the Bouillabaisse Marsellaise.

The Captain's Quarters Bed and Breakfast, located on South Empire Blvd. (Cape Arago Highway) just beyond Newmark Street, is open year-round.

There are several private RV parks on Cape Arago Highway heading toward Charleston. Camping is also available at Sunset Bay State Park and Bastendorff Beach County Park, southwest of Charleston. Both have rest rooms with hot showers.

For motel accommodations try the _Thunderbird Motor Inn/Red Lion_ or the _Best Western Holiday Motel,_ located on U.S. Hwy. 101 in Coos Bay.

Other attractions: The _Oregon Dunes National Recreation Area_ stretches north from Coos Bay more than 40 miles to Florence. There are 32,000 acres of dunes, of which 7,000 acres are open to off-road vehicles. Three- and four-wheel all-terrain vehicles can be rented at concessions throughout the area.

Charleston Harbor, southwest of Coos Bay, is a major fishing port with charter boats available for offshore salmon or bottom fishing.The _Oregon Institute of Marine Biology_ is also located in Charleston.

The _South Slough Estuary Sanctuary,_ on Seven Devils Road south of Charleston, was the first of 20 estuarine reserves established in the United States. The Sanctuary's 4,400 acres are preserved in their wild, natural state. The Interpretive Center has exhibits to help visitors understand the complex and vital role estuaries play in our natural environment.

The road to Cape Arago State Park southwest of Charleston offers spectacular ocean vistas and the opportunity to view sea lions and migrating whales. Several state parks along the way offer camping, picnicking, and swimming. The most impressive is _Shore Acres State Park,_ 4.5 miles southwest of Charleston. This was once the estate of lumber baron Louis L. Simpson, built in 1906 as a Christmas present for his wife. The formal gardens have been preserved and rival the famous Buchart Gardens in Victoria. albeit on a smaller scale.

The Blackberry Arts Festival and the *South Coast Multi-Image Festival* are both held in late August. The first is a tribute to the tasty berries of the briar bush that are ripening along highways and byways throughout the state at this time of year. The second is a photography festival, including exhibits of camera equipment, workshops and multi-image shows in addition to some outstanding photography. The highlight of this festival is the salmon barbeque.

Other important festivals in the Coos Bay area include the *Oregon Coast Music Festival* in late July and the *Charleston Seafood Festival* on Memorial Day weekend.

See also Coquille River and Whiskey Run Beach.

Whiskey Run Beach,

Seven Devils Wayside

★ ★

Whiskey Run Beach is an area of consistently strong winds. Because of this it was chosen by the Pacific Power and Light Company as a wind-powered electrical generation site. The beach at Whiskey Run is wide and unpopulated. There are no beach homes, motels or other residential development in the area – just acres and acres of golden-yellow gorse.

Skill rating: Expert

Location: This site is just north of Bandon on the road to Seven Devils Wayside (Coos County Road 33A). Heading north on U.S. Hwy. 101, turn on Seven Devils Road about 2 miles past Bullards Beach State Park. Whiskey Run Beach is about 5 miles farther. Heading south on U.S. Hwy. 101, turn onto Beaver Hill Road approximately 12 miles past Coos Bay. Look for the highway marker that says "Wind Turbine Project Viewing Area 6 Miles."

Sailing conditions: (Short Board) The beach gets nice shore-breaking waves and side-onshore winds from the northwest. Sailing is best in the summer from May through September. June and July have the most consistent wind.

Access: The access to Whiskey Run has paved parking with an easy walk down to the beach. The beach itself is broad, flat sand without any rocks or other obstacles. There are no rest rooms or other amenities here.

Hazards: Beware of tides and rip currents.

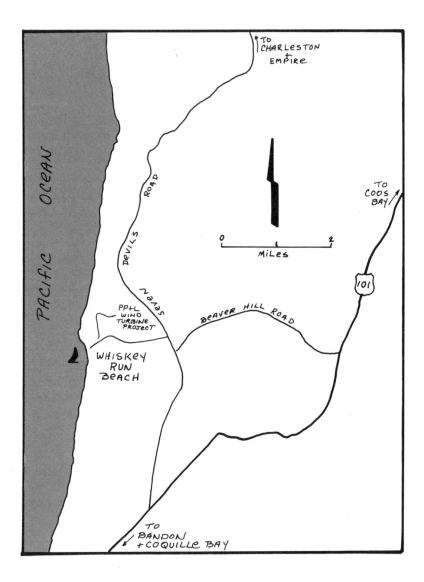

Wind and water reports: 347-9283 – Southern Oregon Sailboards, Bandon · 888-3266 – U.S. Coast Guard Station, Charleston

Food and lodging: The nearest gas, food and lodgings are in Bandon, about 10 miles south (see Coquille River) or in Charleston and Coos Bay, 12 miles and 21 miles north respectively.

The PP&L Wind Turbine Project near Whiskey Run Beach is a testament to the strong, steady winds that blow along the southern Oregon coast.

Other attractions: The *PP&L Wind Turbine Project*, just to the north of Whiskey Run Beach, has 25 wind turbines mounted on 80-foot towers. The project is capable of generating 1250 kilowatt hours of electricity in 30 MPH winds.

See also Coquille River and Empire, Coos Bay.

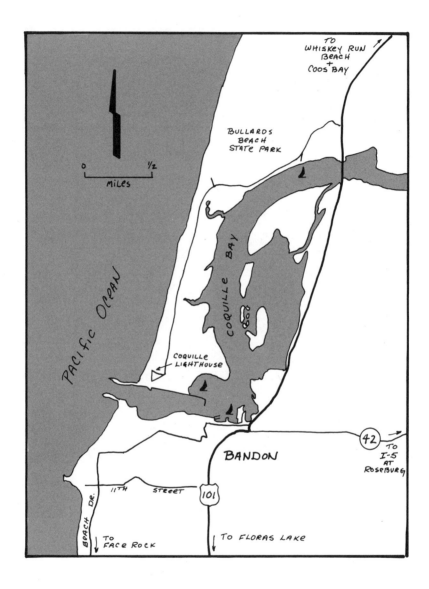

Coquille Bay

The Coquille River enters the Pacific Ocean at the town of Bandon. Like most Oregon estuaries, sailing is possible here year-round. The summer is best for novice sailors. Advanced, intermediate and expert sailors will find winters more to their liking, particularly just before or after a storm front.

"Bandon by the Sea," as the residents like to call their little town, is unique, and the nearby beaches are some of the most picturesque along the south Oregon coast.

Skill rating: Novice to intermediate

Location: Bandon is approximately 25 miles south of Coos Bay and 20 miles north of Floras Lake on U.S. Hwy 101.

Sailing conditions: (Long and Short Board) Bay sailing is great in northerly (summertime) or southerly (wintertime) winds, best on incoming tides.

Access: There are two launch sites on Coquille Bay. One may be better than the other depending on the time of year. In the winter, the best place to launch is from the boat ramp at Bullards Beach State Park. It has plenty of parking, grass nearby for rigging and, at this time of year, little competition from powerboats. The southerly winds will be side-onshore. There are no rest rooms or other amenities at the ramp itself, but rest rooms are located elsewhere in the park, some with hot showers.

In the summer, you can launch at the boat basin in Bandon. The area has plenty of parking and public rest rooms. It is next to Old Town Bandon, so there are plenty of stores and restaurants within walking distance. The only place to rig is in the parking area. Launching is off the docks at the boat ramp, unless you want to climb down the rocky bank.

An alternative summertime launching spot for long boards is

the point of the sand spit across the river from the boat basin. It has a little cove with flat water and a nice sand beach, but no other facilities. The northwest wind will be offshore to side-offshore, making it somewhat difficult to return to the beach, but there is no competition with powerboats. This area is reached by going to Bullards Beach State Park and following the beach road. Turn left on the dirt road just before reaching the lighthouse. The road is rough; vehicles with high ground clearance are recommended.

Hazards: When launching from the boat basin beware of the mud flats directly northeast; stay in the main river channel.

Wind and water reports: 347-9283 – Southern Oregon Sailboards, Bandon · 888-3266 – U.S. Coast Guard Station, Charleston

Food and lodging: *Old Town Bandon,* on the waterfront, is a mixture of galleries, featuring the works of local artists, and quaint restaurants too numerous to mention. All are excellent!

Lodging in Bandon also runs the gamut from typical Hwy. 101-type motels to one-of-a-kind beachfront bed and breakfasts. If you're on a budget and don't mind sharing a room with strangers, try the *Sea Star Hostel* in Old Town. For more elaborate accommodation, try the *Inn at Face Rock.*

Year-round camping is available at *Bullards Beach State Park.* The park has rest rooms with showers and almost 200 tent and RV sites, half with full hookups.

Other attractions: Sample Oregon's finest wines and seafood delicacies at the annual Bandon *Seafood and Wine Festival,* Memorial Day weekend.

Bandon is the center of Oregon's cranberry industry. Tours of the bogs are offered during the fall harvest season and local shops feature fancy cranberry concoctions all year. The annual *Cranberry Festival* is held in September.

The Dixie Lee, a model of an old sternwheeler, makes twice daily cruises up the Coquille River from its berth at the Bandon Boat Basin. Evening dinner cruises are featured on weekends.

Bandon Stables, on Beach Loop Drive just south of Face Rock Wayside, offers horseback riding on the beach, seven days a week, from March to September.

Face Rock Wayside

Face Rock Wayside is named for the large offshore monolith that resembles a man gazing off towards the northwest. It is no doubt looking for wind, symbolic of the boardsailors who now frequent the area. The beach access is difficult, but worth the hike. The broad stretch of sand has lots of large rocks to block the wind for rigging and sunbathing. There are also lots of tide pools to explore if the wind dies out or, heaven forbid, if you get tired of sailing.

Skill rating: Expert

Location: Face Rock Wayside is located about 2 miles southwest of Old Town Bandon on Beach Loop Drive. Coming from the north, turn right off U.S. Hwy. 101 at Eleventh Street, go past the city park, then left on Beach Loop Drive. From the south, turn left off U.S. Hwy. 101 at the Beach Junction Market. Stay on Beach Loop Drive for about 3.5 miles. The Wayside is on the left, just past the Inn at Face Rock.

Sailing conditions: (Short Board) Expect side-shore to side-on-shore winds out of the northwest and great shore breaking surf, making for some great open ocean wave-sailing.

Access: Face Rock Wayside has a large paved parking area, lots of grass, rest rooms and drinking water. It's a long hike down to the water but there are steps part way to make the trek somewhat easier. It's best to launch and sail to the south of the rocks.

Hazards: Beware of rip currents and undertows, especially near offshore rocks.

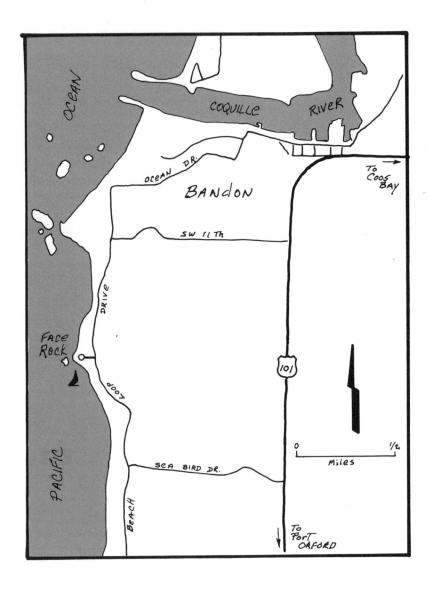

Wind and water reports: 347-9283 – Southern Oregon Sailboards, Bandon · 888-3266 – U.S. Coast Guard Station, Charleston

Food and lodging: See Coquille River.

Other attractions: See Coquille River.

Floras Lake

★ ★ ★

Floras Lake is becoming one of the best spots along the southern Oregon coast for the beginning or intermediate boardsailor. It has excellent flat water sailing and was the site of major speed sailing events in 1987 and 1988. Bay Sailboards of Eugene opened a rental/training concession here in 1988, offering high wind sailing lessons and equipment.

Skill rating: Novice to expert

Location: Floras Lake is approximately 40 miles south of Coos Bay and 9.5 miles north of Port Orford, near the towns of Langlois and Denmark. From U.S. Hwy. 101, head west on Floras Lake Road. The turnoff is not well marked. In the town of Denmark look for the small sign which reads "Floras Lake Public Boat Launch Area." Follow these signs 2 miles west to Boice/Cope County Park.

Sailing conditions: (Long and Short Board) The sailing is excellent year-round. Summer weather along the southern Oregon coast usually begins in August and 70-plus temperatures are not uncommon even in November. Floras Lake is actually a bay that has been cut off from the ocean by low sand dunes. These stop the surf but not the strong, persistent winds common to the Cape Blanco area. The lake is shallow, only chest deep in many places, making it a good place to learn or improve water starting techniques.

Access: Boice/Cope County Park has a public boat ramp, picnic area and pit privies. Camping is allowed in the park but there are no RV hookups. The lake has no beach and the shoreline is very weedy, but there are docks to make water entry easier. Rig in the picnic area where there is plenty of grass. Stairs at the south end of the park lead down to the lake.

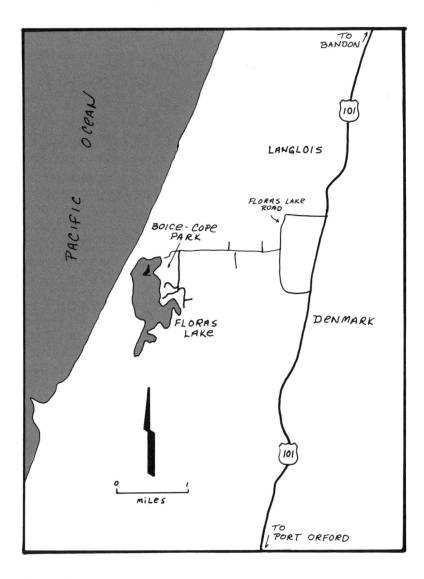

Hazards: This is also a popular fishing lake.

Wind and water reports: 469-2242 – U.S. Coast Guard Station, Brookings · 888-3266 – U.S. Coast Guard Station, Charleston

Food and lodging: The nearest gas, food and lodging are in Port Orford to the south or Bandon to the north.

See also Face Rock and Coquille River.

Other attractions: See Face Rock and Coquille River.

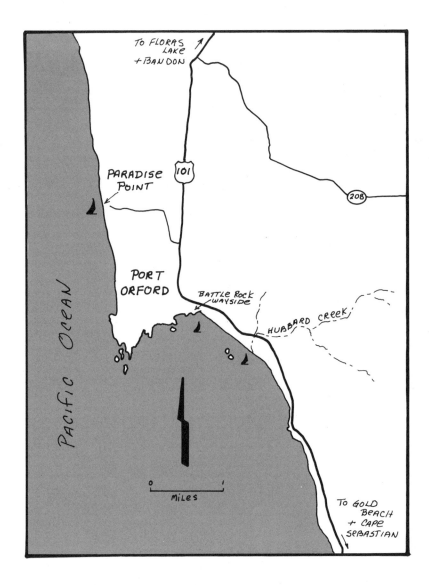

Paradise Point

Paradise Point is located just south of Cape Blanco, the windiest spot in Oregon. This is definitely a spot for short boards and small sails, 4.2 or less. The strong wind is the only attraction. It is a difficult hike down to the beach and there are no amenities.

Skill rating: Expert

Location: Paradise Point is just north of the city limits of Port Orford off U.S. Hwy. 101. The turnoff is not well marked but it is the first road to the west, past the city limits sign. Paradise Point Park is about a mile off the highway.

Sailing conditions: (Short Board) Side-onshore winds are from the northwest. The water is somewhat choppy in the summer with steep, shore-breaking waves. The beach is flatter in the winter and the surf breaks further offshore.

Access: The park consists of a parking lot with a steep trail down to the sand and gravel beach. There is grass near the parking area for rigging but no rest rooms or other amenities.

Hazards: The wind here can become overpowering. Watch out for a series of rock islands about 1 mile offshore.

Wind and water reports: 469-2242 – U.S. Coast Guard Station, Brookings

Food and lodging: See Port Orford.

Other attractions: See Port Orford.

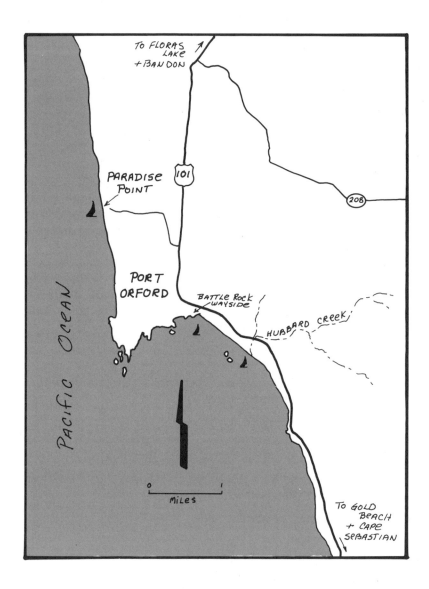

Port Orford

Port Orford is the westernmost incorporated city in the lower 48 states, and Oregon's only open-ocean harbor. The headland to the north breaks the wind and waves, providing some great flat-water sailing.

Skill rating: Expert

Location: Port Orford is on U.S. Hwy. 101, approximately 50 miles north of the California border and 50 miles south of Coos Bay.

Sailing conditions: (Short Board) The warm summer winds tend to be offshore, making it difficult to launch and return to the beach. Boardsailors must paddle or slug out until there is enough wind to plane. The best sailing is in north winds, which are most consistent in June and July.

Access: Launch at Hubbard Creek, about 1 mile south of town on U.S. Hwy. 101. There is parking along the roadside with a healthy walk down to the beach. Rigging is done on the beach. There are no rest rooms or other amenities at this site.

An alternative launch site is at Battle Rock Wayside, a mile north of Hubbard Creek, in the town of Port Orford. This site has a paved parking area, rest rooms, and picnic tables. It is a steeper trek to the beach but the path is paved. Launching and returning to this site can be even more difficult than at Hubbard Creek.

Hazards: There are a number of rocks close offshore south of Hubbard Creek. Fewer offshore rocks will be found at Battle Rock Wayside. Unless you're a great swimmer, this is no place for a sinker board.

Wind and water reports: 469-2242 – U.S. Coast Guard Station, Brookings • 888-3266 – U.S. Coast Guard Station, Charleston

Food and lodging: Port Orford has a good selection of gas, food and overnight accommodations for such a small town.

The Wheel House Restaurant, next to Battle Rock Wayside, and *The Truculent Oyster Steak House and Spirits,* across the highway, both have excellent food.

Gwendolyn's and *Home by the Sea,* both bed and breakfast establishments, offer an alternative to motel accommodations.

Camping is available at *Cape Blanco State Park,* 9 miles north of town. Tent and RV sites are available with electrical hookups. *Humbug Mountain State Park,* 6 miles south of town, has tent and RV sites with full hookups. Both parks have rest rooms with hot showers and RV dump stations. In addition there are several private RV parks located in and around Port Orford.

Other attractions: Scuba diving is popular in the harbor because of the abundance of sea life and the deep clear waters close to shore.

Port Orford Head, north of town, is a fine place for whale watching in the spring and fall.

The Elk and Sixes Rivers, located just north of town, are two of the finest salmon and steelhead rivers in the state.

Cape Sebastian

★

This is one of the few places on the south coast where intermediate sailors can go out into the open ocean. A row of offshore islands help break the waves, making the area feel more protected.

Skill rating: Intermediate to expert

Location: Cape Sebastian is located approximately 8 miles south of Gold Beach on U.S. Hwy. 101, just a few miles north of the Pistol River.

Sailing conditions: (Short Board) Expect good, strong side-shore winds with waves 2 to 3 feet smaller than at other nearby beaches.

Access: There is a highway turnout for parking and only a short walk down to a nice sand beach. A three- to four-foot sand bottom near shore makes this an excellent spot for learning water starts or making land jibes. There are no rest rooms or other amenities here.

Hazards: Beware of rip currents near Hunters Island.

Wind and water reports: 469-2242 – U.S. Coast Guard, Brookings

Food and lodging: The nearest gas, food and lodgings are in Gold Beach, to the north, or in Brookings, about 27 miles south.

Jot's Resort in Gold Beach has 140 waterfront rooms and condominiums. In addition to the fine restaurant and lounge, they have a heated pool and indoor spa. Jot's is a point of embarkation for many ocean charter fishing and upriver jet boat excursions.

The Beach House Restaurant and Lounge in Gold Beach, boasts of the "Best Ocean View in Town."

This Old House features casual dining with an authentic oak pit barbeque.

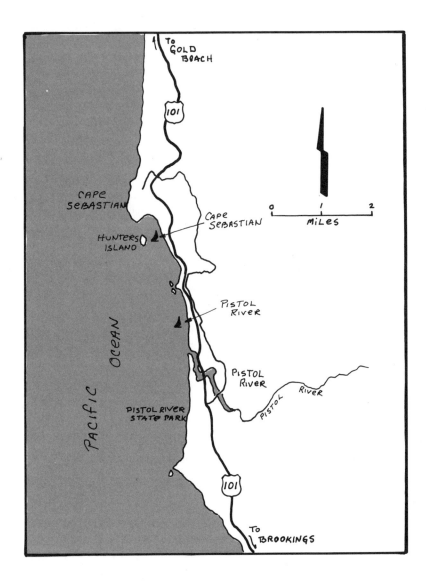

For a unique lodging or dining experience, try one of the rustic lodges in the Rogue River Wilderness Area. Many of these establishments can only be reached by trail or jet boat. Reservations are required. Contact the Gold Beach Chamber of Commerce for more information.

Other attractions: Gold Beach is the jumping-off point for trips into the wild and scenic *Rogue River Wilderness Area*. Jet boat excursions head upriver into the Rogue Canyon, stopping at wilderness lodges along the way for meals and to pick up passengers.

Indian Creek Trail Rides, in Wedderburn, offers trail rides along the Rogue River.

Cape Sebastian State Park, located on top of the cape, offers a breathtaking view of the coastline. Trails leading out to the edge of the cliffs are not for the faint of heart.

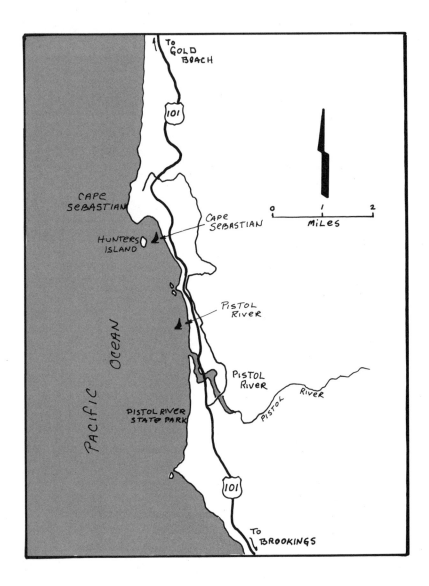

Pistol River

The beach at the mouth of the Pistol River is the southernmost launch site on the Oregon coast. Beyond Cape Ferrelo, approximately 12 miles further south, the coastline curves toward the southeast, effectively blocking the prevailing northwesterly winds. Signs along this stretch of U.S. Hwy. 101 warn motorists of gusty winds so you know you're at the right spot.

Skill rating: Expert

Location: The Pistol River is located just a few miles south of Cape Sebastian on U.S. Hwy. 101, 12 miles south of Gold Beach. The name is misleading; the actual site is a half-mile north of the river mouth. Heading north on 101, it is just past the Pistol River bridge.

Sailing conditions: (Short Board) Expect side-onshore winds out of the northwest with big, shore-breaking waves. Some local sailors come here year-round, but the most consistent months are probably June and July. The Pistol River runs parallel to the beach before entering the ocean. When conditions are right, this area offers great flat-water speed-sailing.

Access: A large rock along U.S. Hwy. 101 marks this site. It's near a parking turnout with a historical marker. From here it's not too far to the sandy beach. Launch to the north of the rock.

To sail in the Pistol River itself, launch at the state park south of the U.S. Hwy. 101 bridge. There are no rest rooms or other amenities at either location.

Hazards: Beware of dangerous tides and undertows.

Wind and water reports: 469-2242 – U.S. Coast Guard, Brookings · 247-2414 – Gold Beach Airport

Food and lodging: See Cape Sebastian.

Other attractions: See Cape Sebastian.

Region Three: _____

_____The Interstate 5

_____Corridor

Interstate 5 Corridor

It is difficult to characterize the lakes along the Interstate 5 Corridor with regard to wind and sailing conditions. The same natural phenomena that control the winds along the coast, in the Gorge, and in the Cascades are present here as well, but they are not as clearly defined. During the summer months a thermal low-pressure area, or "trough," which forms over northern California, begins to move north along the coast with air circulating in a counterclockwise direction. At the same time, a high pressure area is forming over the Olympic Penninsula with clockwise air movement. As a result, a strong north/south flow of air is created along the coast and in the interior valleys, which lie between the Coast and Cascade mountain ranges. These prevailing winds occur three out of four days on the average and tend to increase in strength as they move further south, reaching speeds of 12 to 18 MPH. The increase is the result of thermally generated winds, which are also moving up the valley. In addition to these north/south winds, thermal slope winds move laterally from the valley floor, upslope during the morning hours and downslope in the evening. Southerly facing slopes, which receive more solar radiation, will have stronger upslope winds.

It should be obvious from this generalized discussion that the wind patterns in the interior valleys are very complex. Local terrain and man-made changes will modify the prevailing wind patterns even further, making it difficult to predict which lakes will be best for windsurfing and when. Most of the lakes covered in this chapter are open year-round. For many, the best boardsailing conditions exist in the winter months.

Since the lakes described in this chapter are close to population centers and easily accessible from I-5, they are popular recreation areas and heavily used. The greatest hazards are powerboats and water-skiers. Many of the lakes are were actually built as impoundments for irrigation and flood control. Because of this, the water level fluctuates throughout the year and is usually lowest in late summer and fall. At these times, submerged logs and rocks can create additional hazards for boardsailors. In exceptionally dry years the water level may be drawn so low that recreational use of the lakes is impossible.

Foster Reservoir

Foster Reservoir is located in the foothills of the western slopes of the Cascade Mountains. The west end of the lake is surrounded by low rolling hills, while the east end is in the steep, forested slopes. As a result, the lake is influenced by valley winds, so the best sailing will usually occur in the late afternoon and evening. Because the lake is also oriented on an east/west axis, it is somewhat influenced by pressure differences between the east and west sides of the Cascades.

Skill rating: Novice to intermediate

Location: The reservoir is approximately 25 miles east of I-5 on U.S. Hwy. 20, near the town of Sweet Home. From southbound I-5 take exit 233, or from northbound take exit 216, and follow Hwy. 228 east to the junction of U.S. Hwy. 20. Foster Reservoir is three miles beyond Sweet Home.

Sailing conditions: (Long Board) The sailing season at Foster Reservoir is from Memorial Day, when the parks open for the season, through Labor Day. At the end of September the water level is lowered for flood control purposes.

Access: Several county parks on the north shore of the lake can be reached by crossing the dam and heading east on North River Road. The best launch site is at Lewis Creek Park which is located near the widest point of the lake. This park has plenty of paved parking, rest rooms, grass rigging areas, picnic and barbecue facilities. There is a protected swimming area here with a nice beach and boat docks for easy water entry. It's a long way from the parking area to the water but paved paths make the walk a little easier. The prevailing wind at this site will be side-offshore.

Hazards: A small log boom is the only barrier at the dam spillway. Floating logs and debris are common obstacles early in the

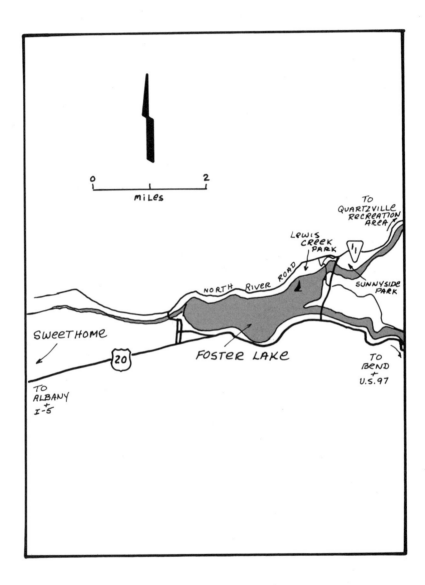

year. Submerged logs, rocks and stumps near shore are also hazards, particularly when the water level is low. Water levels in Foster Lake may fluctuate as much as two feet during the day.

Wind and water reports: 688-9041 – National Weather Service, Eugene Airport

Food and lodging: Gas, food and some lodgings are available in the towns of Sweet Home and Lebanon. A larger selection can be found in Albany, approximately 30 miles west at I-5. Two RV parks are located in Sweet Home. Additional tent and RV camping is available at Sunnyside Park, 1 mile east of Lewis Creek Park, on the Mid-Santiam River.

Other attractions: Sweet Home is the site of the *Calapooia Round-up* each year in July.

The *Quartzville Recreation Area*, located on Quartzville Creek west of Foster Reservoir, provides primitive camping and fishing opportunities. Recreational gold mining is allowed in this area as well. Check with the U.S. Forest Service office in Sweet Home for details and make sure you don't prospect on someone else's claim.

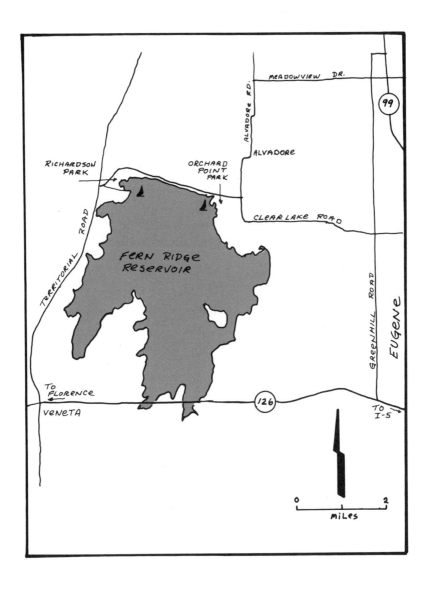

Fern Ridge Lake

★ ★ ★

Fern Ridge is the most heavily used recreational lake in Oregon. It covers about 15 square miles with an average depth of 11 feet. The surrounding area is relatively flat farmland with very few trees to block the wind. This is a great place for long board sailing. It is the site of the annual Mid-State and Mistral Long Board Championships.

Skill rating: Novice to intermediate

Location: Fern Ridge Lake is 12 miles west of Eugene on Hwy. 126.

Sailing Conditions: (Long Board) Sailing is good year-round, but the best months are May through July. The water is warm enough by midsummer that wetsuits aren't necessary. A strong west wind usually develops in the evenings when it's hot in the valley and cool on the coast.

Access: The best access and launch sites are located on either side of the dam at the north end of the lake. Two county parks, Orchard Point Park and Richardson Park, are located on Clear Lake Road at the east and west ends of the dam respectively. Both offer parking, rest rooms, beach and boat launching facilities. Day-use fees are charged by the county. The shore of the lake is covered with concrete to reduce erosion, which also makes water entry extremely easy. Many Eugene area sailboard shops run rental concessions and lessons at these parks during the summer.

Hazards: In late summer, especially in dry years, the water level may be very low, and submerged stumps along shore can be dangerous. At these times it is best to stay near the north end of the lake where the water is deepest.

Be careful not to sail into the reverse wind shadow caused by the dam, particularly if you can't water start. Waves can build up quickly in open waters when the wind is strong, making it impossible to uphaul a sail, and the swift current could pull you over the spillway.

Wind and water reports: 688-9041 – National Weather Service, Eugene Airport

Food and lodging: Eugene offers an excellent choice of food and lodging accommodations in every price range.

Mega Resort, a privately operated campground, is located on the south shore of Fern Ridge Lake.

Other attractions: The *Hult Center for the Performing Arts*, located next to the Hilton Hotel in downtown Eugene, features top-name artists in the theatrical and musical fields.

The *Eugene Saturday Market*, featuring the work of local artists and craftsmen, has been a weekly summertime tradition for almost twenty years.

The *Forgeron Vineyard*, just north of Elmira, and the *Hinman Vineyard*, approximately 10 miles south of Veneta, are open to the public with tours and wine tasting. In mid-July the *Vineyard Bluegrass Festival* is hosted by Forgeron with great food, wine and entertainment.

Other Eugene area music festivals include the *Oregon Bach Festival* in late June, and the *Emerald Valley Dixieland Jazz Jubilee* in late August.

The *McKenzie River* east of Eugene is world famous for fishing and whitewater rafting.

Dorena Lake

Dorena Lake is a good place to learn boardsailing. It is oriented in a northwesterly direction, taking advantage of the prevailing summer winds, and the water temperature is warm, approaching 80° F by August.

Skill rating: Novice to intermediate

Location: Located approximately 20 miles south of Eugene, Dorena Lake is 7 miles east of I-5 (exit 174) near the town of Cottage Grove.

Sailing conditions: (Long Board) The best sailing is in the months of May through July. About mid-July the water level is lowered to provide winter flood storage. If the wind is out of the south, forget about Dorena Lake and try Cottage Grove Lake, which is only 15 miles away.

Access: The best access is at Baker Bay where the northwest winds are side-onshore. The park has plenty of parking, rest rooms with showers, covered picnic areas with barbeque grills and electricity, camping, a small marina and food concession. There is also lots of grass, right down to the water's edge, for easy rigging and entry. The park is open from April through September. An admission fee is charged on weekends and holidays. Equipment rental and lessons are available at the park during the summer months.

Hazards: Submerged stumps, logs and rocks can be a problem late in the year when the water level is low. Dangerous waves can build suddenly. Novices should avoid open water in stronger winds.

Wind and water reports: 942-7669 – Baker Bay Campground

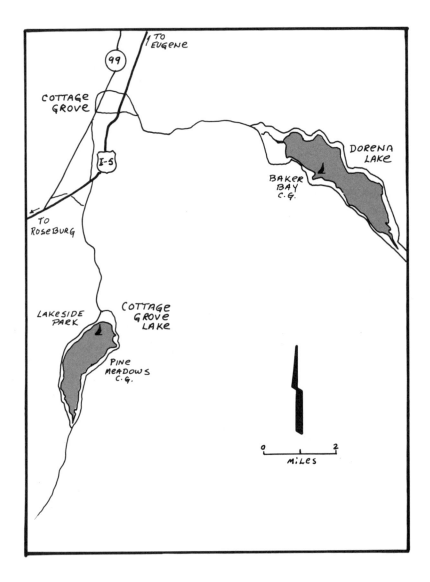

Food and lodging: Gas, food and lodgings are available at the I-5 interchange, as well as in the town of Cottage Grove. In addition to the campground at Baker Bay, camping is available at Schwartz Park approximately 2 miles west of Dorena Lake.

The Village Green, located at the I-5 interchange, has a restaurant, lounge, motel and RV park with full hookups. Tennis courts, a pool and spa are just some of the other amenities offered.

Other attractions: The *Bohemia Mining District*, located southeast of Dorena Lake, was the site of a gold rush in 1905. The old mining district can be visited by automobile but the roads are rough. A better idea is to take a guided tour on "The Goose," a 1914 steam engine operated by the Oregon Pacific & Eastern Railroad. The city of Cottage Grove remembers its pioneer past during the *Bohemia Mining Days* celebration each year in mid-July.

Cottage Grove is the *Covered Bridge Capital of Oregon*. Four of these historic and picturesque structures are located within a few miles of Dorena Lake.

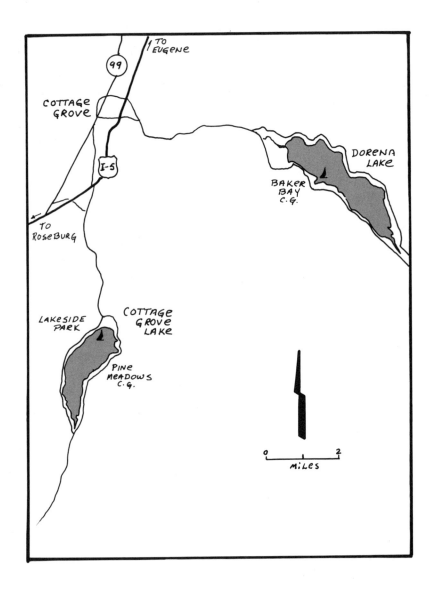

Cottage Grove Lake

★

Cottage Grove Lake is another good place for the beginner. The lake is shallow and relatively warm. It is also accessible early in the season when many of the higher lakes are still snowbound. The lake is oriented in a southwesterly direction, making it ideal for winter and early spring sailing.

Skill rating: Novice and intermediate

Location: Located about 25 miles south of Eugene, Cottage Grove Lake is 5 miles south of I-5 (exit 170), near the town of Cottage Grove. Directions from I-5 are well marked.

Sailing conditions: (Long Board) The best sailing is in the months of May through July. In August the drawdown for winter flood storage begins, but it is not as drastic as at other reservoirs. Fall and winter sailing is good, with less competition from motorboats. If the wind is out of the north, forget Cottage Grove Lake and try Dorena Lake.

Access: The best access is at Lakeside Park, which is located at the north end of the lake next to the dam. The lake is deepest in this area so it is still possible to launch when the water level is lowered. The park has plenty of parking, grass for rigging, a nice gravel beach for easy entry, rest rooms and picnic tables. The picnic area is closed from mid September till Memorial Day but the boat ramp is open year-round with paved parking and chemical toilets.

The southwest wind will be side-onshore at Lakeside Park. An alternative launch site with similar conditions and facilities is located across the lake at Shortridge Park. Several other parks are located on the east shore of the lake but the water is shallow and marshy, making access difficult.

Hazards: Submerged rocks, stumps and logs along the shoreline can be hazardous, especially in the fall when the lake level is lowered for flood control. Dangerous waves can form suddenly when the wind strengthens, beginners should avoid open waters.

Water skiing is popular here. Ski boats are restricted to the center of the lake and required to proceed in a counterclockwise direction.

Wind and water reports: 942-7669 – Baker Bay Campground, Dorena Lake. (If there is a south wind at Dorena Lake, sailing should be good at Cottage Grove Lake.)

Food and lodging: Camping is available at *Pine Meadows Campground* on the east shore from Memorial Day to Labor Day. A primitive campground, located one-half mile south of Pine Meadows, is open year-round. There is also a private campground on London Road just south of Lakeside Park. Additional gas, food and lodging are available in Cottage Grove.

See also Dorena Lake.

Other attractions: See Dorena Lake.

Lost Creek Reservoir

Lost Creek is a large, deep and relatively new reservoir completed in 1977. The lake is almost 2 miles wide and it is possible to sail the entire distance on a full reach.

Skill rating: Novice to intermediate

Location: Approximately 26 miles north of Medford and I-5 on Hwy. 62.

Sailing conditions: (Long Board) The reservoir is large and deep and although the water exceeds 70°F by mid-July, it seems cold compared to the air temperature, which is usually above 90°F. During the day, upslope winds are blocked by the dam, creating a wind shadow on the west end of the lake. Local windsurfers recommend sailing in the evening from about 5:00 PM to dusk, when the downslope east winds can average 20 to 25 MPH.

Access: The best launch site is approximately 2.5 miles east of the Cole Rivers Fish Hatchery. A dirt road leads down to the water's edge from Hwy. 62, just west of Joseph P. Stewart State Park. Parking and other facilities are limited at this launch site but rest rooms, camping and other amenities are available in the park nearby.

Hazards: Powerboats, water-skiers and anglers are the major hazards. There are also lots of stumps and logs along shore. "Floating rocks" are a local phenomenon. These pumice stones are generally not large enough to damage equipment.

Wind and water reports: 560-3334 – Joseph P. Stewart State Park

Food and lodging: The closest gas, food and lodgings are in the town of Shady Cove, approximately 10 miles southeast on Hwy. 62.

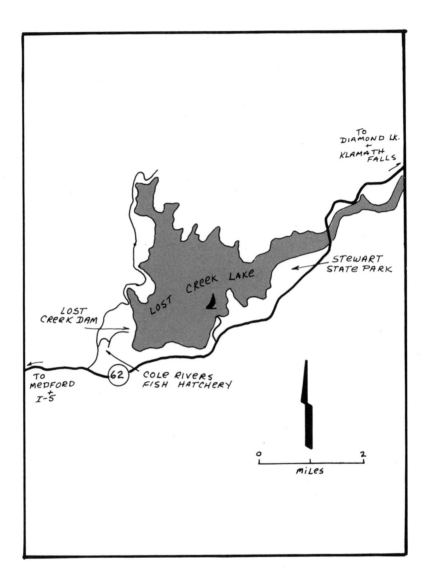

Joseph P. Stewart State Park, on the south shore, has excellent camping facilities with 151 RV and 50 tent sites.

Other attractions: *Cole M. Rivers Rish Hatchery*, downstream of Lost Creek Dam on Hwy. 62, is the largest hatchery in the state and is open to the public.

The Rogue River, a favorite of the late Zane Grey, offers world-class fishing for salmon, steelhead and trout. It is also excellent for white water rafting. A scenic drive east along Hwy. 62 leads to *Mill Creek Falls: Natural Bridge*, where a natural rock formation crosses the Rogue River; and the *Rogue River Gorge*.

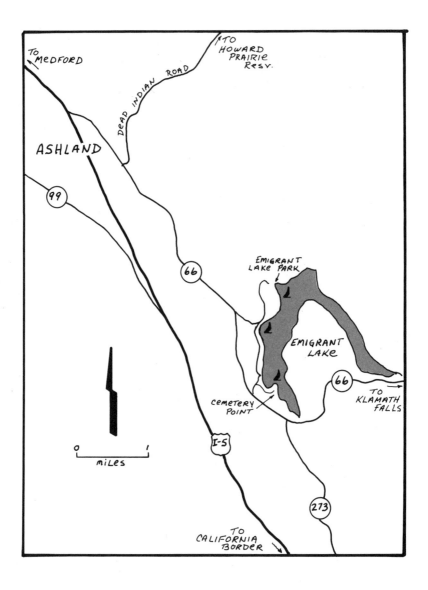

Emigrant Lake

Emigrant Lake is shaped like an inverted **V** with one arm oriented toward the northwest and the other toward the southwest. In the spring and early summer it offers typical long board lake sailing. By late summer, the lake level has usually been lowered so much by irrigation withdrawal that it is unusable for recreation. In the winter, when the lake has refilled, the southwesterly wind screams down out of the Siskiyou Mountains at 40 MPH plus, creating Gorge-type short board sailing conditions.

Skill rating: Novice to expert, depending on time of year.

Location: Emigrant Lake is approximately 6 miles southeast of Ashland on Hwy. 66. The directions from I-5 are well marked. Take exit 14 south of Ashland.

Sailing conditions: (Long and Short Board, depending on the season) Good winds are consistent in spring and early summer when the lake is at full pool. Later in the year, when water is released for irrigation, the wind comes over the top of the dam and conditions get squirrely. In the winter, the southerly winds scream down out of the Siskiyou Mountains at speeds of 25 MPH plus. Local sailors who can't afford to go to Baja or Hawaii come here in the winter months.

Access: In the winter the best sailing is at Cemetery Point on the southwest shore. To reach this site stay on Emigrant Lake Road past the entrance to Emigrant Lake Park. Turn left on the dirt road just before the weigh station and cross over the small rock dam. The road branches after passing the old pioneer cemetery. Keep to the right and you will find a small point of land jutting out into the lake. There are no facilities or improvements here and the beach is mud and cobbles. Local sailors have reported 60 MPH side-shore winds when the winter storms move in.

From April to August (wind and water permitting) Randy

233

Warren of The Hobie House operates a concession with rentals and lessons near the entrance to Emigrant Lake Park. This is a good place to launch in northwest winds, or you can go into the park where rest rooms, plenty of grass for rigging, trees and a beach are just some of the amenities. Swimming floats in the middle of the lake make nice rest stops.

Hazards: Drag boats and water-skiers can be a problem during the summer months. Look out for submerged rocks, logs and stumps near shore when the water level is low.

Wind and water reports: 488-0595 – The Hobie House, Ashland

Food and lodging: Camping is available in the county park at Emigrant Lake, as well as at private campgrounds near the park entrance.

The city of Ashland offers one of the most diverse selections of food and lodging facilities in Oregon. Unfortunately, there is not room enough in this book to describe them all. Motel space is at a premium during the summer months and reservations are advised.

Other attractions: The *City of Ashland* is an attraction in itself. With an almost European atmosphere, it is probably the most eclectic community between San Francisco and Portland. Some of the attractions include:

The *Oregon Shakespearean Festival*, the oldest in the country, runs from February through October. Tickets for the outdoor performances go fast and advance reservations are advised for this world-class event; call: (503)482-4331.

Lithia Park along Ashland Creek was designed by John McLaren, designer of Golden Gate Park in San Francisco. Every Thursday evening during the summer the Ashland City Band puts on a free concert in the band shell.

Medford celebrates the return of spring with the annual *Pear Blossom Festival* in mid-April. The festivities include a parade, carnival, street fair and square dance.

Painted Sky Stables offers trail rides into the hills surrounding Ashland. Trips are by the hour, the day or overnight. Overnight trips feature a hearty chuck wagon dinner around the campfire.

Rogue Valley Balloon Flights offer one-hour hot-air balloon rides including refreshments and brunch.

Howard Prairie Reservoir

Howard Prairie is one of the best sailing lakes in the southern Cascades and the site of many national sailing events. The lake is oriented in a northwesterly direction, taking advantage of the prevailing summer winds. Randy Warren of The Hobie House operates a concession here from July through September (water permitting), with rentals and lessons.

In some years, like 1988, drought conditions have prevented the lake from filling, so sailing was not possible. It is a good idea to call ahead or check with locals before heading to Howard Prairie.

Skill rating: Novice to intermediate

Location: The lake is approximately 22 miles east-northeast of Ashland off Dead Indian Road. From I-5, take exit 14 and head east on Hwy. 66. The junction with Dead Indian Road is well marked. Follow the signs to the reservoir.

Sailing conditions: (Long Board) The northerly winds are strong and consistent from June through September or October. They begin each day around noon and continue until dusk.

Access: The best sailing is near the south end of the lake at Willow Point, also known as Windy Point by local sailors. There is adequate parking and a boat ramp at the Willow Creek campground. The bottom is gently sloping for easy water access. When the lake level is low, usually late in the year, you may have to carry your equipment a long way to reach the water.

Hazards: A rock ridge, extending west from Buck Island, may be exposed or just below the surface when the water level is low. This is a popular fishing lake so watch out for trolling fishermen, particularly along the eastern lakeshore.

Wind and water reports: 482-1979 – Howard Prairie Resort

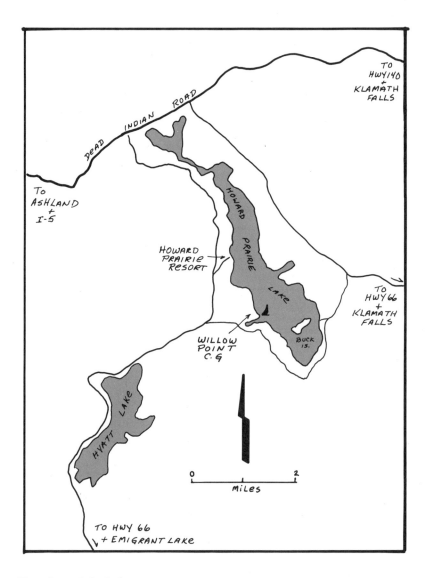

Food and lodging: *Howard Prairie Resort* has an excellent campground with fully equipped trailers for rent by the day, week or month. It also features a marina, gas station, store and cafe. Reservations are recommended; call: (503)482-1979.

Primitive campgrounds are located north of the resort on the west shore of the lake and at Willow Creek. Camping is also allowed on Buck Island. Additional gas, food and lodgings are available in Ashland, approximately one hour's drive from Howard Prairie Reservoir.

Other attractions: Howard Prairie is one of the premier fishing lakes in the southern Cascades, where more than a half-million trout are harvested in some years. _Hyatt Lake_, just south of Howard Prairie, is another outstanding lake for fishing.

See also Emigrant Lake.

Region Four: _____

_____ The Cascade Lakes

Cascade Lakes

The Cascade Mountains are dotted with hundreds of natural and constructed lakes. Many offer excellent sailing and almost all provide unsurpassed scenery. It is not easy to explain the wind and weather conditions that make for the best sailing on mountain lakes. The Cascades, like all mountains, modify the prevailing wind patterns and generate their own weather. Two types of wind occur in the Cascades, forced wind and thermal wind. Forced wind is the prevailing wind modified by terrain. This wind usually occurs when the prevailing wind is strong. Thermal wind, on the other hand, is caused by the movement of air, warmed by solar radiation, rising up the slopes and valleys. This dominates when the prevailing wind is weak. The wind at any given location in the Cascades will be created by a combination of these two wind forces. Some lakes have strong, constant wind patterns almost like the Gorge, while others have fluky winds, swirling around in every direction. Understanding mountain wind patterns can be tricky. Dabberdt, in his book *Weather for Outdoorsmen*, does an excellent job of explaining these phenomena for anyone interested in the technical background. (See bibliography.)

For the benefit of boardheads who are more interested in sailing the wind than understanding it, let me try to simplify things. Mountain lakes located where the forced winds and thermal circulations complement one another will be best for sailing. This includes lakes that are oriented toward the prevailing winds, which in Oregon are out of the northwest; lakes located in mountain passes, where wind forces similar to those at the Gorge are created; and lakes located in broad, deep mountain valleys. Wind patterns will vary throughout the day as different factors come into play. Prevailing winds are normally steady while thermal winds can be turned on and off in an instant as passing clouds temporarily block the sun. As a general rule, good sailing wind in the mountains begins around noon and continues steady until sundown.

The Cascade lakes offer an entirely different type of sailing from that found in the Gorge or along the Coast. The pace is more relaxed and the scenery unsurpassed.

As for the best time of year for sailing the Cascade lakes, many areas are snowbound until June. Man-made lakes are drawn down during the summer for agricultural irrigation or flood control. These lakes are usually pretty low by late August or September, with exposed mudflats and tree stumps. Early winter snowstorms are also possible at this time of year, particularly above 5,000 feet elevation. Despite the short season, boardsailing is becoming more popular in the Cascade lakes, with rental concessions opening up at more and more marinas and resorts each year.

Lost Lake

Lost Lake is the closest of the Cascade Lakes to Hood River and the Gorge. The lake is beautiful with a spectacular view of Mt. Hood. The Indians called it "E-e-kwahl-a-mat-yan-ishkt," which means "Heart of the Mountains." Lost Lake offers a pleasant change from the frantic pace of the Gorge and may be the nearest sailing when the Gorge wind shuts down.

Skill rating: Novice to Intermediate

Location: Lost Lake is located thirty miles south of Hood River on Hwy. 281. Cross the Hood River at Dee and head left on Lost Lake Road, Forest Service Road #13. From U.S. Hwy. 26, Lost Lake can be reached via Lolo Pass Road, which intercepts Road #13 about 4 miles east of the lake. The turnoff from U.S. Hwy. 26 is near the town of Zigzag.

Sailing conditions: (Long Board) Lost Lake is influenced by the same pressure differential between the east and west sides of the Cascades that fuels the Gorge "wind machine." The lake is also affected by thermal and valley winds. These wind forces are funneled between Buck and Preachers peaks, resulting in onshore winds from the west at Lost Lake Resort.

Access: Lost Lake Resort has the best access. The wind is onshore, making it a good place for beginners. A boat ramp on the east shore of the lake has side-onshore winds, for more experienced sailors. Lake access is also possible from the U.S. Forest Service campground. Parking is not a problem. Vault toilets and pumped water are the only other amenities.

Hazards: The bottom is rocky with sunken logs near shore.

Wind and water reports: 386-4367 – Mobile Phone, Lost Lake Resort

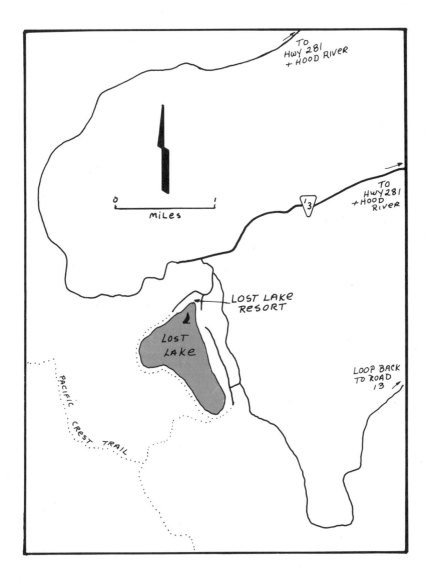

Food and lodging: *Lost Lake Resort* has seven cabins and a furnished apartment for rent by the day, the weekend or longer. The resort also has a general store stocked with all the basic necessities. There is no gas available at Lost Lake, the nearest gas station is in Parkdale, 20 miles away.

The U.S. Forest Service campground at Lost Lake has 80 camp-sites with piped water and vault toilets. There are no RV hookups.
See also Hood River.

Other attractions: Hiking trail #656 circles the lake while trail #616 climbs to a vantage point with a commanding view of five snowcapped peaks. The _Huckleberry Mountain Trail_ (#617) which begins at the organization camp, wanders up 2.5 miles to connect with the _Pacific Crest Trail._

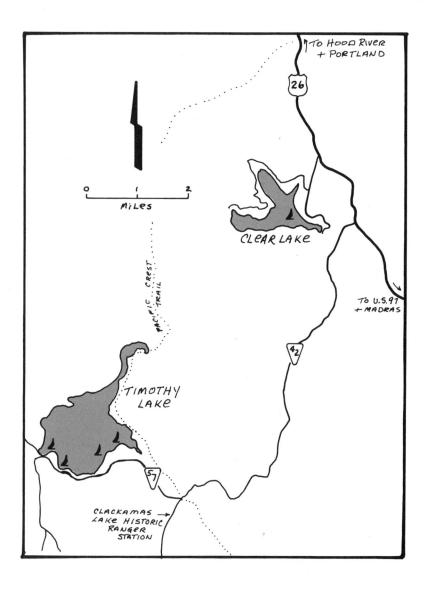

Clear Lake

Oriented to take advantage of the summer northwest winds, Clear Lake is one of the best sites in the northern Cascades. The pressure differential between the east and west side of the mountains that makes the Gorge such a great sailing site also affects this location. The wind is generally strong and consistent, rarely gusty. Short board sailing is often possible here.

Skill rating: Novice to intermediate (sometimes expert conditions occur.)

Location: Clear Lake is approximately 65 miles south-southeast of Portland off U.S. Hwy. 26. From I-84 take U.S. Hwy. 35 from Hood River, then go left on U.S. Hwy. 26 approximately 8 miles. A Forest Service road connects the lake with the main highway. The junction is well-marked. The access is closed from December to April.

Sailing conditions: (Long Board, Short Board at times) Expect good consistent wind, averaging 15 to 30 MPH. The lake is accessible from May through October but the sailing is best either early or late in the season, July and August are generally poor.

Access: Clear Lake, as the name suggests, is clear and cold. It has two arms, one oriented due west and the other in a northwest direction. A U.S. Forest Service campground is located at the junction of the two arms. The boat ramp at the campground is probably the best launch site. Typical winds here should be side-shore. When the water level is lowered, however, it is possible to drive around the shore of the lake to take advantage of varying wind conditions. The campground has vault toilets and pumped water.

Hazards: There are a few stumps which can be hazards late in the year when the water level is the lowest. Local sailors have begun a stump removal program, so the danger from these hazards is becoming less each year. Very low water levels may occur late in July or August due to irrigation withdrawals.

Wind and water reports: None available

Food and lodging: There is a Forest Service campground on the southeast shore of the lake. Dozens of other campgrounds are located within a few miles. Government Camp, 10 miles northwest on U.S. Hwy. 26, has additional gas, food and lodging facilities.

Timberline Lodge, on the south slope of Mt. Hood, is a National Monument with year-round lodging and a gourmet restaurant.

Other attractions: The *Pacific Crest Trail* passes just a few miles west of Clear Lake.

Timberline Lodge offers year-round skiing on the Palmer Glacier. This is the summer training camp for the U.S. Olympic Ski Team. Mountain climbing and hiking trails are some of the other attractions at Timberline Lodge.

Timothy Lake

Timothy Lake is a large reservoir on the south side of Mt. Hood. Because of its close proximity to Portland it gets a lot of recreational use. Motorboat speed on the lake is limited to 10 MPH.

Skill rating: Novice to intermediate

Location: The lake is approximately 75 miles east-southeast of Portland off U.S. Hwy. 26. From I-84 take U.S. 35 at Hood River, then go left at U.S. Hwy. 26, approximately 8 miles, to U.S. Forest Service Road #42 (Skyline Road). The junction is well marked. Stay on Road #42 approximately 8 miles, to Road #57. From here it is approximately 2 miles further to the lake. It's a long way from the main highway but the Forest Service roads are paved.

Sailing conditions: (Long Board) Sailing conditions at Timothy Lake are similar to those at Clear Lake, which is approximately four miles to the northeast as the crow flies. Winds from the northwest average 15 to 30 MPH during the summer months. The lake is accessible from May through October, but the sailing is best either early or late in the season. July and August are generally poor.

Access: There are four U.S. Forest Service campgrounds along the east shore of the lake, with boat ramps for water access and small gravel beach areas. The winds are onshore to side-onshore. Parking is adequate and vault toilets and pumped water are provided.

Hazards: Large rocks and stumps line the shoreline away from the beaches and boat ramp areas.

Wind and water reports: None available

Food and lodging: U.S. Forest Service campgrounds are the only lodging facilities at Timothy Lake. This is a popular area and

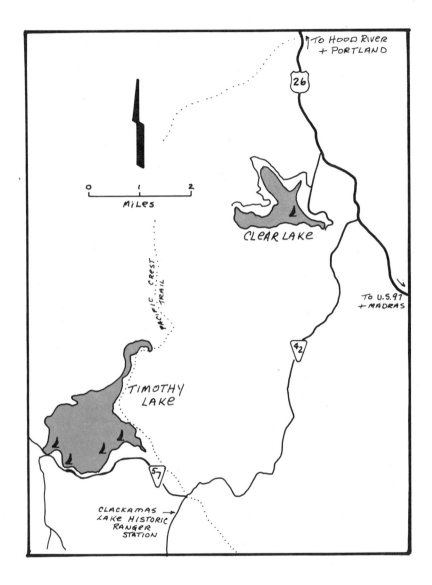

campsites on the lake are hard to come by. Fortunately, there are hundreds of other U.S. Forest Service campsites within a few miles.

The nearest gas, food and lodgings are at Government Camp, approximately twenty miles west on U.S. Hwy. 26.

Other attractions: The *Pacific Crest Trail* passes just east of the lake. In addition, there are a number of shorter trails in the area that lead to other nearby lakes and offer excellent views of Mt. Hood. Hiking and other recreational information can be obtained at the *Historic Clackamas Lake Ranger Station*, located near the junction of Forest Service Roads 42 and 57.

Timberline Lodge offers year-round skiing on the Palmer Glacier. This is the summer training camp for the U.S. Olympic Ski Team. Mountain climbing and hiking trails are some of the other attractions at Timberline Lodge.

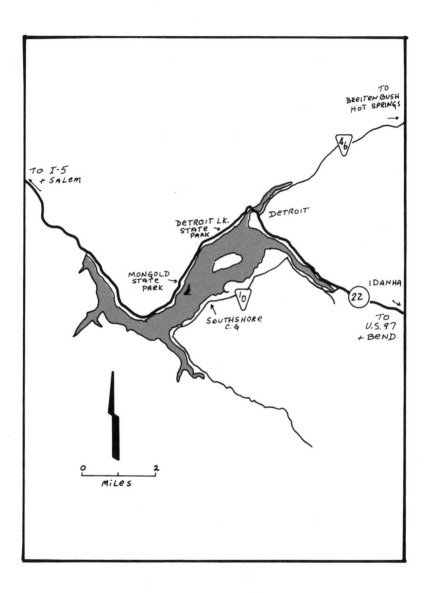

Detroit Lake

Detroit Lake is the closest inland sailing to Salem, the state capitol. This beautiful lake is located on the western slopes of the Cascades, below majestic Mt. Jefferson. Because of the scenery and the close proximity to the Willamette Valley, it is one of the most heavily used lakes in the state for recreational boating.

Skill rating: Novice and intermediate

Location: Detroit Lake is located 52 miles east of Salem. Take Hwy. 22 from I-5.

Sailing conditions: (Long Board) The best sailing is in the months of June through August. After that the water level in the lake is lowered to make room for winter flood storage. The best time of day to sail is in the afternoon as the thermal wind works its way up the valley.

Access: The Mongold day-use area of Detroit Lake State Park, on the northwest shore, is the only point on the lake with sufficiently consistent winds for boardsailing. A large island to the east of this site makes the wind on the remainder of the lake very fluky. The Mongold area has a huge parking lot, rest rooms with changing areas and hot showers, picnic tables and barbeques. A day-use access fee is charged here on weekends and holidays.

The beach at Mongold is paved with asphalt up to the water's edge. This makes for lousy rigging but there is some grass in the picnic area. The lake bottom is sand and gravel. The launch area is in a cove so it is necessary to paddle out to reach clear wind.

An alternative launch site is the U.S. Forest Service South Shore campground, located across the lake from Mongold. To reach this site, take Forest Service Road #10 from Hwy. 22. The turnoff is located approximately 1 mile west of the town of Idanha. The facilities here are not as nice as those at the Mongold Area.

But, because it is more difficult to reach, it will not be as crowded. Also, the wind should be better.

Hazards: Water skiing is very popular at Mongold but restricted areas have been set aside for this use. Because Detroit Lake is a man-made reservoir, there are a lot of old tree stumps along the bottom. These can be especially dangerous when the water level is lowered late in the year.

Wind and water reports: 854-3346 – Detroit Lake State Park

Food and lodging: A limited selection of gas, food and lodgings are available in the town of Detroit.

Detroit Lake State Park has more than 300 tent and RV camp sites, with more than 100 full hook-ups. There are also telephones and rest rooms with hot showers. This is a popular area so it fills up fast. Reservations are recommended: call (503)238-7488.

Other attractions: *Breitenbush Hot Springs* are located approximately 10 miles north of Detroit on Forest Service Road #46. Facilites include natural hot spring baths and sauna, bath house, restaurant and cabins. Reservations are required; call (503)854-3501

Suttle Lake

Suttle Lake lies in a deep, broad, glacial valley approximately 5 miles east of the Cascade summit at Santiam Pass. This long, narrow lake is oriented on an almost perfect east-west axis. Wind generated by the pressure differential from mountain to desert regions is funneled through the pass between Three-Fingered Jack and Mount Washington, combining with the prevailing wind to create excellent boardsailing conditions. A sailboard rental concession has operated here in past years and may operate again in the future.

Skill rating: Novice to intermediate

Location: Suttle Lake is approximately 30 miles west of U.S. Hwy. 97. Take U.S. Hwy. 20 from Bend or Hwy. 126 out of Redmond. Paved Forest Service roads lead from the main highway to the campgrounds and resorts surrounding the lake.

Sailing conditions: (Long Board, Short Board at times) The most consistent wind occurs in the months of July through September. Occasionally, good sailing conditions can be found in May and June when it's overcast in the Willamette Valley and hot in Bend. The best bet is in the afternoons when the thermals start cooking. Winds of 25 to 30 MPH happen in the spring and fall when storm fronts pass through.

Access: The most consistent wind occurs in the middle of the lake. The best launch sites are at the campgrounds along the south shore where the west wind blows side-onshore. In Blue Bay Campground the shoreline is steep and the only easy access is at the boat ramp. South Shore Campground is at lake level and it is possible to launch from shoreside campsites. Both have nice beach areas with boat docks for easy water entry. Facilities include water, vault toilets, picnic tables and barbeque pits.

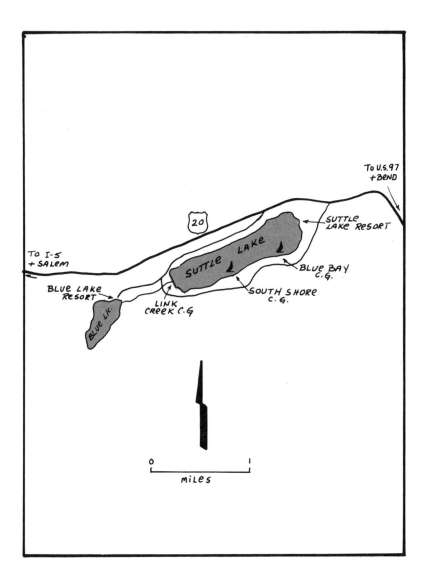

Hazards: Watch out for rocks and logs near shore. This is a popular fishing lake, especially early in the season. Don't sail too closly behind trolling fishing boats.

Wind and water reports: 595-6675 – Alpine Restaurant and Country Store • 595-6662 – Suttle Lake Marina and Resort

Food and lodging: _Suttle Lake Resort_, on the east end of the lake, has a store, marina and campground with indoor plumbing.

Blue Lake Resort is located about a mile west of Suttle Lake, with various lodging accommodations from Indian tepees to A-frame cabins. There is also tent and RV camping, with indoor rest rooms and hot showers.

The Alpine Restaurant and Country Store, at the west end of Suttle Lake, has everything in the way of picnic and camping supplies as well as excellent food.

The nearest gasoline is in the town of Sisters, 13 miles to the east on U.S. Hwy. 20. Sisters offers additional food and lodging facilities in true western fashion.

Other attractions: Each year in early June the Chamber of Commerce sponsors the _Sisters Rodeo_, which includes a parade, barbeques and the "cowboy dance."

Blue Lake Corral, at the west end of the lake, offers scenic horseback rides and pack trip services.

Black Butte Ranch, 5 miles east of Suttle Lake on U.S. Hwy. 20, is another of Oregon's premier destination resorts, featuring golf, tennis and horseback riding, in addition to fine dining and accommodations.

There are a number of hiking trails in the area including the Shoreline Trail around Suttle Lake. The _Pacific Crest National Scenic Trail_, 5 miles west on U.S. Hwy. 20, leads into the _Mount Jefferson and Mount Washington Wilderness Areas_.

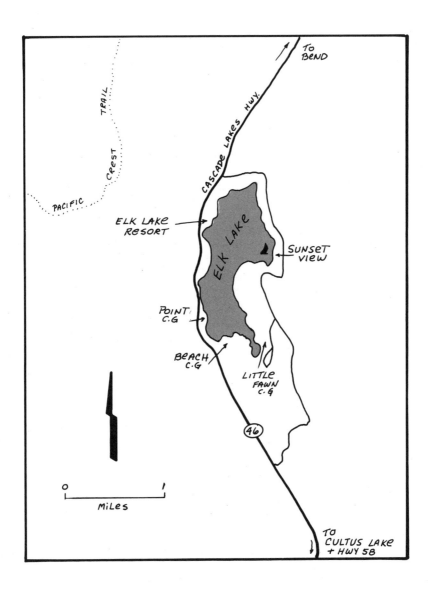

Elk Lake

★ ★ ★

Elk Lake is the closest of the Cascade Lakes to the city of Bend. The scenery here is as great as the boardsailing. Randy Barna uses this lake as a training site for Gorge-bound sailors. The lake is shallow and very warm for Oregon, with summertime water temperatures approaching 70° F.

Skill rating: Novice to intermediate

Location: This lake is approximately 25 miles west-southwest of Bend on the Cascade Lakes Highway (County Road #46). Access points to the lake are well marked. From I-5 take Hwy. 58 from Eugene, which intersects the Cascade Lakes Highway just south of Odell Lake.

Sailing conditions: (Long Board) Expect totally enjoyable long board sailing with afternoon winds from the north-northwest, typically 5 to 15 MPH. Elk Lake is one of the last lakes along the Cascade Lakes Highway to open in the spring, and snow may further prevent access until late May or early June. The lake should remain open through September.

Access: Sunset View Beach on the northwest shore of the lake is the favored launch site. The U.S. Forest Service has provided limited parking, pit privies and changing huts. No camping is allowed here. The beach is sand and gravel with a gentle slope into the water. Winds are onshore, so beginning sailors won't get into trouble. The beach area can get crowded, making it is necessary to paddle out in order to avoid swimmers near shore. For more experienced sailors, there are several other access points around the lake, most of which have offshore winds.

Hazards: Watch out for folks trolling from boats; motorboat speeds are limited to 10 MPH. Some rocks and logs near shore in the unimproved areas can be hard on boards and feet.

Wind and water reports: YP7-3954 – Mobile Phone, Elk Lake Resort

Food and lodging: There are three U.S. Forest Service campgrounds at Elk Lake but the area is very popular and the campsites fill quickly, especially on weekends. Fortunately, there are hundreds of other USFS campsites within just a few miles. *Little Fawn Campground*, near Sunset View Beach, is available for group camping by reservation only; call (503) 388-2715.

Elk Lake Resort, on the northwest shore, offers furnished cabins and a dormitory in addition to a store, restaurant and marina.

For a real vacation experience try *The Inn of the Seventh Mountain*, on the Cascade Lakes Highway just a few miles west of Bend, or *Sunriver Resort*, 22 miles east of Cultus Lake via paved Forest Service roads.

The city of Bend, just a 30-minute drive from Elk Lake, also has a wide selection of food and lodging facilities.

Other attractions: Elk Lake is located in the *Deschutes National Forest*, which has many attractions for the outdoor recreationist. The *Pacific Crest Trail* and the *Three Sisters Wilderness Area* are located just a few miles west of Elk Lake.

The *Summer Festival of the Arts* is sponsored by the Bend Visitor and Convention Bureau each year in late July.

Cultus Lake

Cultus Lake is oriented on an east-west axis, allowing for great sailing on the prevailing westerly winds with scenic views of the surrounding mountain peaks. Frequently the winds here are strong enough to make short board sailing possible.

Skill rating: Novice to intermediate

Location: The lake is approximately 50 miles southwest of Bend, along County Road #46, the Cascade Lakes Highway. A paved Forest Service road leads to the lake. The turnoff is well marked. Early in the year this road may still be closed by snow near Mt. Bachelor. In that case take Forest Service Road #40 from U.S. Hwy. 97. This road rejoins the Cascade Lakes Highway about 22 miles west of Sunriver Resort.

Sailing conditions: (Long Board) Cultus Lake is usually free of snow by May and stays open into October. As with most mountain lakes, the sailing is best in the afternoon and evening. The wind from the south or southwest is effectively blocked by Cultus Mountain, but on other winds the sailing should be great.

Access: Shallow sand bottoms on the east and west ends of the lake make launching easy. Access is best at the Resort or in the Forest Service campground at the east end of the lake. The wind here tends to be onshore, making it difficult to get out onto the lake, but it's a good place for beginners. The West Cultus Lake Campground can be reached only by hiking trail or by boat.

Hazards: Except for the east and west ends of the lake the shoreline is rocky, with trees down to the waterline and very few sand beaches. This is a popular fishing lake, so watch out for trollers.

Wind and water reports: YP7-3903 – Radio phone at Cultus Lake Resort.

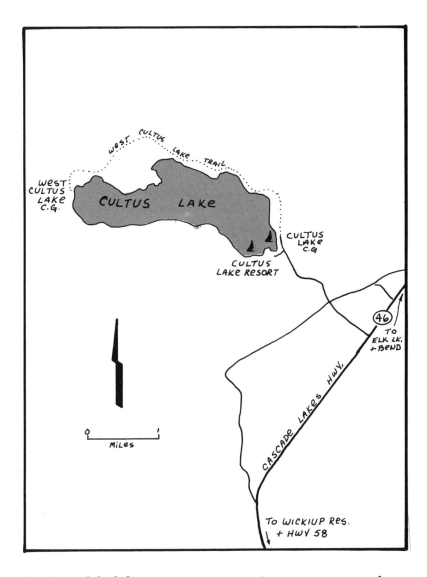

Food and lodging: Two U.S. Forest Service campgrounds are located around the lake. Also, *Cultus Lake Resort*, at the east end, offers modern cabins, a fine restaurant, boat rental and a store. There are several other fine resorts along the Cascade Lakes Highway, and the city of Bend has a wide selection of food and lodging facilities.

The campground at Cultus Lake has a nice beach for launching, and the onshore winds keep beginners out of trouble.

For a real vacation experience try *The Inn of the Seventh Mountain* on the Cascade Lakes Highway just west of Bend, or *Sunriver Resort*, located about 22 miles east of Cultus Lake via Forest Service Road #40.

Other attractions: Cultus Lake is located in the *Deschutes National Forest*, which has many attractions for the outdoor recreationist.

The *Pacific Crest Trail* is just a few miles west, and the southern boundary of the *Three Sisters Wilderness Area* begins at the north shore of the lake.

Wickiup Reservoir

Wickiup is the second largest reservoir in Oregon in terms of surface area but it is very shallow, with an average depth of only 20 feet. This means the water will be warm nearly always and choppy even in the lightest wind. The reservoir is at a lower elevation than many of the other Cascade Lakes so it is usually free of snow from early April on into October.

Skill rating: Novice to intermediate

Location: The reservoir is approximately 38 miles southwest of Bend off U.S. Hwy. 97. Turn west at Wickiup Junction, approximately 3 miles north of the town of LaPine, or take the Cascade Lakes Highway, County Road #46, south from Bend.

Sailing conditions: (Long Board, Short Board on occasion) Sailing is good here on almost all winds except due south, which are blocked by Davis Mountain. Afternoons are best.

Access: The best launch site will depend on the wind direction. Gull Point and North Wickiup campgrounds, as well as the boat ramp on the northwest shore, are recommended. All have nice sand and gravel pumice stone beaches and vault toilets. Access may be difficult along the northern and southern shorelines later in the season when the water level is low.

Hazards: The water is very shallow in the marshy areas along the northern and southern shorelines. There are submerged stumps in these areas that are impossible to see. These can be avoided by staying in the main body of the lake. Watch out for folks trolling from boats.

Wind and water reports: 385-2188 – Twin Lakes Resort

Food and lodging: *Twin Lakes Resort*, located just up the road from Gull Point Campground, offers rustic lakefront cabins, a fine restaurant, a store, a marina, and shower and laundry facilities.

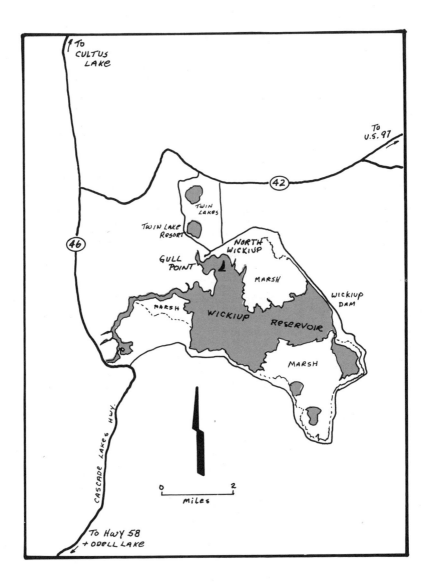

There are more than 125 Forest Service campsites within a mile of the resort, and others are located at several spots around the lake. All have vault toilets, some have running water, but there are no RV hookups.

Other attractions: The _Deschutes River_, which feeds Wickiup Reservoir, is a world-famous trout stream. Several more primitive camp sites can be found along its banks both above and below the lake.

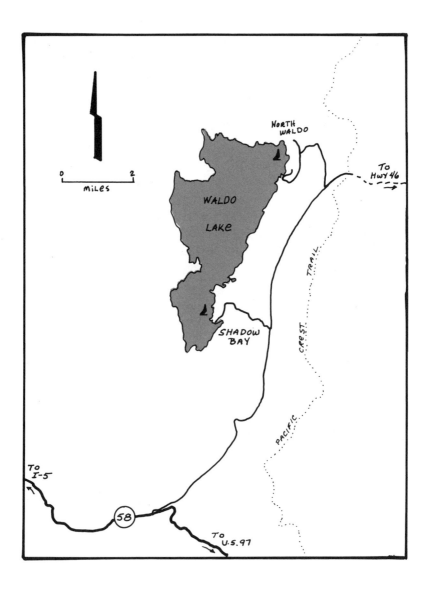

Waldo Lake

Waldo Lake is one of the largest natural lakes in Oregon, having almost 6,300 surface acres. It is also one of the cleanest bodies of water in the world, with the most incredible cobalt-blue color. The sailing here is good and the scenery is outstanding. Windsurfers rarely come here because it is so remote, but anyone who makes the trip will not be disappointed.

Skill rating: Novice and intermediate

Location: The lake is approximately 55 miles southeast of Eugene on Hwy. 58. Forest Service Road #5897 is paved from Hwy. 58 to the lake campgrounds. The turnoff is well-marked. There is a rumor that the Forest Service plans to pave this road all the way to the Cascade Lakes Highway, which would make access to Waldo Lake from the east much easier.

Sailing conditions: (Long Board) The surrounding terrain funnels the prevailing wind into Waldo Lake from the southwest. The lake elevation is above 5,000 feet. Snow may prevent access until mid-June, and early storms can make sailing after August risky. Check weather conditions before coming here.

Access: There are only two access points on Waldo Lake; both are Forest Service campgrounds. The sailing should be best at Shadow Bay on the southeast shore with side-shore winds. At North Waldo, on the northeast shore, the water can be very choppy. The side-onshore wind will be much stronger at this end of the lake. Both campgrounds have rest rooms with running water, plenty of parking and areas for rigging. The shoreline is rocky but the lake bottom is sandy with a shallow entry.

Hazards: Sunburns come easy at 5,000 feet. Watch out for large submerged rocks offshore at Shadow Bay. The mere size of the lake can be a hazard, making it difficult to return to shore if equipment fails.

Wind and water reports: 782-2291 – Willamette National Forest, Oakridge Ranger District

Food and lodging: There is no gas or food, and camping is the only lodging available. The campground facilities are excellent and rarely crowded. In the early summer you may be the only one here.

Other attractions: A network of hiking trails, including the *Pacific Crest Trail*, surround the lake. Fishing in Waldo Lake is poor because it is so clean, but many anglers backpack into the smaller lakes nearby for excellent trout fishing.

See also Odell and Crescent Lakes.

Odell Lake

Odell Lake is, without a doubt, the best boardsailing lake in the Cascades and also one of the largest, with almost 3,600 surface acres. It is located near the summit of the Range and oriented in a northwesterly direction. Willamette Pass and Diamond Peak act as a vortex for the strong summer wind, creating conditions similar to those at the Columbia Gorge. When everything is right, short board sailing is possible. The annual Odell Lake Blowout is held here in mid-August. Check with Randy Barna's Ski Shop in Bend for more information.

Skill rating: Intermediate to expert

Location: Odell Lake is located on Hwy. 58, approximately 20 miles northwest of U.S. Hwy. 97. Heading south from Bend on U.S. Hwy. 97, turn west at the town of Crescent onto County Road 61. This road also intersects the Cascade Lakes Highway. Travelers on I-5 can also reach Odell Lake via Hwy. 58, approximately 70 miles southeast of Eugene.

Sailing conditions: (Short Board) Odell Lake rarely freezes over and the resort is open year-round. The sailing season, however, generally runs from Memorial Day through Labor Day. The best wind, averaging 20 MPH plus, occurs from noon to dusk when the thermals blow. Typically this happens when marine air moves into the interior valleys and the mountains are sunny and warm. If the marine air moves offshore and it's sunny at the coast, the sailing will probably be poor at all the Cascade lakes. The water here is often choppy, even in light air.

Access: There are several launch sites around the lake. Some people like to launch near the marina at Odell Lake Lodge on the southeast shore because of the big waves. However, this area tends to be congested with fishing boats and the wind is dead

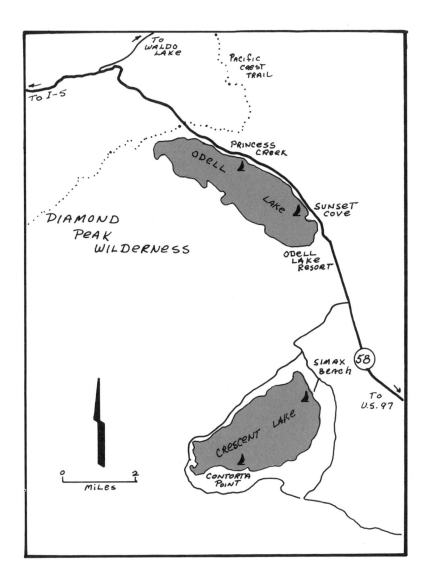

onshore, making short board sailing impossible. Most people launch at Sunset Cove or at Princess Creek campgrounds along the northeastern shoreline. Both sites have vault toilets, water, picnic tables and fire pits. The prevailing wind is side-shore but the beaches are rocky with very little sand. Launching is also possible at Odell Lake Viewpoint, which is located along Hwy. 58 between these two sites. It has a large roadside parking area, picnic tables and a small grass area for rigging. The beach here is also rocky and there are no toilets or other amenities.

Hazards: Odell Lake is very deep and cold, and the shoreline drops off suddenly. The ability to water start is mandatory for short board sailing.

Wind and water reports: 433-2540 – Odell Lake Lodge · 433-2548 – Shelter Cove Resort

Food and lodging: _Odell Lake Lodge,_ on the southeast end of the lake, has guest rooms and housekeeping cabins, and a fine restaurant, store and marina. Reservations are recommended; call (503)433-2540.

Shelter Cove Resort, at the northwest end of the lake, offers RV camping with electric hookups, rustic cabins, a marina, and a "General Store" serving breakfast and sandwiches. Call (503)433-2548 for reservations.

In addition to the private resorts, there are five Forest Service campgrounds around the lake. All have vault toilets, and most have pumped or piped water systems. But there are no RV hookups available.

Other attractions: The _Pacific Crest Trail_ skirts the northwest shore of the lake, and it is only a short hike into the _Diamond Peak Wilderness Area._

Waldo Lake, one of the cleanest in the world, is located about ten miles north of Odell Lake. It has two fine Forest Service campgrounds and there are rumors of excellent boardsailing, with average winds of 10 to 12 MPH and 6-foot waves on the leeward shore. (The author has visited the lake on several occasions and not found these conditions, but Forest Service personnel report differently. This location could be a real sleeper.) It's worth a visit to Waldo Lake just to see its brilliant cobalt-blue color.

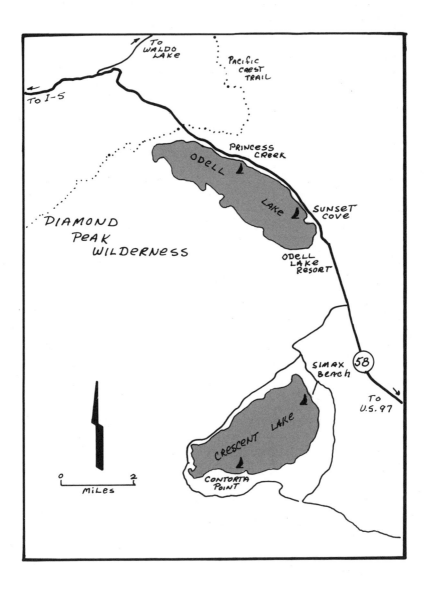

Crescent Lake

Crescent Lake is often overlooked because it is so close to Odell Lake, one of the best short board lakes in the state. It is a great long board location with some of the best beaches, excluding the coast. This is the site of the annual Oregon Long Board Championships in July. Check with Randy Barna's Ski Shop in Bend for more information.

Skill rating: Novice to intermediate

Location: The lake is just off Hwy. 58, approximately 15 miles west of U.S. Hwy. 97. Heading south from Bend, turn west at the Town of Crescent. A paved Forest Service road connects the lake with the main highway. The turnoff is well marked.

Sailing conditions: (Long Board) Crescent Lake is approximately 5 miles long by 4 miles wide. It is very deep, so the water is always cold. The sailing is best on south to southwest winds in the afternoon and evening. Northwest winds will fill in at the southwest end of the lake near Contorta Point. The water level is lowered several feet in late summer by irrigation withdrawals, but because the shoreline is so steep this has little effect on the surface area.

Access: The lake is surrounded by beautiful pumice sand beaches. There are numerous access points, depending on wind direction. The best launch sites are located at Simax Beach on the northeast shore and Contorta Point on the southwest shore. Both have campgrounds with vault toilets and picnic tables. Simax Beach has piped water. The facilities at Contorta Point are smaller and more primitive but camping is allowed on the beach. The wind, if out of the northwest, will be side-onshore.

Hazards: Watch out for trolling anglers.

Wind and water reports: 433-2505 – Crescent Lake Lodge and Resort

Food and lodging: Six Forest Service campgrounds surround the lake. The best facilities will be found at Crescent Lake, Simax Beach and Spring Campgrounds. Additional gas, food and lodging can be found at the Hwy. 58 junction; in the town of Oakridge, 29 miles west on Hwy. 58; or in the towns of Crescent and Gilchrist, about 15 miles east at the junction of U.S. Hwy. 97.

The Crescent Lake Lodge and Resort, on the north shore next to Simax Beach, is open year-round featuring rustic lake front cabins, a restaurant with an old-fashioned soda fountain, a grocery store, gas station and marina.

Other attractions: Crescent Lake is located in the *Deschutes National Forest*, which has many attractions for the outdoor recreationist.

The *Pacific Crest Trail* follows the west shore of the lake and backpackers can follow it into the *Diamond Peak Wilderness Area*, just a few miles northwest of Crescent Lake.

Diamond Lake

If compared with other Cascade lakes on the basis of wind and water conditions alone, Diamond Lake would probably rate average at best. But when scenery, shoreside facilities and other attractions are considered, it has to be rated as one of the best. This is an excellent spot for the recreational boardsailing family. There are activities for every interest and accommodations ranging from tent camping to luxurious beach-front cabins.

Sailboards are available for rent at the marina and lessons can be arranged. Long board lake sailing is the order of the day, with scenic views of snow capped Mt. Thielsen to the east and Mt. Bailey to the west. In the past, this has been the site of the Diamond Cup Race in late August. Check with Bay Sailboards in Eugene for more information.

Skill rating: Novice to intermediate

Location: Diamond Lake is approximately 20 miles west of U.S. Hwy. 97 on State Hwy. 138. The lake can also be reached from I-5. Coming from the north, take Hwy. 138 east from Roseburg, approximately 80 miles. From the south, take Hwy. 62 northeast from Medford, approximately 85 miles.

Sailing conditions: (Long Board) The lake is oriented on a north-south axis. The prevailing northwesterly wind is funneled between Mt. Bailey and Rodley Butte. Winds of 20 MPH are common here but somewhat inconsistent. The lake elevation is 5,182 feet. The water is always cold, so wetsuits are required at all times.

Access: There are plenty of access points around the lake, most along the east shore. The best launch site, in terms of shoreside facilities, is at Diamond Lake Resort at the north end. In addition to sailboard rentals and lessons, this site has public rest rooms with hot showers. Launching is also possible at the public boat

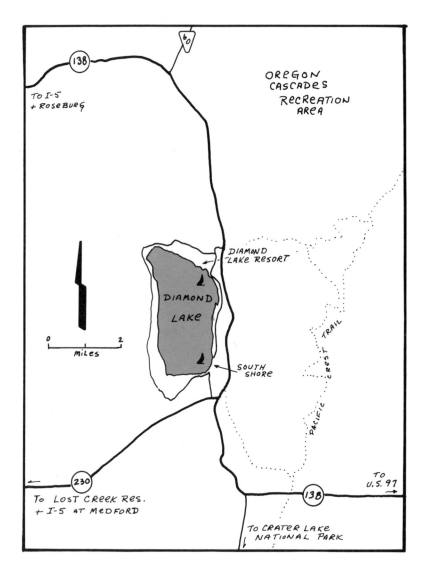

ramp next to the resort. There is plenty of parking and rest rooms but this area is often congested with fishing boats. The bottom drops off sharply at this end of the lake. Beginners might want to try the south shore where the water is shallower. South Shore Park has picnic sites, rest rooms, a boat ramp and nice beach area. This end of the lake is generally less crowded.

Hazards: This is a popular fishing spot, so watch out for trollers. As there is a 10 MPH speed limit on the lake for motorboats, water-skiers are not a problem.

Wind and water reports: 793-3333 – Diamond Lake Resort

Food and lodging: Three Forest Service campgrounds surround the lake with more than 300 campsites. Diamond Lake Campground, on the east shore, offers the best lake access and facilities.

Diamond Lake Resort, on the north shore, has over 100 rental units in every price range, an RV park, grocery store, gas station, marina, lounge and two restaurants.

South Store has gas as well as groceries, moorage and a pizza parlor. _Diamond Lake Trailer Park_, next to South Store, has additional RV camp sites and a boat ramp.

Other attractions: _Crater Lake National Park_ is so close no one should miss it. It is one of the scenic wonders of the world, formed by the volcanic eruption of Mt. Mazama. Unfortunately, windsurfing is not allowed on the lake. Tour boats take visitors for excursions, stopping at Wizard Island, a small volcanic cone that formed after the peak of the ancient mountain collapsed. The park has several campgrounds, a historic lodge, a gas station and a store.

Diamond Lake Horse Corrals rent saddle horses for trail rides into the _Diamond Lake and Oregon Cascades Recreation Areas_. Evening rides and hayrides are also available by reservation.

The _Pacific Crest Trail_ passes 3 miles to the east, through the _Mount Thielsen Wilderness Area_. The trail crosses Hwy. 138 about a mile east of the Crater Lake Park entrance. Side trails lead from the north and south ends of Diamond Lake.

Region Five: _____

_____The Desert Lakes

_____and Points East

The Desert Lakes

and Beyond

The lakes of the high desert and eastern regions of Oregon were the hardest to evaluate because much of the area is so remote. Rumors of outstanding conditions on Abert and Goose lakes in the south central area of the state, for example, could not be substantiated because few if any boardsailors have ever explored them. (If any reader does explore these areas and finds the boardsailing worthwhile, please send a report so that the sites may be included in future editions.)

The high desert plateau is an area of juniper and sagebrush, quite different from the Oregon most people picture. The winters are cold and clear while the summers are hot and dry. Agriculture is the major industry and, since there is little precipitation in the area, irrigation is a necessity. All of the sites covered in this region are irrigation reservoirs. Winter rain and snow runoff is collected for use during the summer. In most years, the reservoirs are full by March and the daytime temperatures are warm enough to permit sailing with a wetsuit. By May or June the water will be warm enough that wetsuits are not required. In late summer the water levels in the reservoirs will probably be too low for sailing, and in very dry years there may be no water at all. In winter, most lakes will be frozen.

The wind in the desert region is governed by the same natural phenomenon that controls the winds in the Gorge and the Cascade Lakes regions, namely, the change in air pressure between the east and west sides of the Cascade Mountains. The main difference is there are no gorges or mountain passes to create a wind tunnel effect. During the summer, the prevailing wind is out of the west, averaging 10 to 15 MPH. There are no trees and few obstacles to block this wind as it blows sweet and clean off the Cascades. Residents of the area tell of the "four o'clock wind." This occurs when the locally generated thermal wind adds to the velocity of the prevailing wind.

Generally speaking, the best boardsailing is from about 2 PM till sunset, during the months of March, April and May, when the wind is from the west. From June through September, the wind direction gradually swings to the north-northwest and the average speed diminishes. This is not to say the sailing will be poor during these months, because actually the strongest winds come from the north-northwest.

The best indication of great sailing in the desert region is the presence of a deep layer of marine air in the interior valleys on the west side of the Cascades. This condition is marked by overcast skies and cool temperatures, with hot sunny weather on the east side of the mountains. When this occurs, the wind on the east side will easily exceed 20 MPH. If the wind aloft in the jet stream is also from the north-northwest, winds at the surface will be even stronger. On the other hand, if it's hot and sunny on both sides of the mountains, the only wind will be the locally generated thermals. Still, these winds are strong enough for recreational sailing.

Most of the sites included in this region are within a few miles of U.S. Hwy. 97, a major route from California to Hood River and the Gorge. Despite this fact, these lakes do not get much use by boardsailors. Klamath and Agency lakes are located in sparsely populated areas where there are not many local sailors. The sites further north near Bend are passed over by the locals, who prefer to sail in the Cascade Lakes along Century Drive. For someone seeking a little diversion as they head to or from the Gorge, these sites deserve a look.

Haystack Reservoir

Haystack Reservoir was rated as one of the best desert sailing lakes by local boardsailors. The other was Ochoco Reservoir. This reservoir was designed for regulatory storage of irrigation water from Wickiup Reservoir. This means it is not drained each year like other reservoirs in the desert area. Sailing is possible here well into the fall months.

Skill rating: Novice to intermediate

Location: The reservoir is ten miles south of Madras on U.S. Hwy. 97. The turnoff, just south of Culver Junction, is well marked. Follow Jehricho Road approximately 1.3 miles east to Southwest Haystack Lake Drive.

Sailing conditions: (Long Board) Sailing is possible from late April well into September. The summer thermals generally begin around noon and continue until sundown. North to west winds are best. If the wind is from the southwest, try Crescent Lake or Wickiup Reservoir.

Access: Locals launch off the point on the south shore of the lake. To reach this site, drive along the shoreline from the primitive camping area just past the dam. There are no facilities here but chemical toilets are available in the camping area.

A U.S. Forest Service campground on the north shore of the lake has better facilities, with a boat ramp, a nice cinder beach, picnic shelters and rest rooms with running water. Most people don't want to drive the extra two miles over a dusty washboard road to reach this site. Both launch sites have sideshore winds.

Hazards: This is a popular lake for fishing and waterskiing. There are some large rocks along the shoreline. A wind shadow created by the dam makes sailing impossible on the northwest end of the lake.

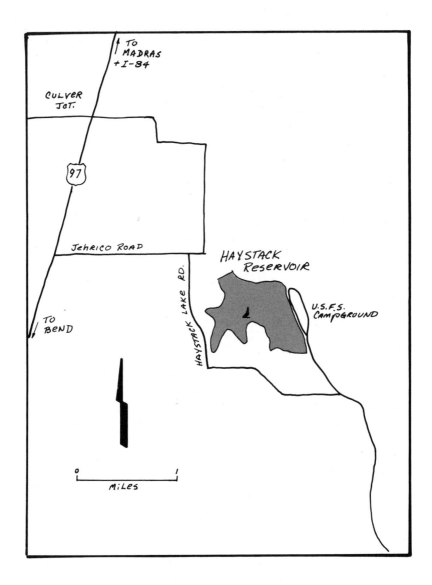

Wind and water reports: 389-0890 – Randy Barna's Ski Shop, Bend

Food and lodging: The nearest gas, food and lodgings are in Madras to the north or in Terrebonne, ten miles south on U.S. Hwy. 97. *Haystack Lake Campground* is nicer than most U.S. Forest

Service campgrounds, with paved RV sites and rest rooms with hot showers. A KOA campground on Southwest Jehricho Lane offers full hookups, showers, a laundry and grocery store.

Other attractions: The *Peter Skene Ogden Wayside,* located approximately 10 miles south on U.S. Hwy. 97, offers a great view of the Crooked River Canyon.

Smith Rock, northwest of Terrebonne, has unusual, multicolored volcanic rock formations above the Crooked River Canyon. The area also boasts of excellent walls for experienced rock climbers.

The *Deschutes River,* from Madras to the Columbia, has world-class whitewater rapids and some of the best fly-fishing in the state for wild rainbow trout.

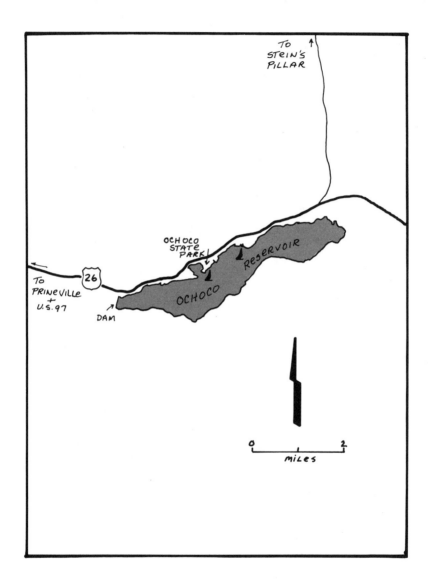

Ochoco Reservoir

Ochoco is a man-made reservoir with steep canyon walls at the west end near the dam. This creates a vortex for the predominantly westerly wind. The wind will usually be side-shore since the lake is oriented on an east/west axis. There are several secluded beach areas on the south shore which have no road access and are undeveloped.

Skill rating: Novice to intermediate

Location: The lake is approximately 28 miles east of U.S. Hwy. 97, near the town of Prineville. Heading south, take U.S. Hwy. 26 at Madras. Northbound, take Hwy. 126 east from Redmond to U.S. Hwy. 26, then head east to the lake.

Sailing conditions: (Long Board, Short Board on occasion) The strong thermal wind moves up the valley and is funneled through the canyon at the west end of the lake, creating excellent sailing conditions. The afternoon wind can reach 20 MPH. The center of the lake and the south shore generally get the strongest wind. Sailing is possible at Ochoco Lake from early March through September, but it is best early in the season when the lake is at full pool. Later in the year, when the water level lowers, the west end of the lake will be in the wind shadow of the dam.

Access: There is a boat ramp at the west end of Ochoco State Park. The ramp itself is in a small cove out of which it is difficult to sail, especially on a short board. When the water level goes down, however, it is possible to drive along the shoreline around the cove to launch into the main body of the lake. Other than parking, there are no facilities near the boat ramp. Rest rooms are located in the campground area.

According to locals, the Lakeside Steak House, located about 1 mile east of the state park, allows rigging and launching on the beach out front. Check here first since this is a better launch site and there is a marina and RV park right next door.

Hazards: Water levels fluctuate considerably throughout the year because of irrigation withdrawals. Large rock outcroppings near the west end may be submerged when the lake is at full pool. Extensive mudflats will be found at the east end of the lake in late summer when the water level is at its lowest.

This is a popular fishing lake, so watch out for trolling anglers.

Wind and water reports: 447-5394 – Ochoco Lake Boat Rentals · 447-1160 – Lakeside Steak House

Food and lodging: *Ochoco Lake State Park* on the north shore has a nice campground with running water and flush toilets.

The Crystal Corral RV Park, located across from the state park, has a store and cafe.

The Lakeside Steak House has a lounge for relaxing after a day's sailing.

Additional gas, food and lodging can be found in Prineville, 7 miles west of the lake on U.S. Hwy. 26.

Other attractions: Prineville is the site of the annual *Crooked River Rodeo* in mid-July.

Stein's Pillar, a huge stone monolith, is located northeast of Ochoco Lake along Mill Creek. This area of Oregon is a rock-hound's paradise, with thousands of acres of digging sites on the public lands surrounding Prineville, the "Agate Capital of the U.S."

The *Morning Glory Balloon Company* in Redmond offers sunrise hot-air balloon rides for a spectacular view of the high desert and surrounding rimrock.

Ochoco Lake is a prime location for viewing bald eagles. Alaskan and Canadian birds winter in the area and are a common site from December through April. March is the best month. Check with the local U.S. Forest Service office for tips on spotting bald eagles.

Agency Lake

Agency Lake, which is actually the north arm of Upper Klamath Lake, is a short board sailor's dream. Locals say the sun shines and the wind blows hard here almost every day. There are no mountains or trees to interfere with the "nor'westers" that rip down off the eastern slope of the Cascades. The average depth of the lake is only three feet, which makes it a great place for practicing water starts. Because the lake is so shallow, the water is warm and choppy even in the lightest winds.

Skill rating: Intermediate to expert

Location: This site is approximately 28 miles north of the city of Klamath Falls, off U.S. Hwy. 97. Turn west at Modoc Point at the north end of Klamath Lake and follow County Road #427, Agency Lake Road, approximately 6 miles to Henzel Park. Heading south on U.S. Hwy. 97, turn at the Texaco station at the south Chiloquin Junction and head west. This road crosses Hwy. 62 approximately 2 miles west of the turnoff, Henzel Park is about one-quarter mile beyond.

Sailing conditions: (Short Board) Sailing is best from March through May when the wind is from the north-northwest. During this period, the wind averages 20 to 25 MPH and the lake has constant whitecaps. At Henzel Park the lake is 5 to 6 miles wide, making for long, screaming reaches. This is a good area for learning water starts and high wind sailing. If the wind gets too strong, you'll be blown down to the dam and can always walk back. Like Klamath Lake to the south, Agency Lake supports a large growth of algae from July on, turning the lake to pea soup and making boardsailing and other water-contact recreation unpleasant.

Access: Most of the shoreline of Agency Lake is in private ownership. The best access is at Henzel Park at the southeast corner.

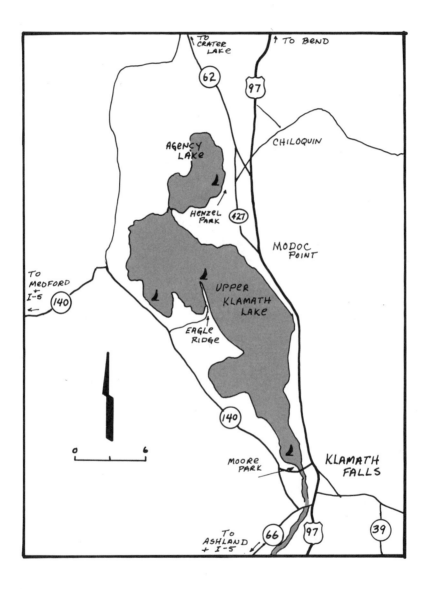

The park has plenty of paved parking, a large grass area for rigging, picnic tables, rest rooms and a boat ramp. A small sand beach on the north side of the boat ramp breakwater makes launching easy.

Hazards: There are no known hazards in Agency Lake. The lake is large but it is so shallow that if you break down you can walk to shore.

Wind and water reports: 882-5060 – National Weather Service, Klamath Falls Airport (recorded message)

Food and lodging: There is no camping at Henzel Park. _Neptune Park Resort_ on Lakeside Road just to the north has tent sites and RV camping with full hookups, rest rooms with hot showers, gasoline and a snack bar. There is also a grocery store and marina, with RV camping located about 3 miles south of the park on the road to Modoc Point. Additional gas, food and lodgings can be found to the north along Hwy. 62, and south along U.S. Hwy. 97, as well as in Klamath Falls.

Other attractions: Just east of Agency Lake on U.S. Hwy. 97 is _Collier Memorial State Park_, with one of the largest logging museums in the country. The junction of _Spring Creek_ and the _Williamson River_ at this site offers some of the finest trout fishing in the world.

Fort Klamath Frontier Post is located on Hwy. 62 about 8 miles north of Henzel Park. Originally built in 1863 to promote peaceful relations between the Indians and white settlers, it became a staging area and hospital for the Modoc Indian Wars. The graves of Captain Jack and other individuals executed after the war are here, along with a reconstructed guard house containing displays and exhibits of the era.

See also Upper Klamath Lake.

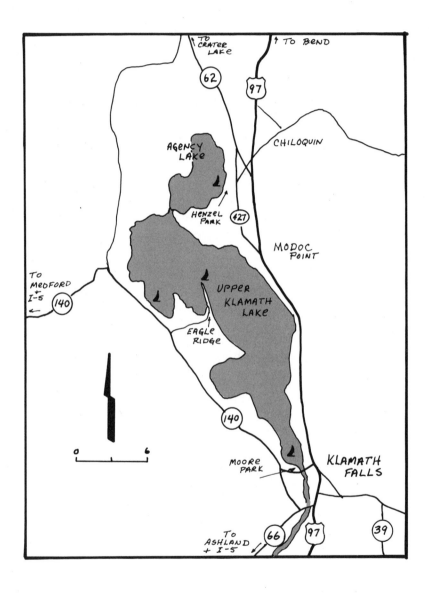

Upper Klamath Lake

Klamath Lake offers outrageous sailing with high winds, warm water and huge waves. It is the largest freshwater lake in Oregon, having more than 61,000 surface acres and more than 100 miles of shoreline. The average depth of the lake is only 10 feet, so whitecaps are common even in the lightest winds. The lake is so large that it has a major influence on the local weather. Meteorologists at the Klamath Airport report that the lake adds 5 MPH to the average wind speed.

Skill rating: Intermediate through expert depending on conditions

Location: Klamath Lake extends north from the city of Klamath Falls for almost 30 miles. U.S. Hwy. 97 parallels the east shore and Hwy. 140 follows the west shore.

Sailing conditions: (Long and Short Board) The lake is more than 12 miles wide in some locations, providing for seemingly limitless reaches. While it is possible to sail here year-round, the best time is from early March through the month of June. The wind usually picks up around 2 PM and continues until sunset. From July until the winter frost, the lake experiences large blooms of algae. During these periods, the water resembles pea soup and smells terrible, so most boardsailors go elsewhere.

Access: With such an extensive shoreline there are any number of good launch sites on Klamath Lake. For the best high wind sailing, Eagle Ridge is recommended. Located off Hwy. 140 approximately 18 miles northwest of Klamath Falls, the Eagle Ridge Road turnoff is difficult to spot. It is located between mileposts 51 and 52, at the bottom of a steep hill, just before Hwy. 140 rejoins the lakeshore next to Rock Creek Ranch. The road is rough but passable. Stay to the left at all intersections. The road ends in a loop near the ruins of an old resort, at the point of Eagle Ridge. From here a steep, overgrown trail leads down to the lake water, where there is a grassy rigging area. From Eagle Ridge it's a 5-mile reach across to Agency Lake Dam. There are no facilities here but toilets are available at nearby Eagle Ridge Park. Local sailors report a hot springs near Eagle Ridge, which they use for warming up while winter sailing.

Moore Park Marina, on Lakeshore Drive in Klamath Falls, is a good launch site for the less experienced sailor. The winds here are not as strong as at Eagle Ridge and the lake is much narrower. Moore Park has rest rooms, picnic areas with barbeque pits, tennis courts, plenty of parking, and lots of grass for rigging.

There are also a number of turnouts along Hwy. 140 northwest of Klamath Falls with parking, boat ramps and chemical toilets. Any of these may be a good launch site depending on the prevailing winds.

Hazards: The mere size of the lake can be hazardous in the event of equipment failure or fatigue. A large chop can build up rapidly, especially in open water. The ability to water start in 4-foot waves is a must under these conditions.

Wind and water reports: 882-5060 – National Weather Service, Klamath Falls Airport (recorded message)

Food and lodging: A wide variety of gas, food and lodgings is available in and around Klamath Falls.

Molatore's in downtown Klamath Falls has great Italian food, nice rooms and a heated pool.

The Klamath Spice Company, also downtown, specializes in freshly prepared seafood.

The Stockman's Social Club, on South Sixth Street, specializes in fine American cuisine, steak and seafood.

Odessa Marina and RV Park, located approximately 5.5 miles north of the Eagle Ridge turnoff on Hwy. 140, has full hookups, laundry facilities, and showers.

Rocky Point Resort, located off Hwy. 140 approximately 26 miles northwest of Klamath Falls, has a grocery store, marina, restaurant and lounge. The campground has tent sites, full RV hookups, restrooms with hot showers, laundry facilities, and lodging units with kitchens.

Other attractions: The *Favell Museum* of Western Art and Indian Artifacts, located in downtown Klamath Falls, is rated as one of the finest museums of its kind anywhere.

Each year in late May the Klamath County Visitors and Convention Bureau sponsors the *All Indian Rodeo and Powwow Days*. A highlight of this event, the Indian dance contest, is an opportunity to witness America's native cultural heritage.

The *Mountain Lakes Wilderness Area* is located just west of Hwy. 140 near the Eagle Ridge turnoff.

The *Sprague* and *Williamson Rivers*, which feed into Klamath Lake from the northeast, are two of the best flyfishing rivers in the world.

Wildlife is abundant at Klamath Lake. This is the wintering area for the largest concentration of bald eagles in the lower 48 states. White pelicans, one of the largest of North American water birds, are also common in the area from March through November. Several National Wildlife Refuges in and around the Klamath Basin help to preserve these and other wildlife species.

See also Agency Lake.

Appendixes

Appendix A

C = custom equipment
D = demos
I = instruction
M = mail order

RN = equipment rental
RP = equipment repair
S = equipment sales
V = vacation packages

Region 1: Columbia River and "The Gorge"

Big Winds (D,I,RN,S,V)
505 Cascade Street
Hood River, OR 97031
(503)386-6086

Cascade Sailboards (C)
704 First Street
Mosier, OR 97040
(503)478-3441

Columbia Windsurfing Academy
(C,D,I,RN,RP,S,V)
202 Cascade Street
Hood River Village Mall
Hood River, OR 97031
(503)386-5423

Dill Sailboards (C,D,RP,RN,S,M)
1020 Wasco Street
Hood River, OR 97031
(503)386-6202

Front Street Sailboard Company
(D,I,RN,S,V)
207 Front Street
Hood River, OR 97031
(503)386-4044

Gorge Animal (C,D,M)
101 N. Second Street
(Below Alice's Restaurant)
Hood River, OR 97031
(503)386-5524

Gorge Gear (RP)
4th and State Street
Hood River, OR 97031
(503)386-2037

Gorge Sails (C,D,RN,RP)
210 Oak Street
Hood River, OR 97031
(503)386-4464

Guess What Precision
  Sailboards (C)
400 N. 2nd Street
Hood River, OR 97031
(503)386-4737

Gorge Windsurfing
  (D,I,M,RN,RP,S)
319 East Second Street
The Dalles, OR 97058
(503)298-8796

Hi-Per Tech (C)
416 Cascade Street
Hood River, OR 97031
(503)386-6608

Hood River Windsurfing
  (C,D,I,M,RN,RP,S,V)
4 Fourth Street
Hood River, OR 97031
(503)386-5787

Hurricane Sails (RP,S)
207 Fourth Street
Hood River, OR 97031
(503)386-4240

Life Cycles The Dalles
  (C,I,RN,S,V)
112 East Second Street
The Dalles, OR 97058
(503)296-9588

Meadows Windsynergy
(C,D,I,RN,RP,S)
Port Marine Park
Hood River, OR 97031
(503)386-9463

Mid-Columbia Watersports Center,
  Inc. (D,I,RN,RP,S,V)
260 Dock Road
Hood River, OR 97031
(503)386-3321

Mr. Bill's Boardsailing
  Adventures (V)
111 Oak Street
Hood River, OR 97031
(800)426-4981

Northwave Sails (RP,C)
1020 Industrial Street
Hood River, OR 97031
(503)386-6156

Promotion Wetsuits (M,RP,S)
416 Cascade Street
Hood River, OR 97031
(503)386-3278

Rushwind Sail Loft (M,RP,S)
416 Cascade Street
Hood River, OR 97031
(503)386-1428
(503)386-4978 (FAX)

Sailboard Warehouse, Inc.
  (C,M,RP,S)
4th and Oak Street
Hood River, OR 97031
(503)386-1699

Sailboards Hood River
  (D,I,M,RN,S)
4th and State Street
Hood River, OR 97031
(503)386-5363

Schuler Custom Boards
(C,D,RN,RP)
64937 Hwy. 14
White Salmon, WA   98672
(509)493-3733

Second Wind Sports (D,RP,S)
210 Oak Street
Hood River, OR   97031
(503)386-4464

Sporty's (C,I,RN,S)
11855 Colvin Road at Hwy. 30
Clatskanie, OR   97016
(503)728-2847

Windance Sailboards (C,D,RP,S)
108 Hwy. 35
Hood River, OR   97031
(503)386-2131

Washington Shops

North Shore Windsurfing
(C,D,RP,S)
116 West Steuben Street
Bingen, WA   98605
(509)493-3340

The Pro Shop (C,I,RN,RP,S)
916 15th Avenue
Longview, WA 98632
(206)577-1580

Region 2: The Oregon Coast

Cleanline Surf Company
(C,I,RP,RN,S)
719 First Street
Seaside, OR 97138
(503)738-7888

Newport Surf Designs
(C,I,RN,RP,S)
213 S.E. Bay Blvd.
Newport, OR 97365
(503)265-7334

Northwest Divers (I,RN,S)
1119 Newmark Street
North Bend, OR 97459
(503) 756-3483

Schuler Custom Boards (C,S)
237 Hamlet Route
Seaside, OR 97138
(503)738-7651

Southern Oregon Sailboards
(C,I,RN,RP,S)
U.S. Hwy. 101 South
Bandon, OR 97411
(503)347-9283

Waterfront Sailboards
(D,I,RN,RP,S)
85289 Hwy. 101 South
Florence, OR 97439
(503)997-2457

Region 3: Interstate 5 Corridor

Bay Sailboards (I,RN,S)
388 West 6th Street
Eugene, OR 97041
(503)345-7589

Boardsports (C,D,I,RN,RP,S)
2475 Jefferson Street
Eugene, OR 97405
(503)484-2588

Gorge Performance (D,I,RN,RP,S)
7400 SW Macadam Blvd.
Portland, OR 97219
(503)246-6646

High Tech Ski & Surf (D,I,RP,S)
616 Crater Lake Avenue
Medford, OR 97504
(503)779-9623

Hobie House (D,I,RN,RP,S,V)
170 Emigrant Lake Road
Ashland, OR 97520
(503)488-0595

Larry's Sport Centers (RN,S)

Cedar Hills Shopping Center
10120 S.W. Parkway
Beaverton, OR 97225
(503)297-5575

Oregon City Shopping
Center #60
Oregon City, OR 97045
(503)656-0321

Gresham Square
310 E. Burnside Street
Gresham, OR 97030
(503)665-6102

Peak Sports (D,I,RN,RP,S)
129 NW 2nd Street
Corvallis, OR 97330
(503)754-6444

Rivers West (I,RN,S,D,M)
1565 West 7th Street
Eugene, OR 97402
(503)686-0798

Sailboards On The Go
(I,RN,RP,S,C,D)
4235 NE Cully Blvd.
Portland, OR 97218
(503)281-9628

Ski Rack U.S.A.(D,RN,S)
12705 S.W. Beaver Dam Road
Beaverton, OR 97005
(503)643-7300

West-Marine (S)
12055 N. Center Avenue
Portland, OR 97217
(503)289-9822

Windoggie Sailboards (C,D,I,RN,S)
2414 N.W. Raleigh Street
Portland, OR 97210
(503)228-0945

Windjammers West (C,D,RN,RP,S)
1521 N. Jantzen Street
Portland, OR 97217
(503)289-9011

Regions 4 and 5: Cascade Lakes, Desert Lakes and Points East

Anson Ski Shop (D,I,RN,S)
112 Depot Street
LaGrande, OR 97850
(503)963-3660

Powder House (RN,RP,S,D)
311 S.W. Century Drive
Bend, OR 97702
(503)389-6234

Randy Barna's Ski Shop
(D,I,M,RN,RP,S)
345 S.W. Century Drive
Bend, OR 97702
(503)389-0890

Stowell's Ski Haus (RN,RP,S,D)
926 NE Greenwood Avenue
Bend, OR 97701
(503)382-5325

Sunriver Sports (C,D,I,RN,RP,S)
Sunriver Village Mall
Sunriver, OR 97707
(503)593-8369

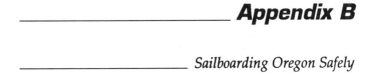

Appendix B

Sailboarding Oregon Safely

(The following material is reprinted with the kind permission of the Oregon State Marine Board)

Introduction

Sailboarding is a relatively new and exciting sport, but there are certain precautions sailors should take in learning this sport. This pamphlet will provide you with the basic safety considerations.

Starting Out

The Oregon State Marine Board strongly recommends that beginning sailors receive proper instruction from experienced sailors or instructors. Small lakes make excellent sites to learn how to sailboard. With proper instruction, equipment and environment, the beginning sailor can then move onto less sheltered waters.

Sailboarding is physically demanding, and the sailor should be aware of the problems that can occur and the steps to prevention. Expect to swim to your board many times during an outing, especially during winds that may carry the board away. The sailor should realize the physical exertion required and avoid becoming fatigued.

Safety Equipment

Personal flotation devices (life jackets) are required by the Oregon State Marine Board. Falls into the water are inevitable and the life jacket will provide flotation. Specially designed life jackets that incorporate a harness have been recently approved by the U.S. Coast Guard for the advanced sailor. When sailing in cold water (less than 70 degrees), wet suits or dry suits are strongly recommended as they provide additional flotation and warmth.

Sailboards should have a "mast leash" that connects the mast to the board and prevents the two from separating during a fall. Use of a mast leash will allow the fallen sail to keep the board from drifting away from the sailboarder. If the board and sail do separate, the sailboarder should swim to the board first, since it provides flotation, and then paddle back to reconnect the mast and board.

Wear protective footwear to guard against cuts from broken glass or sharp rocks.

In places like the Columbia Gorge and the Oregon Coast, it is highly recommended that sailors carry pocket flares.

Getting Underway

Let someone know where you are going and when you plan to return.

Never sail alone, and be sure to have a rescue plan. The current or wind can carry you and your board a long distance. Be sure your sailing friends will pick you up should you get into trouble.

To alert someone that you are having difficulty, use a two-handed wave over your head. Do not sail to exhaustion.

Watch other sailors, and check the equipment and sail size they are using. Remember, the wind conditions on shore are usually lighter than on the water.

A common mistake sailors make is to try a long reach and then realize that something has gone wrong. By tacking or jibing close to shore, you are able to test your equipment, your body, your skills, and the conditions. Any problems can then be easily remedied onshore.

Notice if you are moving rapidly away from shore. Mark your position with landmarks.

Maintain a safe distance from sailors in front and near you. Before you jibe, look down-wind and behind you.

Sailboarders should avoid congested areas, especially areas where waterskiing or other high-speed power craft are in operation.

Self rescue is mandatory. If you are caught in high winds with a sail that is too large, don't panic. If you can lift your sail out of the water, point your board and rig towards shore, and luff your sail. You may be carried downwind by the wind or river current, but you will make progress.

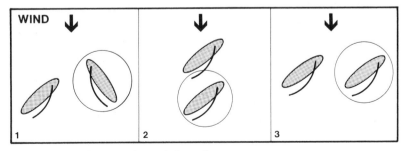

Right hand forward = right-of-way

If the water conditions are too rough to stand on your board, you may have to unrig and paddle in. Be sure to roll your sail tightly around the mast. Center the furled mast and boom on the board and paddle to shore.

In an emergency situation, abandon the sail rig and paddle to shore, diagonally to the wind and current.

Sailboards are boats. Sailors should respect the rights and privileges of all craft. One way of doing so is to follow the rules of the road.

Rules of the road

1. A boat on starboard tack (circled) has right-of-way over a boat on port tack.

Right hand forward in normal sailing position = starboard tack.
(Right hand forward = right-of-way)

Left hand forward is on port tack.

2. A leeward (downwind) boat (circled) has the right-of-way over a windward (upwind) boat on the same tack.

3. An overtaking boat must keep clear of the boat being overtaken (circled). Don't insist on your right-of-way if it means a collision. You are obligated by law to avoid a collision even if you have the right-of-way.

Columbia Gorge and Oregon Coast

Strong, unpredictable winds, large waves, cold water, tide and current movements are reasons only sailors with considerable experience or proper guidance (lessons, classes, etc.) should try either the Gorge or the Oregon Coast. Sailboard Information signs have been placed at popular sailboarding sites in the Columbia Gorge. Sailors should take a few minutes to read the material before starting out on the Columbia.

Watch for Hazards

Sailboarders should be aware of underwater obstructions and avoid sailing in shallow water. Check with a knowledgeable local sailor to avoid area hazards. In Oregon, most water is cold year-round. Cold water can cause a person to become hypothermic in a very short time. Boardsailors spend considerably more time in the water than most other boaters, therefore are exposed to a greater risk of hypothermia. A hypothermic person loses coordination and may be unable to swim back to his overturned sailboard.

Barges -

In bays, and in the Columbia and Willamette Rivers, large, deep-draft vessels travel confined to the channel. They have limited maneuverability and are unable to change their speed significantly. Very large vessels require several miles to stop. **It is the sailboarder's responsibility to keep clear of large vessels.** Get into the habit of checking in both directions for traffic at every tack, jibe or fall. Remember:

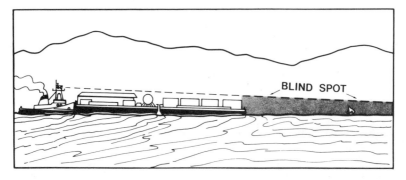

- Commercial vessels have a blind spot which may extend up to 10 boat lengths in front.
- Sailors should be aware that a large vessel can block the wind – leaving the sailboarder unable to maneuver.

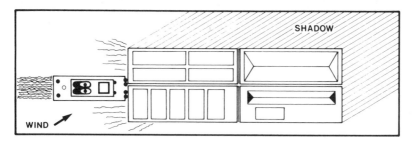

- A large vessel's propeller causes suction and its stern wakes can be dangerous.
- Slow-moving tugs may have a cable extending several hundred feet, attached to a partially submerged log-raft.

Sailors should check the river regularly. Before sailing onto the water, find out where the river traffic passes. If a commercial vessel is sighted:

- **Warn other sailors of its approach; and**
- **Clear the river and wait until the vessel passes.**

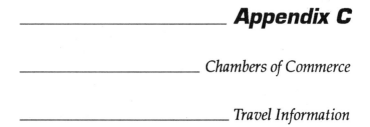

Appendix C

Chambers of Commerce

Travel Information

Region 1: The Columbia River and "The Gorge"

Clatskanie Chamber of Commerce
P.O. Box 635
Clatskanie, OR 97016
(503)728-2134

Gresham Area Chamber of
  Commerce
P.O. Box 696
Gresham, OR 97030
(503)665-1131

Hood River Visitor's Council
Port Marina Park
Hood River, OR 97031
(503)386-2000

Columbia Gorge Boardsailor's
  Association
P.O. Box 887
Hood River, OR 97031

Mt. Adams Chamber of Commerce
Daubensbeck Park
Bingen, WA 98605
(509)493-3630

The Dalles Chamber of Commerce
404 West 2nd Street
The Dalles, OR 97058
(503)296-2231

Greater Hermiston Chamber of
  Commerce
P.O. Box 185
Hermiston, OR 97838
(503)567-6151

Umatilla Chamber of Commerce
P.O. Box 59
Umatilla, OR 97882
(503)922-5456

Skamania County Chamber of
  Commerce
Stevenson, WA 98648
(509)427-8911

Maryhill Information Center
(509)773-4395

Region 2: The Oregon Coast

Oregon Coast Association
P.O. Box 670
Newport, OR 97365
(503)336-5107

Astoria Area Chamber of
   Commerce
P.O. Box 176
Astoria, OR 97103
(503)325-6311

Seaside Chamber of Commerce
P.O. Box 7
Seaside, OR 97138
800-452-6740

Cannon Beach Chamber of
   Commerce
Second & Spruce Street
Cannon Beach, OR 97110
(503)436-2623

Manzanita Merchants Association
P.O. Box 164
Manzanita, OR 97130

Garibaldi Chamber of Commerce
202 Hwy 101 North
Garibaldi, OR 97118
(503)322-0301

Tillamook Chamber of Commerce
3705 Hwy 101 North
Tillamook, OR 97141
(503)842-7525

Pacific City - Woods Chamber of
   Commerce
33315 Cape Kiwanda Road
Pacific City, OR 97135
(503)965-6161

Lincoln City Chamber of
   Commerce
P.O. Box 787
Lincoln City, OR 97367
(503)994-3070
In Oregon 800-452-2151

Depoe Bay Chamber of Commerce
P.O. Box 21
Depoe Bay, OR 97341
(503)765-2889

Greater Newport Chamber of
   Commerce
555 S.W. Coast Hwy.
Newport, OR 97365
(503)265-8801

Waldport Chamber of Commerce
P.O. Box 419
Waldport, OR 97394
(503)563-2133

Yachats Chamber of Commerce
P.O. Box 174
Yachats, OR 97498
(503)547-3530

Florence Area Chamber of
   Commerce
P.O. Box 712
Florence, OR 97439
(503)997-3128

Lower Umpqua Chamber of
    Commerce
P.O. Box 11
Reedsport, OR 97467
(503)271-3495

Lakeside Chamber of Commerce
P.O. Box 333
Lakeside, OR 97449
(503)759-3011

North Bend Information Center
1380 Sherman Street
North Bend, OR 97459
(503)756-4613

Bay Area Chamber of Commerce
P.O. Box 210
Coos Bay, OR 97420
800-824-8486
In Oregon 800-762-6278

Bandon Chamber of Commerce
350 S. Second Street
Bandon, OR 97411
(503)347-9616

Coquille Chamber of Commerce
119 N. Birch Street
Coquille, OR 97423
(503)396-3414

Port Orford Chamber of
    Commerce
P.O. Box 637
Port Orford, OR 97465
(503)332-8055

Gold Beach - Wedderburn
    Chamber of Commerce
P.O. Box 55
Gold Beach, OR 97444
(503)247-7526
In Oregon 800-452-2334

Brookings - Harbor Chamber of
    Commerce
P.O. Box 940
Brookings, OR 97415
(503)469-3181

Region 3: Interstate 5 Corridor

Greater Portland Convention
    & Visitors Association
26 S.W. Salmon Street
Portland, OR 97204
(503)222-2223

Forest Grove Chamber of
    Commerce
2417 Pacific Avenue
Forest Grove, OR 97116
(503)357-3006

Sweet Home Chamber of
    Commerce
P.O. Box 61
Sweet Home, OR 97386
(503)367-6186

Eugene - Springfield Convention
    & Visitors Bureau
P.O. Box 10286
Eugene, OR 97440
800-547-5445
In Oregon 800-452-3670

Cottage Grove Chamber of
Commerce
P.O. Box 587
Cottage Grove, OR 97424
(503)942-2411

Greater Medford Visitors
& Convention Bureau
304 S. Central Street
Medford, OR 97501
(503)772-5194

Southern Oregon Reservation
Center
P.O. Box 477
Ashland, OR 97520
800-547-8052
In Oregon 800-533-1311

Ashland Visitor & Convention
Bureau
P.O. Box 606
Ashland, OR 97520
(503)482-3486

Region 4: The Cascade Lakes

Mt. Hood Recreation Association
P.O. Box 342
Welches, OR 97067
(503)622-3101

Sandy Area Chamber of
Commerce
P.O. Box 536
Sandy, OR 97055
(503)668-4006

Sisters Chamber of Commerce
P.O. Box 476
Sisters, OR 97759
(503)549-0251

Oakridge Chamber of Commerce
P.O. Box 217
Oakridge, OR 97463
(503)782-4146

**Region 5: Central and Eastern
Oregon**

Central Oregon Recreation
Association
P.O. Box 230
Bend, OR 97709
(503)389-8799

Madras - Jefferson County
Chamber of Commerce
P.O. Box 770
Madras, OR 97741
(503)475-2350

Redmond Chamber of Commerce
427 S.W. 7th Street
Redmond, OR 97756
(503)548-5191

Prineville - Crook County
Chamber of Commerce
P.O. Box 546
Prineville, OR 97754
(503)447-6304

Bend Visitor & Convention Bureau
164 N.W. Hawthorne Street
Bend, OR 97701
(503)382-3221

Klamath County Visitors
  & Convention Bureau
125 N. 8th Street
Klamath Falls, OR 97601
(503)884-5193

Lake County Chamber of
  Commerce
Courthouse
Lakeview, OR 97630
(503)947-2249

Milton - Freewater Chamber of
  Commerce
501 Ward Street
Milton - Freewater, OR 97862
(503)938-5563

Pendleton Chamber of Commerce
P.O. Box 1446
Pendleton, OR 97801
800-547-8911
In Oregon 800-452-9403

Wallowa County Chamber of
  Commerce
P.O. Box 427
Enterprise, OR 97828
(503)426-4622

Joseph Chamber of Commerce
P.O. Box 13
Joseph, OR 97846
(503)432-8411

LaGrande - Union County
  Chamber of Commerce
P.O. Box 308
LaGrande, OR 97850
(503)963-8588

Baker County Chamber of
  Commerce
490 Campbell Street
Baker, OR 97814
(503)523-5855

Ontario Chamber of Commerce
173 S.W. 1st Street
Ontario, OR 97914
(503)889-8012

Vale Chamber of Commerce
P.O. Box 661
Vale, OR 97918
(503)473-3800

Nyssa Chamber of Commerce
P.O. Box 2515
Nyssa, OR 97913
(503)372-3091

Burns - Harney County Chamber
  of Commerce
18 West D Street
Burns, OR 97720
(503)573-2636

Port Districts

Region 1: The Columbia River and The Gorge

Port of Arlington
P.O. Box 427
Arlington, OR 97812
(503)454-2868

Port of Cascade Locks
P.O. Box 307
Cascade Locks, OR 97014
(503)374-8619

Port of Hood River
P.O. Box 239
Hood River, OR 97031
(503)386-1645

Port of Kalama
380 W. Marine Drive
Kalama, WA 98625
(206)673-2325

Port of Klickitat County
P.O. Box 1429
White Salmon, WA 98672
(509)493-1655
(800)222-8660

Port of Longview
10 Port Way
Longview, WA 98632
(206)425-3305

Port of Morrow
P.O. Box 200
Boardman, OR 97818
(503)481-2695

Port of St. Helens
P.O. Box 598
St. Helens, OR 97051
(503)397-2888

Port of Skamania County
P.O. Box 413
Stevenson, WA 98648
(509)427-5484

Port of The Dalles
P.O. Box 457
The Dalles, Or 97058
(503)298-4148

Port of Umatilla
P.O. Box 871
Umatilla, OR 97882
(503)922-3224

Region 2: The Oregon Coast

Port of Alsea
P.O. Box F
Waldport, OR 97394
(503)563-3872

Port of Astoria
1 Portway
Astoria, OR 97103
(503)325-4521

Port of Bandon
P.O. Box 206
Bandon, OR 97411
(503)347-3206

Port of Bay City
P.O. Box 228
Garibaldi, OR 97118
(503)322-3292

Port of Brookings
P.O. Box 848
Brookings, OR 97415
(503)469-2218

Port of Coos Bay
326 Front Street
Coos Bay, OR 97420
(503)267-7678

Port of Gold Beach
P.O. Box 1126
Gold Beach, OR 97444
(503)247-6269

Port of Nehalem
P.O. Box G
Manzanita, OR 97130
(503)368-5401

Port of Newport
P.O. Box 1065
Newport, OR 97365
(503)265-7758

Port of Port Orford
P.O. Box 145
Port Orford, OR 97465
(503)332-7121

Port of Siuslaw
P.O. Box 1220
Florence, OR 97439
(503)997-3426

Port of Umpqua
P.O. Box 388
Reedsport, OR 97467
(503)271-4888

Select Bibliography

Boden, Clive and Angus Chater. *The Windsurfing Funboard Handbook.* Woodbury: Barron's Educational Series, Inc., 1984.

Dabberdt, Walter F. *Weather for Outdoorsmen.* New York: Charles Scribner's Sons, 1981.

Hall, Major. *Sports Illustrated Boardsailing.* New York: Harper & Row Publishers, 1985.

Johnson, Daniel M., Richard R. Petersen, D. Richard Lycan, James W. Sweet, and Mark E. Neuhaus. *Atlas of Oregon Lakes.* Corvallis: Oregon State University Press, 1985.

Northwest Sailboard Magazine. *1987 Gorge Guide.* Seattle: Windsurfing Northwest Inc., 1987.

Northwest Sailboard Magazine. *1988 Gorge Guide.* Seattle: Windsurfing Northwest Inc., 1988.

Olney, Ross R. *Windsurfing – A Complete Guide.* New York: Walker Publishing Co., 1982.

Oregon Division of State Lands. *Oregon Estuaries.* Salem: 1973

Oregon State Parks and Recreation Division, and The Windsurfing Study Committee. *Columbia Gorge Windsurfing Study.* Salem: 1986.

Smith, F.G. Walton. *The Seas in Motion.* New York: Thomas Y. Crowell Co., 1973.

Christmas at the Lakeside Resort

The Lakeside Resort Series (Book 1)

SUSAN SCHILD

CHAPTER 1 — BAH HUMBUG

WALKING DOWN MAIN STREET IN the small town of Shady Grove, Jenny looked up from her to-do list and stopped abruptly in front of Frank's Friendly Hardware Store, her eyes narrowing. Though Halloween was weeks away, ghosts and goblins floated in one window while a recording of an organ played dirges with a spooky *bwa ha ha* tossed in every now and then. In the next display window, the Pilgrims and the Native Americans were sharing a feast. Good gravy. In the third window, a full-sized Santa was boogying to *Rockin' Around the Christmas Tree*. Jenny huffed out a sigh. What was wrong with merchants these days? It was just mid-October. Most people were starting to think about pulling together their kid's Wonder Woman or Batman costumes. At the grocery store, parents were eyeing the economy-sized bags of Snickers Bars and Twix, wondering which they'd enjoy munching on most if they didn't get many trick-or-treaters. But Frank's Friendly Hardware was cranking up Halloween, Thanksgiving *and* Christmas.

The premature Christmas display galled Jenny the most. Just because Douglas, her ex-fiancé, had broken their engagement nine months ago as she was in the throes of planning their Christmas Eve wedding didn't mean she needed to hold a grudge against holidays. But a Christmas display on October 15th? That was too much. What was that *Me Booster* affirmation about staying calm? *I can stay centered in a golden orb of calm. All good things come to you at the right time.*

Jenny pushed back her shoulders and felt a little better. But three smiling, fit women who looked to be about her age strode by, coffee cups in hand and yoga mats over their shoulders, and paused to admire Santa. They chatted cheerfully, and the graying brunette chirped, "We're having both of our families at the house for Christmas this year, and John plans to cover the house with lights..."

Oh, the happy couples, already planning a merry and bright day, blah blah blah. Jenny scowled. That steamed her, too. At forty-two, she wanted to be part of that happy wives club, saying *we* and *our* and talking about plans with *her* husband. Was that too much to ask?

With her daddy as a role model, Jenny had developed a real knack for picking men who would let her down: her husband of seven years who was a fierce-eyed passionate workaholic who'd come on strong when he courted her, intent on sweeping her off her feet. After they'd married, his ardor cooled immediately and he'd zealously returned to his workaholic ways. Jenny was still bewildered at the change in him when he announced he was leaving her for his boss, the skinny, intense, Vape smoking, archery champion Natalie. Jenny had dated a few other men, but she was a bad picker. In a crowded room, Jenny could pick the slippery commitment-phobes, the me-me-me narcissists, and the men who'd flirt with waitresses. Cal said he traveled for work, but really had a wife and kids in Chapel Hill. Laid-back Lou gardened for a hobby, which Jenny thought was cool until she went to pick tomatoes at his house and found a bumper crop of marijuana mixed in with his zucchini, squash and pole beans. Vowing to steer clear of men, for years Jenny filled her life with work, good girlfriends, and occasional trips to Topsail Beach or Black Mountain. When she was thirty-nine, Jenny was ruminating about her upcoming fortieth birthday when her beloved but rickety old Labrador retriever, Chief, died. Jenny was achingly sad. At that vulnerable point, she'd met Douglas and thought she'd found her happily ever after. But look at how that had turned out. Jenny shook her head and walked faster. Never again.

From the corner of her eye, Jenny caught a movement. She walked closer to the Christmas window. Inside, a man put the finishing touches on the display, fluffing Santa's beard and placing a plate of what she hoped were fake cookies and a fake glass of milk on the fake fireplace mantel. She'd liked to have given him a dirty look and stalked off, but on her to-do list was a problem that could only be solved at the hardware store. Reluctantly, she pulled open the door.

Jenny strolled around, pretending to be interested in electrical tape and weather stripping. Before she approached him, she needed to size up the clerk's tolerance for odd questions. Jenny tried to look engrossed in an array of paint color chips as she eavesdropped. The man who'd been fluffing Santa's beard was now behind the counter, where a gray-haired woman with arthritic knuckles and the fuzz of white dog hair on her navy blue sweater had questions about light bulbs.

"My kids say I should switch to the new light bulbs, but I liked the old ones just fine." The woman frowned, examining the contents of her blue shopping basket. "It's all so complicated these days."

The dark-haired man, whom she assumed was Frank, stood behind the counter wearing a cotton tool apron. Frank *did* seem friendly as the store's name indicated, answering her questions patiently and in a kind tone. "Ms. Ida, we've had a lot of folks wish we could go back to the good old regular light bulbs, but over time the new ones will save you a bundle on your light bill."

"Well, then," the woman said, brightening. "Let's give them a whirl." Rummaging in her big purse, she pulled out a checkbook. "Can I call you if I have any questions?" she asked.

"Any time," he said with a gallant half bow. He packaged up her bulbs and handed her a business card from the stack on the counter. The woman gave him a twinkly smile and a wave as she left.

Abandoning her faux paint perusing, Jenny walked up to the counter and pulled her measurements from a scrap of paper in her purse. But then she looked at the man, thought about that darned Santa and just blurted out, "Don't you think you're rushing the holidays with Christmas decorations up so soon? I sort of get Thanksgiving. But Christmas?" she huffed out indignantly. "Why don't you have the Valentine's Day display up, too? Did you run out of windows?" Jenny knew she sounded churlish and mean, but she couldn't stop herself.

The man raised a shoulder. "My mom and sister love when we put up the Christmas display early. It's their favorite time of year. They start the baking, decorating and holiday music in early November." He gave a good natured shrug. "If that makes them happy, that's okay by me."

Jenny felt her face heat up. She was being mean to a man who was trying to indulge the women in his family. "I am so sorry," she said. "That was rude of me."

"No offense taken," the man said mildly. "Let's start over. How may I help you?"

Jenny had to smile. This had to be Friendly Frank, an open faced, good-looking guy with mesmerizing blue eyes. Were they indigo blue, peacock blue, or Prussian blue? Realizing she was staring, Jenny gulped in a breath, and made herself concentrate. "Could you give me any advice on a...pet door I'd like to get installed?"

"Sure," he said, pulling a pen from his apron pocket. "What sized dog?"

Jenny eyed him, trying to decide how much to tell him. "Large."

"Like Lab large, Great Dane or mastiff type large?" the man asked, looking thoughtful.

Jenny leaned forward and spoke in a confidential tone. "It's actually a miniature horse. Levi weighs about one hundred fifty pounds. He was neglected so I...bought him. At the time, there weren't any other animals on the old farm where I live, and he got lonely. I could tell," she said feeling a pull as she thought about how the little guy used to run toward her when she pulled up in the car and how he still leaned his head against her and gazed at her soulfully whenever he had the chance. "I've since adopted two other big dogs and he pals around with them now, but he still likes to hang out with me in the house. He's completely house-trained, and I'd like to get set up so he can come in and out of the house without me playing doorman."

Jenny looked away, afraid she'd see the widened eyes, the

skepticism, or the *this chick is crazy* smirk that some men liked to give. But he just slipped on black-framed reading glasses. "Minis are great little animals. We had one when I was a kid," he mused and started tapping away on his keyboard. He brightened and turned the monitor around so she could see it. "Here's something that might work."

Jenny examined the screen. A couple watching television on their couch smiled indulgently as a happy, two-foot-high horse poked his head through a dog door into the living room. She broke into a smile. "That's what I want. Is that hard to do? Is it expensive?"

"No and no," he chuckled. "Have you thought about an electronic door? They make ones with large enough openings for your mini, and the guy would wear a special collar that signals the metal grate to raise to open when he approaches. You need to consider your security," he clarified, looking serious.

Jenny had been considering security a lot lately. Though she'd been a good money-saver, at forty-two years of age she drew a modest salary from her one-woman tutoring business, lived in a converted chicken coop that she rented, had sketchy health insurance, and had become un-engaged from Douglas, whom she'd been seeing for almost two and a half years. Though money was not a driver for her, her ex owned a successful commercial property leasing and sales business. Once she'd slipped on the ring and said yes, Jenny was surprised at how fast she had become used to the idea of a secure future. Now, no Douglas, no ring, no pretty Christmas wedding.

Jenny gave herself a mental shake and looked more closely at the man across the counter. Gracious. A tall, rangy fellow in his early forties, he was broad-shouldered and looked fit in his black-and-white checked flannel shirt and jeans. Jenny's brain melted a little and she made a show of peering at the computer screen. "That would be great. Will you order that for me?"

"I will." His fingers flew over the keyboard. "We can have it shipped here by tomorrow."

"And do you know anyone who can help install it for me?"

5

If Jenny looked at the spot between his brows, she wouldn't get so rattled by his eyes. If he thought she was cross-eyed, so much the better.

The man hesitated. "I'm a licensed contractor, and my sister, Alice, and I do small home improvement jobs on the side."

Jenny broke into a tentative smile. "I know an Alice who does carpentry on the side." She pointed at him. "Does your sister teach at White Pine Middle School?"

He broke into a grin. "She does."

"She's referred several students to me. I tutor middle school and high school kids," Jenny said, feeling more trusting of him. Alice couldn't have a mean brother. "I don't know her except from phone calls and emails, but she seems to have this pleasant way of cajoling those kids into good grades and polite behavior."

"She does. Alice's a pistol, and she's handy with a hammer, too," he said affectionately and stuck out his hand. "I'm Luke Hammond."

"Jenny Beckett," she said and pointed at the Frank's Friendly Hardware Store sign on the wall behind him "Not Frank?"

"That's my daddy. This is a family business. Alice and I help him out. I've been on a...sabbatical from work," Luke said with a studied casualness.

"Are you a college professor?" she asked and immediately regretted her question. Maybe *taking a sabbatical* was the new euphemism for being unemployed.

"No," Luke said quietly and looked away. "I worked in IT, and I'm taking some time off to figure out what I want to do with my life." His face closed. "Alice is just substituting now. She's headed back to school in January to start a master's program." Luke held his hands palms up. "We both have free time. How about Wednesday mid-morning? I can check if Alice is free."

"That'd be great." Jenny thought of all the small repairs she could get their help with if she could afford it.

"So, do you teach?" Luke asked, his eyes bright with curiosity.

"I did for seven years but then got into tutoring. One-on-one

6

suited me better than the classroom," she said, trying to sound breezy, editing the part about her growing dislike of her work.

A man approached with a question, and Luke held up a finger. "I'll be right back." He walked with the customer to the plumbing section.

While she waited, Jenny thought about it. For nine years she'd reliably trotted off to the tiny office she'd rented near the school and helped her students develop better study habits. Her kids usually improved their grades and moved on, graduating from high school, then college. And there she was, still in her small office, cheerily greeting the next anxious parent's distracted, unfocused, or just plain lazy child. Now, Jenny dreaded her next tutoring day. Maybe it was the shock of the roughly broken engagement, or maybe she was just rethinking everything in her life and trying to get to happier because she was itching to close up shop, leave Shady Grove in her rearview mirror, and start fresh somewhere else.

The two men chuckled about something, and Luke strode back toward her.

Luke was pleasant to that customer, too, Jenny noted. Taking a business card from the sloping stack, she scribbled her contact information and address on the back.

Stepping behind the counter again, Luke gave her a wry smile as two men in paint – spattered jeans and sawdust-flecked jackets ambled in and headed toward them. "Busy today."

Jenny nodded. "Do I pay you for the door now or when you put it in?"

"You can pay for it when we install it," he said.

Jenny handed him the card. "I'm glad you can get it done soon before it gets too cold, and I may have a few other things I need your help with besides the door."

"I'll double check if Alice is free and shoot you a text to confirm." Luke gave her a level look. "Nice to meet you, Jenny Beckett. You're a nice lady to take in that little horse."

"Thanks," Jenny said, inordinately pleased at the compliment. She almost got caught in a full-on blast of his blue eyes, but zeroed in on the corner of his brow. Whew. Close call. She turned to go, fighting a smile.

The chicken coop cottage she called home was an outbuilding on a rambling, ramshackle farm out in the country, so she'd best shop while she was in town. She'd swing by the Food Carnival, she decided, and pointed her SUV toward one of the nicest shopping centers in Shady Grove. After a satisfying whirl up and down the aisles of the upscale market, Jenny loaded the bags into the cargo area of her supposedly fuel efficient crossover SUV. It was ten years old, but cranked every time she started it and never left her stranded. Glancing at her crossed-off shopping list, she felt like patting herself on the back. Jenny had stuck to her budget and to her list, mainly, except for the little tub of exotic olives, Lovely Olivia's homemade pimiento cheese, a box of wine, and Dove chocolates had somehow fallen into her cart.

Feeling good at the prospect of a full cupboard, Jenny fastened her seatbelt and paused a moment before starting the car, sipping her creamy latte. Jacked-Up Coffee was conveniently located next door to the grocery store, and she'd been lured in by the smoky scent of roasting beans. She patted the froth off her lip. Jacked Up made the best lattes with just the right amount of whip in a flower swirl on the top. The drink came to almost five bucks, and Jenny felt guilty when she thought about it. But lately, she'd been giving herself more little inexpensive treats to boost her spirits and *celebrate her glorious self,* as her friend Charlotte would say. Charlotte followed blogs with names like *My Phenomenal Fluffy Life, Curvy and Groovy,* and *Be Proud of Your Big Girl Build,* which is where she got the *Me Booster* tips that she had been enthusiastically offering Jenny since the big breakup. Jenny had been through a lot and deserved little pleasures but as she took another delicious sip of the brew, she glanced up and gaped.

Her ex-fiancé Douglas walked out of the coffee shop she'd just left. His head thrown back in laughter, he was newly trim and looked positively jaunty as he walked toward the parking lot holding the hand of his dewy-skinned girlfriend, Aiden. Through Shady Grove's small town grapevine that ran faster than any high speed internet, Jenny had heard that Douglas was serious about Aiden, and that the woman was referring to him as her fiancé. Sliding down in the seat, Jenny lowered the visor, slipped on sunglasses. Her pulse raucous, she tried to peer at the woman's hand as she considered the possibility that Douglas might be engaged again already. If so, would he be cheap enough or insensitive enough to recycle the engagement ring she'd given back to him just nine months ago? Her eyes fixed on them like a hunting dog on point, Jenny didn't think she saw a ring, but couldn't be sure. Snaking an arm into the back seat, she snagged the chocolates and popped a few in her mouth as fast as she could unwrap them.

Now, her ex-fiancé solicitously opened the door of his shiny new Lexus for the woman he'd referred to in his breakup speech as *the love of his life*. His show of good manners irked her, too. He'd opened the car door for Jenny only in the early days of dating and after that, just started calling out the rhetorical, "You got it?" as he swung into his seat.

She rubbed her forehead, still not quite believing how fast her relationship with Douglas had fallen apart. The day after his forty-fifth birthday, Douglas had brought a leaf blower out to her cottage and helped with yardwork. He'd pulled the cord and it roared to life. Lifting the heavy backpack blower onto his shoulders, he'd taken two steps and fallen to the ground writhing in pain. Muscle spasms put him in bed, and that weekend, Jenny had gone to his apartment each day, dutifully alternating the heating pad and the ice pack.

Two days later, Douglas had limped into his orthopedic doctor's office and got a prescription for a muscle relaxant and six weeks of physical therapy. He'd winced as he walked out the door for his first therapy appointment. Soon, he was back on his feet again, and he announced that Aiden, his physical therapist, was a lifesaver.

Taking a long draw of her creamy coffee, Jenny shook her head at her own stupidity. She'd been so supportive of his new fitness regime. At the end of his second week of physical therapy, she'd been cooking dinner for them and asked, "What's Aiden like?"

"Young, strong as a bull and tough on me. Says I need to build core strength to keep my back from going out again," he'd said, pounding his stomach with a good-natured grimace.

"Good." Jenny patted his arm encouragingly, picturing a strapping, young, ginger-haired man with a delightful lilt of an Irish accent. As she scooped the chicken breasts onto the bed of charred leeks and pulled the broccoli from the microwave, Jenny dreamily wondered if Aiden played the bagpipes or did Irish dancing. She just loved both.

So, Douglas began his physical fitness obsession, Jenny discovered Aiden was a woman, and that was the beginning of the end.

CHAPTER 2 — SMALL TOWN BLUES

WHEN JENNY FINALLY FOUND OUT the truth, Douglas manned up and broke things off without even apologizing. And the cheapskate immediately asked for the engagement ring back. In hindsight, that seemed beyond tacky. She had twisted the ring off her finger, told him she never wanted to see him again and whizzed over to her best friend's house. Charlotte hugged her until she stopped crying, handed her a box of tissues and started baking the chocolate chip cookies she claimed were medicinal. When Jenny asked *Isn't it awful? And how could he do this to me?* for the tenth time, Charlotte had wrinkled her nose and said diplomatically. "I never thought Douglas was the right man for you."

As the glamorous couple glided away in his new white Lexus, Jenny groaned aloud and hit her head softly on the steering wheel. This town was just too small. Last weekend, she'd almost bumped into the two of them while buying popcorn at the movie theater. She'd had to hustle into the ladies room and peek out until the coast was clear. "I need to get out of this town." Crumpling up the gold foil wrappers in her lap, she stuffed them in her coat pocket and jerked the car into drive.

Early Wednesday morning, Jenny wrestled open the front door, and let the boys out. Standing on the porch in her flannel pajamas decorated with cherries, she watched Buddy and Bear race across the yard, nose to the ground, before taking care of business. Levi stayed in the stall in the barn at night, but would be in and out visiting her throughout the day. She was so glad she had the boys for company.

After the big breakup, she'd moped around for weeks, lonely to the core. One Saturday, she'd taken the urn containing Chief's ashes, sat on the couch and conjured up his image, letting herself cry. Remembering the games of catch, the snuggling and the devotion that shone in his eyes, she sent up a prayer to Chief and promised to see him again down the road. Wiping her tears, she'd given herself a bracing pep talk and gone to the animal shelter. When the lady there told her that big dogs and older dogs were hardest to adopt out, Jenny drove home with two sixty pound plus dogs with gray muzzles breathing down her neck from the back seat of her car. Buddy was a Lab mix, and Bear a Shepherd mix. After they settled in with her, both were sweet tempered and loving. The raids on her kitchen trash can were happening less often, the limited-ingredient dog food helped with the air-quality problems and if she draped a throw just right, the gnawed wooden couch leg wasn't that noticeable.

Stretching and yawning, Jenny started the coffee and dumped kibbles in the dogs' bowls. Back inside, she picked up her phone and pulled up her calendar for the day. She didn't have a tutoring client until after two. Luke and his sister, Alice, were coming by at ten to size up the door switcheroo. Smiling, she held open the screen door for the dogs who careened in, churning up two kitchen rugs in their race to get to their bowls. Jenny was hungry, too, she decided and no kale-laced flax and chia seed smoothie would do. She'd *affirm her self-worth* by running into town for a warm, fresh baked sausage, egg and cheese biscuit. Scraping her hair into a messy topknot, Jenny threw on jeans and a fleece, stopped at the barn to give Levi breakfast and a pat and whizzed off in the car.

In the snaking line of Biscuit World Drive Thru, Jenny glanced in the mirror and saw the wrinkles fanning out from around her eyes. Mother of pearl. She needed to stop smiling and start slathering on more face cream. Her roots needed attention, too. Several silver gray strands mixed in with the brunette. Her mother's hair had been streaked with gray when she was thirty, but she'd lived with Jax until she couldn't anymore and that would have given premature gray hair to a saint. Jenny hoped she wasn't on the same path. She needed to do a hair touch up, soon. Maybe instead of the home kit she used to save money, she'd splurge and get her hairdresser, Star, to put in new highlights.

Two cars ahead, Jenny gasped as she spied the white Lexus driven by Douglas with Aiden in the passenger seat. They were chatting and laughing, and Jenny could see Douglas's hand reach over and tousle the redhead's mane. Jenny slouched way down in her seat, and thought about easing out of line and driving off. But this was her town, too. Plus, she was starving. The counter girl gave her a guarded smile as she stretched her arm down and handed Jenny the white bag. Zooming away in her car, Jenny chewed and stewed.

Back home, Jenny took a quick shower and dressed, let Levi in and poured herself a second cup of coffee, trying to forget about seeing Douglas and Aiden. At the computer, Levi leaned into her side as Jenny determinedly scrolled through a site called *Best Places to Live in America*. Maybe she could buy a small house and start fresh. San Diego's beachy vibe and amazing shoreline were alluring, but the median home prices made her almost choke on her coffee. Yikes. She'd have to tutor a ton of smart-alecky, homework-ditching students to afford life there.

Dickinson, North Dakota had hiking galore and easy sightings of aurora borealis. Sitka, Alaska had meteor showers, eagles gliding overhead and majestic snow-capped mountains. Jenny considered it. Maybe she'd buy a faux fur-trimmed parka and train her champion team of mushing dogs, led by Bear and Buddy of course. Minnetonka, Minnesota had 196 clear days per year, but the photo was of a fresh-faced, wholesome-looking family cross-country skiing, blizzard-like snow blowing around them. She shivered. Born and raised in milder climes, she threw on a sweater when the temperatures dipped below seventy degrees. No, ma'am. No town above the Mason-Dixon Line.

But she'd better get cracking now. Luke and Alice would be

coming by to install a new door with a dog door for Levi so he could swan in and out whenever he wanted to.

Her landlady's cheapskate son was handling her rental now, and Earl Evans would be slippery as an eel if she tried to get him to pay for any upkeep at all much less an upgrade. Six months ago, she'd asked him to replace several of the hole-pocked screens so she could open the windows without inviting in flies and mosquitos. Sounding irritated, he'd left her a voice mail. "I've taken care of your windows. Keep in mind this is a rental and we need to keep unnecessary costs down." Irritated, she'd stabbed the delete button, and her eyes were drawn to the windows. Earl had taken clear packing tape and taped shut the holes.

Opening all the windows to invite in the crisp morning air, Jenny started another pot of coffee. She brushed her teeth and was dabbing on eye cream with a pinky when she heard the crunch of gravel on the driveway. A swarm of butterflies fluttered in her stomach as she thought about Luke. Pasting what she hoped was a confident smile on her face, she opened the front door to Luke and Alice. Avoiding eye contact with Luke meant she instead noticed his disarming smile, broad shouldered build, and the muscles on his forearms and legs. Whoops. Big mistake. She smiled at Alice, a curly-haired blonde in her thirties with creamy skin, an open face and a friendly smile. Wearing no makeup, she had her hair in a ponytail that looped out of her ball cap. "Good morning," Jenny said, suddenly feeling shy as she held out a hand to the woman.

But Alice broke into a smile and gave Jenny a quick hug. "I feel like I know you. You've done such a good job with the students I've sent you."

Jenny felt her face grow pink, pleased at the praise. "I've heard good things about you, too. Thank you for all the referrals." She pointed at the burbling coffee maker. "How about a quick cup before we talk about all the work I need done?"

Alice put her hands together as if in prayer. "Please, please, please. I accidentally ran out of regular coffee this morning and had to drink decaf."

Luke gave a good-natured smile and nodded.

Soon, they each held a freshly brewed cup and sat at the kitchen table. Jenny went to the door and called up Levi, who strolled into the kitchen, sniffing and nuzzling Luke and his sister.

"He's adorable," Alice cooed, rubbing the bridge of the little horse's nose.

"Hey, guy," Luke said softly as he scratched the wiry hair of the horse's back.

Levi groaned with pleasure.

"So, the door..." she began but heard a car approaching. Puzzled, she pulled back the curtain and groaned as she saw a gleaming Cadillac SUV pull up in front of the house, followed closely by a silver truck. The sedan belonged to Earl Evans with the mean, beady eyes and puffed up sense of his own importance. "That's my landlady's son, effectively my landlord now. I'll just be a minute." Jenny stepped out the door, wishing for the hundredth time that she'd not been so spooked at the thought of a thirty-year mortgage and bought her own house or condo long ago.

Nodding at Earl, Jenny said stiffly, "Morning, Earl."

"Hey, girl," he said with a smile that didn't meet his eyes. "You're not skipping out on the rent are you?" Earl chuckled at his own lame joke.

Some woman had actually married Earl and put up with his idiocy. "I put the check in the mail yesterday. It'll arrive right on time, just like it always does," she said evenly.

Her landlord put a hand on his hip, and tilted his head at her small SUV and her beat up, silver Airstream parked beside the barn. "When you going to get rid of those buckets of rust and get nice, new vehicles?"

"They're paid for, Earl," she said, eyeing his gleaming Cadillac, which she'd bet her pearls was leased.

Unfazed, Earl unwrapped a piece of hard candy, popped it in his mouth and sucked it wetly. With his thumb, he gestured over his shoulder to the silver truck behind him, where a short fellow wearing a chartreuse safety vest took a yellow tripod from the truck bed and fixed a piece of technical looking equipment to the top of it. "That there's Randolph. He's my surveyor. Mama's

15

pneumonia got worse, she had a stroke, and they moved her into skilled nursing this weekend."

Jenny gasped quietly. Both of them respected each other's privacy, so she never knew her landlady all that well, but Jenny had liked Mrs. Evans.

"We got her okay to sell the farm." Earl said, rocking back on his heels, looking proud of himself. "You're going to need to find a new place to live, little girl."

Jenny winced inwardly, picturing Earl's meaty paw holding his vacant-faced mama's bird-like hand and guiding it over the documents. Fighting a knee-weakening wave of panic, Jenny worked hard to keep her voice from trembling. "Would the new owners be interested in a renter?"

"Hah!" Earl scoffed. "Not likely. The buyer is Great Southern Development. The farm and your chicken coop will be torn down. They're going to build upscale apartments," he said, his eyes glittering, cash registers in his head probably ka-chinging.

Jenny felt like she'd taken a punch to the gut. The chicken coop cottage that had been her home for ten years, gone. Mrs. Evans's leaning, asbestos shingled old home with the trotting horse weathervane, gone. "You're just going to let them bulldoze it all? This farm has been in your family for generations."

"We close the second week in November. We need you out," he said in a matter-of-fact tone as he hitched up his pants, which were trying to slip below his barrel stomach. "Can't stand in the way of progress." Earl shook his head regretfully as if he'd been forced at knifepoint to sell his family's home place.

Surely his wife had had the opportunity to push a pillow over his head or quietly turn off his CPAP machine while he slept, but maybe she was slimy, too. Jenny crossed her arms and gave him a level look. "So, you're giving me less than thirty days to move?"

"It's not me. It's what the new owner wants." Earl looked away, scratching his chin. "If you get out within two weeks, I might be able to refund your security deposit."

Realizing her fists had clenched at her side, Jenny tried to be casual about unclenching them. She needed to keep her composure the best she could. "Why do you think you're entitled to the security deposit?" she asked in a no-nonsense tone, determined not to show fear to a man like that.

"Wear and tear. Horse in the house, blah, blah, blah." He shrugged.

Neither Levi nor the dogs had ever had one accident inside and the cottage was pin neat. This was a bully move. "You're talking about supposed damage to the house, but your plan is to tear it down?" she asked tightly.

Earl held his hands palms up. "It's in the lease."

"There's no lease, Earl. Just a handshake agreement between me and your mama," Jenny said wearily. There was no use talking to this man.

Earl glanced behind her and his eyes shifted. He seemed to lose some of his swagger. "Three weeks, and I'm being generous," he said. Hiking up his pants, Earl stalked off.

When Jenny turned, Luke and Alice stood behind her stone-faced, watching her landlord approach the surveyor.

"What an odious little man," Alice said, her eyes flashing. "Can he really do that to you, evict you like that?"

Jenny put her hands around her waist and hugged herself. "I think he can."

Luke rubbed his chin and the muscle in his jaw worked. "You want me to talk with him?" he asked, a note of menace in his voice.

Jenny felt a swell of gratitude for their support, and these were people she hardly knew. "It's okay," she said thickly. "He's a piece of work, but I think he holds all the cards."

Looking uneasy, Alice glanced at her brother. "Is she right, Luke?"

"Probably," he said, grim faced.

Jenny pushed her shoulders back, trying not to cry. "I guess I don't need your help with the door now. I'm sorry to get you all the way out here for nothing,"

"Oh, shug," Alice said sympathetically, and reached around to hug Jenny's shoulder. "You let us know if we can help at all. We'll put the word out and see if we can find another place for you to rent, one that will let you keep all your critters and won't charge you out the wazoo."

"Movers, lawyers, landlords. We know a lot of good people in this town. You don't need to deal with the likes of him," he said, jerking his head toward Earl. Fixing his eyes on hers, Luke spoke with quiet intensity. "Anything you need, Jenny. Call or come see us at the store."

Jenny just nodded. "Thanks," she managed to croak out.

The rest of the day, Jenny felt strangely languid, like she was swimming underwater. She drank peppermint tea, nibbled chocolates and took the boys on meandering walks. Though the day was as gorgeous as fall got in North Carolina, with red and magenta leaves on the trees and the sky a blue only seen in Monet paintings, Jenny barely noticed. She didn't read the essays she'd assigned her students, stepped over laundry, and smashed down the overflowing detritus in the kitchen trash can.

In such a short time frame, where was Jenny going to find a place to stay with two large dogs and a small indoor/outdoor horse? And the rent she'd paid, a deal she'd struck with Mrs. Evans while she was still compos mentis, was very reasonable for the almost on the brink of coming into its own town of Shady Grove.

Later that afternoon, Jenny was listlessly perusing the Apartments4U and Craigslist ads for rentals when her phone rang. She perked up when she saw it was Charlotte calling.

"I got your text about becoming a homeless person," Charlotte breathed dramatically.

Jenny had to smile. She'd texted her earlier, saying Earl had given her the boot, not that she was on the streets. "That's a tad overstated, but close enough to the truth."

"I can help," Charlotte said, all business now. "Between my home staging classes and my many, *many* previous places of employment, I know a ton of people. I'll put feelers out for a place..." She hesitated, probably remembering all of Jenny's complications.

"With space for two big dogs, a miniature horse and rent of under eight hundred dollars a month," Jenny said, rubbing a spot on the bridge of her nose.

"Oh, dear." Charlotte wilted but then her voice brightened.

"I'd love to have you and your beasts camp out with me. That would be so much fun," she said with that eternal enthusiasm that Jenny usually loved but could drive her mad.

Charlotte lived in an apartment above the four-car garage attached to her parents' massive plantation style house. Nell and Beau Perry were the un-flashy, modest-living kind of moneyed people. Both drove old cars, sported rumpled khakis and smelled faintly of dog. The Perrys were fond of Jenny, but even they might balk at her moving in with her menagerie.

"You're sweet," Jenny said. "But your place is upstairs. Levi doesn't do stairs."

"We could work something out. Ramps or elevators or pulleys," her friend said airily.

"Thanks, girl." As impractical as the offer was, at least Jenny had a backup plan.

"I'll call you later. I'm off to my Dieters Anonymous meeting." In a confidential tone, Charlotte added, "I've been on the ketogenic diet. No desserts, more butter, full-fat milk, too much kohlrabi and radishes. No wine, either, but I'm viewing that as sort of optional."

"Good for you." Jenny said and ended the call. She'd used the enthusiastic tone she always used for every diet her friend went on…and off. Charlotte was not like the wraiths on the magazine covers, but who was? Jenny thought she was beautiful, like one of the Greek goddesses who rode around in chariots and threw lightning bolts at people who deserved it.

Levi butted her hand with his head. Ruffling his mane, Jenny gazed into Levi's chocolate brown eyes and kissed his muzzle. She was running low on the good, clean alfalfa grass hay and sweet feed that the mini ate. Jenny stood and slung her purse over her shoulder. She'd hit the Farmer's Co-op for Levi's grub and pick up kibble for Buddy and Bear, too.

As she thunked the last bag of dog food into the back of her SUV, Jenny's phone rang. She didn't recognize the number, but maybe it was a new tutoring client. "Jenny Beckett," she said crisply, secretly hoping the caller was a telemarketer so she could be snappy with him.

"Good afternoon. This is Ashe Long with Guardian Assets," a man said politely.

Jenny had never heard of them. "Will you please take my name off your call list?"

The man cleared his throat. "We're the law firm that worked with your father, Jackson Beckett, handling his investments and his estate."

"Let me guess. Daddy needs money." Grimly, Jenny remembered bounced checks, race horses that came up lame and hot new business ventures that flamed out. Jax was always on the brink of being rich, and though he'd had a few wild successes, he was broke more often than not. Growing up, Jenny had fielded enough calls from collection agencies to know the drill. "If you want money, I can't help you. I don't even know where he lives now."

The man paused for a long moment. "We were contacted by the Green County Sheriff's Department. I'm sorry to tell you this, but your daddy had a heart attack and passed away."

CHAPTER 3 —
BREATHING ROOM

BLOOD THRUMMED BETWEEN JENNY'S EARS and felt the burn of an unexpected lump in her throat. She'd not heard from Jax in six years and, though she felt a stab of guilt, knew she'd been relieved about their estrangement. The last time she'd seen him, he'd come to spend the weekend with her to *reconnect with my beautiful daughter.* While he was getting settled in, Jenny made a quick run into town to pick up charcoal for the cookout she'd planned. When she came back, Jax's big truck was gone but the battered Airstream he'd been towing, the one he fondly called the Silver Belle, was still in her driveway. He'd left her a hastily scrawled note of apology:

> Baby Girl, just got a call from a buddy of mine. I've got to go out west. There's a gold mine in the Superstition Mountains that they thought was tapped out but still holds a motherlode. Opportunity of a lifetime. Take the Silver Belle and have adventures of your own. Sorry. Your loving Daddy

Jax had taken off like he'd done countless times before. She'd grown up being let down by Daddy and thought she'd steeled herself against being disappointed by him, but Jenny had been crushed. She'd vowed to never speak to him again.

A blunt-spoken big guy with a captivating laugh and an uncanny resemblance to Tom Selleck, Jax was a speculator, a charmer and a world-class breaker of promises. Jenny put a finger on her temple where a vein was starting to pulse and tuned back in to what the attorney was saying.

"…and so, we'll need to meet with you as soon as possible," the attorney was saying "We've had a hard time locating you. Your father passed two weeks ago."

"Was there a funeral?" she asked, still trying to take in the fact that Jax was gone for good.

"At his request, he was cremated and he instructed his friends to spread his ashes where they saw fit," he said, sounding apologetic.

"Okay," Jenny said, relieved. She shivered inwardly, glad she had missed the experience of cruising down 1-64 with an urn strapped into the seat beside her.

Ashe Long hesitated. "You were the only person named in the will."

"I was an only child, he was an only child, and my mother washed her hands of him," she explained. When Jenny left for college, Mama quietly divorced Jax, and soon married Landis Collins, a retired banker she met in the waiting room of her dentist's office. They moved to Summerville, South Carolina. Mama seemed happy with her new life, though, and regularly sent her postcards from the trips and cruises she went on with Landis.

Ashe went on. "We're in the process of getting updates on his retirement accounts and other investments. He lived in a modest home here in the small town of Celeste just north of Hickory. He owned it free and clear and deeded it to you. You can sell it, rent it, or live in it."

"Okay." Jenny sat up straighter, feeling a glimmer of hope. Selling the house might give her financial breathing room while she came up with a plan for the rest of her life.

"I'd like to go over the will with you at your earliest convenience," Ashe said. "We'll have to see where we stand with regard to assets and liabilities, of course."

"I can't clear up any of his debts," Jenny said flatly, rubbing her forehead. "I just can't. I'm not in a financial position to do it, and I've done it too many times before."

"Understood," Ashe said, not sounding the least bit judgmental.

"I can drive up to Celeste tomorrow morning," she said reluctantly.

Back home, Jenny felt strangely calm as she sent texts and made calls to reshuffle her tutoring calendar, clearing her schedule for Thursday. One irreverent thought kept coming back, no matter how she tried to shoo it away. Jax was dead and she was still cleaning up his messes.

At the desk in her tiny living room, office and bedroom combination, Jenny sat chin in hand and gazed out the window to the rolling fields, feeling teary, not so much for the love she'd lost with him, but for the love she'd never had a chance to have. Deep inside, when she hadn't hidden her hurt with cynicism, Jenny had secretly dreamed of a grand father-daughter reunion in which Jax would look anguished and say, "I was so foolish for letting those years slip by without spending time with you, my beloved daughter." No chance for that, now. Jenny brushed away brimming tears with her fingers.

Behind her, the door pushed open and Levi strolled in. Jenny rose to shut it, and called to him, "Wipe your feet, young man."

Practicing a move they'd been working on, the miniature horse made a show of pawing at the mud mats that came with a guarantee they would *stop the dirt at the door*. Levi ambled over to see her, giving a friendly nicker and shoving his muzzle in her lap so she'd pet him. Jenny gave him a good scratch and a quick kiss.

When she'd rented the chicken coop turned cottage that stood a hundred yards from a farmhouse on thirty acres, she'd been thrilled when she spied the miniature horse grazing in pasture beside the house. But upon closer inspection, Jenny saw that the little guy's hooves were curled up like elf shoes, making it painful for him to walk. Jenny read up on it, and learned that most unshod horses needed their hooves trimmed regularly by a professional called a farrier. The little horse's owners had been too neglectful or too cheap to have had it done in way too long.

Angrily, she'd tracked down the neighbor who owned him and insisted that the mini's hooves be attended to. When he'd scoffed at her in his rough voice, Jenny told him she'd hate to have to call the S.P.C.A., and offered him a hundred dollars to take Levi off his hands. So that's how she came to own a miniature horse that thought he was a house pet.

After a quick call to the teenaged girl who lived at the next farm and who loved pet sitting for her, Jenny closed her eyes for moment, dreading the trip. Every time she thought about Jax dead, she shooed the thought out of her brain. She imagined herself waking up in a darling house in a happier town, and tried to remember what she'd read in the article *Best Towns Ever in the U.S.* In forty-eight hours, she'd be back home planning a move and getting on with her life.

After a night of thin sleep, Jenny grabbed an insulated to-go cup of coffee, put the address in WAZE and tooled down the highway.

Just as she merged onto I-85, the phone rang. Charlotte. She hit hands free and called out, "Hey, there."

"Hey yourself," Charlotte said. "My class just let out. Tall sconces draw the eyes upward. Don't put huge armoires in small ranch houses," she advised. "Your text said you had even more news?"

Jenny filled her in on the news of Jax's death and the reason for her ride to Celeste.

Charlotte gasped, "I am so sorry. Poor you. Your daddy let you down way more than he came through for you, but the few times I met him, I could always tell how much he loved you. That has to be hard."

"I don't feel anything right now," Jenny admitted. "It hasn't sunk in, and we weren't all that close."

"He was your one and only daddy," Charlotte said firmly.

Jenny snorted, but felt a wave of sadness.

"Cynicism is the cloak of the true romantic," Charlotte said quietly. "Call me when you get home."

That afternoon, Jenny gazed across the oak roll-top desk at Ashe Long, a lawyer with thinning red hair and wire-rimmed half glasses. "I'm truly sorry for your loss," he said gravely, his eyes kind. "This must be a shock for you."

24

"It is, but it isn't," she admitted, raising a shoulder. "Jax and I lost touch years ago, and before that, I didn't hear from him much." Jenny remembered three pages of her address book devoted to Jax, crossed out phone numbers and addresses filling each page. "He was never the kind of dad they write the Father's Day cards about." She felt heat rise in her face, sure the attorney thought she was a bad daughter.

But the attorney just nodded his understanding and held his hands palms up. "These things happen. Your daddy led an adventuresome life, and I'm sure it was difficult to keep up with him at times."

It was hard to not roll her eyes, but she managed. Ashe was trying to be diplomatic.

He took a finger and pushed up the glasses that had slipped down his nose. "An estate, even a fairly simple one, can take up to two years to settle, but we've started work on it." He handed her a summary sheet of Jax's debts and assets. "Over the years, your father had some strong profits and significant losses. He's at about net zero."

"Hmmm," Jenny said, relieved he'd not accumulated a boatload of debt. Low expectations had always been the key to dealing with Jax. But even a small amount of money from a house sale could be a big help to her, especially given her dicey housing situation.

Ashe looked out the window. "Don't write off living here. Celeste's a good town. I like it here. I moved back from Chapel Hill to take care of my folks and ended up staying," he explained. "People are nice. You can leave your door unlocked. The pace of life is slower and your money goes a long way. The property taxes...." He droned on.

But Jenny stopped listening because, despite the gravity of the meeting, she was matchmaking in her head. Ashe was good to his parents and held a decent job. He didn't wear a gold band. He wasn't as old as she initially thought. If a woman fed him right so he wasn't so skinny and helped him pick less stodgy clothes, he'd be attractive in a nice, family guy way. Not her type by a long shot. She liked them skeevy and unpredictable. But maybe he could be Charlotte's future husband.

Ashe waved a hand in front of her face. "You okay? You drifted a little. Would you like a glass of water?"

"Thanks, I'm fine," she said sheepishly. "Just a lot to take in."

Resting his elbows on the desk, Ashe tented his fingers and gazed at her. "So, do you have any interest in living here or would you like to rent or sell the house?"

Jenny mentally tried on the idea of the sad spinster settling into Celeste, which seemed like a sleepy town. She'd give up trying to watch her weight, join the church choir for the companionship, and sit on the front porch wearing a zip-up housecoat, rocking in a glider and watching traffic. Maybe she'd start waving at cars and get a write-up in the town newspaper, an article called *The Friendly Waver: Southern Hospitality Still Means a Lot in Celeste*. Jenny shuddered inwardly and opened her mouth to tell Ashe she'd decided to sell.

But Ashe jumped in, holding up his palm. "Do me a favor. Before you head home, will you just drive by your dad's house before you decide?" He held up a jangling bunch of keys looped to a motorboat shaped key ring with Billy Bob's Bait printed on the side, and handed it to her. "The furniture is...well...lived in, but please take anything you'd like. Your dad also left a box of personal items he'd want you to have. It's on the floor right inside the door of the glassed – in porch."

"Okay." What could he have wanted her to have? "I'm leaning toward selling, but I'll take a look at the place."

Ashe gazed at her, a half-smile playing on his lips. "I saved the good news for last."

"Oh?" Jenny said, but tried to glance surreptitiously at her phone to catch the time.

Ashe hesitated. "The attorney I bought the practice from worked into his eighties before he retired and his filing system got... haphazard. After we talked, I double checked all the records we held on your dad and just this morning, I found another asset." He leaned forward, his eyes sparkling. "Your daddy owned a large waterfront lot with almost four hundred feet of shoreline on Heron Lake that he acquired in the `70's. Last year, he began building eight small cabins on it, but ran out of money before he could finish them." He paused, running a hand through what was left of his hair. "I'm not sure what his plans were, but he was excited about the project."

The lot could be worth serious money. Jenny's heart thudded so loudly she thought the attorney might hear it. Though she'd never been to Heron Lake, some of her students had wealthy parents who owned second homes there. If Jenny sold the lot, she'd have the means to start over in a place where she didn't run into her ex and that wench Aiden everywhere she went.

"Heron Lake is ten thousand acres with one hundred seventy miles of shoreline. It's considered one of the most scenic, pristine bodies of water in North Carolina." Ashe's face growing animated. "The property you now own is not in a subdivision, has no zoning and no covenants. The lake used to have a lot of mobile homes and modest weekend cottages on it, but it's gotten discovered in the last twenty years. There are many expensive houses on the lake and prime lots are sought after. You may be able to sell it and realize a tidy gain." He clicked his pen open and shut and the corners of his mouth quirked up. "I wasn't sure why or how he bought it. His finances could be...erratic."

Jenny nodded at that colossal understatement.

"But then I found this." Ashe plucked a piece of paper from a folder and held it up to her. It was a messily scrawled note written on a torn off piece of a brown paper grocery bag. Ashe broke into a grin. "This is the record of the sale. Jax won the lot in a poker game."

Jenny cracked a smile. "That's my daddy."

He thrust the crumpled paper bag closer to her and pointed at what looked like an addendum. "Last year, he signed the lot and cabins over to you. He's up to date on taxes on the property, and you own it free and clear. You can take possession now. No need to wait for us to settle the estate."

I own a valuable lakefront lot, Jenny thought wonderingly and put a hand to her mouth. After believing for years that he never thought much about her, one of his last acts had been to give her this gift. Tears pricked her eyes. Suddenly weary, she rubbed her eyes with her fingers. "I need to get back home. This is a lot to take in."

"I understand," he said, and gave her a sympathetic look, probably imaging her dealing with the bleak grief a daughter feels when she loses her beloved father.

Jenny would let him think that, but it was way more complicated.

"Heron Lake is on your way back to Shady Grove, so you might swing by there as well." Ashe fixed his gaze on her and gave a half smile. "I had the pleasure of meeting your daddy on several occasions. He was a fine man. And he talked about how smart you were and how proud he was of you for having your own business. He could go on and on about you."

Jenny blinked. What? The man who was MIA for much of her childhood went *on and on* about her? "That's good to hear," she said, skeptical, guessing Ashe was just being nice.

Walking her to the door, he gave her an encouraging look. "Keep me posted." The lines around his eyes crinkled nicely when he smiled, and Jenny sensed that he was rooting for her.

Outside, the day was sunny but the wind had a bite. Fallen leaves blew around her and Jenny zipped her jacket. Dutifully, she put Jax's address in WAZE, and set off. She'd do what Ashe had asked her to do, but she had an odd mix of dread and curiosity about the place her rolling stone father had finally called home. Right on Main, left on Skyview, and there was 901 Prospect, on a quiet, tree-lined street with small, well-maintained looking older homes that might have been built in the `20's or `30's. Jax's house was a Craftsman-style bungalow with peeling paint and one cockeyed shutter. The lawn was shaggy and high, and a storm must have split two of the three Bradford pears that used to grace the side yard. But the air of neglect could not hide the simple beauty of the house, with its broad gabled roof, dormer windows, and inviting front porch.

Jenny pulled up to the curb, lowered the window and turned off the engine. A crow cawed as she gazed at the house, and she got the sense that the home had been a calm refuge for Jax but she had no desire to go inside. She trudged around to the glass enclosed porch behind the house, and under a blue tarp found the box Ashe had told her about. She lugged it to the truck. On impulse, she walked around the house taking several photos of the exterior and held the phone to the windows to get interior shots. Peering inside, Jenny saw that the rooms were sparsely furnished. There were no pictures on the wall, the couches looked sprung and the furniture was mismatched. Jenny hugged herself, feeling a wave of sadness. Hard to believe that her glamorous, larger-than-life father had spent the last years of his life in this shabby house. Jenny shivered, and got back in the car.

Her key in the ignition, Jenny glanced at the house one last time, and brushed away tears that welled up in her eyes. She sent up a quick prayer to her dad. *Hey, Jax. I'm glad you found this pretty home and I hope you were happy here. Thank you for the gifts. They mean a lot. I'm still mad at you but we'll talk about that later. For now, Godspeed, Daddy.*

An hour later, Jenny was cruising down the interstate, sorting through a confused churn of feelings. The WAZE lady spelled out turns from the address the attorney had given her, and finally, Jenny turned down a long and winding two-lane road. Finally, she saw the hand-lettered green sign with the peeling paint. It read: *The Lakeside Resort.* Underneath it, an arrow pointed to a gravel lane off to one side. A large pine tree had fallen across the driveway, so Jenny pulled in as far as she could. Hopping out, she peered ahead, her view obscured by the overgrowth of bushes and branches. The breeze picked up and Jenny paused, listening hard, and grinned delightedly. She could hear the sound of waves lapping onto the shore. Hurrying now because of her excitement, Jenny broke into a trot.

Peering ahead through the dense brush, Jenny gasped as she caught a glimpse of Heron Lake, a dancing, gleaming, expanse of blue. The land sat high on a bluff, and the view took her breath away. She inhaled a deep breath of clean air, catching a delicious hint of wood smoke. Jenny spun around to take it all in. The wind kicked up and the waves were now small whitecaps. For the first time in a long while, Jenny felt like she was on top of the world.

CHAPTER 4 — LAKESIDE FIXER UPPERS

JENNY DUCKED LOW-HANGING BRANCHES AS she hurried toward the cabins arranged in a semi-circle facing the lake. Rustic and adorable, they reminded her of the small tobacco curing barns that used to dot the countryside of North Carolina. With big windows facing the lake, rocking chair front porches, stone chimneys, and curved doorways like hobbit houses, these cabins had real charm. Jenny guessed them to be about three-hundred square feet each, perfect for a weekend or even a month-long rental. Each cabin had a dark green metal roof. At the front door of the one on the end, Jenny's tricky knee twinged as she climbed up the stacked cement blocks that served as temporary steps, rubbed away dirt from the window with the sleeve of her jacket and peered inside. It looked like a construction site. The studs were up but there were no interior walls, and no kitchen cabinets, appliances, light fixtures, sinks, or toilets.

As she continued snooping, she thought about the sign out front, *The Lakeside Resort*. There were no upscale amenities and it looked like none were in the works, so *resort* seemed grand and inaccurate. Why hadn't Jax called this place *The Lakeside Cabins*? This was a real head scratcher.

The cabin on the far end had wires strung to it from a pole. Had Jax run power to it and made it habitable so he could stay on site while working on the other cabins? She strode down to investigate. On the porch, she peeked inside and her heart lifted. The place was seriously cute.

Her hands shaking with excitement, Jenny snapped several photos. This cabin was furnished with the bare-bone essentials. She saw a blue wood stove, a futon type couch, a rag rug, a bed in a loft, floor lamps and lights on the wall. The kitchen sinks had faucets. Plumbing was a real plus.

Jenny could picture herself, actually, a sunnier version of herself who looked a lot like Jennifer Aniston, living in the adorable log cabin with jaw-dropping view of Heron Lake. Walking to the clearing, Jenny stood and looked at the eight cabins, scarcely believing she owned such an appealing spot. She took several more photos and then took shots of the glittering lake. Slipping her phone back in her pocket, Jenny pinched her lip, thinking. So, Jax's idea had probably been to rent them out to summer tourists. This could have been his retirement plan. But a thought nagged at her. Maybe, just maybe, Jax had always intended to pass the cabins on to Jenny as a legacy, to ensure she was financially secure and to make up for all the times he'd let her down.

But Jenny gave her head a quick shake as if to clear it. Nah. Despite Ashe telling her Jax went on and on about her, Jenny wasn't sure she was buying it. These cabins came under the category of the lucky break of being related to a man with no relatives who hadn't planned on being felled so young by a heart attack.

The cabins were magical and the views from them were amazing, but she needed to be practical. She owned a large lakefront lot free and clear and that was the big moneymaker. Selling would give her financial security for a while, and cash in her pocket was Jenny's ticket out of Shady Grove and on to a new town, a fresh start, and a hopeful new life.

Thoughts and feeling swirling around, Jenny headed back to the SUV and motored home. This morning on the drive to Celeste, Jenny remembered thinking about her to-do list, her head swimming with all the decisions she had to make. With a strong hand of cards and a quick stroke of his pen, Jax Beckett had added a whole wheelbarrow full of other options and decisions she needed to make. Jenny had a lot to think about.

That evening, Jenny's mind kept racing and she was too

buzzed with all the latest developments to curl up in bed with a book and drift off to sleep. She had another big problem to solve: where to live once she had to leave her cottage. At the computer, she skimmed the online ads for rental houses. The pickings were slim. Slumping, she looked again at the possibilities. Helping with chores in exchange for lower rent was the common theme. One required the tenant to help out with the haying, chicken feeding and cattle roundup. She shuddered and deleted that one. Even though she tried to work out with Jillian Michael's DVDs three times a week...well at least once a week...she couldn't see herself tossing around bales of hay with a hook like she'd seen the ruggedly good-looking rancher use in the Dodge commercials, or leading an unsuspecting cow to....well. Jenny shuddered, wishing she could quickly squeegee that image out of her brain.

Scratching her head with a pen, she studied the two best options. The first one was a cute small house and the price was right, but the owner required the tenant to be able to drive a tractor and *help out from time to time*. Hmmm.

The second rental required the tenant to *occasionally prepare meals and help take care of an elderly man* who was bedridden. If he liked salsa and chips for supper, or spinach and blueberry smoothies for breakfast and if caring for him in the evenings meant eating boiled peanuts, trailing his fingers down the wiry fur of Levi's back while patting dogs and watching HGTV or The History Channel, it might just work. But she suspected the deal might involve adult diapers and patience. She didn't feel like taking care of anyone. She hit DELETE, and rubbed her forehead with her fingers. Enough for tonight.

As she closed her eyes and snuggled into bed, Jenny thought about it. If she were brave enough, could she make The Lakeside Resort work? She could get excited about her life again, and give herself financial security for her future.

But Jenny pulled a pillow over her face and groaned aloud at that half-baked idea. The possibility of pulling off that big a do-over in her life was as low as winning big on the scratch – off lottery tickets her father had bought for her when she was a girl, the ones with names like *Rolling in the Dough* or *Hey, Big Spender*. And one thing Daddy had taught her by his example was to pay attention to the odds. Lady Luck wasn't likely to smile on her just because she had a cockeyed idea. If she was a real estate lady with a building contractor's license and money to spend, the cabins might be a go. But a burned-out school tutor with moths in her wallet, no building experience and zero background in the innkeeper, cabin keeper or whatever you called it industry? The odds weren't in her favor.

Friday afternoon, Jenny stepped out of the baggy sweatshirt and pants she wore around the house and reluctantly put on her work clothes: khaki slacks, a white high-collared shirt and a thick wool cardigan in case the heat in her small office wasn't working. Though she talked to the landlord several times about the faint-hearted heat and he always promised to *get a guy to look at it*, the problem never got fixed. Jenny just dressed in layers and brought a space heater when it got really cold. On the short drive over, the car behind her was inches from her bumper and, irritated, Jenny looked at the speedometer. She was driving ten miles under the speed limit. Shaking her head at herself, Jenny sped up. She did not want to go to work.

Jenny's day began when the kids finished classes. Her three o'clock, Kaylee, usually arrived ten minutes late, full of attitude and wearing scarves, bangles and a cape. Her parents were both doctors and were pushing hard for their only child to follow in their career path, but with Kaylee's anime creations and love of reading fantasy, Jenny guessed that the girl was headed down a more artistic path. Today, Jenny planned on doing career and interest testing to find out if her hunch was right.

As was her habit, Jenny arrived a half-hour early to water her anemic peace lily, check her email, and mentally prepare for work. As she pulled up beside the squat brick professional building that was one block from the middle school, she spotted a white Lexus parked out front. Her heart started thudding. Why was Douglas here, and what did he want?

Jenny stepped out of the car, slamming the door as he stepped out, looking trim and buff as he waved. "Hey, Jenny. Do you have time to talk before your first appointment?"

"Douglas, I'm busy," she clipped out, hurrying by him.

"Wait," he called. "I just need ten minutes."

"You've got five," Jenny said brusquely and didn't slow her pace as she hurried up the sidewalk to her office.

He followed behind like a puppy, holding the door open for her and trying to take her canvas briefcase for her. She wrested it away from him and swatted him with it. "I've... got... it," she said through gritted teeth.

Looking chastened, Douglas stood by the door, his hands thrust in his pockets, jingling change. Change jingling was his tell for nervousness, she knew, and felt good about it. Let him be nervous. Jenny eyed him. Unfortunately, he looked good. He'd lost about twenty pounds and was wearing a sharp-looking hounds tooth sports coat and a tie. He wasn't wearing his glasses. Maybe he'd gotten contacts. Spiffing up for the way-younger girlfriend/fiancée.

Thumping down in a chair, she gracelessly pointed to the chair on the other side of the desk. "Sit. What's this about?"

"You know what yesterday was, right?" Douglas sat in the chair and leaned forward, his tone doleful and his face as solemn as a doctor about to deliver bad news.

Everything about him just irritated her. Knitting her brow, Jenny was baffled. "Don't step on a bee day? Hug your cat day?"

Douglas smiled sadly. "I think you know as well as I do that it's the anniversary of our first date."

His tone was mildly reproving, and it made her want to smack him again with her briefcase. "If a couple is broken up, which we are, they don't celebrate anniversaries," she said in the tone she reserved for her slower students. "There's really nothing to celebrate."

Douglas held up a hand. "I know. I know. It's just that I thought about you...about us... a lot yesterday. We had so many happy memories. We were such a comfortable pair." He gave her a long, doleful look and gazed off into the distance. "We were like a pair of old shoes."

Jenny rolled her eyes, but he was too busy reminiscing to notice.

"I always could count on you. You knew me inside and out. You knew my flaws and always supported me," Douglas said wistfully. "You were like a good old hound dog. Loyal and faithful. Like a little brown wren, quiet, cheerful, always there for me."

An old shoe, old dog, a brown wren. Jenny glowered at him and tapped the watch on her wrist. "Hate to interrupt this reverie, but I have a client in ten minutes." She shot him a hard look. "Why are you here?"

"My little Jenny. So many sharp edges these days." Douglas shook his head sadly.

"I'm not your little Jenny anymore." She could feel her scalp prickle as her blood pressure rose. "Now what is it you wanted?"

Reaching in the pocket of his jacket, Douglas pulled out a black jewelry box, opened it and tilted it toward her. "Remember these, Jenny? You gave me these cufflinks shortly after I proposed. I... I wanted you to have them." Snapping the box, he slid it across the desk to her.

Jenny closed her eyes for a moment and touched her forehead with the heel of her hand. How had she almost married this man? "Why would you think I'd want these, Douglas?"

Douglas recoiled, his eyes grew wide. "I was cleaning out some of my old things and came across them. Aiden is big on minimalist living and helping me declutter my apartment. She suggested I take what I don't need any more to the thrift store."

Yup. Douglas had never said the words *minimalist* or *declutter* before in his whole life. Jenny knew whose words he was parroting. So Aiden wanted all traces of the ex-fiancée gone so she could pretend that she was Douglas's first big and only love.

Douglas went on, oblivious. "I knew these were expensive and had sentimental value and wanted to offer them to you. I don't need them anymore," he said magnanimously.

Jenny picked up the black leather box, jerked her arm back and launched it at him.

He ducked but she'd grazed his temple. Rubbing his forehead

he scrambled to his feet, looking affronted. "What is wrong with you, Jenny?"

She'd never ever thrown anything at anyone, and Jenny kind of liked the scared look in his eyes. Maybe she'd start throwing things and smacking people more often. Crossing her arms, she glared at him. "Why would you think I'd want your stupid old cufflinks? So I could gaze at them mournfully and regret losing you? Well, guess what? I don't miss you."

"Aiden said you'd be bitter." Eyeing her carefully, he straightened his tie and picked the jewelry box off the floor. "I was just trying to be nice."

"Well, stop it," she said. "And Douglas, I was never a brown wren or a faithful old hound dog. Never." Standing, she stabbed a finger toward the door. "Go."

He huffed out, an indignant look on his face.

Waiting for the adrenaline to dissipate, Jenny rocked back in her chair and thought about it. Douglas's first wife, Karen, had left him after six years of marriage *for no apparent reason* he'd always claimed. Jenny now guessed it was because of his emotional cluelessness, but was it that another long-legged young nymph had caught his eye and helped him out of his marriage? But Jenny's gut told her he wasn't a real cheater. There was truth in what he said. He and Aiden *did* have a special connection Jenny and Douglas hadn't. She shut her eyes and rubbed them with her fingers. Douglas had a daughter Hannah who lived with her mother and spent as little time as she could with Douglas. Why hadn't Jenny asked more questions about all of these relationships? Another regret to add to the tall pile.

Jenny rose, stretched and rolled her shoulders, then inhaled and exhaled a few deep breaths. She'd just calm down and think about her day. Her next student after Kaylee would be Riley, who skimped on studying and played video games with names like *Dragon Warriors* and *Eternal Apocalypse* until the early hours of the morning. He was sleepy in his classes and had drowsed off during their last session.

Her last client was Caleb, one of her success stories. When he first came to see Jenny, the young man had been barely passing despite having an IQ of 130. Because Jenny had worked with him on organization and study habits, Caleb had just made honor roll.

Staring out the window at nothing, Jenny tipped her chair back on two legs and thought about it. All the young people she worked with would make some progress. There were predictable kinds of parents: The overinvolved ones. The ones who pushed the kids hard to be all they hadn't attained in their lives. The status seekers laser focused on getting their kids into an Ivy League school. The neglectful, preoccupied or clueless parents. Some would defend or explain away their child's bad habits. Others would yell at their kids or berate Jenny about their child not improving rapidly enough. Often, these were the parents who ended up crying in her office about their disintegrating marriages. Jenny knew the signs and symptoms for learning disabilities, eating disorders, autism, depression, and substance abuse. She wasn't afraid to make the call to the parents and refer a student to a mental health professional. In the years she'd been tutoring, Jenny had seen most everything and was good at what she did.

Here's how it would always go. Jenny would make progress with the kids, their grades would improve and they'd move on. A few would text her over the next year, but she'd fade from their memory as they got into the University of North Carolina or N.C. State, landed a good job, married and moved into their first home. They'd build joyful, rich, rewarding lives and she'd...be stuck here.

With coolly assessing eyes, she glanced around her office, the one that she'd been so proud of when she'd first signed the lease. The sun had faded the swirls of blue paisley fabric on the couch, the carpet had a dingy path worn into it by kids who never wiped their feet, and her framed diploma from N.C. State hung slightly crookedly on the wall. Jenny picked at a cuticle, and felt a wave of sadness. Her little office had gotten dumpy and worn and smelled faintly of teenaged boys' feet.

Jenny raked her hair back with her fingers and shivered as she thought about her likely future. Was she going to keep doing what she'd always done year after year and wait for the next crop of students until she was stoop-shouldered and even grayer? Would she beaver away until she was drained of all the joy and juice God had allotted her and drew her first Social Security check? Maybe she was too old to make a change.

Tipping back in her chair, Jenny looked around the room moodily and her eyes rested on the postcard from Mama that she'd taped to her computer monitor. Peeling it off, she examined it more closely. The Greek island of Mykonos was bathed in golden sunlight, and whitewashed homes with bright blue doors surrounded a harbor full of colorful fishing boats. Flipping it over, Jenny re-read the message her mother had scrawled.

> *Our Adriatic and Greek Isles cruise is heavenly. Traveling on small ship this time, The Seafarer.*
>
> *Mikonos achingly lovely. Landis enjoying seeing sights, but highlight for him so far: he found a fellow college football fan and managed to watch the South Carolina - Florida game Saturday. Ah, men! Embrace your life, darling. Mama*

Jenny tapped the card on her palm and thought about it. After living with Daddy and knowing she could not count on him, Mama had finally found a good man when she was in her mid-fifties and made a happy life. Though her communication with Jenny consisted mainly of cheerful lines from various ports of call, each postcard contained a message about the importance of making yourself happy. *Embrace your life.*

Jenny thunked her chair back down on all four feet and felt a crazy, wild excitement burning in her chest. No, ma'am, she was not going to keep on doing what she had always done.

Pushing her shoulders back, Jenny felt a surge of determination. She had a SEP-IRA that she'd never ever touched and a little nest egg in a CD at the bank. She'd been hardworking and dutiful, and she was sick of not being happy. Jenny put a hand to her mouth

38

as it all sunk in. Holy Moses. Now was the time she needed to get living.

She'd give notice on this dumpy little office and move to the lake. Jenny Beckett was going to hunt down joy and a sense of freedom and do whatever she wanted to do. Little brown wren, her behind. She was a free soaring bird, like the osprey she'd seen gliding gracefully across the sky at Heron Lake.

CHAPTER 5 — MONEY, HONEY

S ATURDAY EVENING, JENNY PUT THE clean butterhead and red leaf lettuce in the salad spinner, whirled them around, and dumped them into a large bowl. With Levi standing beside her watching her every move and the dogs' looking hawk-eyed at her from their beds hoping she'd drop a tasty morsel, Jenny shook her head. "You're greedy men," she called affectionately as she handed them each a carrot. Adding roasted pecans, sliced beets, mushrooms, carrots, and bell peppers, Jenny tossed the salad and scraped in the shredded rotisserie chicken she'd bought at the grocery store. Charlotte was on another diet, and though Jenny couldn't keep up with the food requirements that changed every two weeks, she could at least fix a spread that was fairly healthy.

Jenny heard a car and stepped outside, the dogs and Levi following closely behind. Grinning, she stood on the porch and raised a hand as Charlotte approached.

The apple hadn't fallen far from the tree with regard to living frugally, Jenny thought with a smile as she watched her waving friend wheel up in an older model car that her father had helped her buy from the rental car company when they retired their fleet. The sedan was a faded green four-door, with a basketball-sized dent in the right driver's side panel. None of this fazed Charlotte one bit. Yes, she drove a beater of a car, and few but Jenny knew that her friend was wealthier than her parents, thanks to the Berkshire Hathaway stock that Beau and Nell had bought their daughter every year for each of her forty-five birthdays. Charlotte never needed to work a day in her life, and that was without taking into account the bundle she'd inherit from her parents. But she shopped with coupons, and every week, always knew where the cheapest place in town was to buy gas.

"Hello, girly girl. Hello, you handsome men," Charlotte called, stepping out of the car and raising her sunglasses to her head as she grabbed bags of groceries from the back seat.

Dressed in black jeans and a heavy Icelandic sweater the color of Damson plums, Charlotte had glossy black curls and rosy skin. She was perfectly proportioned in a lush, Sofia Loren way. Jenny shook her head, mystified as to why Charlotte berated herself about her weight. Knowing that pointing this out would lead to her friend's detailed explanation of what her ideal weight should be for her height and why men did not like big girls, Jenny just hugged her. "You look wonderful, as always."

Charlotte waved away the compliment, but gave her a grateful look. "I can't wait to hear all your news." The dogs swarmed around Charlotte as she followed Jenny into the house.

The two loaded up their plates, grabbed glasses of wine and, since the temperature had risen to the low-fifties, they decided to bundle up and sit at the small bistro table on the back stoop to eat their suppers. Not quite ready to talk about her possibly wacky decision, Jenny tucked her napkin in her lap and said, "Tell me something good. How are your classes coming?"

"Great," Charlotte said with a smile and paused for a moment to take a sip of wine. "Despite all the time I put into my beauty consultant career..."

Four months, Jenny thought but wisely took a forkful of salad instead of speaking.

Charlotte touched her thumb enumerating. "Selling cosmetics was just not for me." She rolled her eyes. "My friends started dodging my calls, and I never got even remotely close to the pink blazer sales circle. Not my thing." Squinting, she counted off on her forefinger. "Soy candles. The fire was not my fault." Middle finger. "Real estate. I had to work weekends." She shuddered prettily. Ring finger. "Landscape design. They expected me to dig in the dirt, and work even in the rain." Pinkie. "Dental hygienist school. I am not cut out for cleaning other people's teeth, especially ones who I assure you did not floss every night. Gack." Charlotte's nose scrunched and she looked pained at the memory. "But I think this staging/designer thing might really be right for me."

"Tell me about your classes," Jenny said, using the toe of her boot to rub Bear, who had managed to squirm his bulky self underneath the tiny table.

"I like the fact that we are mainly using the client's own stuff, instead of going out and spending a ton of money buying new and fancy furnishings. And when you see the difference..." Charlotte rattled on, her face animated. When she wound down, she smiled at Jenny and, looking like she was afraid she sounded fatuous, said, "This just feels like I've finally found the right fit."

"Good," Jenny said encouragingly. Charlotte's career path had been a real zig-zagger up to this point. "Sounds like the perfect blend of creativity and practicality." Charlotte *did* sound excited about her courses and had rearranged Jenny's cramped living room twice, improving the feel of the space each time. "No point in working a job you don't like, not if you can help it," Jenny said slowly, thinking about her freshly-hatched and possibly foolish decision to jettison her tutoring business. She looked at Charlotte. "I need a new career. I need a fresh start."

"You do," Charlotte said in a matter-of-fact tone as she poured more salad dressing. "Your hound dog of a fiancé swans off with a big-haired man-stealer and Earl-the-rat kicks you out. You're tired of your work life. Then you get the inheritance from the grave." Crunching a crouton, she gave Jenny a mischievous smile. "Being friends with you is better than watching those family sagas on Netflix. But it makes sense that you're ready for a change."

Jenny sipped the delicious Margaret River Chardonnay, a *Me Booster* purchase she'd found on sale for eight bucks. Hesitating, she met Charlotte's eyes. "I have an idea that's kind of crazy."

"Those are the best kind." Eyes wide, Charlotte leaned forward. "Do tell."

"What if I changed every single thing in my life?" Tilting her wineglass, Jenny gazed at it as if it were a crystal ball. "I'm thinking about putting Jax's house on the market and selling it, transferring all my clients to other tutors and shutting down the business. Then, I could move to the Lakeside Resort, finish the cabins and rent them as weekend getaways."

Charlotte's face fell. "Oh, no. You can't move out of town."

Jenny felt a pang of sadness at the thought of not living so close to her friend. "Heron Lake is just over an hour away and you and I will always be friends. We'll be in touch all the time, just like now. I promise." She patted Charlotte's hand reassuringly.

"You better mean that." Squint-eyed, Charlotte glared at Jenny, then broke into a smile and rubbed her hands together. "So, show me pictures of the cabins and your daddy's house."

Relieved that her best friend didn't think her idea was a huge mistake, Jenny slid her chair closer to Charlotte's. Pulling the phone from her pocket, Jenny scrolled through the shots. "First, the lake."

Charlotte flipped through and whistled appreciatively. "My stars! Those views will take your breath away, and the cabins are super precious. I mean it." She put a hand to her chest. "And those cabins were built by your very own daddy."

"The same daddy who ditched me on his last visit?" Jenny smiled crookedly.

"Good point." Charlotte forked in the last bites of her salad and chewed slowly, looking contemplative. "You know the Pinterest board I have for my favorite places to honeymoon?"

"I do." Jenny felt a pang of compassion for Charlotte who dearly wanted to marry again, but mucked it up every time. On her last date, she'd pulled up her *Honeymoon Ideas* board right after the entrée. The fellow went to the men's room and slipped out a side door.

Charlotte was spinning through her phone. "Here is one I made for *Cabins and Cottages for Honeymoon*. Guess how much these rent for a night?"

"No idea," Jenny said, guessing she'd soon know.

Her friend showed her pictures of small cabins with a long-range view of a valley. "One fifty a night and you're off a busy highway." The next was a small Victorian cottage. "This one's on a big chunk of land. Two hundred a night off season, and they don't have waterfront or your amazing views."

Doing the math in her head, Jenny's pulse quickened. She leaned in, peering more closely at the photos.

A charming ski chalet-styled guest cabin was next. "Three fifty a night. It's on the side of Black Balsam Bald up in the mountains and they cater to honeymooners. The place has a small Jacuzzi tub. They strew rose petals on the bed, throw in a bottle of Prosecco and bump up the bill by fifty or sixty bucks," Charlotte said with a knowledgeable nod.

Jenny stared at the screen, incredulous. "Summer lasts about ninety days. If I charge one twenty five or one fifty and only rent three for every night, that's thirty or forty thousand dollars?"

Charlotte bobbed her head. "Once you get established, you could probably rent more of them, make even more per night during the summer, and work on getting off-season guests."

Jenny rubbed her chin, ideas whirling around in her head. "Maybe we could do a Valentine's Weekend, an Anniversary Weekend, or a Busy Couples' Retreat."

Charlotte nodded enthusiastically, but then scowled. "Let's not get all carried away with the couples and forget about the single folks. That steams my grits when everyone makes a big fuss over the marrieds and treats us singles like we're pathetic leftovers."

Jenny agreed. "How about getaways for sisters, girlfriends, or authors writing for a deadline?"

"I love it!" Charlotte held up her hand for a high-five, and Jenny slapped it, grinning.

The dogs milled about her feet, and Levi ambled over to rest his sweet head on her knee. Jenny gently scratched his soft muzzle. "These boys want us to go for a walk before the sun sets. Help me keep brainstorming."

In the galley kitchen, they dropped their dishes and silver in a pink tub of warm soapy water and headed down the long driveway. Levi kept pace with the women, but the dogs darted off, yipped and barked their heads off and then circled back to them, smiling and panting.

Jenny stuck her hands in her pocket, frowning. "On most of those cabin shows and DIY shows, the buyers are all young, attractive, fit, and hip. That's not the crowd I want us to target in our marketing."

"We could put a *Plain Folks Only* sign out," Charlotte suggested helpfully.

Jenny ignored her. "We want to welcome all ages and all types of singles, couples, and families." She paused. "We want the readers, the campfire-sitters, the peace-seekers."

"Don't forget the curvy girls and the husky guys." Looking serious, Charlotte held up a hand. "Here is a rule. No ladders to the cabin lofts. They pose a hazard for anyone who needs to tee-tee in the middle of the night without falling."

"Noted. No ladders to the loft bedrooms." Jenny matched her pace with Charlotte's, and pulled her to one side to avoid a pothole. "We need to make the cabins handicapped accessible with wide doorways and ramps."

"I love that." Charlotte pointed at Jenny. "How's this? Every once in a while, we could have disability friendly weekends. All the parents of kids with autism and developmental disabilities can relax and not worry about anyone being upset by their kids' quirks."

Jenny knew Charlotte's nephew had high-functioning autism and was a part of the population dear to her heart. "I agree. Our website and marketing materials should show all sorts of regular people."

"We'll do that." Charlotte gave an excited little skip.

Jenny noticed they were both using plural pronouns and hid a smile. "So, it's *we* and *us* now?"

"Of course it is," Charlotte said indignantly. "I love, love, love this idea and I want to help you in any way I can." She beckoned with her fingers in a gimme gesture. "Show me Jax's house."

Jenny stopped, fished the phone from her pocket and pulled up the photos.

"Whoa," Charlotte said in a reverent tone. "She's a neglected Plain Jane now, but this bungalow has great bones." She fanned her face with her hand in excitement. "I cannot believe how cute,

cute, cute this house could be! This has so much potential for someone's happily ever after home." Charlotte held up a hand and partially closed her eyes. "I'm seeing an older professional couple with money. They'll want a fire pit, a she-shed and an endless pool so he can swim laps and not have a heart attack and die young."

Jenny grinned, and enlarged the pictures of the yard. Easy-peasy, there was room for a pool and a shed.

"Did you know that a staged house with curb appeal and fresh paint will get a seller twenty percent more than a house that's sold as is?" Charlotte asked importantly and then grinned. "Learned that in my *Setting the Stage for the Sale* class." She peered more closely at the photos. "This house is an absolute dollhouse and, woo hoo, do people dig Craftsman homes these days. I don't care if it's located in Hicktown."

Jenny thought about it. "The lawyer said I could get more money for the house if I updated it instead of selling it as is, but I don't have the five thousand dollars he said it might cost to do that."

Charlotte grabbed Jenny's wrist, her eyes wide. "This is what I *do* now. I could turn this house into a cream puff for a lot less money than that. Remember, the more money you get for the house, the more you have to finish the cabins."

Jenny considered it. "I know you're talented, but the market isn't good in Celeste."

Ignoring that pesky detail, Charlotte's face lit up. "A before-and-after deal would be perfect as the big final project in my *Staging Masters* class. I could take a bunch of photos along the way and build my website and album for my staging and design business."

Jenny rubbed her other fingers against her thumb. "Money, honey. I'll need money."

"You give me thirty-five hundred dollars for supplies, and I'll do it for free. I need credibility if I'm going to get my future business off the ground." Charlotte shot her a speculative look, and kicked her way through a pile of leaves. "Here's the deal. Ask your lawyer to have two realtors suggest a list price as is, and give me a couple of weeks. I'll go up with a few of my teammates from class, we'll spruce it up. Any money you make above and beyond the number the realtors' suggest, I'll take a ten percent cut."

Jenny looked out across the meadows. "Twenty percent, and you've got yourself a deal."

"Deal." Charlotte beamed. "My first real gig as a designer/ slash stager."

"I'll need all the help I can get." Jenny quickened her pace, buoyed by a feeling a fizzy excitement. But reality started to seep in, and she felt a jittery thrum of anxiety. "I'm planning on moving to a lake out in the middle of nowhere, taking on a big renovation, and managing rentals when I have no experience at all. And then I'll need beds and a website and who knows what else." Jenny put a hand on either side of her head, feeling like it could explode.

"You'll figure it out. I'll be your designer, sheet changer, reservation taker, or whatever you need," Charlotte promised.

Jenny kicked a rock with the toe of her boot and looked at her friend. "Am I foolish to think I could make this idea work? Is it too late for a do-over?"

Charlotte gazed intently at her. "You can do this, Jenny Beckett. I know you can. This will be the adventure of a lifetime and a chance for a fresh start."

Jenny nodded slowly, wanting to let herself be reassured by Charlotte's words. But the doubts crept back even stronger as they headed home.

After Charlotte left, Jenny changed into her nightgown, poured the last of the Margaret River into her favorite Flintstone glass and slipped into bed. The dogs jumped up to join her and Jenny clicked through her favorite shows she'd DVR'd. On the show about the tiny houses, a couple who were traveling nurses wanted to build what looked like a tiny farmhouse to tow around so they wouldn't have to find a short-term rental for their out-of-town jobs. Soon, the grinning couple sat on top of their portable, red-roofed farmhouse, their legs dangling over the side. The *Barn Salvagers* carefully dismantled an old barn in Pennsylvania, and put it back together in Georgia. Newly rebuilt around a tree, the new/old barn turned out to be a stunner with a recording studio and a retractable dance floor. On her favorite show, *Maine Cabin Masters*, Chase, Ashley, Ryan and the crew rode jet skis to the work site, sized up repairs and brought the decrepit-looking summer camp back to life.

So smart, Jenny marveled as she turned off the TV. People on these shows were not rule followers. They were following their hearts, trying something that intrigued them, following a dream that other people might think was crazy.

Jenny felt a fizzy buzz of excitement as she imagined finishing the cabins and living on the property. She'd be out of this fishbowl of a town and get to look at that glorious lake any time she wanted to. She brushed her teeth, her mind racing. She could tow the Airstream up there and put it closest to the finished cabin. Until she had a chance to install fencing, Jenny could walk Bear, Buddy and Levi. The trailer would give the boys a place to bunk as the temperature dropped. Later, she could fix it up and make it her living space. Then, all eight of the cabins would be income producing. Smoothing coconut oil on her arms and legs, Jenny smiled as she pictured herself wearing a gingham dress and a red calico head scarf, loading a bumper crop of vegetables from her raised-bed garden into a red Radio Flyer wagon and pulling it back to her Airstream home. Outside, a big handsome guy who was, in fact, her new husband would be chopping firewood in a very manly way and he'd smile a special smile at her. *Let me help you with that, sweet pea,* he'd say and take the wagon handle from her.

Climbing into bed, Jenny closed her eyes and smiled as she replayed that delicious domestic scene. If she were brave enough and worked harder than she'd ever worked in her life, she just might be able to make that dream come true. The Lakeside Resort could give her financial freedom and a new home sweet home.

But before she drifted off, Jenny had one last thought. What if I'm about to make the biggest mistake I've ever made in my life?

CHAPTER 6 — THE GREAT ESCAPE

JENNY'S SLEEP WAS RESTLESS, PUNCTUATED by vivid dreams. The chinking that seals the gaps between the logs of cabins and makes it watertight turned out to be made of flour and the logs collapsed when a hard rain fell. Next, she was begging for a living, standing at an intersection, holding a sign that read, *Old. Need money. Failed at my business. Bless you and have a nice day.* Jenny woke tired and with gut-wrenching doubts about her plan.

After she let the boys out and fed them, Jenny decided she'd stay in her flannel pajamas and work on shaking off her fears. Making a to-do list always helped. Jenny took a cup of coffee back to bed. The dogs hopped up to join her and she propped herself on pillows, breathing slowly in and out and trying to vanquish thoughts of collapsing cabins and a begging career. Clicking her pen open and closed, she wrote:

- Close tutoring practice and refer clients.

Jenny would make calls this afternoon. She'd miss her students, and they'd miss her until they moved on to the next mini-drama in their lives. Her colleagues would be thrilled to inherit her clients.

- Tell office landlord that you're leaving. Clean out office.

Jenny had been renting so long that the landlord had her on a month-to-month lease, so no great loss or complicated situation there.

- Call Ashe and get ball rolling on sale of house. Ashe and Charlotte ♡ ???

Jenny grinned, picturing Cupid with his bow drawn. She'd work on it.

- Apply for a construction loan. Need cash for renovations until Daddy's house sells.

Wincing, Jenny pictured a staid banker flipping his toupee at her request, but she had to do it.

Taking a last sip of her lukewarm coffee, Jenny thought nervously about the big missing piece of the puzzle. She needed construction help, and it couldn't cost a fortune,

Picking up the phone, Jenny found Luke's number. Was he just being polite when he offered to help in any way he could, or did he mean it? To whet Luke's curiosity, she texted him two long-range shots of the cabins and, screwing up her courage, called him. Though she was hoping it would go to voice mail so she wouldn't have to hear one more man tell her *no*, Luke picked up.

"Hey, Jenny." Luke's voice had a warm timbre. "I just got your cool pictures."

Good. He thought they were cool. Jenny tried to sound confident. "Hey, Luke. I've inherited eight small cabins at Heron Lake and am hoping you and Alice could help finish them out." He may as well know the whole problem so he could run for the hills if he wanted to. "I have a shoestring budget and I need the cabins to be ready for renters by December 15th, two weeks before Christmas." Jenny's heart was trying to pound its way out of her chest as she waited for his answer.

"Let me just double check my calendar." He paused, apparently glancing at his Outlook. "This works. We might well be interested. I'd be glad to take a look at the place,"

Jenny tried to sound matter of fact as she made plans to meet him at the cabins on Tuesday morning, while inside she was cheering and doing cartwheels. His quote could be too high or he might decide he didn't want to take it on, she reminded herself. But his interest and his calling the pictures *cool* had buoyed her spirits.

Next, Jenny dialed Ashe Long. "I'm going to take your suggestion about staging." After she relayed her plan and he'd responded with restrained enthusiasm, Jenny went on. "And Ashe, my friend Charlotte is a fledgling stager and designer who is coming up Tuesday with some helpers to size up the work. Although she seems friendly, she is almost cripplingly shy." Jenny choked a bit, telling that big `ole lie. "Charlotte needs a lot of encouragement and praise. I hate to impose, but if you could be especially supportive of her, I'd be so grateful." Ashe readily agreed to help Charlotte out in any way he could. Such a nice man. With so many worries weighing on her, Jenny knew she was looney to be matchmaking but she just had a feeling about the two of them. Charlotte deserved to be happy.

Jenny made herself go down to the barn, where the old Airstream sat parked under a blue tarp. Hands on hips, she stood a few feet away and gave herself a pep talk. It's just a trailer, not Jax's inner sanctum. She wasn't rifling through his private possessions. The night he skipped out of his beautiful, father-daughter reunion, he'd left a bill of sale for the Silver Belle on her kitchen counter and a note signing it over to her. The beat up Airstream was all hers.

Outside, Jenny unhooked the bungee cords that held the blue tarp on the trailer like an old lady's plastic rain bonnet and pulled it off, ducking away from the slimy cold water that poured from pockets and sags in the heavy plastic.

Unlike the brightly gleaming silver Airstream trailers with the whitewall tires that she'd seen on Pinterest, the ones that had been lovingly restored by starry eyed, cool-cat young couples, this one was dented and looked like it'd been through a golf ball-sized hail storm like the ones on Weather Channel.

But if Jenny squinted her eyes and didn't look at the details, the shape of the trailer was graceful and had a fifties feel to it, like an old Cadillac with extravagant fins or the gleaming, pearly Lockheed Electra that Amelia Earhart had flown. Though it wasn't much to look at, the trailer was the answer to her need for a temporary bunk house for Levi in the cold weather. Maybe Buddy and Bear would hang out with him and it would become a man cave.

Gathering courage, Jenny stood up straighter and found the key. She'd never been in the Silver Belle. Once she realized that Daddy had taken a runner, she'd been so mad at him that she'd just had a neighbor maneuver the RV in beside the barn, locked it, and decided to let it sit until she had the energy to figure out how to sell it.

Unlocking the door, Jenny tried to open it, but it was stuck. Jiggling the key, she grasped the lever with two hands and yanked it open. Feeling shaky, Jenny hesitated, picturing a hoarder's lair with stacks of old newspapers as walls and bags and bags of molding garbage. Maybe a pair of raccoons or copperheads had moved in and started families. Bracing herself for anything, Jenny stepped inside.

No trash or animals or reptiles. Whew. The trailer was tidy and well laid out, but looked empty. The stove, refrigerator and cabinets had been removed from the kitchen area. A jackknife sofa was attached to the wall, and Jenny guessed it pulled down and served as Jax's bed. A turquoise blue Formica table and two matching leatherette chairs were secured to the wall with straps. In a basket on the floor was a stack of magazines called *Airstream Renovation Today*. Jenny picked up one from the pile and blew the dust off. It showed a clean cut, dad-looking man in a plaid shirt and a tool belt installing new cabinets in an Airstream. Jenny smiled. In addition to the cabins, Daddy was planning on fixing up the trailer, too. He just ran out of time to finish his dreams. She leaned against the door frame and looked around. This would do fine.

Back in the cottage, Jenny drew a deep breath, took the boxes she'd collected from the ABC Store and the grocery store, and started packing. She'd take a load down when she met with The Hammonds.

Grunting, she managed to heave a velveteen armchair and Ottoman that had belonged to her grandmother into the back of the SUV and slowly tucked full boxes around it. Finally, she shut the cargo door, tired but pleased with her progress.

When the sun moved lower in the sky, Jenny put her rice, cheese, and beans frozen dinner in the microwave and mentally reviewed her plan. As much as she hated to leave her sweet chicken coop haven, she had to get moving. Jenny would take a load when she met with Luke and Alice. Tomorrow, she'd finish packing what she could and make sure she spoke with every tutoring client's mom or dad to finish closing her practice. Tuesday, she'd tow the Silver Belle to Heron Lake and leave it for now. Later, she could build a pole tent for Levi just like the one she'd seen being built on YouTube.

But for now, she and the boys were going to have to be as flexible as Gumby and not whine when they had to rough it. They *would* be roughing it. Jenny sat down with her steaming dinner, shook her head, and sent up a quick prayer that Luke and Alice would agree to help with the cabins. She still couldn't believe she was committing herself to such a shaky plan. But she was. One thing she knew for sure, these next couple months were going to be doozies.

Bright and early Tuesday morning, Jenny filled her stainless steel travel mug with coffee, freshened the boys' drinking water, and squeezed one more box into the SUV.

Charlotte's green sedan pulled into the driveway. In the misty light of morning, her friend bounced over to Jenny. Instead of saying hello, she burbled, "I'm tickled pink about this staging project." Charlotte hooked a thumb toward her car. "Two of the smartest cookies in my class agreed to come along to help me with Jax's house."

"Good. I asked Luke and his sister to help finish the cabins." Jenny held up crossed fingers.

"Yay!" Charlotte bounced on her toes like a kid who'd gotten into their Trick or Treat stash. "I hope they say yes."

"Me, too. I'll know later on today," Jenny said, an unexpected stomach clench making her realize just how keyed up she was about them agreeing to help. "So, y'all can follow me until I take the lake exit. When you get to the house, keep in touch and you can do all that you talked about with me but remember our skimpy budget."

"Oh, I promise on my parents' graves," Charlotte breathed.

Jenny grinned. Beau and Nell were alive and kicking and eating All Bran and drinking coffee about now, but she caught her friend's gist. "Remember to check in every step of the way with the attorney, Ashe Long. He needs details and updates regularly to comply with the terms of the trust." She had no idea what *comply with terms of the trust* meant and might have seen it on *For the People*, but she said it gravely.

"Oh, I will," Charlotte said earnestly.

Jenny climbed back in her car, shaking her head at herself. If there was chance of a tiny spark developing with Charlotte and Ashe, the constant contact might be enough to get it ignited. "I am an evil genius," she said quietly, toasting herself with her coffee.

Their small convoy set off. The headlights of the green sedan were welcome company on the drive. As Jenny turned on her blinker at the turnoff for Heron Lake, Charlotte gave a cheerful toot-toot of her car horn and the girls hooted and waved wildly from the rolled down windows as they exited I-40 and continued north up Route 468 to Celeste.

Jenny stuck an arm out the window and waved. Those two would be high-energy, fun helpers for Charlotte's fix up. They would begin work today and hopefully have Jax's house ready to put on the market soon. Ka-ching. Money was crucial, especially after Luke's visit today when he gave her the go or no go and the estimated cost for finishing the cabin.

Jenny held her breath as she pulled the heavily laden SUV into the driveway of the Lakeside Resort. She was gambling her whole future on cabins she'd seen only once and never even been inside. What if they weren't as charming as she remembered? What if she'd been overly optimistic on her first visit and they were dumpy, ugly, or even unsalvageable?

When she stepped out, she felt weak with relief. The cabins were just as darling as she remembered. The last of the morning mist hugged the lake like a delicate Angora sweater and the wide blue view from the bluff was phenomenal. Jenny paused for a moment and let herself feel the peace and beauty of the spot.

Feeling like a trespasser, Jenny unlocked the cabin Jax had finished. It was dark and a damp cold inside. Shivering, Jenny kicked herself for not remembering to get the power and water turned on. A woman with a long to-do list, Jenny didn't waste any time looking around. She worked quickly, unloading boxes and furniture. Huffing with effort, she humped and wrestled her belongings inside and pushed them into a pile in the living room. When she finished, she was damp with perspiration but was proud of what she'd accomplished. Without a backward glance, Jenny headed back outside.

The wind off the water was chilly as she scoured the ground for dead limbs and branches and started a pile. With a shovel she'd brought from home, she dug a shallow pit in a sandy spot a safe distance from the cabins and laid a small fire. As the flames licked the twigs and caught, Jenny warmed her hands, feeling inordinately proud of herself. From a box she'd brought from home, Jenny pulled out a jug of water, mugs and a Coleman stove. She *fired up the stove,* as the camping guys drinking beer on the YouTube video had said, and heated water.

Beside the fire, Jenny arranged the two short lawn chairs she'd found in the Silver Belle. Both had a few pieces of broken webbing, but she tried one out. Jenny's bottom touched the sand and both knees clicked when she sat down, but the smell of burning wood reminded her of a happy two weeks she'd spent one summer at Girl Scout camp in the mountains. She touched the metal arms. The chairs would do fine.

Jenny made a cup of Joe with a coffee teabag, and sipped it. Pretty darn good. Back home, she'd have turned up her nose at coffee like this, but not here on her lofty perch on Heron Lake. It was a glorious, crisp, fall morning, she was on the water, and, so far, her plan was on track.

When Luke's dark blue Chevy truck pulled into the clearing and he stepped out, Jenny's heart lifted. Her knees cracking as she rose from the low chair, Jenny hurriedly brushed sand off the seat of her pants. "Morning, Luke," she called, her voice hoarse with nerves.

"Morning, Jenny." He lifted his sunglasses to the top of his head and gazed at her with those blue eyes of his. He gave the cabins an appraising look. "I like this rise here, and the cabins sit perfectly on the lot. Great little project your daddy had going." Luke took his glasses off and polished them with the hem of his shirt. "How big did you say the lot was?"

"I'm not exactly sure," Jenny said. "There's almost four hundred feet of shoreline."

Luke whistled. "That's a lot of waterfront. If you haven't gotten a recent survey, you need one before we even start."

"Okay," Jenny said, adding a *Do Now!* section to her running mental to-do list. A thought that had been bugging her surfaced. "Why do you think it's named the Lakeside Resort instead of the Lakeside Cabins? I wonder if Jax was planning on making it fancy, like putting in a pool."

"Maybe. Or maybe your daddy or the previous owner wanted to put RV's on it. Lots of RV folks call campgrounds *resorts*." He hesitated and gave her a sympathetic look. "Not sure I said this, but I'm real sorry about your dad."

"Thanks." Jenny poured hot water in a mug and handed it to him along with a coffee bag. She sipped her coffee and then met his eyes. "My daddy, Jax, was a good guy, but my relationship with him was ...complicated."

"That can happen with people you love the most." Luke slipped his glasses back on.

Grateful he didn't pry and ready for a distraction, Jenny pulled the Billy Bob's Bait key ring from her jacket pocket and held it up. "You ready?"

"I am," he said. "Give me one minute." Luke strode over to the permits box, examined the papers inside and closed the door. "Everything is permitted and up to date," he said with satisfied nod.

"Good," Jenny said uncertainly. She hadn't even known to be concerned about permits.

The two of them headed to the cabin on the far end of the crescent.

Jenny unlocked the door. "I haven't even been in any of them except briefly in the one wired for power," she called to him from over her shoulder.

"Why not?" Luke pulled a notepad from his pocket and a small flashlight from his jacket.

"I was afraid I'd find a major problem and couldn't face it alone," she admitted, her face heating up. "On those house flipping shows, they find expensive problems like rotten foundations, or black mold, or terrible work." Jenny winced. "I also saw the shows with the boa constrictors loose in the house and the scorpion infestation. I just wanted someone to be here with me in case I..." She trailed off, feeling foolish.

"In case you got scared." Luke gave a half smile. "We can handle what comes up."

Luke had no idea how much she needed to hear those words. But he was not her rescuer, she reminded herself, and she knew nothing about him. He seemed nice, but so had Douglas at the get-go. Jenny wouldn't let herself be attracted to him. She hoped Luke whined, had foot odor and chewed with his mouth open. Bow legs and a hairy back would help, too.

Luke walked around inside, shone his flashlight in a few dark corners and whistled. "Sweet. Excellent view from any window. He's got the studs up. These metal roofs are top notch and everything looks dry." Luke pointed to a pile of sheet rock. "Looks like he was getting ready to start interior finishes."

Jenny perked up at that, fervently hoping this *we* meant he'd take on the project.

Luke tapped a finger on the glass of the small bay window that looked out at the lake and nodded approvingly. "Your dad sprang for double-paned windows. He was going for quality, not a cheap and fast build." Pointing to the robin's-egg blue, cast-iron wood stove on the rectangular, raised stone-work slab, he seemed impressed. "A Nilsson wood stove. I always wanted one of those. It burns efficiently and is easy on the environment."

Jenny felt a rush of pride about Daddy's work, but then that new sorrow of having underestimated him. She jammed her hand into her pockets.

Luke stuck his head into the next cabin, and she peeked in from behind him. The layout was the same as the one before. "Good layout. Solid workmanship," Luke said and moved on to the next.

At Jax's cabin, Luke worked around the heap of her stuff, poking around, taking notes, and muttering to himself while Jenny crouched outside, feigning nonchalance but feeling almost sick with anxiety. Though encouraged by Luke's comments about the work, she still had a knot the size of a tennis ball in her stomach, worrying. On the outside chance he said yes, how much would it cost? If Luke's quote was too high, she couldn't afford to finish the cabins, and her dreams about a new life would go up in smoke.

Athletically hopped off the stoop, he hooked a thumb over his shoulder. "You were right about this being a foreman's cabin. You're all wired up, you've got plumbing, and it's finished work. A good spot for you."

"Thank goodness." She tilted her head. "Can we make the cabins disability friendly?"

Luke tapped a finger on his chin. "It'll cost more, but we can widen door frames, install door levers and make the flooring easy for wheelchair use." He pointed to the back of the cabins. "We can add ramps on the side closest to the driveway."

"Good," Jenny said.

Examining the figures he'd scrawled in his notepad, he looked solemn. "Jenny, I have to tell you…"

His phone rang, though, and with an apologetic smile he answered it. Jenny breathed shallowly. Tell her what? That she should bulldoze the cabins and start from scratch? That they cost a million dollars to finish?

CHAPTER 7 — FIRESIDE CHAT

L UKE PRESSED THE PHONE TO his ear as he gazed out at Heron Lake. "Hey, sis. Yeah, I'm here." He paused. "No, you take a left at that fork. The one by the grain silo. Yeah." Luke glanced over at Jenny, giving her a crooked smile. "You'll dig it, Alice. It's a cool little project." He ended the call, giving Jenny a slow, sweet smile that sent a tingle up her spine.

Jenny blew out breath she didn't know she'd been holding and felt wobbly with relief. "So the job didn't scare you off?"

"The tight schedule does," Luke admitted. "Let's go sit by the fire and talk about it."

When Luke eased himself into the short lawn chair, his rear end, a particularly cute one, Jenny noticed, sat squarely on the ground but he didn't seem to mind. He gripped the aluminum arms of his chair and gazed appreciatively at the water. "I love this lake."

"I do, too." Jenny looked over at him. "I was so afraid you were going to say no."

"We'd be up for the job, but the December 15th deadline could be unrealistic." Luke squinted, and thought about it. "This is one tight time frame. Why do you want it done so quickly?"

Jenny just blurted it out. "Because I quit my job. I was burned out and closed down my tutoring practice." She pushed both hands through her hair and held it back a moment, afraid Luke thought she was flighty, but then plowed on. "I've got some savings, potential proceeds from a small house that may or may not sell quickly, and that's about it. I'll need to get a construction loan," she said, trying to sound braver than she felt.

Luke nodded slowly. "So you need to get the cabins ready for guests and the rental fees rolling in as quickly as you can, and thought there'd be a draw to spending the holiday on Heron Lake."

Hearing the blood in her ears thrum, Jenny was almost afraid to meet his gaze. Was this a cockeyed idea? What if everyone in the world wanted to be home for Christmas, enjoying their families, relatives, dogs and their own holiday traditions? What if she finished the cabins and no one came? "Do you think people would want to come here for Christmas?" she asked in a small voice.

Luke rubbed his chin. "I think they might," he said solemnly.

"But is it doable timewise?" Jenny held her breath, every muscle tensed.

Luke looked at his notes, his brow furrowed. "The cabins are basically sound and about sixty percent finished. We may be able to get the job done by December 15th if the weather holds, everything goes right, and we get lucky. But I'm not promising you anything, and Alice has to be in agreement about doing this or it's a no-go."

"Understood." Jenny let herself consider the very real possibility that the cabins wouldn't be ready for Christmas. Her words came out in a rush. "I'm a novice, but I'm going to pitch in and do whatever you need me to do. I'll carry things for you, pound nails, haul lumber, or shovel dirt. I promise I'll be a help to you." Out of breath now, Jenny held up crossed fingers. "Now tell me how much it'll cost."

Luke fished a pencil out from behind his ear and did math. "So we finish adding decks and porches and get to the interior work. We'll hang drywall, install hardwood floors downstairs and in the loft, and do trim work. We'll add cabinets, get contractors in to install countertops in the kitchen and bath, and finish out the electrical and plumbing. We need appliances and fixtures in the kitchen and bath, water heaters, and wall heat and AC units." Underlining his final tally, he showed her the figure. "Does this work for you?"

Jenny held her breath while she looked at the figures and they *were* high, but not astronomical. She'd done some research and known that finishing the project would be expensive. But the main thing was, Luke had agreed to take it on. Elated, Jenny fought the urge to throw her arms around his neck and hug him. Nodding vigorously, she leaned back into her lawn chair. "The numbers are workable. I'm hoping Alice is on board because I'd be thrilled if y'all helped me with this."

"Alice will be here in about ten minutes. If she's all in, we'll take the job." With a slow smile, he blasted her with his eyes, which looked cerulean today.

"Great," Jenny said but was distracted by a jolt of attraction. Alarm sirens starting going *whoop-whoop-whoop* in her head. No, ma'am. This was not happening. Best to nip it in the bud. "Just so you know, I don't much like men these days," she blurted, giving him a hard look.

"As long as you can work with one," Luke said mildly. Reaching for his mug, he poured himself another cup of hot water and snagged a coffee bag to dunk in it. "This coffee hit the spot. I'll bring my own cream and sugar when we start work, though."

Embarrassed now that she'd practically taken a megaphone and blared out her personal business, Jenny got up and tossed another log on the fire.

"So you're going to pull up stakes and move out here to the lake. Nothing holding you in Shady Grove?" Luke asked.

"Nope," Jenny said with more confidence than she felt. "I'm ready for a change in my life, work, living situation, everything." She looked away and then met his eyes. "My fiancé dumped me about nine months ago. We were planning on marrying at Christmas."

Luke grimaced. "I'm starting to get why you're not a big fan of Christmas."

"Christmas magic, my eye," she said grimly, sinking down in her chair. Jenny gave him a challenging look. "Do you want to know why he dumped me?"

"Only if you want to tell me." Luke's look conveyed interest, not judgment.

Jenny had no idea why she was talking so unguardedly this

morning, dishing up the lurid details of her life and offering them to a man she'd just met. But, she wanted to talk. "He lost interest in me. Called off the wedding because he thought he might be falling for his twenty-seven year old physical therapist. A month later, he told me she was the love of his life."

"Ouch," he winced. Looking thoughtful, he stretched out his legs and crossed his ankles. "Kind of a blow to the old pride, but if he even gave another woman a second glance when he was engaged to you, he was not the man for you."

Jenny looked at him, picking up on how definite he sounded. "You really think that?"

"I do." Luke spoke conversationally, as if commenting on the weather. "The guy's a fool."

Did Luke mean Douglas was a fool for missing out on her or because he'd been engaged and jilted her? Jenny felt the color rise in her face, guessing there was an implied compliment in what he said but doubting him. "Maybe we were too much of an odd match."

"How so?" Luke took a sip of coffee.

"Douglas was more outgoing, a guy who could talk with anyone and was a lot of fun. He was a people person. He even charmed the wary ones."

"Doubt he'd charm me," Luke drawled, half smiling but steely-eyed. He looked out at the lake. "How about you? What are you like, besides being adventuresome?" He tilted his head toward the cabins.

Hmm. Jenny tried on adventurous and liked it, picturing herself as Annie Oakley standing on a cantering horse shooting an apple off Wild Bill's head. "I like one-on-one talk, not crowds. I'm the quieter type who cares too much about things. I can't watch the news because it upsets me. I donate too much money to the SPCA. My ideal night is curled up in bed reading a novel with a happy ending." She gave a wry smile. "Douglas liked going out to dinner or having drinks with his friends and clients from work. But then he got into running big time and all he talked about was BMI and training schedules and weight work." She tried to smile but guessed it came out crooked. Yup, Douglas was popular and vital and she was boring. No wonder he'd bolted.

But Luke just lifted his shoulders in a noncommittal shrug. "Odd matches can work. What did you have in common?"

"Well," Jenny said lamely, feeling blood rush to her face. Her thoughts careened around. She couldn't think of one thing. "We both liked....shrimp," she said, triumphantly. "And Christmas lights and ..." Jenny furrowed her brow in concentration but she'd run out of gas.

"How about deeper things, like values?" he asked mildly, as he rested his coffee mug in the sand.

Jenny stared at her shoes and flushed, embarrassed. "We didn't talk much about values, but they must have been different. Like, faithfulness is really important to me."

"To me, too," Luke agreed.

"Why didn't we talk about those things?" she asked him, her voice coming out more plaintively than she'd intended.

"Maybe you just assumed you both had the same values," he said quietly.

She gave him a tight smile. "Douglas would claim he was a big fan of faithfulness, but then he met a woman that he said he was *destined to be with and you can't fight destiny.* Yuck." Jenny shook her head and looked at Luke with narrowed eyes. "I've been talking for one whole cup of coffee, and I don't know one thing about you."

"Fire away." He gave a half-smile, and leaned back in his lawn chair.

Jenny didn't like feeling so raw and vulnerable, though she was the one who'd volunteered so many personal details. "How about you? I'll bet you married young, are crazy about your wife."

"No wife," he said tightly, the muscles in his jaw working.

Jenny felt the heat of shame. She probably came off like a smart aleck when he'd been through a gut-wrenching divorce. "I didn't mean to sound flip. I know divorce can be..."

He held up a hand to stop her. "I'm widowed. I *did* marry young. I was *crazy* about my wife. Then I lost her almost three years ago. Chloe got an odd bloodwork result during a routine physical. No symptoms at all except for tiredness. We thought maybe she was anemic, but it turned out to be a rare form of cancer. They treated it, Chloe improved, it came back, and it got her. From the first test to her death, it was four months." His face was etched in stone.

Jenny winced, feeling a stab of sadness for him. "I'm so sorry," she said softly.

Luke stretched out his long legs and crossed one foot over the other. "Chloe was so healthy, too – a nutritionist and a part-time Pilates instructor. She had us eating healthy before it even got popular." His lips twitched as he thought about it. "Kale, chia seeds and cauliflower six different ways."

Jenny picked up a white pebble from the ground beside her chair and touched its smooth edges. "She sounds lovely."

"She was," Luke said softly and studied his palms.

"Any kids?" Jenny guessed this could be the only silver lining.

"No. We couldn't. We were just starting to investigate adoption when..." Luke trailed off, and looked into the distance with a thousand-mile stare.

Jenny paused. "Is that why you've taken a sabbatical? You wanted time to regroup?"

"Yes," he began but a horn sounded and a small, turquoise hybrid pulled in the clearing, *It's Beginning to Look a Lot Like Christmas* resonating from the speakers. It was Alice and she was grinning, her head poked out of the driver's side window, a wide indigo blue band holding back her wildly curling blonde hair. With a jaunty wave, she strode over to them. Jenny and Luke rose from their chairs. Jenny watched Luke raise a hand to greet his sister. Still a bit shaken at the serious ground she and Luke had covered in just a few minutes, Jenny smiled.

"Good morning, my lovelies," Alice called. She wore a lightweight blue down jacket, sturdy boots and overalls. Walking over to Jenny, she gave her a quick kiss on the cheek, punched her brother in the arm, and spun around wide-eyed. "This place is fantastic. The view is unbelievable and these little cabins are precious as could be. I just want to pick one up, put it in my pocket, and bring it home." Her hands on her hips, she got a dreamy look in her eye. "Maybe my honey and I could get married here." She gestured to the space in the center of the crescent of cabins. "We could set up a rose-covered trellis and have the ceremony outside. I've always wanted an awesome setting like this." Alice waved her arm in a looping motion to take in all the property.

Noticing the sparkler on her hand, Jenny smiled, trying to push away disappointment at the memories of her own ring, which was probably on the redhead's finger. "Congratulations, Alice. Who's the lucky guy?"

"Mike Hayes. We work together at the school. He teaches math and physical education and is a great guy," she said, sounding pleased, but Jenny thought she heard an undertone of wistfulness.

Gently taking Alice's hand, Jenny admired the ring. "So pretty. Now when are you getting married?" she asked, too late to catch the warning shake of the head Luke sent her.

Alice's shoulders slumped. She touched the ring, and looked away. "We're not sure. Well, Mike's not sure. He's one of those low-key guys who goes with the flow." Shaking her head, she gave a wan smile. "So, we've been engaged for almost a year and no sign of a wedding date." She held her hands palms up and looked exasperated. "We are like two peas in a pod and we're crazy about each other. I don't understand the holdup."

"Oh, dear." Jenny glanced at Luke for help but he had his hands shoved in his pockets and was whistling tunelessly. "That's frustrating," she said mildly.

"Really frustrating." She stomped a boot on the hard ground. "Mike says he'll know when the time is right, but I've known since I backed my car into the bumper of his truck on the first day of school." A smile played at the corners of her mouth at the memory. But her sunny look passed and she gave a wan smile. "If we want kids, we need to get a move on."

As Jenny racked her brain about how to change the subject without seeming too obvious, Luke saved her. He clapped his hands together. "Al, let me give you a rundown on what work

65

needs to be done." When he'd finished detailing the job, he looked at his sister questioningly. "So are you up for taking this on?"

Her eyes sparkling, Alice bobbed her head. "Absolutely. These cabins are adorbs and I think we'll have a blast fixing them up."

Jenny clasped her hands together and looked at Alice. "Thank you, thank you, and thank you. You don't know how much this means to me."

"We'll have a great time working together," Alice said, all smiles.

"We've got work to do and we're jawing away." Luke's words were softened by the twinkle in his eye. "We've got our deadline. We need to come up with a schedule, measure, get materials, fixtures and appliances ordered, line up subcontractors and get going." He walked purposefully toward the closest cabin.

"I'll tell you more about my soap opera later." Alice zipped up her coat and linked her arm in Jenny's as they followed Luke.

Luke and Jenny gave Alice the tour. "The plumbing, electrical, framing, and HVAC are roughed in."

"Good," Alice said.

Remembering Charlotte being so adamant about hazardous trips to the ladies' room in the middle of the night, Jenny asked, "Can we do wide, safe stairs instead of ladders? The cabins need to work for everyone."

"I think so." Luke scratched his head as he looked around at the space under the loft. "Let's get measurements, Al." Pulling a black and yellow tape measure from his pocket, Luke shot out tape and Alice held it, calling out specs to Jenny, who wrote the numbers down carefully and repeated back what she'd written to make sure she got it right.

"Ah. A measure twice, cut once kind of girl. Good," Luke said approvingly.

Jenny's pulse kicked up because of that small off-the-cuff compliment. Pitiful.

Alice was just as capable as her brother, correcting him mildly when she caught a mistake. Jenny liked the way Luke paused, rubbed his chin, and asked Alice what she thought would be the best way to handle a problem. Working with these two might be a lot of fun.

After finishing the tour of the last cabin, they stood in the clearing reviewing their plan.

"Jenny, how about you and Alice go to the big box home improvement store, and establish a line of credit. Put Alice and me down on the account as being authorized purchasers. Check with the store to make sure they can start delivering in just a few days." He paused, jotting down items in his notepad and ripping off the page to hand to Jenny. "If you can research online tonight and tomorrow and start making a list of the wood flooring, appliances and fixtures you like, I'll check your picks and we can order what you need."

Alice cocked her head at Luke. "Do the permits look good?"

"They do," Luke nodded. "We'll schedule final inspections for early December." He gazed at Jenny. "You'll need to get up with a banker and set up a construction loan."

"Okay." Jenny picked at a ragged fingernail as she considered the possibility of the bank turning her down for a loan. What would she do then? She wasn't tutoring anymore, so she had no income. Purchasing seven refrigerators, stoves, toilets and everything else on her to-buy list, she'd fast burn through her modest savings. Charlotte and her staging pixies had better be geniuses, because she'd need every penny she could make on the sale of Jax's house. "If you were a betting man, what would you say my chances are to be open for business by December 15th?" she asked, trying to keep the note of panic out of her voice.

Luke rested a hand on his hip. "75-25," he said. "That work for you?"

"That's fair," Jenny said. She could live with those odds.

He pulled his keys from his pocket. "We'll start Friday morning at 7:00."

"Oh, thank you so much, you two," Jenny breathed, flooded with relief.

"We'll have a ball," Alice said with a puckish grin and headed

67

toward the turquoise car. "I'll follow you over to the store in my car."

"Sounds good." Jenny paused to program the address for the store into her phone. As Luke walked away, she admired the scenery from behind her sunglasses. He was lean, rangy and athletic. She shook her head as if to clear it. The man was adorable, but strictly off limits. Jenny would keep things light and friendly, keep imagining he had a back as hairy as a brown bear's and terrible foot odor. When she paid him at the end, she'd never have to see him again.

CHAPTER 8 — GOODBYE CHICKEN COOP COTTAGE

J ENNY STEPPED IN HER CAR. As she pulled on her seatbelt, a bird flew toward her windshield and she froze, hoping it wouldn't crash into the glass. But the bird landed and just perched on the hood of her car. The pretty Carolina wren slanted her head almost shyly and gave Jenny an inquisitive look. "Hey, there," Jenny said softly. The wren had subtle but rich bronze plumage, a long, graceful tail that cocked up optimistically, warm brown eyes and white striped eyebrows. Riveted, Jenny watched the little bird hop toward the windshield, tap on the glass several times with its beak, and flutter off.

Jenny shook her head, marveling at the bird's friendly visit. Maybe Jax or God or the universe was sending her a promising sign. The wren was beautiful – not in a showy, pink flamingo way like a redhead with washboard abs and toned, mile-high legs but in a quiet, richly hued, understated way. If Douglas thought Jenny was a boring, run-of-the-mill wren, he'd never seen one close up because they were lovely. Still, when Jenny glanced in the rearview mirror and saw those gray hairs, she grimaced.

On the drive home from the big box store, Jenny planned to call her stylist, Star, who was a hair magician, amateur psychologist, and motivational speaker wrapped up in one. She could add some cinnamon to Jenny's shoulder-length brown hair and a few face-brightening highlights. Jenny had neglected herself, and it was time that stopped. She was, after all, a lovely Carolina wren.

The next afternoon, Jenny sat in a chair at the Sassy Southern

Gal Salon, eyeing herself in the mirror with distaste. Her hair was mousy, she had circles under her eyes, and she looked washed out. "Thanks for fitting me in, Star. This was kind of a hair emergency."

"Good to, sugar lump. Haven't seen you in a long while." Smiling encouragingly, Star whipped the red cape around Jenny like a matador and gave her hair a once over. She tutted. "We need to trim these ends and cut some shape back into your hair," she said, holding a hunk of Jenny's dark brown mane. "What were we thinking for color, darling? A few subtle highlights?" she asked, hip cocked as she gazed at Jenny in the mirror.

"I need some…pizzazz," Jenny said, holding up a magazine to show Star a picture of Isla Fisher and Emma Stone radiating auburn-headed beauty at a charity event. "If you can get me to look like any of these women, I'll be happy."

Star tutted. "I'm not going to let you get carried away. You have beautiful sable brown hair, just like Princess Kate. So pretty and thick. If you go *red red*, you'll be in here all the time needing touch ups." The stylist's eyes narrowed. "All right. What's up? Why the radical change?"

"I'm ready for a fresh start. My ex-fiancé left me for a young, big-haired athletic redhead," Jenny admitted.

Star rolled her eyes. "I swear, men can be dumb as dirt. I had another client two gals before you, the exact same story except the new girlfriend was the kids' babysitter. Barely legal," she snorted. "So I'll say to you what I said to her. No drastic revenge haircuts or colors. It'll come back and bite you in the fanny. Move on and let karma play out."

Jenny pinched a lip, doubtful.

Confiscating the magazine Jenny had been studying, Star put it on the counter. Twirling the chair around to look at her, the hairstylist spoke with quiet intensity. "You listen to me, sweet cheeks. You don't need to look like anyone else. You're pretty as a peach and just perfect the way you are. We'll just take off a few inches and add wisps of color to frame your face with light. You'll look even more gorgeous."

Jenny broke into a smile. "Good."

Star gave her one more pat and turned her chair back around to face the mirror. "Now sit back and enjoy the ride, honey bun. We're going to put some shine back on you."

An hour and a half later, Jenny's brown hair was silky and had shimmers of chestnut that shone through every time she turned her head. She practiced a few times. *Swish, swish.*

"Slow down, girly. You'll get whiplash." Star grinned as she gave Jenny's do a shot of spray. "Now go out and be yourself, Jenny Beckett. You're beautiful, inside and out."

"Star, you're the best," Jenny said. "I needed this."

"Thank you, darling. I have a man like your ex-fiancé in my rearview mirror," Star said with a cackling laugh. "Should have backed over him when I had the chance." With a mischievous grin, she pecked Jenny on the cheek and pushed her out the door. "Go toss that beautiful hair around."

Her shiny hair swinging around her shoulders, Jenny felt a new confidence. Time to go to the bank to apply for the construction loan.

Sterling Fairwood, the senior loan officer, was finishing up a phone call when the teller delivered Jenny to his door. He waved her in, holding up an *I'll-be-done-in-one-minute* finger. His corner office had lots of windows and a credenza strewn with pictures and plaques. In one, Sterling was on the beach with his pretty, platinum-haired wife, two towheaded boys and a pair of English cream golden retrievers. The man liked blondes. There he was in a tux standing beside former Governor Pat McCrory. The banker was a Rotarian and belonged to Ducks Unlimited. He wrapped up his phone call. "You know your word is good enough for me, Cade. We'll see y'all tonight at the fundraiser."

Jenny wilted a little. The good 'ole boy network was still alive and well in Shady Grove.

"Good afternoon," Sterling said smoothly and shook her hand.

"I'm Jenny Beckett and I called you about applying for a loan." Giving herself an internal pep talk, Jenny launched into her description of the Lakeside Resort.

When she'd finished, Sterling was quiet for a moment.

"Well, interesting little project you've got going." Picking up her application, he studied it and frowned. "You're not currently working?"

"No. I'll be involved in the renovations of the cabins." Jenny bumped up the volume of her voice and tried to sound confident. "But we plan to be open by Christmas and generate revenue from holiday rentals."

"We?" His eyes swept at her left hand, probably registering no big diamond ring. "Are you working with a business partner?"

"No," Jenny said, her shoulders creeping up toward her ears. "I meant me and my construction crew."

Sterling gave her a patronizing little smile. "And Ms. Beckett, do you have any experience in construction, renovation or the hospitality industry?"

"No," Jenny admitted, her heart sinking. Things were going south fast.

Sterling tapped the application with the knuckle of his finger. "You've got some savings and your SEP-IRA to collateralize the loan, but I'm not convinced underwriting will go for this." He reached for his computer, slipping on tortoise shell glasses. "Let me run the numbers."

Jenny fumed silently as he clicked away on his mouse, studying the screen. Another *no* from another man, and there went her dreams up in smoke.

In a prominent place on the wall behind his desk was a photo of a group of men and women in suits standing side by side. The plaque under it read, Board of Directors, Goodlife Bank 2018. Jenny stared at it and blinked, her heartbeat drumming in her chest as she saw her best and only chance.

Rising, she walked over to the picture and made a show of leaning in to look at it.

Sterling glanced up from his screen, looking startled. "Uh, anything I can help you with..." he began, eyeing her warily.

Jenny went for a Mona Lisa smile and pointed at the tall, bespectacled man on the end of the back row. "My stars. That's Landis Collins, isn't it?"

"Yes, it is." Looking uncertain, he rose. "He's the chairman of the board here."

"That's my sweetie pie stepdaddy. He and Mama are in Greece for a few months, you know." Jenny shook her head fondly. "What a small world."

When she left the bank, Jenny was floating on air. Sterling Fairwood was her new best friend. Practically fawning over her, he'd approved the loan. Jenny leaned her forehead on the steering wheel and sent up a fervent *thank you*. Fingers shaking with exultant relief, she texted Luke and Alice: "Loan approved!!"

Immediately, her phone started dinging. A big blue thumbs up from Luke. A GIF from Alice with middle-aged, dad-type men in coats and ties dancing with hips gyrating and fingers snapping.

On Thursday morning, sunlight dappled her room and a cool breeze puffed in the open bedroom windows, ruffling the white eyelet curtains. Pulling the down comforter around her ears, Jenny snuggled under it for a few last minutes before she got up. Beside Bear's whiffling snore and Buddy's muffled yips as he chased rabbits in his dreams, the only sounds she heard were the chirping of the birds and the wind rustling through tree branches.

Jenny felt a wave of sadness, realizing she'd never again sleep in her snug and homey chicken coop cottage. Touching the soft fur of Bear's ears for comfort, she glanced at the bead board on the walls, the tiny but cozy rooms, and views of rolling farmland. Jenny tried reminding herself to be grateful for having been able to make a home in this magical, quiet spot for a good long while but all she felt was a poignant ache of homesickness. One of Charlotte's *Me Boosters* popped into her mind. *Home is where your story begins.* Jenny had a new story to begin at Heron Lake. Time to move on.

Stretching, Jenny groaned as she discovered just how sore she was from packing the day before. Last night, she'd worked hard neatly fitting pots and pans, books, and bedding into boxes. Jenny had sorted through clothes she didn't wear anymore and made decisions about furniture. The lake cabin was sparsely furnished, but Jenny wanted her own bed and familiar things around her.

Jenny had pushed two ladder-back chairs from the corner of the house she'd designated as the Thrift Store area over to her Keep area, and back over to the Thrift Store area. Her mother's maple dresser had to come with her as did the ruby-red leather wingback chair that had shown up on her doorstep four years ago on her birthday. The surprisingly comfy chair came from the finest furniture store in Shady Grove. After the men in the delivery truck had brought it inside, they handed her a note. It was from Jax and read: Nothing like a wing chair in front of a fireplace for a reader. Never mind that the chicken coop cottage had no fireplace. She wasn't sure how he knew she was a reader or where she lived. Plus, she couldn't believe he'd remembered a birthday. The chair was firmly in the Keep area.

After Jenny let the boys out for a quick trip, she fed them and jumped in the shower, hoping the hot water sluicing down around her would ease the muscles in her aching back. The unseasonably warm temperature had changed. This morning was gray and chilly. Throwing on jeans and a heavy fleece, she kept an eye out for her helper.

When they'd heard of Jenny's getting asked to leave the cottage, Charlotte's parents, Beau and Nell, had offered her the help of their gardener, Harlan. He'd be by soon to help her load the rest of her possessions into the Silver Bell and the back of her SUV. Then, he'd cart a load of her castoffs to the thrift store for her. Afterward, Jenny would pack up the boys and haul her life to the lake. Tonight, she planned on staying in the cabin.

Just after she'd scarfed down her lunch, a peanut butter and raisin sandwich, a box truck from a car rental company pulled up beside the house. Jenny had never met Harlan but expected a gardener to be a serious man with glasses wearing a floppy hat to protect himself from the sun. Instead, the fellow who swung down from the driver's seat had an Elvis-inspired swoop to his black hair. His sleeves were rolled up to reveal arms filled with bulging biceps, and he had sleeves of tattoos, including one that featured the face of President Lincoln. Jenny tried not to stare and was glad to be distracted from her homesickness for the cottage she was leaving. "I'm Harlan, the Perry's landscape guy. So, we're moving?"

"That's right." Jenny nodded and from underneath her eyelashes, tried to sneak a better peek at his tat, zeroing in on the stovetop hat, beard, and piercing eyes. It *was* Lincoln. The tough guy looking gardener was also a history buff, and that made Jenny like him.

"Let's hitch the trailer to your rig and load up." Harlan took her keys and, with little effort, hooked the Airstream to her SUV and backed them both as close as he could to her front door. Jenny pointed out what she wanted to take and Harlan swung into action, lifting an overstuffed yellow toile chair over his head like it was a child's plastic seat. He moved fast, and Jenny scrambled to lend a hand with her desk and the wing chair from Daddy. The dresser wasn't so bad once she pulled the drawers out, and the kitchen table was a breeze. She huffed as she helped maneuver her memory-foam queen mattress into the Silver Belle.

When they finished, they sat on the porch drinking from icy water bottles. Harlan eyed her. "Ever hauled that trailer?"

"Never," she said, chagrinned that she'd not thought about that before now.

He waved her over to her SUV. "Come on. Let's have you take her up and down the road a few times. Get the feel of the weight, learn the turns."

Her palms sweating, Jenny took the wheel and Harlan encouraged her as she slowly turned on to the state road. "Nice and easy. Slow and steady acceleration. That's the way you do it," he said. "You're doing great. You've got to get the feel of it. You need wider turns, no sudden stops, and no lanes changes until you account for the extra length you're hauling."

Harlan was a calm and confident teacher, and on the third trip back from the turnaround point at the Gas Up and Go, Jenny began to breathe more normally and relax her death grip on the wheel. Back at the cottage, Jenny put the SUV in park, turned to Harlan and smiled. "Thanks so much for …"

But Earl jerked his gleaming Cadillac into the driveway and

pulled it right in front of her SUV. Jenny groaned while Harlan raised a bushy black brow and looked at her questioningly. "It's okay. It's just my landlord," she explained. Just a prince of a guy.

Slipping Harlan four fifties, she watched him drive off with her thrift shop load and suddenly felt bereft. The move was really happening, and now she had to endure another conversation with Odious Earl.

"You getting cleared out?" Earl curled his lip as he eyed the SUV and trailer as if it were the Beverly Hillbillies truck with Granny in her rocker.

"That's right." Jenny gave him a cool look. Today, Earl sported a green and raspberry checked button-down that he must have ordered from a catalog called *Upwardly Mobile Gents* or *Wealthy Landowner Today*. He also wore a wide-brimmed hat that he probably thought was sporty but Jenny thought looked decidedly Canadian Mountie.

Her landlord nodded, his jaunty Mountie hat bouncing up and down. He needed a chin strap. "I got fellows with a bulldozer and a front-end loader coming in a few days to tear down the barn. We've inked the deal and the buyer wants to use that space to set up a cement plant for the job," he said importantly.

The reality of it all finally registered for Jenny. Everything was getting torn down: the farm house with its rusted, sloping roof and her tiny, shabby gem of a cottage. Neither were great beauties or of any architectural value, but she felt sick at heart picturing them destroyed.

Crossing her arms, she looked at the small, faded crimson barn that leaned to the left and was over a hundred years old, according to Mrs. Evans. The red barn that had sheltered animals, crops and people over the past century would soon be reduced to rubble. In the soft morning light, the barn looked like a small version of the ones imagined by Andrew Wyeth or Currier and Ives. She lifted her chin. "You're tearing down that beautiful barn?"

Earl's brow flew up and he looked at her as if she were crazy. "Beautiful? It's got holes in the roof and will likely blow the rest of the way down the next big storm."

"But it's got amazing old wood. What are you going to do with that?" Jenny persisted.

Earl sniggered, pulled a tin of tobacco from his pocket and, with fat fingers, put a pinch between his cheek and gum. "Take it to the landfill. Darn fool environmental people fine us if we burn these days." He looked disgusted. "It's hardly a barn, more like a shed painted red."

"Maybe we could call that show *Barn Salvagers*. Those guys could save it and rebuild it somewhere else." Jenny was talking too fast but she couldn't help it.

Earl snorted and gave a dismissive wave of his hand. "Harebrained, yuppy TV. New wood is good wood. I like treated lumber, not rotted boards," he said with a savvy look.

Unable to stop herself, Jenny asked, "If they tear it down, can I take the wood?"

He cocked his head. "What do you want with it?"

"I don't know," she admitted, her thoughts careening around. Maybe they could repurpose the wood at the Lakeside Resort and use it for flooring in the lofts, accent walls, or the pole barn she needed to have built. The wood would live on at the property. "I'll bet those landfill fees are high," she said, thrusting her hands in her pockets and gazing off into the distance. "Tell you what. You can keep my security deposit if you give me the wood. That could save you the cost of hauling it out of here and the dump fees."

"Nah." Earl waved a beefy hand. "No deal. You owe me the security deposit."

"You know, it's funny." Jenny tried for a cynical chuckle the way the tough women detectives did when questioning lying perps on the TV shows. "I talked to a lawyer and he said us arguing about the security deposit could gum up the works for you. If I took you to small claims court, the whole land sale could get delayed," she said. If he lied about a lease and supposed damages, she could lie about a lawyer.

Earl gave her a hard look, rubbing his chin and trying to decide if she was bluffing.

"I can get him on the phone," Jenny offered, speed dialing her hair stylist Star and praying she didn't pick up.

"You need to get that pile of kindling out of here fast," he growled.

Her thoughts flashed to her daddy's paper bag contract and Earl's fondness for lying. She held up a hand and smiled as pleasantly as she could, "Let's make this official, Earl." Stepping over to the SUV, she tore a corner from the paper bag full of her shoes, and scrawled out a line about their deal and signed it with a flourish. Handing him the pen, she tried to look nonchalant, making a show of retying her boot that was already perfectly tied.

Looking disgusted, Earl signed it and practically threw the paper bag scrap back at her. He put a finger in her face. "Work starts November 5th. If the wood's not gone by Friday the 2nd, you can kiss your deposit good-bye." He stomped away, his hat jouncing. The SUV sped off, spewing gravel as he screeched out.

Her heart racing with excitement, Jenny hurried down to the barn and took several pictures. She leaned against the SUV, her heart swelling with exhilaration. She'd bought a barn. Somehow, her purchase eased the aching sadness she felt about the demo of the farm.

Praying he wouldn't think it a cockamamie idea or, worse that the lumber would create more work that would make their deadline unattainable, she sent the pictures to Luke along with what she hoped was a cheery text. *Guess what I just bought for the lake? Won't the wood be amazing?*

Holding her breath, she waited for his response.

A big blue thumbs up. She exhaled. No letter of resignation. No questions about her sanity. A moment later, another text arrived. *Alice says there's a saw mill not far from your spot at the lake. We'll check it out.* Jenny smiled. Thank goodness he *got* her.

Back inside the cottage, Jenny made one final sweep through, making sure she'd not left anything behind. She'd take the memories with her. This was the place she'd lost herself in books and dreams and spent time with her boys. Her desk had sat there, and that was where she'd conceived the idea of the tutoring business. Her love seat had been there, and that's where Douglas had proposed, and later, looked anguished as he broke their engagement. Jenny rubbed her face with her hand and stood in the doorway, thinking. She took pictures inside and outside. Standing in the doorway, she blew it a kiss. "Goodbye sweet house. Thank you for everything."

Brushing away tears, Jenny rounded up the dogs and watched them jump happily into the SUV. Pulling out the telescoping ramp she carried for Levi, she couldn't help but smile as she watched the little horse step confidently into the back of her SUV and take up his usual position standing between the seats. Jenny put the heavily laden car in gear, felt the weight of the Silver Belle, and slowly turned onto the road, nice and easy like Harlan had taught her. She'd be back for the barn wood, but her time at the chicken coop cottage was over. *Home is where your story begins,* Jenny reminded herself and she stepped on the gas.

CHAPTER 9 — THE STORY BEGINS

T HE AIRSTREAM WOVE MORE ON the road than Jenny had expected. Her heart banging, she vowed that next time she hauled it, she'd load it with more ballast. Maybe boulders, pianos, or anvils. Driving hunched and white-knuckled, Jenny began to relax when she finally nosed into the Lakeside Resort about four thirty, feeling somehow like she was coming home. Turning off the engine, she paused for a moment, watching as the late autumn sun – the color of an apricot – slowly sank toward the slate blue waters of Heron Lake. After taking the boys for a walk, Jenny let herself into Jax's cabin, deciding she'd try to start referring to it as *her* cabin.

Jenny fed the boys, lit her favorite balsam-scented candle to try to claim the space, and unloaded all the food and paper goods she'd stocked up on at the store. Though she was tired, she brought in several boxes, stacking them neatly in a corner. She climbed up the ladder to the loft, stripped the linens and blanket off Jax's bed, and shoved them into a large plastic bag for the thrift store. Tossing it down, she unrolled her old sleeping bag on the mattress. That would do for now. Jenny hoped Luke and Alice wouldn't mind helping her haul in her bed and the rest of her bulky items from the Silver Belle the next day.

Jenny got a fire going in the pretty little wood stove and, as it caught, backed up to it. The heat warmed her to her bones. Lovely. Arranging the dogs' beds on the floor, she pulled Bear's gnawed-up rabbit and Buddy's baby whale from her canvas tote bag and gave them to the dogs. She made up the pallet bed that Levi favored, and the animals promptly investigated their spaces and settled in as if they'd lived there forever.

Glancing around the cabin, Jenny noticed a large, primitive pine shelf brimming with books. She blinked, trying to pull up a memory of Jax with a book and came up empty. He was so full of restless energy, Jenny would have never guessed he was a reader. Curiously, she crouched and examined his shelves.

Jax read guy books but had a range. Beside the expected John Grisham, Stuart Woods, and a whole shelf of Lee Child's Jack Reacher novels, Jenny discovered Earnest Hemingway's works, six of the Sir Arthur Conan Doyle's Sherlock Holmes series, Zane Gray's *Riders of the Purple Sage* and *The Lone Star Ranger,* and Louis L'Amour's *Last of the Breed* and *Son of a Wanted Man*. Serving as bookends were stacks of magazines: *Mechanics of Airstream Campers* and *Family Man Fix It Guy*. She examined a cover that depicted a smiling father working with his son to replace a water heater. That was the second magazine she'd seen with a family man fix – up theme. Maybe that's who Jax wished he was, and that seemed sad. Her father could fix anything except his family. Jenny tossed the magazine back onto the shelf.

On the bottom shelf were magazines on investing. The one on top was called *The Eleven Proven Keys to Winning Business Investing,* and on the cover was man in a navy blue blazer stepping out of a private jet, grinning, and holding up a set of oversized keys. Jenny rubbed the spot on the bridge of her nose, remembering all the businesses that Jax had invested in, including the company that manufactured stones to look *exactly like* sapphires and the *can't miss* chain of laundromats with karaoke bars inside. Not wanting to, Jenny felt a stab of pity for her father. Jax had meant well, but sure managed to foul up the things that she was starting to suspect were most important to him. She gave herself a talking to. *Move on. What's past is past.*

Popping a frozen burrito in the microwave, she poured herself a glass of wine and sat at the small kitchen table, scrolling through her phone. It looked like she had signal, but Jenny did an experiment. If she stepped to one side of the cabin, the bars disappeared. In the bathroom, the signal was weak.

The phone rang, startling her so that Jenny bobbled it and caught it just before it fell to the floor.

"Hi, sweets," Charlotte called, the hum of road noise loud in the background.

"Hey, girly girl," Jenny called, happy to hear her friend's voice.

"I'm about to get to your exit. Can I visit and stay over?" Charlotte asked.

"Oh, yes," Jenny said, elated.

"Good. I drove home yesterday morning for Daddy's birthday and I'm on my way back to Celeste, but do you have the energy for an overnight visitor? I'd have to leave at six tomorrow to be on the job bright and early, but I'd love to visit."

"Come on. I'd be grateful for the company on my first night's stay here," Jenny admitted. "GPS will lead you in. Call me if you get turned around and watch out for deer in the road."

"I will," Charlotte promised. "I can't wait to see the cabins."

Fifteen minutes later, Jenny saw headlights bouncing down the driveway and walked outside with a flashlight, waving and grinning.

Charlotte enveloped her in a hug, and paused to give all the boys sugar talk and pats. "You handsome men. Such good watch dogs and horse," she said patting each on the head.

"Let's get you settled," Jenny said and the two women grabbed a brightly flowered duffle and a sleeping bag from the back seat. "Let me show you the best spot to take the cabins in." Jenny led her around to the front of the crescent of cabins. The lake slapped against the shore, and the moonlight shone a golden path on the water. A three-quarter moon had appeared, and the cabins looked dreamy.

"Oh, wow. Just wow," Charlotte said, shaking her head in amazement. "These cabins are fabulous. I can't wait to see them in the daylight, but right now I need a tall glass of wine and an update on every little thing. I'll fill you in on Jax's house. We three have a great plan."

"I want to hear all about it," Jenny said with a grin.

Inside, Charlotte stepped from the bathroom in a long, flannel gown and a fleece jacket. "This place is amazing," she breathed, and reached over to touch Jenny's hair. "And your hair looks fab. Good for you. You were getting drab."

"Why didn't you tell me?" Jenny groused, handing Charlotte a glass of wine and an afghan her grandmother had crocheted. The two relaxed on the sofa. Jenny filled Charlotte in on her news.

"My parents used to be friendly with a family called Hammond, and I thought they had a son named Luke," Charlotte mused, taking a long swallow of wine and somehow making wiping her mouth with the back of her hand look graceful. "But he was a math genius and turned into some big muckety-muck company owner."

"This Luke is or was in information technology, but I don't think he's a muckety-muck," Jenny said.

"The man sounds *interesting*." Charlotte raised her eyebrows up and down like Groucho Marx.

"He is, so I'm going to work to steer clear of him romantically," Jenny said firmly. "I'm not a big fan of men right now, and Luke's face when he talks about his late wife makes me think he's still... I don't know.... haunted by her death or by regrets."

Her face serious, Charlotte twirled a lock of hair. "I read in a recent *Big Girl Looking for Big Love* blog that dating widowers can be tricky. As opposed to widows who tend to have women friends and family they can talk to about their loss, widowers can take longer to grieve because the late wife was the only real friend they talked to. They can get stuck in remembering her as a saint. No other women measure up."

Jenny gave it some thought. "I can see that." The timer on the oven dinged and Jenny hopped up. She returned carrying two paper plates laden with large pieces of cheese, mushroom, and spinach pizza and handed one to Charlotte.

"Oh, yum," Charlotte said and took a bite.

For a few moments, the two munched pizza and discussed its deliciousness.

Jenny swallowed and patted her mouth with her napkin. "So, tell me about Jax's house."

"The house is a sugar baby and we're having a great time," Charlotte said. "I made this like a documentary." She put down her second piece of pizza and held up her tablet so Jenny could see Charlotte's two young helpers wearing dust masks as they hauled rolls of torn-out carpet from the house. Charlotte swam back into view and gushed to the camera, "You won't believe what good shape these oak floors are in. All we need to do is clean and buff them. They'll come back to life and just gleam." The camera panned to the floors so suddenly that Jenny started to feel queasy. Charlotte put the tablet down. "So, we're going great guns. That yummy attorney Mr. Long stopped by yesterday afternoon. Such a nice man. So supportive." Charlotte shook her head, blushing. "He's so complimentary."

Yummy, huh? Jenny took a swallow of wine to hide a grin. "Well, there you go. Do keep up with him because of the whole terms of the trust issue."

"Oh, yes," Charlotte agreed, looking serious. "If you want to see exactly what we've done already, it's on YouTube. I'll send you the link. These young girls are so smart."

"Are you camping out there?" Jenny asked, having trouble picturing the cheerful women at the bleak-looking house.

"We are. No motels for us. We're living on a budget." Charlotte got a dreamy look in her eyes. "Mr. Long had the power and water turned on and bought three air mattresses for us."

"Smart," Jenny said. Ashe Long *was* a nice man.

Charlotte spoke in a confidential tone, "I shouldn't mention this, but I've lost three pounds in a few days without even trying."

"Good for you," Jenny said casually. Charlotte wouldn't want her to make too big a deal about it, especially if she slipped up later. "You still on that Keto diet?"

"Nope." Charlotte tipped back the last of her wine. "We're working hard. I'm hanging out with fun women and ..." she trailed off, flushing prettily.

"And that nice Ashe Long is helping you," Jenny finished, giving her a knowing look.

"Maybe that's part of it," Charlotte admitted with a wisp of a smile. Brows in a v, she peered at Jenny. "So you're going to be okay? I've been worried about you. What's lake life going to be like?"

"Good, I hope," Jenny said thoughtfully. "Different for sure, but good. I just bought a barn and am bringing it up here."

"Goody." Charlotte clapped her hand excitedly. "I've always wanted my own barn."

Jenny smiled but fought a yawn. "I'll send pictures. But I need to get to bed. I'm beat."

"Me, too." Charlotte patted the couch cushion. "I'll bunk here."

"Actually, if you don't mind, how about sleeping up there in the bed? I don't know why, but it feels too personal for me to sleep in Jax's bed."

"That's because you're still mad at him, silly billy," Charlotte said. "But I'll happily take the comfy bed, even with the ladder of death." Holding the afghan around her like a shawl, she rose, tossed her sleeping bag up to the loft, and carefully climbed the ladder. Tossing Jenny's sleeping bag down to her, she called drowsily, "Have you looked in that box Jax left for you?"

"Not yet." Jenny felt a flash of guilt as she glanced at the box pushed to the furthest corner of the room. Slipping into her sleeping bag, she turned off the light.

"You will when you're ready." Charlotte yawned loudly. "Sweet dreams, Jen."

Before light the next morning, a still bleary-eyed Jenny stood at the door in robe and slippers and handed a mug of steaming coffee to Charlotte, who kissed her on the cheek and whisked out the door. The temperature had dropped twenty degrees from yesterday. Slipping a down parka over her robe, Jenny walked the dogs and Levi as her breath hung frozen in the air.

Back inside, Jenny put on layers of clothing, beginning with a long-sleeved undershirt. She made a big pot of homemade hot chocolate and poured it in an insulated thermos, and whipped up four man-sized turkey and cheese sandwiches and tucked them in the fridge. She wasn't sure how Luke and Alice usually handled meals when they were on the job, but with the nearest fast food restaurant being twenty miles away, she'd already decided she'd feed her help and feed them well.

Outside, Jenny started another campfire and went in to brew a fresh pot of coffee. The sun grew brighter, the air was crystal clear and cold, and the smoke from the fire curling into the morning sky smelled heavenly. Geese called as they flew overhead and Jenny watched them glide by. Even though her life was jumbled in the back of a trailer and she'd had trouble locating the bathroom in the middle of the night, Jenny's step was light as she did her morning chores.

After pulling a heavenly smelling pan of blondie brownies from the oven, Jenny began to unpack a box of her toiletries, watching out the window for her helpers. At quarter to seven, Luke stepped out of his blue truck and she hurried out to greet him.

This morning, he looked disconcertingly handsome in a deep purple down jacket, a plaid flannel shirt, jeans and work boots. Luke smiled at her warmly then cocked his head, looking at her more closely. "Morning, Jenny. Your hair looks...swingy and bright. I like it."

"Thanks," Jenny mumbled, feeling hot color rush to her face. She hoped he didn't think she was primping for him.

Luke began to unload tools from the silver toolbox in the truck bed but stopped to pat Buddy, Bear and Levi who were swarming around him in a friendly way. "Hey there, guys," he called in a gravelly morning voice and inclined his head toward the Silver Belle, his eyes bright with interest. "What a great trailer. That's a real classic."

"Thanks," she said, suddenly feeling shy. "That was my dad's, too. He called it the Silver Belle and it's a little worse for wear."

Luke eyed it appreciatively. "Still, the shape of it and that retro look are special."

Jenny nodded her agreement. "It needs love but you can see the potential."

Alice's little hybrid wheeled in silently, *Let it Snow* blaring from the car radio. She grinned as she breezed toward them wearing brown, insulated coveralls and a seasonal red and green plaid mad bomber hat. "Morning. Just sixty days until Christmas," she called cheerfully.

Instinctively, Jenny winced though the grudge against Christmas was beginning to fade. "Morning, Alice."

The young woman leaned down to kiss Bear, Buddy and Levi and pointed at Jenny.

"Love the new do."

The three of them grabbed coffee and stood around the fire. Luke pulled a piece of paper from a folder. "Did you know you've got four acres and three hundred and eighty-seven feet of waterfront?"

Jenny's eyes widened. Rushed, she'd forwarded the new survey to Luke without even looking at it. "That much?"

"Yes, ma'am," Luke said with raised brows. He outlined the plan. "We'll get the construction site set up, and do more measuring. We'll start work on porches and decks. We'll build one handicap ramp at the end of the job and build more ramps after the opening when we have more time." Luke hooked a thumb to his blue truck. "I've got lumber in the truck and more being delivered. We'll start at the cabin on the far end and work our way this way, one cabin at a time."

The three worked companionably unloading the truck and setting up. Luke and Alice worked well together, one sibling seeming to sense what the other needed. Jenny helped measure and carried boards, and Alice taught her how to use the power saw. Luke showed her how porches were built, and how the frames and joists supported the decking.

A little after one, they took a break for lunch. As Luke pulled a protein bar and a box of raisins from his jacket pocket and Alice snagged a pack of almonds from her backpack, Jenny held up a hand. "Oh, no, no, no. I dragged you two all the way out here and asked you to take on a rush job. The least I can do is feed you a decent lunch." She hurried into the cabin and came out with the sandwiches, crisp apples from the mountains she'd bought at the farmers' market, and the blondie brownies she'd baked this morning.

"Oh, wow." Alice grinned in delight. "I wouldn't say no to that offer."

Luke broke into a slow smile. "Man, oh man. You're spoiling us."

Jenny divvied up the meals. Luke goosed the fire and dragged a log to sit on, and the two women sprawled onto the short lawn chairs. The three munched their sandwiches silently, gazing at the sparkling waters of Heron Lake.

Jenny's phone rang. Douglas's number came up. With a jabbing finger, she declined his call. Why was he calling? More gifts to return? Maybe he wanted to give back the worn pair of running shoes she'd bought him for his birthday last year.

"Who was that?" Alice asked. "You gave that phone a big `ol poke."

"My ex. Not sure what he wants, but I'm busy," Jenny said with a grimace.

"My old boyfriends never call me. I wish they'd pine more and regret losing such a gem," Alice said mournfully. She raised a brow at Jenny. "When did you all break up?"

"Douglas broke up with *me* nine months ago," Jenny clarified. Carefully, she wrapped her sandwich back up in wax paper, her appetite gone.

"Wow. Sorry, Jenny." Alice shook her head sympathetically and shot her brother an accusing look. "Men. And they say women are fickle."

Luke rolled his eyes. "So he's having trouble letting go?"

"Douglas couldn't let go fast enough, and now rumor has it he's going to ask the new girlfriend to marry him." Jenny gave what she hoped was a casual shrug. If he *was* engaged, it would hurt hard but she was working on feeling nothing for him. "Let's not talk about it."

CHAPTER 10 — TROUBLE

L UKE EXCHANGED A QUICK LOOK with Alice and took a large bite of his sandwich.

"Subject change. We can't keep calling the cabins *that one* and *the one on the end*. They need proper names." Alice wiped a bit of mayonnaise from the side of her mouth with a napkin.

"I agree." Jenny caught a piece of lettuce that fell from her sandwich and popped it in her mouth. "Should we just number them one through eight?"

"Boring." Alice wrinkled her nose. "They deserve better names than that. How about nautical terms like The Lighthouse, The Sea Kelp or The Tides?"

Jenny caught Luke's quirked brow, and tried to use a diplomatic tone. "Well, there aren't any lighthouses, kelp or tides on this lake."

Alice laughed. "Right. Sorry."

"How about birds?" Jenny asked. "The Hummingbird, The Skylark, The Goldfinch…"

Luke held up a hand. "Manly guys won't stay in The Hummingbird or The Skylark."

Alice smirked. "How about The Mud Bog, The Red Clay, or The Motor Oil?"

"The Poison Ivy or The Copperhead are nice and manly, too," Jenny pointed out.

Luke fought a smile and held up his hands in surrender. "Go for the girly names."

Jenny looked at the cabins appraisingly. "They're so pretty. They deserve pretty names."

Alice bobbed her head in agreement. "How about Southern

flowers, bushes or tree names like The Magnolia, The Gardenia, The Camellia, The Azalea..." She paused to take a large bite of her brownie and rolled her eyes in pleasure. "So good," she mumbled.

Jenny chimed in. "The Redbud, The Mimosa, The Hydrangea and The Dogwood."

Grinning, Alice clapped her hands together. "I love those names."

Jenny sent them a questioning look. "Can my cabin be The Dogwood? I love that tree."

"Done." Luke toasted the women with his water bottle.

At the sound of tires on the gravel driveway, Jenny glanced up. A white four-door sedan with black and white North Carolina plates came to a stop, and a man stepped out. Slipping on a pair of glasses, he opened the permit box and examined the papers inside.

Jenny gaped, but Luke was already on his way over. "Can I help you?" he called in a tone that sounded more like "Move along, buddy."

Still holding her hammer, Alice walked over to join him, and Jenny hurried along after them. Ignoring them, the man slowly looked through the papers, then looked up at them and blinked. "I'm Merle Woods from the Lake County Planning and Zoning Permits Department. I need to speak to Jennifer Beckett, the owner of this property."

"That's me," Jenny said, eyeing him.

"I'm Luke Hammond, Ms. Beckett's general contractor," Luke said pleasantly.

Mr. Woods handed them each business cards. "I'm auditing all of the build sites that were previously approved by Mr. Ralph Jenkins from Inspections." He looked like he'd just sipped curdled milk. "Mr. Jenkins, who is no longer with Planning and Zoning, approved rough-ins on projects with little oversight. Willy-nilly." He looked grim. "Shoddy work poses threats to public safety."

Jenny shot Alice a questioning glance but she just widened her eyes, looking baffled.

Luke nodded and crossed his arms. "What are you telling us, Mr. Woods?"

"You need to stop work until all the rough-ins are re-inspected by our permits crew – the electrical, plumbing, framing and HVAC inspectors," he announced. "They'll be out at the end of next week or early the following week. If we find any irregularities, you'll need to correct them and we won't be able to re-inspect until mid-January."

Jenny's heart lurched as she pictured every calamity she could. The electrical inspector could turn on a light and the shock would make his teeth chatter and his hair frizzle. The plumber would shine his flashlight under a cabin and find a pool of water creating a sinkhole that swallowed the cabin before his very eyes. Mr. Woods would lean against the handsome rough-hewn log post in the living room and the loft would collapse behind him. She tried to fortify herself with a calming breath but her nerves were so taut that it didn't help.

By the time she tuned back into the conversation, Luke was nodding gravely at something Mr. Woods had said. "We're happy to have you all re-inspect and think your crew is going to find everything is in order. Now the problem is, Ms. Beckett is on a tight time frame with an even tighter budget and needs the revenue from her Christmas guests."

"Everyone wants us to get to their job first," the man said with a world weary sigh, looking like he'd heard that request a hundred times before. "We may be able to get back out here end of next week. We'll get to it as soon as we can."

"You're having to clean up messes caused by a less than competent employee. The job needs to be done right and the buck stops with you," Luke said in a man to man tone.

Mr. Woods looked relieved to be understood. "That's correct."

Luke rubbed the back of his head. "Trouble is, Mr. Jenkins has put us in a real bind." He shook his head slowly. "If you could get back out here sooner than later, we'd sure appreciate it."

Jenny and Alice both gave Mr. Woods beseeching looks and his face softened. "I'll see what I can do, but no promises. My inspectors stay extremely busy and we are short staffed," he said curtly and tromped off.

As the car cruised away, Jenny looked at Luke and then at Alice. "What if they find a big problem that needs to be fixed?" She hated that her voice quavered. "What are we going to do?"

Luke studied the tree line for a moment, then pulled back on his work gloves. "These things happen," he said evenly. "No need to panic."

Jenny gaped at him. Seemed like there was gracious plenty to panic about. She pictured numbered days flying off the calendar like in the old movies when they showed the passing of time.

"We can't close up anything before the inspection. They need to be able to see inside." He passed a hand across his jaw. "Let's get our own contractors in to double check that the job was done right before the folks from the county come back."

But Jenny was fighting the urge to hyperventilate, talk ugly about Mr. Merle Woods, and threaten to write an angry letter to the County Council that she'd never get around to.

Luke must have seen her anxiety on her face and sent her a reassuring look. "We won't sit and wait for them. Let's focus on what we can do."

Alice gestured toward the jungle of underbrush and low hanging limbs that lined the driveway. "Let's get brush cleared and cut back so we have a more workable driveway."

Jenny inhaled deeply and blew out her breath slowly. "Let's work on the front lawn and the sides of the lot, too. It's wild looking and branches are obstructing the view of the lake."

Luke held up his phone. "I'll try to round up contractors. Y'all get started." He strolled off, already punching in numbers on his phone.

Alice was chuckling at her phone, probably a text from Mike. "Horses playing with beach balls. So cute," she said softly and tapped a response, her thumbs flying.

These Hammond siblings might have a thing or two to teach her about staying calm.

A few hours later, Jenny rolled her shoulders and swallowed a few Ibuprofen she'd tucked in her pocket after lunch. If she was this sore on day one, she'd be gimping by day two. Jenny looked around with satisfaction. The driveway, sides of the lot and the lakeside lawn area were almost clear, and guests arriving would be welcomed by a 180 degree view of the lake.

Luke had already managed to line up a few contractors to check the work, and a licensed electrician had already come by and deemed the electrical "done right." No hair frizzling shocks. A plumber was coming by later in the day, and other contractors would be by Monday. Jenny's stomach finally was beginning to unclench. She and Alice had made good progress and Luke had been busy pre-cutting whatever boards he could.

As the sun lowered in the sky and they knocked off for the day, the three sat fireside. Luke and Alice peered at the screen of Jenny's tablet as she showed them the preliminary choices she'd made. Brother and sister offered input, letting her know what would or wouldn't work in the space.

Jenny started scrolling, starting with the pretty choices. For the walls in the bathroom and walls of the cabin that weren't wood, she was leaning toward Benjamin Moore's White Dove, a soothing, soft white with just a hint of gray. Though it would be a tight fit, she picked a white bathroom vanity with clean lines, two square sinks and plenty of storage underneath. Husbands and wives, siblings, and best friends always did better with two sinks, she decided. A curved shower rod cost seven dollars more than a straight standard bar and would make the shower seem bigger. The toilet was tall, a water miser, and pretty. For kitchen cabinets, Jenny decided to go with white to make the space look larger and picked the same white for the bathroom vanity. She'd spring for large, rectangular farmhouse sinks and swooping faucets that looked like they belonged in a glamorous Italian chef's kitchen but were a surprising bargain. For the backsplash, Luke said she couldn't go wrong with white subway tile.

Alice swooned over the countertop, a white gray granite with a wildly swirling pattern that reminded Jenny of waves and cost almost as little as the Formica. For the water heater, stove, fridge, microwave, toaster, and coffee maker, she made decisions based on their energy efficiency, price tags and customer reviews.

Jenny hit TOTAL for the items she'd placed in the online shopping cart and gasped quietly as she saw the number. "Gracious," she said, her voice cracking with nerves. She looked at the Hammonds. "I know we were very careful with the budget, but I need to send this on to my designer friend, Charlotte. She's great at making things stylish while saving money."

"Just let us know what you decide," Luke said.

"I know a few other discount sites where we might shave dollars off that total," Alice said with a knowing look and then smiled. "Everything is going to turn out so beautifully."

Feeling more hopeful, Jenny waved at Luke and Alice as they headed out.

A truck with *Jed's Plumbing* emblazoned on the side lumbered into the clearing and Jenny went to greet him. The driver stepped down, and raised a hand. "I'm Jed. Sorry I ran late," he called and a few sunflower seeds escaped from his mouth. Jed flushed. "Sorry about that. Trying to quit chewing tobacco," he explained as he unloaded tools from the truck.

"Good for you," Jenny said as she walked with him to the clearing. "We need to check that the plumbing was done right on all the cabins."

"Will do." Jed caught a glimpse of the view and stopped short, pushed his ball cap back on his head and sighed. "I never get tired of this view. Beautiful blue everywhere you look and fish out the wazoo. A fellow caught a one-hundred-seventeen pound catfish last year."

"Wow." Jenny swallowed loudly as she pictured that monster fish.

"They like shad," Jed said with a knowledgeable nod.

Jenny shuddered. Come summer, if she floated on an inner tube in the lake, would a whiskery monster catfish think her legs and nether areas looked like a shad?

"You care if I drop a line in the water after I finish up? I've got my fishing license and I always carry my gear," the man said with a hopeful look in his eye.

"Sure," she said, hooking her hands into her back pockets.

With a nod of thanks, the plumber headed off toward the cabins.

The stir fry was sizzling and Jenny was knee deep in dogs, scooping kibble into their bowls when a knock sounded on her door.

Jed stood, hat in his hands. "All finished up. The plumbing looks fine and dandy. You're not going to have any problems with that inspection."

Jenny blew out a sigh of relief, handed him a credit card and they settled up.

As he turned to go, Jed paused, looking uncomfortable. "Hate to tell you bad news, but I wouldn't let anyone on that dock until you get it looked at. It needs to be braced, a few boards are rotted, but the whole deal may need to be replaced," he said with an apologetic grimace.

"Oh, no." Jenny pictured unwitting guests plunging through boards into icy waters and felt a cold knot of dread form in her stomach. "How much do new docks run, Jed?" she asked, trying to keep her voice steady.

"Twenty-five to fifty grand," he said. "Depends on what kind of bells and whistles you want, double or single slips, boat and Jet Ski lifts, upper decks, boat houses, tiki bars." He gave her an apologetic look. "I'm no pier guy, though. But you need to check it out."

Jenny thanked him, closed the door and leaned against it.

Slumping down on her couch, Jenny put her hands on top of her head. That's what she got for starting to let herself feel hopeful. The dock and inspections could totally blow the budget for the project. "Stupid, stupid, stupid," she muttered and began to cry. Buddy and Bear leaped up beside her, and Levi trotted over and butted his head against her knees. Panting and whining, the dogs gazed at her anxiously. Snap. She needed to get a grip. She was even scaring the animals. Jenny buried her face in Bear's fur and then Buddy's. Brushing tears from her face with a shaking fingers, called Luke.

When he said hello, Jenny told him about the dock in a quavering voice. "As a complete rookie, am I making a huge mistake taking this on, Luke? We've already had major setbacks and we haven't even started the work."

"Jenny, unexpected things come up during a renovation. We'll have more. We'll do what we can, and try to stay calm at setbacks," he said, sounding annoyingly reasonable.

"Okay," Jenny said, mildly reassured but skeptical. How exactly did staying calm work?

"I should have noticed the dock, but didn't," Luke said, sounding apologetic. "I think I've got a guy I can get over there tomorrow to size it up, and fix whatever needs to be fixed quickly."

Relieved, Jenny tried to knead the knot out of her shoulders, and then thought about it. "How do you manage to get all these qualified guys out here so quickly?"

"I told you there were some good folks in Shady Grove," Luke said, a smile in his voice. "My daddy had a building business when we were growing up, and some of the guys who used to work with him are still in the business. Others are buddies I went to school with who Daddy used to hire to help out during summers."

"Well, you've got quite a network," she said admiringly but then remembered the costs of having all these guys size up the cabins or do repair work. Maybe the Celeste house would sell soon. "I'm sorry I bothered you on the weekend."

"You're not bothering me," he assured her, sounding good natured. "I'm glad you thought to call."

Feeling lighter as she said goodbye, Jenny brushed the rest of the tears from her face, and gave herself a pep talk that she'd try hard to believe. "This is a setback, not a tragedy. We can sort all of this out," she told the boys who sat watching her anxiously. "We can do this. We will push onward, boys." That last line came from a movie she'd watched on Churchill the night before, but still. Jenny needed all the help she could get.

Was there anything else *she* could do to get this problem solved? "Think," she said and raked her fingers through her hair. Suddenly, she thought about mornings she'd been shocked when she looked in the mirror and realized her roots were way overdue and she looked like a fishwife. She'd call Star and beg for the first cancellation she had. Lots of times, she got slipped in early. Jenny sat up straighter. Did begging work with county employees, too? Before she lost her nerve, she grabbed her phone, looked up Mr. Wood's number and waited for voice mail.

Her voice still a little shaky, she left a message. "Hello, Mr. Woods. This is Jenny Beckett from the Lakeside Resort. I am so worried about delays in construction. If you get a cancellation, will you please call or text me and put us in that earlier time slot? I'd be so grateful."

As she ended the call, Jenny sent up a quick prayer and hauled herself up to get ready for bed.

Saturday morning, Jenny was stiff and sore when she rolled out of bed. After ten minutes on the floor stretching, she could walk with just a slight limp. Groaning aloud, she sank into a chair at the kitchen table, went online and ordered a jumbo-sized bottle of Ibuprofen, Blue Emu Cream, Epsom Salts, a muscle and joint pain relief salve Native Americans swore by and an extra-large heating pad that went the length of her torso. Tough. She needed to be tough.

A shower made her feel better. Bundling up, she gathered up the boys and stepped into the crisp morning and paused to admire the broad expanse of gentle waves and reminded herself of how lucky she was to be able to look out at this breathtaking view every morning.

Inspired by yesterday's cabin naming, Jenny found a can of royal blue paint in a junk box she'd brought from home and hand lettered the names of each cabin on a scrap board. She'd put them up tomorrow. They were nothing to look at, but they'd help during their work. Later, she'd get someone artistic to paint handsome, permanent signs. She pressed the lid back on the paint can and rested the signs on two sawhorses to dry.

The dock man arrived and said he could repair the dock and shore it up safely for a thousand dollars, and since she was a friend of Luke's, he'd come in Monday and knock it out. A week ago, an estimate for a thousand dollars would have sent Jenny into a twirling faint. Today, Jenny felt so relieved that she could have hugged the man.

CHAPTER 11 — ACCIDENTAL BISCUIT BRIBES

A T 10:00 ON MONDAY MORNING, Luke was helping his buddy unload lumber and carry it to the dock, Alice had run out for supplies and Jenny was gathering downed branches from a dead cedar they'd cut down Friday when her phone sounded. She saw the Lake County number and held her breath as she read the text from Mr. Woods:

Ms. Beckett, We've had a cancellation. My inspectors and I will be by at 7:30 tomorrow morning for our re-inspection. Thank you.

Jenny whooped happily, Bear jumped up on her and they did a crazy waltz, two step combo. Her fingers flying, she texted Luke and Alice with the good news. Luke looked up at her from the dock, his wide grin easy to see from two hundred feet away. Her phone dinged twice. Blue thumbs up from Luke. Alice texted a smiley face, two dogs, fireworks exploding, a rocket launching and a GIF of two flappers wildly dancing the Charleston.

They were busy the rest of the day. Jenny put up the signs with the cabin names, Luke helped out with the dock, and Alice delivered supplies to each cabin, bopping and twirling every once in a while to a tune playing in her ear buds. Despite the stop work order, the three got a lot of work done. After Alice glided off in her hybrid and Luke pulled away, Jenny headed inside. She'd fix herself a bowl of soup for supper and hit the hay early. She quickly scanned her phone for messages and paused to read the text from Charlotte. After she'd moaned to her friend about the delays during a phone call Saturday, Charlotte had sent her even more

Me Boosters mental health tips she found on the *My Phenomenal Fluffy Life* blog. This latest text read:

I'm worried about your stress level. Check out this YouTube clip. Zion the Serenity Coach is so fab!!! Here's the link. No scoffing or deleting. Just do it. XOXO

With a half-smile, Jenny opened the YouTube video. The *fab* Zion was a bald fellow with a long braid sprouting from the back of his head who wore an outfit that looked like a cross between a saree and a toga. With a placid look on his face, he smoothly intoned, "Peace, my followers. I've just returned from a spiritual journey to India and my soul is refreshed." Zion smiled beatifically. "Now, last year we attained serenity with adult coloring books, tapping, soap cutting and snake massages."

Snake massages? Jenny backed up the video to make sure she'd heard it right. Yup.

Zion held out his arms. "Now, with fresh wisdom I learned from the great enlightened guru, Swami Dasa Babaji, I'm introducing you to the latest serenity technique which are bird poses with chanting and diaphragmatic breathing. Best if practiced outside in the tranquility of Mother Earth, today we'll learn the Great Egret pose."

Rolling her eyes, Jenny was about to close the app, but Zion explained, "An egret is a great white heron and a graceful and serene creature."

Jenny glanced out the window at the sparking blue water of the Heron Lake and watched as a heron glided gracefully across the water. "All right, all right," she muttered. Somebody upstairs was giving her a heavy handed message. Heaving a sigh, Jenny pulled on her coat. She'd go outside and give it a try.

Closing the door, she glanced around just to make sure she was alone. The coast was clear. Starting the clip again, she began the breathing Zion was demonstrating. The air was cold, but bracing and fresh. It felt good to breathe deeply. She needed to do it more often.

As Jenny began stretching her arms out in the wide wingspan

move Zion was demonstrating, she glanced at the windows of the cabin. The animals had noses pressed to glass and were watching her. Bear and Buddy were in one window, heads tilted curiously. Levi gazed at her unblinking from the other. Jenny started laughing.

Now, Zion wanted her to *flap her wings, preen proudly* and *shake her tail feathers.* Jenny did so, feeling foolish but the back stretching involved in preening and shaking did ease some of the muscle stiffness that she had in her back. "Shake harder," Zion urged. "Pretend you are a graceful bird twerking."

Jenny had never twerked, but she did her best booty gyrating Miley Cyrus imitation. It *did* seem to help her sciatica. For a bad dancer who'd accidentally broken the eyeglasses of the woman dancing beside her while attempting the Electric Slide and falling doing a line dance to *Achy Breaky Heart* and creating a domino effect of downed dancers, she just might be getting the hang of it. Zion sure had some moves.

A man coughed, and Jenny dropped the phone, whirled around and saw Luke standing behind her, brow raised and a bemused expression on his face.

Color rushed to Jenny's face. "Just stretching," she called in a too-bright voice, and whirled her arms around like a helicopter to support her claim.

His face deliberately neutral, Luke gave a matter of fact nod and held up his cell. "Left this here. See you tomorrow." The corners of his mouth twitching, he walked off.

"See you in the morning," Jenny called in a peppy tone and rolled her shoulders exaggeratedly in case he could still see her.

As soon as the truck pulled away, Jenny covered her face with her hands, mortified. Picking her phone up, she jabbed at the clip, deleting it. But as she walked back inside, Jenny began to chuckle and shook her head. Unfortunately, she thought Luke was hunky. Twerking like a bird was probably a good man deterrent.

At 5:00 the next morning Jenny woke from a thin sleep, her nerves jangled with worry about the inspection. What if they'd missed something? She thought about Luke's words and repeated them to herself as if they were a mantra, *Stay calm at setbacks.* But she still felt like snakes were writhing in her stomach.

When she stepped outside to air the boys, she gasped. The temperatures had to be in the low teens. Levi, who had tender feet and more than a few quirks from being neglected for so long, refused to step in the frozen grass to pee. Jenny tried jollying him along, pointing to the other dogs who were invigorated by the cold and watering everything. "All the other guys are doing it," she said but he just looked affronted and turned his head away from her.

Jenny shook her head and led him inside. Hopefully, he'd feel more carefree when the grass thawed a bit. Back inside, she goosed the glowing embers in the Nilsson and added new logs, fed the animals, and showered quickly. Jenny frowned when she glanced at the weather app on the phone. The high today was going to be only twenty degrees. Shivering, Jenny dressed in her warmest work clothes and stepped back outside. Laying twigs and shavings for kindling, she started a fire in their makeshift fire pit. They'd need the warmth today, and the smoky, earthy scent of a wood fire always comforted her.

Jenny sipped coffee and paced beside the fire, waiting for the Hammonds, and for Mr. Woods. She was driving herself crazy. It was only 5:45. Cooking sometimes settled her down, so Jenny stepped back inside, pulled out her cast iron skillet and began frying sausage. Right away, she began to feel calmer as she watched the fragrant meat brown up. Once she'd finished frying a pound, she sliced up another roll and threw those in the pan. While the patties were sizzling away, Jenny whipped up two batches of scratch made buttermilk biscuits and an egg and cheese casserole and slipped them in the oven. A good warm breakfast of sausage, egg and cheese biscuits would start them off right on a day that promised to be cold and busy. After twenty minutes, she pulled buttery smelling golden brown biscuits from the oven and quickly assembled sausage, egg and cheese biscuits. Jenny shook her head at herself. Because she was anxious, she'd baked enough for a small army. Pulling out a roll of aluminum foil, Jenny wrapped the biscuits loosely in aluminum foil, put them on a cookie sheet and stuck them back in the turned off oven to stay warm.

Luke's truck pulled up and Alice's hybrid was right behind him, *Jingle Bell Rock* blaring cheerily from inside her car. As the two gathered their gear, the white county car and two white trucks pulled in and Mr. Woods and five other men stepped out. The Hammonds and the county men all converged at her cabin at once. Flustered, Jenny threw open the door. "Good morning," she called, trying to sound calm and look law abiding.

"Ms. Beckett," Mr. Woods said stiffly.

"Thank you so much for fitting us in. I know you all stay so busy, and we're so lucky you were able to work us in." Jenny said, knew she was gushing but couldn't seem to stop herself.

"Not lucky for the builder who had this time slot. A sixty-foot loblolly pine fell through his new house yesterday," he said, grim-faced.

"Oh, dear," Jenny said. Men standing behind Mr. Woods began looking hungrily toward her kitchen, apparently catching whiffs of the just cooked sausage.

Luke stepped in smoothly. "Alice and I are going to go get these men started. How about you stay here, and take care of those calls you're expecting."

Thank goodness. Luke was giving her a chance to get distance from the anxiety of watching the men do their inspections.

"Good. Can't miss those... er... calls," Jenny said lamely. As the group of men turned away, their frozen breath hanging in the air, Jenny impulsively called out, "Hold up, guys."

Hurriedly she grabbed the cookie sheet loaded with wrapped biscuits and proffered them to the men. "I got carried away cooking and made too much food. I can't let these go to waste."

The County men all watched Mr. Woods for his reaction. He hesitated for a moment and took a biscuit. "Thank you, Ms. Beckett," he said curtly and turned away, unwrapping the foil. The rest of the crew grinned and jostled each other good naturedly as they reached for the biscuits.

Alice smiled sweetly at Jenny as she helped herself, and said softly, "Jenny Beckett.

Bribing county officials. What a grand idea." She winked, took a bite of her biscuit, and groaned aloud. Mumbling through her next bite, she pointed at the last half of biscuit she held. "You need to take pictures of these pretty biscuits and save them for your future website. Let guests know what deliciousness awaits them." Popping the last bite in her mouth, Alice sauntered off after the men.

Why hadn't she thought of that? Jenny snapped a few biscuit close-ups and uploaded them. Good to have such smart friends.

Glancing at the time, Jenny wondered how much longer the inspectors would take. An hour later, Jenny heard a quick knock on the door, and pulled it open. Luke and Alice were flanked by the inspector. "Oh, hello." Jenny held her breath, bracing for the man's verdict.

The inspector cleared his throat. "Ms. Beckett, all the work appears to have been done in a workmanlike manner and according to code. You may carry on. We'll be back for the final inspection in December per your general contractor's request. If any work does not meet code, we'll have to re-inspect before we can sign off on the work. That could take weeks. Do you understand?"

Jenny got his message loud and clear. If they made mistakes, they'd have guests arriving and no place for them to stay. "I understand."

"Good. Thank you." Mr. Woods turned to go, but paused and looked at Jenny. "Of course, your biscuits played not the smallest part in our inspections today, but I have to say, they were tasty." With a wisp of a smile, he turned and walked away.

Luke, Alice and Jenny waited until they heard all the vehicles pull away before the gleeful chatter and high fives began. The dogs milled around, wagging their tails. Jenny put her hands on her cheeks and stared wonderingly at Luke and Alice. "Can you believe it? We caught a lucky break."

"But you heard what the man said. If we don't get it right, there'll be no room at the inn on Christmas," Luke reminded her. He grabbed another biscuit from the stove and took a bite.

The rest of the day, they hit the work hard, hustling to finish the decks and steps that Daddy's workers had started, and starting from scratch on the cabins where they'd not even started. Because they were small, Luke estimated the job would take just over a week.

On Wednesday, the three of them were sprinkled with sawdust as they sprawled out in front of the campfire, enjoying the sandwiches Jenny had made for lunch, peanut butter and jelly sprinkled with crunchy Virginia peanuts and freshly sliced bananas. For dessert, she'd baked chocolate chip cookies and brought the fat, sweet black grapes she'd found on sale at the store.

When they'd finished, Alice patted her stomach happily. As she retied the elastic scrunchy holding back her glorious blonde mane, Luke thanked Jenny for the meal, and leaned against a nearby tree to make phone calls.

"How are you feeling about graduate school?" Jenny asked.

Alice broke into a smile. "I'm floating on cloud nine. It's going to open up career pathways for me, and let me inspire teachers, something I think I'd be good at."

"I understand," Jenny said, liking the young woman even more for wanting to help others.

Grasping the iced tea with her red mitten, Alice poked the fire with her boot and looked over at Jenny. "My brother said you were engaged, so you know all about men."

Jenny hid a smile at the thought of herself as a man expert. "Did he tell you the man I was engaged to broke it off with me right after the save-the-date cards went out?" Jenny felt the heat of embarrassment just remembering those awkward calls and emails.

Alice leaned toward her, undeterred. "But you had a wedding date picked out, right? How did that conversation happen?" she asked, her eyes bright with interest.

Jenny winced, remembering. "After Douglas proposed, we picked a date for the following year, which would have been this Christmas. I got carried away with the wedding planning, looking for the perfect dress and arranging the fairytale wedding and honeymoon." She held her hands to her cheeks. "I made such a big production out of the wedding. At my age, I'd given up on it ever happening, so I turned into an obsessive bride-to-be." Jenny rolled her eyes, and thought about that white velvet, pearl-encrusted confection that she'd for some reason packed up and kept stored in her small closet here. "Instead of pouring over wedding websites, I should have been getting to know my future husband better. I'm not sure we were a great match."

Alice blinked. "But picking a date was not a big deal for you all?"

"No, it was a detail." Seeing her crestfallen face, Jenny reminded her, "But I'm no role model. I'm an example of what not to do."

Alice pressed her lips together, looking determined. "I know Mike and I are a perfect fit. I just need to get him to the altar."

Jenny sent her an encouraging look. "I hope you do that, then."

Alice smiled wryly.

The three of them had usually had a last cup of coffee fireside as they made plans for the day, but Friday morning when the Hammonds arrived, Luke gave a tight smile, raised a hand and walked directly to The Mimosa to start work. Jenny watched him go and sent Alice a questioning look. "Is he okay?" she called, tipping her chin toward Luke's retreating form.

Alice had a frown on her usually sunny face and rubbed the back of her neck. "He is, or he will be. Today's the anniversary of Chloe's death. Always a hard day for him."

Jenny imagined the reels of her death that must be running through his mind and her heart ached for him. "I'm so sorry," she murmured. She looked at Alice. "What's the best way to be around him on these days?"

Alice paused to think about it. "Just give him space, but try to act normal. Let's find work that you and I can do together and let him be on his own."

Jenny nodded, and the two of them carried boards to the cabins.

Throughout the day, Jenny anxiously stole glances at Luke. He spoke little to her and Alice, and when he did, his voice was flat and his eyes stony. Jenny knew that there was a deep well of grief inside the man.

Late that afternoon around quitting time, Jenny and Alice were nailing the last board into the steps of The Azalea while Luke finished up on The Camellia. From the corner of her eye Jenny saw Luke hammering, and heard his yelp.

"Son of a gun," Luke called loudly. Dropping his hammer on the deck, he shook his hand repeatedly.

Jenny and Alice both hurried over to check on him.

Luke tried to wave them away. "I'm fine," he called. "No big deal."

But Alice grabbed her brother's hand and turned it up so they could examine it. The thumb was red and angry looking and already turning purple. She whistled and looked at Luke. "You smacked the tar out of that thumb. You'll lose your nail for sure."

"No biggie," Luke insisted, but winced as he tried to pull his hand away from his sister. "You Florence Nightingales need to get back to work."

But Jenny was already trotting to the cabin to bring him gauze pads dabbed in water, antibiotic ointment and a cup of ice to stick his thumb in on the ride home.

"Quitting time," Jenny announced, as she hurried toward them.

Alice doctored her brother, the whole time teasing him gently to keep him from feeling foolish about a rookie mistake. "Wasn't this on your general contractor's exam, boss man? How to deal with malfunctioning hammers? Hacks for keeping digits intact?"

As Jenny watched, she remembered how accident prone she'd been for the month after Douglas dumped her. She'd backed her SUV into a fence post, put a slice in her thumb while chopping vegetables, and burned her hand picking up a cast-iron skillet that she should have known was hot since she'd just fried bacon in it. Again, she felt that wave of sympathy for him.

Alice must have sensed the same thing because as she and Luke walked to the truck, she gave him a side-arm hug and leaned her head against his shoulder before releasing him.

Avoiding looking at Jenny's eyes, Luke swung into the truck, lowered the window and waited for Alice to pull away.

Jenny watched him. Luke's jaw was tight and he looked stoic.

Impulsively, she reached in the truck window and briefly touched his shoulder. "I'm sorry, Luke," she said softly.

Wordlessly, Luke gazed at her and his face softened. In his sadness, Luke's eyes looked as blackish blue as the lake did before a thunderstorm. He inclined his head, put the truck in gear, and slowly pulled away.

Jenny stared moodily at the lake for a moment, then hugged herself and headed home.

CHAPTER 12 — LOOKING BACK

MONDAY MORNING WAS DAMP AND cold. Jenny lit a match to the kindling she'd gathered and watched the morning fire crackle to life. Today, Heron Lake was moody dark blue with small whitecaps kicking up. But the weather couldn't dampen Jenny's excitement about the day ahead, an excitement she never felt when she used to tutor.

When Luke arrived, his mood had lifted and he seemed like his old self though his thumb was thick with bandages he'd taped on. With each day that passed, Jenny quickly grew to know the Hammonds. Luke was serious and focused, but could have a wacky sense of humor. Alice was cheerful and, though she could come across as flighty, was first to see how a construction problem could be solved or to engineer a clever work-around. Jenny's nervousness about her inexperience being a burden to them quickly faded away, and she began to feel like she knew what she was doing.

Because of the noise of nail guns and the whine of the saws, the three often worked silently together, but on lunches and brief breaks, the conversation was loose or philosophical and could start and end anywhere. Luke called Alice *butterfly* because she tended to get distracted and start a new task before finishing the last. His sister liked using the *boss man* moniker she'd given him after the thumb-mashing incident. Today, they had a lively and controversial discussion about what kinds of cars Bear, Buddy and Levi would drive if animals could drive.

At lunch on Wednesday, Alice sat on the lawn chair and stretched her long legs out in front of her as she scrolled through her tablet. Jenny sat beside her, a snoozing Buddy's head lolling in her lap.

Alice held up her tablet for Jenny to see and wrinkled her nose. "Is this the website you built for the cabins? Do you want feedback?"

Jenny braced herself. "I do. I know it's not good. I just kind of whipped it up from a build-your-own website place and stuck it there until I had time to have a decent one built."

"It's time," Alice announced. "You've been working hard, but social media rules. We don't have a lot of time and we need to get people here. You don't have one picture of this gorgeous lake. You have dark interior shots of unfinished cabins and your copy is wishy-washy."

Jenny held her hands palms up. "Stop flattering me, Alice. Tell me the real truth."

Alice burst out laughing.

"I know it's not enticing," Jenny said, thinking about the gray, overcast day she'd picked to take photos for the website. Not smart.

Alice wrinkled her nose and flicked a finger toward the screen. "Have you gotten one inquiry from this website?"

Rubbing the nape of her neck, Jenny shook her head no.

Luke had walked over and heard the tail end of the conversation. "Do you have a Facebook page for the business and are the cabins listed on the Vacation Rental by Owners site?"

"No and no," Jenny admitted.

"Let's fix that, right sis?" Luke raised a brow at Alice.

"I will. I taught a web design class to my super smart sixth graders in the Techie Challenges after-school club I ran," Alice told Jenny, pride in her voice. She gave one final glance at the screen. "Goodbye, sad little website. We're going to make you rock." Stowing the tablet in her backpack, she helped pull an aching, creaky Jenny up from her chair and walk her toward the porch they were finishing. "Let's go, sugar pie."

They'd made good progress on the decks and porches. The cabins looked less utilitarian and more welcoming. Alice called them "glamorous" and Luke rolled his eyes.

After lunch, Luke lay on a patch of grass, his bunched-up coat serving as a pillow. Closing his eyes, he lifted his face to the sun. Jenny tried not to notice how much he looked like the rugged but sensitive cowboy towing the vintage airplane for his aging father in the truck commercial. She concentrated on scratching behind Bear's ears.

Alice did a long, slow, back-arching stretch and turned to the others. "You know what kind of people really annoy me? Gum smackers, interrupters, humble braggarts, and people who leave their grocery carts in the parking lot instead of walking twenty feet to put them in the rack."

"I so agree," Jenny said as she retied the laces of her boot.

Luke sat up and took a swig of water from an aluminum cold cup and jumped in. "I'll add drivers who don't wave when you let them in, and highway crews that mow right over trash instead of picking it up first."

Alice held up a hand. "How about people at movie theaters who put their feet up on the seat in front of them?"

"Those are good ones." Luke finished peeling an orange and popped a slice in his mouth. "Any for you, Jenny?"

"Liars and cheaters," Jenny said, and it came out as a little growl. Seeing their raised brows, she hurriedly added, "And litterbugs. I can't stand litterbugs."

Alice studied Jenny. "Ahem. Where did that come from?"

Her chest tight, Jenny chewed her thumbnail and spilled what she'd been trying not to think about all day. "I got a text from my ex this morning, and he told me that he's getting married to his new girlfriend this Christmas, the same day he and I were to have married."

"Why would he tell you that? He's a dolt." Alice eyes flashed. "We ought to let the air out of his tires or hide a dead fish in his car or tell a bunch of Amway agents that he wants to become part of a successful team."

Jenny managed a wan smile. "You're devious, and I like that."

Alice's text sounded and she wandered off, probably to coo at Mike.

Luke turned to Jenny and fixed her with a gaze. "He's still in love with you."

Jenny shot him a skeptical look. "He's marrying someone else and very soon."

Luke just pulled on his tool belt and headed over to The Hydrangea. Jenny watched him walk away and rubbed her forehead with her fingers. Could Luke be right? Nah. Her guess was that Douglas was just being an insensitive guy who was either trying to get under her skin or who actually thought she'd be over the moon to hear his big news.

Maybe she'd buy them a wedding gift. Jenny brightened, remembering an article she'd read online about the worst wedding presents ever. She chuckled as she pictured the two lovebirds opening a twenty pound box of bacon that the veggie bride might enjoy, an ant farm, a self-help book on how to deal with divorce, or towels monogrammed with the wrong initials.

She'd dismissed Luke's theory about Douglas, but maybe it was true. As Jenny walked back to where they'd been working, she thought about her ex's demeanor when he returned the cufflinks. Underneath his bumbling and fatuous talk about his new life, he seemed nostalgic. Why hadn't he just given the cufflinks to charity? Strange as it seemed, Douglas *did* seem to want to stay connected with her.

Thursday, more supplies arrived and delivery trucks from Lowes, Home Depot, FedEx and UPS pulled in and out. Alice directed the delivery men to The Magnolia, the cabin in the middle that they used for their staging area.

"What's the schedule for tomorrow, boss man?" Alice asked.

Jenny racked her brain, trying to remember what day it was. Since the work had started, the days had run together. She glanced at her phone, realizing tomorrow was the 2nd. She had to go pick up the barn lumber at her old place. Her mind raced. She'd make a quick call to Nell and see if she could borrow Harlan for an hour or two. Would the barn wood fit in The Silver Belle?

"Jenny and I need to go into town and bring home a barn," Luke said. "Alice, how about you stay out here, direct the delivery guys and work on getting that new website up and running?" He glanced over at Jenny. "Sound good?"

"Sounds great," Jenny said, amazed that he'd remembered the date for a deadline that she'd just mentioned in passing and glad she didn't have to deal with Earl by herself.

Alice had a happy glint in her eye. "I get to hang out in Jenny's cabin with the dogs and Levi, and keep a toasty fire going in the wood stove." She rubbed her hands together gleefully. "I'll drink hot spiced cider and play Christmas carols while I work."

The next morning, Jenny heard the toot of the truck horn and gave the boys a kiss as she slipped on her coat. Grabbing work gloves and the goodies she'd left to warm on the stove, she hurried outside.

Luke's blue truck was hauling a long utility trailer. Perfect for barn boards, Jenny thought happily as she jumped in. "I love your trailer," she said, handing him several warm aluminum packets and parking her to-go coffee cup in a holder on the console.

"Thank you," Luke said gravely, the corners of his mouth twitching. Unwrapping the foil, he saw the three warm bacon, egg and cheese biscuits and grinned. "The working conditions on this job are brutal." Putting the truck in gear, Luke slowly pulled away. Taking a huge, flaky bite of biscuit, he groaned appreciatively. "Good grub, Jenny."

Jenny smiled and nibbled her biscuit. "I looked at the bank statement this morning, and we're just burning through money. We so need to be ready to open by mid-December."

"Gotcha." Luke rubbed the back of his head. "If all keeps going well, we're still on track to finish on time. If we get the permits signed off on, we may be good to go."

Jenny smiled weakly. The *if all goes well* and *maybe* made her nervous.

For a while, the two of them rode without speaking. Jenny liked the way he drove, keeping a good distance between him and the car ahead of him, staying at the speed limit, and signaling before he changed lanes, something Douglas always viewed as a sign of weakness.

Jenny enjoyed riding so high, and felt comfortable being Luke's passenger. Sipping coffee, she watched as the morning mist lifted and soft morning sunlight began spangling the countryside. "One thing I've noticed. I've been oversharing about my life, my romantic missteps, the gory details of my eviction, and some about my daddy." She looked over at him. "I hardly know anything about you at all. Fill me in. What was your work like? How was it being married?"

Luke glanced over at her. "It's hard to tell you one without telling you about the other."

"So tell me both." Jenny took a sip of coffee. "We've got plenty of time."

"Georgia was home for the past twelve years. I graduated from University of Georgia at Athens and ended up staying there."

"Wow." Jenny wondered how she'd not known he'd lived out of state for so long. The man held his cards close.

"Athens is a hub for tech companies and startups," Luke explained.

"That's what you did, right?" Jenny asked. "Charlotte said she thought you were a big muckety-muck."

Luke chuckled. "A small muckety-muck at best." He drummed his fingers on the steering wheel. "A friend and I developed an app to make it easier to order groceries online and we accidentally hit a growing need in the market. We were no boy geniuses like Bill Gates or Steve Jobs. We put together a team of smart techie minds and developed other products. Our timing happened to be good."

Luck and timing, he'd said, but Jenny noted Luke's humility and liked it.

Double checking all his mirrors, Luke passed an older gentleman driver going way under the speed limit. "I was a world-class workaholic. Weekends, no problem. Holidays, sure thing. Whatever works for the client." He touched his forehead with the palm of his hand. "My personal motto was, *Whatever it takes*." Luke rubbed a spot on his forehead, looking pained at how off the mark he'd been. "I built our mission statement around that phrase and put in on a plaque that hung on the wall of the conference room. How stupid was that?"

"Or maybe just ambitious," she said quietly.

"Driven. Obsessed," Luke said darkly. "We started out with three employees and ended up with sixty. The clients were happy. I was providing jobs for people, making money, and enjoying the challenge. I was riding high, just full of ambition....and full of myself."

Jenny nodded, starting to get the picture. "You're not an arrogant man, though. Maybe you just got your priorities mixed up along the way."

Luke gave her a ghost of a smile. "You're being too kind. I was a bad husband," he admitted. "I worked until eight or nine each night. When I was home, I was either on the computer working or so tired I couldn't listen to my wife. Right before we found out Chloe was sick, I was so late for our dinner reservation on our anniversary that the restaurant canceled and we had to eat at a fast-food restaurant. I was on a job in Nashville on her last birthday." Luke shook his head, looking grim. "I told myself it was for her, for us, and for the future, but it was just me getting caught up in ego and competition. Chloe was so supportive for a good while but the distance between us grew." He looked pained at the memories. "Then, Chloe got the bad bloodwork and test results. She responded well to treatment and I thought I'd been granted a reprieve. I left work, turned everything over to my partner, and took a leave. I drove her to doctors' appointments. We went to matinees in the afternoon and took long weekends on the Outer Banks; all the simple things she'd asked me to do with her before but I was too busy."

"You were there for her." Jenny imagined how painful this had to be for him to talk about.

"I was, but it was too late," Luke said. "After Chloe passed, I sold the company to my partner. Once I got so I could function again, I moved back here, worked part-time in Dad's store and tried to take stock of what was most important in my life. I can never change what happened. But I can be a guy who really understands and cherishes what's important in his life." He gazed at her. "Now I know love and family are central to my happiness, but I'll never marry again if it means I'll treat a woman the way I did my wife."

"You never set out to hurt Chloe," Jenny said softly. "I would guess she knew that, too."

"She did," he said in a husky voice.

"You've been learning from your mistakes but are you still beating yourself up?"

"Some," Luke admitted with a half-smile.

"Good," Jenny said. "From what you've said about her, I can't imagine Chloe would want you doing penance the rest of your life."

"She wouldn't." Luke shook his head quickly.

"So have you been back in the dating pool?" Jenny asked, trying to sound nonchalant.

Luke groaned. "Yes, but I'm a dating disaster."

"Yippee," Jenny said gleefully. "I can't wait to hear every bad dating story."

"I'll tell you later, but for now, I don't want to spoil my debonair image." Luke lifted his chin and pretended to smooth back his hair in a preening gesture. Pausing, he finished off the last of his biscuit and gave her a sideways glance. "What was complicated about your relationship with your dad?"

"Now you see him, now you don't. Poof." Jenny touched her fingertips together and then spread them.

Luke looked over at her. "Did he live with you all or were your folks divorced?"

"They stayed married for a while, but it was an odd arrangement. Jax was always off chasing the next business that was sure to be a winner and missed out on a lot. Mama is a sweet woman so she covered for him, or tried to. These days, they'd call her an enabler, but I think she didn't know what else to do." Jenny looked out the window and picked at a cuticle. "It wasn't until I was in fourth grade that I realized all dads aren't like that."

"That's all you knew," Luke said in an understanding tone. "Give me some examples of what Jax would miss."

Jenny tried to keep her tone light, not self-pitying. "Oh, there was the promised trip to Disney on Ice on my tenth birthday that never happened. Jax no-showed at my high school graduation when I was the valedictorian. He promised to pay for college and never sent a penny so I took out student loans and worked two part-time jobs to pay for school."

"Good for you," Luke said, turning on a blinker.

"When I left for college, Mama got fed up and quietly divorced him. She remarried and moved to South Carolina." Jenny felt a tightness in her chest, a reminder of just how sad she still felt about those letdowns.

"Were you married before?" Luke asked with a sideways glance.

"Briefly, when I was thirty. He was a workaholic and left me for his female boss." She gave a dismissive wave. "Ancient history."

Luke reached over, took her cold fingers in his warm ones, and held her hand. He didn't speak or even look at her. He just held her hand. Jenny blinked back tears, afraid she'd start crying in earnest if she looked at him. He gave her fingers one last squeeze and pointed. "Almost at the farm, Jenny girl."

CHAPTER 13 —
STURDY IN PARTS

J ENNY SQUIRMED IN HER SEAT, suddenly filled with dread about coming back to a place that had been home. "Seeing my old house or the barn torn down will upset me," she said in a voice that wobbled. "If they're still standing, they'll seem forlorn and that will be so sad."

Luke patted her shoulder. "Just keep your head down, try not to look around, and focus on getting that barn wood loaded up."

"I need to get my mail," Jenny said, as they turned into the farm driveway.

Luke stopped and Jenny ran to scoop up her mail from the crooked mailbox, reminding herself to do a change of address when she got home.

Jenny scarcely breathed as Luke eased the truck to the back of the property. She felt like she'd taken a punch to the gut when she saw the bulldozed heap that was the barn. But once she got over the shock, Jenny realized Earl's man knocking down the building made their work that much easier. As Luke expertly backed the long trailer up, Jenny buttoned up her coat, took a swig of water and squared her shoulders.

Luke hopped out, pulling on work gloves. "Let's get this done," he said bluntly.

Her thoughts exactly. Jenny and Luke worked steadily for almost two hours, stopping only for water breaks or to tighten tie down straps on the towering load in the trailer. The pile that was the barn was diminished now. Jenny and Luke loaded the rest of the boards into the truck bed and secured them. Just as the two of them loaded the heavy red cross-beamed barn door over the truck bed, the shiny Cadillac SUV glided in, pulling up directly in front of Luke's truck. Jenny sent Luke a warning look, and he gave an almost imperceptible nod as they loaded the other half of the door and strapped it down.

Odious Earl stormed up to them, glaring. He stepped too close to Jenny, an intimidation move, she decided, so she stood her ground. But Luke suddenly shifted a board so that it came within inches of knocking off Earl's Mountie hat.

"Watch where you're going," Earl bellowed.

Luke began to whistle tunelessly as he ratcheted the strapping on the barn door. "Good and tight on your side, Jen?"

Jenny wished she was confident enough to ignore Earl who was huffing like an angry bull not two feet away from her.

"What do you think you're doing with my wood? I'll have you arrested for theft," Earl shouted, spittle shooting from his mouth. His face the color of a blood orange, he pointed a finger at her.

Jenny felt the hair on the back of her neck stand up and she was angry at herself for still being cowed by the bully. "I paid you for the wood, Earl. You kept my sixteen hundred dollar deposit. We agreed on this." Reaching in her pocket, she pulled out her brown grocery bag corner and waved it at him, proud of herself that she'd finally found her backbone.

"That was before I went on the internet and saw how much some of those old barns are going for," Earl snarled. "Some of them go for fifty grand or more."

Luke rolled his eyes. He stepped over to Earl. "I'm a general contractor. A fifty thousand dollar barn is large and historical with hand cut beams and is in good shape. This was no fifty thousand dollar barn." He stood almost two heads taller than Earl. "I have seen this barn close up before it was knocked down. It was less than twenty by twenty, a shed really, and it had partially collapsed. A lot of this lumber is rotten, and it was dismantled with a piece of equipment that broke a lot of boards. We are moving it for you. All in all, I'd say you and Jenny struck a fair deal."

"I don't think so," Earl said, drawing himself up. "You all stay right here. I'm going to call my attorney." He stabbed at his phone with a pudgy finger.

Jenny gave Luke an imploring look, but his face was flinty. He dipped his head toward the truck and she raced around, scrambling inside. Luke swung up in the cab, and turned over the big engine.

Earl held up a finger at them, still talking furiously in the phone.

Luke backed the rig up a foot or so, and pulled forward, just slicking by Earl's Cadillac with inches to spare. Earl roared in fury when he saw them gliding away. He threw his phone on the ground and began jumping up and down.

"A grown man having a temper tantrum is not a pretty sight," Luke observed. A smile played at the corners of his mouth as he gave one more glance in the rearview mirror and accelerated down the two-lane.

Jenny leaned back in her seat and heaved a sigh of relief. "Earl is a bully. You helped me stand up to him." She looked over at Luke and grinned. "That was kind of fun."

"His blood pressure seemed iffy," Luke said deadpan.

Jenny burst out laughing and held an inch of space between her thumb and forefinger. "You came so close to hitting his precious Cadillac."

"I had lots of room to spare." He sent her a pirate's smile that made her breath catch.

"Thanks, Luke. I couldn't have done it without you," Jenny said fervently.

"You could have handled Earl," he said. "I just drove the getaway truck."

As they pulled on to the interstate, Luke sent her an apologetic look. "Sorry to burst your bubble Jenny, but your barn is really a shed and I'm not sure it's as old as you think."

Jenny thought about it. "It's a good shed though. Somewhat old. Sturdy."

Luke just raised a brow, looking like he was fighting a smile.

119

"Sturdy in parts. And it's red," she added firmly. She was elated with her barn whether it was the real McCoy or not.

"Well, there you go." Luke rested his hand over the steering wheel and tooled down the highway.

When they stopped for gas, Luke reached in the console for his wallet, and after a brief tussle over who was paying for gas that ended with him promising he'd add the fuel cost to his bill with a hefty surcharge, Jenny let him pay.

Slipping out his credit card, Luke tossed his wallet on the seat. When he turned to lift the hose from the gas pump, the wallet slipped to the floorboards, and Jenny picked it up. It had fallen open, and Jenny inhaled a sharp breath when she saw a picture of Luke, his arm draped around the neck of a lovely young woman. He looked at her with passionate intensity and she gazed back at him with equal ardor. Jenny felt like she'd had a bucket of cold water splashed in her face. Who could compete with that kind of tender, aching love?

Closing the wallet, Jenny put it back on the seat and took a few deep breaths, trying to compose herself. For the rest of the ride home, she was thoughtful. Luke had that picture in the middle of his wallet where he'd see it every time he opened it. The guy had a long way to go before he was ready for any kind of relationship.

Just after three, Luke pulled the truck and the heavily laden utility trailer into the clearing at Lakefront Cabins and blew the horn.

Alice stepped out from The Dogwood, and greeted him with the enthusiastic waving usually reserved for a returning war hero. Bear and Buddy barked madly and ran in circles, Levi joining right in doing his madly circling dog imitation. "How was it?" Alice asked, holding the boys back from getting in the way. "Any problems? The truck and trailer do okay?"

"The whole thing went fine," Luke said and reached over to pat Levi.

Jenny caught Alice's eye, raised her eyes to heaven and grinned.

"Oh, goody." Alice clapped her hands together. "I feel a story coming on. Let me get my coat, we'll unload the wood, and you can tell me all about it."

Jenny and Luke told the story of the incident with Earl, and Alice snickered as she chucked a crumbling piece of wood in the scrap pile. "That man needed to know he wasn't the boss of you. Good job."

The winter sun was setting fast. By dusk, they'd taken all the boards from the truck and trailer and were busy sorting it. In her schoolteacher voice, Alice called out, "This pile is good for siding, this one goes to the saw mill for planing or shaping and this is scrap."

Toting board after heavy board, Jenny soon peeled off her jacket and pulled off her hat, sweating. After the last board had been sorted, they all paused for a moment, worn out. Jenny felt a wave of doubt. The wood just looked old and beat. "It'll be pretty wood, won't it?" she asked plaintively. "Do you think it was worth all the trouble?"

"Absolutely," Alice said staunchly.

"I do," Luke said, looking like he meant it.

"Come on inside and warm up. I've got a lot to catch you up on, too," Alice said, beckoning them toward The Dogwood.

Stepping inside, Jenny was struck by the mouthwatering aroma of something wonderful cooking. Alice lifted the lid on Jenny's crockpot and stirred it with a wooden spoon. "Hope you don't mind, but I commandeered your kitchen. I knew I was going to be here all day and I felt like cooking a pot of my mama's famous chicken soup."

Luke stopped unzipping his coat and looked puzzled. "Mama might have opened a can of Campbell's soup but I don't remember any special recipe," he explained to Jenny.

Alice turned Jenny's laptop around and pointed to a recipe on the screen for *My Mama's Famous Chicken Soup.* "Hah. Sit." Ladling out heaping bowls of soup for each of them, she folded her hands on her flat stomach and watched proudly as they tasted it.

Jenny swallowed a spoonful of flavorful broth, carrots and potatoes and tender chicken and savored it. "This is delicious."

"It is." Luke patted his mouth with a napkin.

Alice slid into a chair and looked at them, her eyes dancing. "I had a big morning, too. I finished your real life, professional looking website with amazing photos and prosaic copy." Tapping the keyboard, she turned the laptop around so Jenny and Luke could see the screen.

Jenny put a hand over her mouth. Reaching over, she squeezed both of Alice's hands. "This is the most beautiful thing I've ever seen."

"I'm glad you like it," Alice said simply.

"I love it." Jenny put a hand on her heart, taking in the photos of smiling couples in canoes, friends' gold-lit faces as they sat around a blazing campfire, a single woman smiling as she floated on an inner tube, and happy families playing board games. Per Jenny's instruction about making the cabins inviting for everyone, there were mixes of ages and races. A man was bald, a woman was a size fourteen or sixteen, and the kids were average looking. No gorgeous creatures here. Just normal people enjoying the lake.

Luke grinned. "Good job, sis."

After Luke and Alice drove off, Jenny walked back to the cabin, feeling lonesome. She missed them when they left, especially Luke. Besides the whole broad shouldered, square jawed, eyes as blue as Heron Lake thing Luke had going on that would appeal to some women, talking with him was so easy. But he was the grieving widower who hadn't finished beating himself up for being a bad husband. Then, there was that photo of the lovebirds. And Jenny knew she was a bad judge of men. She'd be smart for once and keep her distance. Maybe she'd stop brushing her teeth and showering just to be on the safe side.

With a wry smile, Jenny turned back to her house. Levi, Bear and Buddy would be starving and she needed to get a grip. If she could find any photos of Douglas and her that she'd not angrily deleted, maybe she'd make herself look at them. That stroll down memory lane ought to remind her that men who seemed like nice guys could let you down the hardest.

While eating a frozen dinner, Jenny flipped through the bundle of mail she'd picked up at the farm. Flyers for pizza delivery, maid services, and concrete driveway repairs. Final payments from two parents for tutoring. Whew. Jenny kissed the checks, folded them and stuck them in her pocket. Next came catalogs with preppy, beautiful families having snowball fights and wearing red or green plaid bathrobes and furry leather moccasins as they happily ate waffles together. With more vigor than was technically necessary, Jenny pitched them toward the recycling pile. At the bottom of the pile, she spotted a vivid palette of pinks, tangerines, and corals. A postcard from her mother. Jenny's spirits lifted.

Ciao, sugar. We're in Brindisi, a charming port right on the heel of the boot of Italy. Landis has been a good sport about sightseeing, but he says he's "cathedralled out." We made our own mozzarella at a family owned restaurant. Delizioso!

I'm wondering if you're blue this Christmas. A much better man is out there for you. I'm praying you find your true love soon. Be on the lookout because he might be right around the corner! Your loving Mama

Knowing she was being silly, Jenny rose and tentatively pulled back the curtain to see what stud bolt might walk right around the corner. With her luck it would be Jed with his sunflower seeds. But not a soul was there.

Jenny shook her head at herself. She'd keep her eyes open, all right. But still, Jenny taped the postcard to her refrigerator where she'd see it every day.

By nightfall, the temperature had dropped fifteen degrees. In her toasty cabin, Jenny listened to the wind and worriedly glanced at the weather app. Her stomach clenched. The ten – day forecast was for much colder weather and a greater percentage chance for precipitation. Jenny fretted that bad weather would throw off their renovation schedule.

After she changed into a flannel nightgown and robe, Jenny eyed the cardboard box that she'd been avoiding since she had brought it home from Jax's house. Pouring herself a glass of wine for courage, she edged toward it and with a sense of surrender, pulled it open. It appeared to be filled with papers. On top was a folded up envelope, stamped and addressed to her. It had never been mailed. With shaking fingers, she slipped it open.

The card was a beautifully done pen-and-ink drawing of a mare and young foal. There was no greeting in the card, just a note in Jax's scrawled printing that read:

"Happy twelfth birthday, baby girl. Sorry I can't be there to celebrate it with you and your mama. You are the best thing that's ever happened to me. Sorry I haven't been a better daddy for you. Someday, I'll try to explain. You are in my heart. Your loving daddy."

Jenny felt a lump in her throat, and turned the card over in her hands. Jax had remembered her birthday, somehow known she was horse crazy then, and just never mailed the card. She rubbed her forehead. Why not? As she gingerly reached in the box for the next piece of paper, the SKYPE tone rang. Charlotte. Thank goodness. Saved by the bell.

Jenny picked up her phone, sank onto the sofa and grinned. "Hey there," she called.

"Hey yourself." Wearing a thick black fleece, Charlotte had her hair in two braids and wore glasses instead of her usual contacts. In one hand, she held a hamburger. "Hold on one sec, I'm starving." Her friend took a large bite and rolled her eyes in pleasure. "I'm sorry to eat in front of you. Miss Manners would shake a finger at me, but we've been working so hard since six this morning and my blood sugar is getting low. I'm on the verge of getting crabby."

Jenny nodded, enjoying hearing her friend's voice. "So how's it going at the house?"

"Amazing," Charlotte said, nibbling a fry. "Let me give you a little tour." Walking from room to room, she held up the tablet to show off their progress. "We tore out the carpet, had the wood floors sanded, painted the house an inviting neutral, and changed out dated fixtures. Next, we work outside. We'll get the yard mowed and the gardens mulched. The trees and shrubs will be cut back so the house doesn't look haunted."

Jenny's eyes widened. The house looked amazing. Shutting her eyes intermittently to keep from getting nauseated at the camera views that went up, down and around, Jenny marveled, "It looks like a house in a magazine."

Charlotte nodded proudly. "We've made so much progress, and we've taken a ton of before and after pictures for our portfolios." Her eyes sparkled. "Big deal stager designer jobs, here I come."

"I'll write a glowing recommendation," Jenny promised.

Charlotte hesitated. "I hate to be tacky, but can we have a yard sale with what's left of Jax's stuff? There are lots of small items, a good recliner and a large screen TV. If we can sell it, that'd save us from having to haul it to the thrift store and get you more cash for your cabins."

"Go for it," Jenny said.

"Fab. We'll do it next Saturday. Ashe is going to help us."

Jenny grinned. "Wait, its Ashe now? Y'all sound friendly."

Charlotte spoke quietly. "It is eight o clock at night and he's in the next room working, and he brought us all hamburgers." She leaned closer to her tablet and whispered, "Ashe is a real *me booster*. He's been so helpful. He painted all the ceilings. Can you believe that? I hate painting ceilings."

"He's not afraid of dirty work and he's trying hard to help you," Jenny said fighting a smile. She'd never heard her friend this enthusiastic about a man.

Charlotte put her mouth close to the device and whispered, "He's still single. Can you believe that? What is wrong with the women in this town?"

"Maybe they're all older or married," Jenny said. "He struck me as a great guy."

"Me, too." Charlotte's face was soft and she looked like she couldn't believe her luck. "Two realtors have seen the house and we've got a list price we want to run by you." She named a figure that Jenny thought was wildly optimistic.

"Go for it. I'll cross all my fingers and toes. Email or fax me what I need to sign and I'll get it right back to you," Jenny said.

"We'll be ready to put it on the market as soon as we finish and stage it. We're planning on holding an open house. Hope we get a big crowd." Charlotte held up crossed fingers.

"With all that sprucing up you're doing, it will be stellar," Jenny said.

"How is it going there?" Charlotte sank back in a chair, getting comfy.

"We're getting there. Luke and Alice are doing such a great job. We're all working hard and gaining ground." Jenny showed her the website and new pictures of the cabin interiors.

"Holy moly. Things are jumping down there, too," Charlotte said. "You've landed on your feet, honey."

Jenny shook her head. "Don't count those chickens yet. We've got a long way to go."

"How about Luke? What's he like?" Charlotte asked.

"Nice guy, hard worker, competent," Jenny said, deliberately keeping her voice neutral. If her friend knew Jenny was fighting an attraction to him, she'd be on it like white on rice.

Charlotte spoke to someone over her shoulder and smiled at Jenny. "I need to run. I've got to paint more trim before bed. Keep sending me pics of your progress." Putting paint – speckled fingers to her mouth, Charlotte blew a kiss. "Sleep tight, Jen."

"You too, sweets," Jenny said. Ending the call, she forwarded a few more pictures. Jenny must have caught Luke in a few shots because Charlotte's text flew back to her, all in large caps. LUKE IS A HUNKA HUNKA!!

CHAPTER 14 — RESERVATIONS

MONDAY MORNING WHEN JENNY LET the dogs out, she rubbed her arms briskly and pulled her down jacket tighter around her bathrobe. Her breath made clouds in the air. The lake looked gunmetal gray and the geese sounded mournful as they flew overhead. It was feeling like winter.

When the Hammonds arrived, Alice was bundled up like an Icelander and had pulled down the ear flaps of her hat. Luke wore a fleece cap, insulated coveralls, and fingerless gloves. Trailing a long orange extension cord with them, they carried the yellow portable heater with them as they moved from one cabin to the next.

The task now was hanging drywall, a tough and sloppy job. Although Jax had partially sheet-rocked one or two cabins, Luke estimated it would take two full weeks to finish the job. The drywall was heavier and trickier to handle than Jenny imagined. As they slowly installed and finished it, rooms appeared and the cabins started to look like homes, not construction sites. Once they'd finished hanging it, they mudded it, gave it time to dry, sanded it and started again with second and third coats of mud. Then, they'd move on to the thousand other things on their list.

While Luke walked around on stilts mudding the high walls, Alice handed up supplies and summarized an article she'd read on the internet called *Ten Ways to End Up in the Emergency Room while Hanging Sheetrock*. Jenny took Luke's truck and drove to the mill to pick up the barn board that they'd dropped off. The grizzled foreman said, "You've got a good mix of oak, pine and hickory. A lot of the pieces turned out real pretty. A few were beyond fixing, but we're sending them back with you to use for special projects." As he and his two helpers helped load the lumber into the truck, they ran their calloused hands over the wood and spoke to one another almost reverently. *Those beetle pocks are special* and *That old grain just jumps out.* As she drove back to the lake, Jenny's heart felt light. Maybe her decision to haul a bunch of barn boards to a building site wasn't such a ditsy one.

Brother and sister helped unload the truck and bring lumber to each cabin. "These are gorgeous." Alice stroked a flat, straight piece of wood with honey brown knots.

"We'll use these for loft floors, and the old, rough ones for accents," Luke said, touching a piece of heart pine admiringly. "The old wood will add gravitas to the cabins."

Around three o'clock, they were taking a quick water break when a Blue Volkswagen Beetle pulled up and a petite brunette with cascading curls stepped out. Wearing a white faux fur coat, a ruffled dress, and red boots, she looked a little like Snow White. The young woman waved energetically and hurried over to greet them. With a red bow of a mouth, wide-set eyes, and a dusting of freckles, the young woman was a fresh-faced stunner. Jenny tried not to gawk and snuck a glance at Luke, who was not gawking. Thank goodness.

The woman gave a twinkly smile. "I'm Lily Buckley and your precious little cabins are the talk of the town." She frowned. "Well not really the town, more like the grocery store, gas station, and town hall. I'm the new county librarian and I'd like to rent one," she said with a self-assured smile.

Jenny blinked. "I'm Jenny. This is Luke and Alice."

"Pleased to meet you." Lily gave then each a dazzler of a smile. "Mama and Daddy have a place just up the lake and I've been coming here since I was a girl. I just got my master's in library science, and I heard about this job up here and jumped on it. Mama and Daddy want me to live in a nice place, but not necessarily with them," she said, sounding amused. Opening her leather clutch, she pulled out a roll of bills. Touching her finger to her mouth, she eyed the sawhorses and the stacks of lumber. "Will the cabins be finished by the first of the year?"

"Yes, ma'am," Luke said smoothly. "We're just putting on the final touches."

And the toilets, sinks, and appliances, Jenny thought but zipped it, trying not to glance again at the wad of cash in the young woman's hand.

"I'd like to rent that one on the end." Lily pointed with a blue fingernail.

"Ah, The Gardenia," Luke said fondly. "A good choice."

"May I rent it for a year?" Lily asked, tipping her pretty head.

Jenny blinked and stammered out, "My plan was to rent these as holiday cabins on a weekend or weekly basis."

The young woman held up a hand. "I know how high the rates are up here on the lake, so you're not going to give me sticker shock when you tell me how much you're asking. I'm willing to pay the going rate. Daddy gave me money, too. First place on my own and all," she said proudly.

Alice fixed Jenny with a look. "We were just talking about the upside of renting to a longer-term tenant, weren't we, Jenny?"

"Um, yes," Jenny murmured. The rent check every month would help tide her over as she grew the business. She'd rent the cabin. Hesitating, she flashed back to the numbers Charlotte had shown her on her Pinterest site for honeymoon rentals. Jenny couldn't in good conscience charge Lily what she'd intended to charge holiday renters, but didn't want to regret a too-low long-term rent when business picked up. Jenny threw out a number that she was afraid was astronomical. "I'll need three months' security deposit and references, too."

"That seems more than fair," Lily said, and peeled off hundred dollar bills with the confidence of someone who was used to handling larger denominations. "Here's my deposit. I'll text you references. I'd like to move in January 1st if that suits you."

Jenny liked the feel of the money in her hand, but then winced inwardly at the thought of renting to someone so young about whom she knew nothing. "Lily, we're going to run a quiet place here. No parties or no loud music, okay?"

"Oh, no. I'm the quiet type." Lily paused, looking glum. "I was serious with a guy who is in graduate school out in Montana, but we split up." She gave Jenny and Alice a woman-to-woman look that conveyed something like *Men, can't live with them, can't smother them.* "He said long distance romances don't work, blah, blah, blah." Lily rolled her eyes.

Luke opted out of the men-are-rats conversation by pretending to retie his boot.

"My job will keep me busy, and I also teach Saturday and evening classes in yoga and meditation at the recreation center and the senior center."

"Oh, my." Delighted, Jenny put a gloved hand to her chest. "I was thinking about offering retreats like that here at the cabins. If all goes well, that may be something we can work on together."

"Yay! I adore that idea. I'm going to call my folks and tell them the good news." With a cheery little wave, Lily walked off toward her Bug, phone pressed to her ear. "Mama, you won't believe the darlin' little cabin I just rented only two coves down from y'all."

Alice's phone rang and she stepped away to take the call, dimpling like a besotted woman as she softly crooned, "No, I miss *you* more."

The little blue Bug slowly pulled away. Still stunned by Lily's whirlwind of girlish enthusiasm, brightness, and cash, Jenny looked at Luke. "Did I just rent that cabin for a year?"

"Yup." Luke adjusted his cap to shield his eyes from the sun. "You'll have that rent as a buffer in your slowest time of year. That'll help big time until you get your advertising going, and you'd be staying on the opposite end of the lot, so you'll have plenty of privacy." He pointed to the right. "If she gives you any trouble, her mama and daddy are just two coves over."

"Thanks for the...coaching." The thought of steady income made her exultant. Impulsively, Jenny reached out and gave Luke a quick hug. She felt his work-hardened body and sinewy, broad shoulder and an involuntary *ah* escaped her mouth. The feel of him made her short of breath, and Jenny made herself pull away.

Luke fixed her with a look, his eyes dark and his expression inscrutable. "You're welcome," he said, his voice husky. He pointed a finger at the Bug that was whizzing away.

"Another woman off men. Imagine that. Men are terrible," he said deadpan except for dancing eyes.

Jenny gazed back at him, and let herself get lost in those denim-blue eyes. "Not all men are terrible," she admitted, slowly letting out the breath she didn't know she'd been holding.

Luke just handed her a hammer. "Come on, Jenny. We've got to hustle if we're going to finish by the time Ms. Lily moves in."

Jenny flashed him a grateful smile. "At least you're not drooling over a pretty young thing like my ex did."

Luke tapped a finger on his chin and pretended to think about it. "She is pretty if you like that sort of fluffy girlyness, but *you're* beautiful." Grabbing the handles of the wheelbarrow, he rolled away. Jenny stood stock still for a moment, happily digesting what he'd just said. Trying not to grin from ear to ear, she followed him back to the work site.

They were making good progress in the kitchen and bath of The Mimosa when her phone sounded. Jenny hurriedly took off her gloves and yanked the cell from her pocket. Could it be a potential renter?

Alice met her gaze and held up crossed fingers. She waved her arms to get Luke's attention and gave the finger across the throat signal for him to cut off the whining saw.

"Good morning, Lakeside Resort," Jenny said silkily. Though her safety goggles were pushed up on her head and she wore a full set of long underwear under her clothes, she tried to sound relaxed and welcoming, like she was sitting behind a burled oak reception desk at a fully finished resort instead of standing in a freezing cold construction site. "In fact, we do have one or two openings for the holidays. Oh, yes. The cabins are all lakefront and are very festive at the holidays," Jenny said eagerly as she looked wide-eyed at Luke and Alice. "You certainly can. We'll book you in The Hydrangea which is just so cozy and adorable."

Pretending to look panicked, Luke threw up his hands and Alice covered her mouth to quiet her chortling.

Currently, The Hydrangea had no heat, no toilet and no stairs to the loft bedroom. Jenny gave the siblings a wink. "Yes, of course. Yes. If you'd just fill out the registration form on the website, we will see you on Saturday the fifteenth."

Sticking the phone back in her pocket, Jenny wiped the sawdust off her face and stared at them, disbelieving. "We've booked our first cabin for December fifteenth through New Year's Day." Grabbing Alice, she hugged her, jumping up and down.

Alice threw back her head and laughed delightedly. "The Lakeside Resort is almost open for business."

At six, Luke called it a day. For a few moments, the three of them sat beside the crackling fire and sipped hot chocolate. Alice fished a marshmallow from her mug, popped it in her mouth and chewed it looking thoughtful. "I didn't say this, but I wasn't sure at all that we'd finish this project on time. Now I think we might."

"I've had my doubts every step of the way," Jenny admitted and sent grateful looks to Luke and Alice. "I don't know what I would have done without you two," she said, a catch in her voice.

"We're not at the finish line yet," Luke reminded her and sipped the frothy chocolate.

"Tell me again what we have yet to do?" Jenny asked nervously. When she'd looked at her bank statement that morning, her palms had gone clammy and her heart started beating double time. They'd gone through so much money so fast.

Luke rubbed the back of his head. "After we finish drywall, we install wood floors, get flooring done in all the lofts and get stairs built. We need to get the cabinets, vanity and countertops in. Then, we can get the painters in, install appliances and move in furniture. If the weather holds and we get the permits signed off on, you should be done by the 15th." Luke gave her a crooked smile.

Still only allowing herself to feel marginally more optimistic about an on time finish, Jenny smiled but her smile faltered.

The project ending meant no more daily contact with Luke. Feeling almost bereft, Jenny realized she'd miss the Hammonds, and probably long for Luke. She'd grown to love their easy camaraderie, his quiet intelligence and his competence. The man could do anything. And Alice was like a Labrador retriever puppy, cheerful, bright, warm and funny. Jenny felt she'd made a real friend in Alice.

Jenny must have looked sad because Luke caught her look, and held her eyes until she had to look away. Almost breathless at her connection to him, Jenny gazed out at the choppy lake. Though she didn't want to be, she was drawn to this big man with the piercing blue eyes, a two-day growth of beard, and hat that sat a little crooked on his head.

As Luke loaded up the truck, Alice lingered for a moment by the fire with Jenny. "What about you and my brother, Jen?" she asked, looking hopeful.

"Hmm," Jenny murmured, looking at the cold glistening waves of the lake. She took a sip of now cool chocolate, trying to hide the fact that she'd been having the same wildly hopeful thoughts and trying to tamp them down.

Alice leaned forward, and spoke sotto voce so Luke wouldn't hear. "You two are good together. You'd make an amazing pair."

Like an old pair of shoes. Jenny winced inwardly, remembering Douglas's assessment of their compatibility. *Little brown wren, old shoe, faithful hound dog.* She shook her head slowly. "I don't know, Alice. I'm not sure I'm ready, and I think your brother's still grieving his wife."

"He's getting past Chloe. And you'll be ready soon. You're just resting," Alice said hopefully, but a cloud passed over her normally sunny face. "I'd just like somebody to get their happily ever after," she said. Gently, she patted Jenny's arm and rose.

The next morning, The Hammonds stopped by the cabin to grab a cup of coffee before starting work.

Blowing on her hot coffee, Alice looked at Jenny. "Mind if I take a shower and get gussied up at your cabin before I leave tonight? Tonight is Mike's and my anniversary."

Jenny's brows shot up, and Alice clarified. "It's been a year since Mike proposed."

"The day you rammed into him with your car," Luke added helpfully.

Alice swatted him with her gloves. "It was fate," she said solemnly.

"Well, congratulations and of course you can use my cabin," Jenny said. "Clean towels are in the sliding drawer under the bed, and the hair dryer is in the linen cubby."

"Thanks," Alice said, a lilt in her voice. "Mike made reservations at that new Korean barbecue fusion place in town that's won all the food awards. It's hyper-local with an onsite brewery, goats rambling in the garden patio, artisan soft drinks, and croissushi. I don't know what any of that means but the foodie crowd digs it." Alice's eyes shone with anticipation. "Tonight might be the night we set the date for the wedding. Mike said he wanted to talk to me about something important." She held up crossed fingers.

Jenny put an arm around Alice, and gave her shoulders a squeeze. "I hope you have a fairy tale night. We want to hear all about it tomorrow."

"I don't," Luke groused, looking pained. "Just give us the highlight reel."

Alice shot him a menacing look. "I'm going to talk about the date ad nauseam tomorrow. Every bite of food, every sip of wine, every word and nuance of conversation, and my detailed analysis of what it all meant." She smirked. "I'll talk a lot about feelings."

Jenny grinned and patted Alice's arm. "I can't wait."

Luke just shook his head. "Come on, sister. Let's stop jawing and get back to work. We're burning daylight." He opened the door and headed back out into the cold.

While the two started work, Jenny stayed behind to respond to two online inquiries from potential guests. People were responding to Alice's website and social media posts.

Closing the laptop, Jenny pulled on a wool hat, zipped her coat, and stepped outside to join the others when a familiar white Lexus pulled into the clearing.

Jenny's heart and breathing stopped. Douglas stepped out of the car, raised his sunglasses onto his head, glanced around the work site, and frowned. He wore an impeccably cut camel hair overcoat with a Burberry plaid wool scarf and loafers that gleamed as shiny as his car.

What was he doing here? For a moment, she considered trying to quietly skitter back to the cabin, but her heart dropped when she saw him spot her. Snap. Pulling off her wool cap, Jenny tried to casually smooth her mashed-down hair but knew it was of no use.

"Hey, there." Douglas raised a hand and gave that disarming smile of his that made people trust him and want to sign contracts. It was that very smile that had made Jenny's heart squeeze when she'd first met him at Trivia Night at The Full Moon Café. "Jenny," he called in his rich, warm baritone.

"Hi, Douglas," Jenny said flatly.

Looking foreign and out of place, Douglas walked toward her. His eyes swept over her and his brow furrowed.

Jenny flinched inwardly, knowing exactly what Douglas saw. Her face was red and blotchy from working in the cold and her lips were chapped. The old Jenny wouldn't have stepped outside without makeup. Now, her morning beauty rituals were cleaning her face, putting on SPF 50, and gathering her hair into a ponytail. Her boots were scuffed and mud – dabbed and her puffy down jacket made her look like the Michelin man.

Embarrassed, Jenny's face suffused with heat, but then she pushed her shoulders back.

Why should she care what Douglas thought about how she looked? Crossing her arms, she waited for him to approach her. She'd be darned if she was going to wag on over to him like a friendly dog.

CHAPTER 15 — VEXING EXES

Taking a deep breath to try to compose herself, Jenny smelled *Bold Adventurer,* the aftershave Douglas always wore, the one she used to think was sexy but now smelled cloying and not at all masculine. These days, she much preferred Luke's scent, a combination of wood smoke, pine, coffee, and clean man.

Douglas slipped his hands in the pockets of his coat. "You're looking...comfortable." The hint of condescension in his voice made her want to kick dirt on his perfect shoes, pull his hair, tell everyone that he was deathly afraid of snakes and getting older, and announce that he cheated when he counted his crunches.

"You're looking... fancy," Jenny said, deliberately uncrossing her arms. "What brings you all the way out here? Trust things are going well with Aiden," she said silkily.

Douglas flinched just a hair, not enough for someone who didn't know him to notice but Jenny saw. "She's well. I'm well."

"Good," Jenny said graciously.

"Jimmy Watson told me that you ended the lease on your office and closed down your tutoring practice." Douglas shot her a questioning look. "And I heard from my buddies at Great Southern that they're about to tear down your old place."

Picturing those bulldozers scraping down her cottage, Jenny felt a pang of sadness that made her want to cry, but she tried to not let herself think about it. "True," she said. "But back to my question. Why are you here?"

He rubbed the back of his neck. "I was worried about you, Jenny. You can't just throw away your life because I disappointed you."

Remembering his arrogance, Jenny didn't respond, but her blood began a slow boil.

Douglas shook his head sorrowfully. "I'm sorry I let you down. I really am, but it was for the best."

Jenny stared at him blankly and tried to look bored, a look her teenaged tutoring students had mastered. She let the silence spin out.

Puzzled at her lack of reaction, Douglas shifted his weight from one foot to the other and plowed ahead. "Life is all about overcoming disappointments and setbacks, and I never wanted to hurt you, Jenny."

He held his hands palms up. "Believe me, if there'd been the right connection between the two of us, I would never have noticed Aiden," he said. "But there was a magnetic pull between Aiden and me when we became running buddies. I tried to fight it, but it was undeniable. That's why I had to break things off with you, Jenny."

Douglas almost sounded noble, Jenny thought, putting a finger on a spot on her temple that was starting to throb. What had she ever seen in this man?

"Douglas, maybe you came out here to apologize for breaking the engagement. However you've justified it in your mind, it was shabby behavior. And I do not want to hear about your stupid magnetic attraction to Aiden."

His face reddening, Douglas looked away. "I'm sorry I hurt you, Jenny."

There was pity in his eyes, and Jenny did not need his pity. Drawing herself up, Jenny swept an arm around the property. "I own this beautiful spot. When the cabins and grounds are finished, they'll be amazing."

Douglas glanced around, taking in the construction debris around the cabins, the piles of scrap wood and brush, and the empty appliance boxes. He looked unimpressed, and shook his head slowly. "Please don't throw your life away in this backwater place. There are no restaurants here, no nightlife, no culture, no gyms. And do you really think people are going to drive all the way out here to rent a Tinker toy cabin?"

Jenny bristled, but felt a wave of self-doubt. What if he was right?

Luke stepped into the driveway and pulled a level from his truck. Jenny wondered how much he'd heard when he ambled over, looking hunkily adorable in a black watch plaid flannel shirt, dark green down vest, and jeans that fit him particularly nicely.

Jenny sent Luke a tight smile. "Luke, this is Douglas, an old friend. Douglas this is Luke, my general contractor and friend." Stiffly, the men shook hands briefly. The two eyed each other and Luke wore a granite-faced John Wayne expression.

Nervous at the tension, Jenny remembered when Buddy and Bear first met, all low growls, bared teeth, raised hackles, and lifting their legs on everything in sight to claim turf. She bit the inside of her cheek to keep from giggling.

Luke scratched his chin. "Jenny has got eight sharp little cabins, almost four hundred feet of prime waterfront, and a dock with deep water. Heron Lake is turning into a big second home and vacation destination for Hickory, Charlotte and Gastonia." He nodded as if it had been settled. "She's got herself a sweet little spot that'll likely be real successful."

Jenny sent him a grateful look. "Our website just went up, and I've already booked six reservations," she said, rounding up from two reservation. "At Christmas, in the middle of nowhere on a backwater."

Douglas looked at the cabins again and then back at her, a new light of respect in his eyes. "Well, sounds promising." His phone rang. Douglas glanced at the screen and silenced it. "I need to head back to town." Reaching in, he gave Jenny an awkward cross between a hug and a shoulder squeeze and in her ear, murmured, "I want you to be happy."

Luke watched Douglas stride off to his car and hooked his hands in his back pocket. "I told you he was still in love with you," he said coolly.

"He's not," Jenny said, remembering the gaga expression on

her ex-fiancé's face when he'd announced Aiden was the love of his life. "Douglas just came out to check on me."

Luke shot her a skeptical look. "Why would he do that?"

She hesitated, starting to wonder if there might be more to his visit than concern for her well-being. "Because he feels guilty about what he did? Because he cares about me as a friend?"

Luke raised a brow. "Guys don't do that. He wants you back," he said in a factual tone, and walked off.

Jenny raked her fingers through her hair and weighed his words. Douglas had come to apologize and check on her, but was he having regrets? Maybe, but Douglas had never understood her and sure didn't understand the Lakeside Resort. Jenny watched his car pull away and looked at Luke's retreating back, her thoughts racing. Could Douglas want her back and, if so, how did she feel about that? It only took a second for her to answer that question. Nothing. Jenny felt absolutely, positively nothing for Douglas except exasperation. One day soon, she might even wish him well.

Pulling out her phone, she texted Charlotte. You won't believe who stopped by. Douglas. Apologized for dumping me. Luke says D's still in love with me but I can't believe. Any theories?

Almost immediately, her friend texted back.

Thru grapevine, heard trouble in paradise between Big D and A. She's a take charge gal i.e. controlling as Ft. Bragg drill sergeant. Has D on a vegan diet and taking yoga class to help with back problems. Can you see uptight D in downward dog? Karma is beautiful. Namaste.

Jenny shook her head, meanly pleased, and tapped out:

True.

A parting missive came from Charlotte.

If D does want you back, please, please, please tell me you'd say no.

Jenny hesitated just a moment, remembering the luxury of being taken care of, the sweetness of revenge on that homewrecker Aiden, and the luxury of a well mapped out and secure future in front of her. That, she'd miss. She replied:

I'd say no.

Stopping inside to get the bottle of water she'd forgotten, the phone rand. "Good morning, Lakeside Resort. This is Jenny," she said in her newly minted relaxed and welcoming behind-the-burled-oak-reception-desk voice.

"Good morning. My name is Daniel Wise. I just found your website, and I'd like to rent a cabin for Christmas though New Year's day."

"Wonderful," Jenny said, scrambling to find a pen and a scrap of paper to write on. She needed a better system than taking money and scrawling details on random scraps of paper.

The man hesitated. "I'll be bringing my thirteen and fifteen year-old daughters."

Jenny thought about what she knew about teens. "I have to warn you. The Wi-Fi signal can be spotty. Most of the times, it's pretty strong and other times it's not. If your girls are big on devices, this might not be the spot for your family."

Daniel gave a mirthless chuckle. "I wish that you had no Wi-Fi at all."

"Okay," Jenny said, puzzled.

The man was quiet for a moment. "We lost their mom right before Christmas last year and we need to make new holiday traditions. We need low key family time with no devices at all." He sounded hesitant. "I read that there are great parks near Heron Lake. Maybe we could pack lunches and do some winter hiking."

How sad. "The parks are amazing," Jenny said with the confidence of one who'd never actually stepped foot in the parks but had thoroughly skimmed that Chamber of Commerce Guide to Heron Lake. "Hiking in December would mean great views with the leaves having fallen, and there are lots of birds and waterfowl to see this time of year."

"Birds," he said wonderingly. "I'll bet the girls would love that,"

"I'll stock the cabin with board games. Your cabin has a wood stove and an incredible view of the lake. The Heron Lake Christmas boat parade goes right by our dock on the 22nd. All the boat owners string up lights, and decorate and cruise by. It's a great night to bundle up and watch the show," Jenny said. That flip through the Chamber Guide was time well spent.

"Wow," Daniel Wise said, his voice more animated. "This sounds just like what I had in mind."

Jenny warmed to the subject of the holiday traditions at the Lakeside Resort, the ones that had never ever happened before. "We'll have a bonfire and hot chocolate out on the banks of the lake and the lighting of our big Christmas tree. Tell me what dates you're thinking about and we'll work hard to make this a wonderful Christmas for you and your girls," she said, feeling determined to make good on that promise.

Jenny scribbled details on the back of the hardware store receipt and asked Daniel to complete his registration online. As she ended the call, Jenny got that familiar panicky feeling about the work that remained to be done by the 15th, but gave herself a mental shake. Going into Chicken Little mode was not going to help. Grabbing a fresh legal pad from a drawer, she sat and wrote down a list of all the work that remained and every detail that needed to be attended to before guests arrived. The list was two pages long and when she put the pen down, she pinched the bridge of her nose. More needed to be done than she'd thought.

She'd show the list to Luke.

Water bottle in hand, Jenny had pep in her step as she walked outside again, ready to get to work. A white SUV pulled into the clearing and jerked to a stop. Curious, Jenny walked over to greet her visitor.

A woman in her mid-fifties stumped toward her. Wearing an oversized pink puffy down jacket, sweat pants and leather Moccasins that might or might not be slippers, the woman had a pair of reading glasses perched on her head and another pair dangling from a bejeweled leash around her neck. Her blonde-gray curls sprang straight out from her head and she looked harried. "You must be Jenny Beckett, the owner. I'm Ella Parr." She hooked a thumb over her shoulder. "My husband and I live two miles away on an off water lot. I looked at your website this morning and just had to drive right down and see you about renting a cabin."

"Nice to meet you," Jenny said, noting the desperate look in the woman's eyes and making herself not take a step backward. "I'll have cabins available to rent soon, but we're still finishing renovations. We won't be open until December 15th."

"Here's my problem. I just can't think." Ella put a hand on either side of her head.

Jenny blinked, wondering if the woman was mentally stable. "Okay."

"I'm a mystery writer and I'm working under a deadline with my publisher. I need a clean manuscript in her hands by February 15th. Problem one. My daughter and her husband and three small kids are coming in from Denver to stay with us for Christmas. I won't get any writing done. The grands are darling but loud and into everything, and my daughter and son-in-law just sit there and watch the chaos with benign expression on their faces, and say things like, 'Aren't they smart?' and 'So much initiative.'" Ella snorted. "Discipline, people, discipline."

Jenny broke into a grin, starting to get the woman. Genuinely curious now, she asked,

"What's problem number two?"

Ella Parr closed her eyes for a moment as if willing herself to stay calm. "My husband Paul is an Episcopal minister who just retired in September. He's driving me insane."

Jenny grimaced, remembering Charlotte's mother's complaints about her husband when he retired. "I've heard that retired men can be..." She trailed off, trying to find the tactful words.

"Overbearing? Irritating? Infuriating?" Ella Parr suggested, nodding so firmly that her curls bobbed. "Newly retired men will tell you how to load the dishwasher properly, follow you around like a puppy, or act like they got promoted to Boss of the House."

Jenny nodded her understanding.

Ella Parr huffed out a mighty sigh. "I love Paul to death, I really do. But when I'm trying to write, he interrupts me constantly. 'Where is the yellow mustard? Do we have any pickles?'" She rolled her eyes. "Male refrigerator blindness," she explained. "So I answer the question and remind him I'm working. Then, I'll just start picking up steam on a scene and he'll tiptoe into the study and whisper to me, 'Where do we keep the car registration?' or 'Have you fed the cats?'" she explained grimly. "Do you know how it is to get back into the groove when you've been stopped for questioning? Very hard." Ella threw up her hands.

Jenny gave her a crooked grin.

"I'm only halfway through this book and I need to step on the gas. If I can't find a quiet place to work during the day, I'll never finish on time." Ella ran a hand through her hair, making the curls stand up. "I've had daydreams about my husband that involve slow death by poisoning or driving off a cliff because of cut brake lines," she said darkly.

"Well, we can't have that." Jenny grinned, liking Ella more and more.

Ella held up her forefinger. "All I need is one month of uninterrupted writing. Can I rent a cabin from you for the month of January?"

January would be the hardest time for her to find renters, so Ella's check would be a big help. Jenny felt a wave of relief. "Yes, and I can promise that you won't be interrupted."

After they discussed terms and move in date, Ella scrawled out a deposit check, handed it to Jenny and threw her arms around her. "I can't even tell you how much this means to me," she burbled. "I'll name a character in the book after you, and not one that gets murdered. One of the heroines," she promised. Ella turned and trotted back to her car, a lightness to her step.

Patting the pocket that held the check, Jenny walked toward the sound of the nail guns, smiling.

"Amaze balls," Alice said when she heard Jenny's report about the new reservations, but Luke's reaction was oddly restrained. "Good news," he said flatly and turned away. He put on safety glasses, turned on the whining chop saw, and started cutting wood.

Today, they were finishing wood floors. Jenny cut the straps of the bundles of prefinished hardwoods, a butterscotch oak with slightly varied grains and colors that would added richness to the cabins. Helping Alice rack the wood, Jenny put long pieces against short ones and made sure no seams lined up beside each other so the floors would be more durable. Luke tapped the boards in place with a big rubber mallet and used a heavy pneumatic flooring nailer to secure the boards. Both women ran the saw, cutting boards to lengths that Luke called out to them. By late afternoon, they'd already finished the floors in the Gardenia, covered then with brown paper to protect them, and moved on to start work on The Camellia, the cabin next door.

Though the three of them worked well as a team, Luke avoided eye contact with Jenny all day, and any overtures she made to be friendly were ignored. Was he mad about the visit from Douglas?

Though it was just after 5:00, the sun was setting. Alice was in the cabin primping, and Luke and Jenny finished the last task of the day, toting seven new toilets into the cabins.

The growl of a large motor sounded and a combat-worthy black truck pulled into the clearing. With extra-brawny tires and a frame that was jacked up high from the ground, the truck looked menacing. Jenny lifted her sunglasses to get a better look.

Luke just held up a hand. "That's Mike."

Jenny had pictured Alice's math-teacher fiancé driving a fuel-efficient, conservative vehicle like an electric car, not this macho machine. "Mike's truck is a little intimidating," she said to Luke who'd been uncharacteristically quiet since Douglas's visit.

"It's big and bad. Very cool looking," he said, a smile playing at the corner of his mouth. "You wouldn't understand. It's a guy thing."

Jenny raised her eyes to heaven, wishing that, for once, the course of love would run smooth for the couple.

Alice stepped out of the cabin looking beautiful and chic in a black velveteen pant suit and black boots, her freshly blown hair falling to her shoulders like shimmery satin. As she walked toward the monster truck, Alice couldn't stop smiling.

Mike grinned when he saw Alice. Holding her hand, he solicitously helped her scooch up in the big truck and they rumbled off on their big date.

Luke was all business as he packed up to go. No easy smiles, no banter, and he drove away with an offhand wave. Could Luke really be jealous? Jenny was troubled by the thought.

Back inside, Jenny switched on the radio for company. The Zen Life station was relaxing with chimes, Native American flutes, birds calling and waves breaking in the background. Jenny felt her breathing slow and her shoulders drop as she chopped vegetables for a salad. Just as she was about to scrape carrots, cukes, baby bella mushrooms, artichokes, radishes into a wooden bowl filled with lettuce, the music stopped and a commercial came on. A woman with a voice that sounded almost catatonically relaxed intoned, *"This holiday, join us for a transformational meditation week on the white sands of Jamaica. The healing week of rejuvenation is an all-inclusive package that ..."*

Jenny stopped listening. All inclusive. She'd promised to make the holiday at the Lakeside Resort inviting to all, but she needed to do more on that front. Hurrying to the computer, she logged into the website. Though she'd had a close friend in college who was Jewish, she was rusty on the meaning of the holidays. After a quick google search, she typed:

To our friends in the Jewish community. Please join us over the holidays. On one of the joyous times of the year, join with family and friends to celebrate the festival of lights. Light the Menorah and celebrate the miracle of the oil. In your lakeside cabin, bring your chocolate gelt and throw a family Hanukkah party. Potato latkes? Yes, please. Mouth-watering rugelach for dessert, I believe I will. Play the dreidel game, relax fireside, and enjoy the beauty of Lake Heron. Come see us, and bring your family and holiday traditions with you. Shalom.

As she watched the post appear, Jenny sat back in her chair and smiled proudly. There. She copied and pasted the update to the Facebook Page, too. Tomorrow, she'd extend an invite to the spiritual but not religious folks. Jenny really did want the Lakeside Resort to be a place where everyone could relax and enjoy themselves.

Her cell rang and Jenny's spirits lifted when she saw the name. "Girl! How are you?"

"Hey, honeybun!" Charlotte chirped. "Guess what? I'm right up the road. I ran home today for a family supper, but I need to be back in Celeste early tomorrow. Have a bed for a weary traveler?"

"Always," Jenny said grinning. "I'll open a bottle of wine."

"Don't make me speed," Charlotte teased and ended the call.

CHAPTER 16 — COLD FRONT

C AR LIGHTS BUMPED INTO THE clearing and Jenny and the boys went outside. She waved excitedly as Charlotte stepped from the car. The two women hugged and chattered as they grabbed Charlotte's canvas overnight tote and went inside. After pouring themselves generous glasses of a smooth Sauvignon Blanc, they sat on the couch.

"Tell me all," Jenny said. "How's the house coming along?"

"Swimmingly, perfectly, amazingly," Charlotte fluted in a high-pitched, happy voice. "The house is just about done and it turned into a little jewel box. Remember how sad it was?"

Jenny did. Sad was the word.

Charlotte opened her tablet and pulled up photos. "Well, look at it now." She showed Jenny pictures. The front porch was painted a crisp white. The two skinny posts supporting the porch had been replaced by fieldstone-covered columns. The front door and the antique cobbler's bench arranged beside it were both painted a striking, lacquered ruby red. Inside, the buffed wood floors gleamed a honeyed gold. An inviting fire burned in the showstopper of a fireplace with white brick framed by iridescent tiles in a basket-weave pattern and topped by a handsome, primitive-looking wood mantel.

Jenny looked more closely at the shot. "That fireplace wasn't remotely that pretty."

Charlotte looked proud. "We re-did it completely, and on the cheap. I got working gas logs and a mantel at Habitat for Humanity for a hundred bucks. We repainted it all and put up cool tiles."

"Genius," Jenny murmured.

Charlotte left swiped through more interior pictures. "Everything else came from Craigslist, lucky Saturday yard sales, and the thrift shops in town," she said proudly.

Jenny shook her head, impressed. "You're doing an extraordinary job. The house is so homey and welcoming, but it's sophisticated, too." She reached over to give Charlotte a quick hug.

"Thanks, Jen." Charlotte turned pink with pleasure. "When we're ready to put it on the market, we'll hold open houses. The realtor is going to let me and my design women work them with her. We're going to bake chocolate chip cookies and sign in the prospective buyers."

Then, trying to sound casual, Jenny asked, "How's that nice Ashe Long?"

Charlotte put a hand to her heart. "He's just a precious man and I think he really likes me. I don't want to talk too much about it so I won't jinx it, but I'm just crazy about him."

"I'm glad." Jenny could scarcely believe that her matchmaking was working.

Charlotte leaned toward her, eyes shining. "He's been unbelievably helpful with the sale of the house and not just kind to me but kind to my two helpers. He thinks I'm smart and funny and pretty. Can you believe it?"

"I can, because you are," Jenny gently reminded her.

Charlotte rewarded her with a quick smile but went on. "And Ashe doesn't mind that I'm....not a size eight. When I told him my weight had always been a problem for me, he looked mystified. And then he said I remind him of Wonder Woman or Mandy Moore. Can you believe *that*?" she asked, her eyes wide with amazement.

"I can," Jenny said staunchly. "Sounds like you've found a good one."

"Well, don't be printing the wedding invitations yet because we're still new, but Ashe seems promising." She shook her head, a look of wonder on her face. "I thought I'd missed my chance at finding love. I thought it would never happen for me, but it might." Pausing to take a long swallow of wine, Charlotte pointed at Jenny. "I need a quick flashlight tour of one of the cabins. You need to update me on how ready you are for your grand opening, and then I want to hear all the details about that hunky Luke."

Later, after they'd taken the tour and were back in her toasty cabin, Jenny gave her friend the rundown on Luke. Winding down, she gazed at Charlotte. "I have no idea where I stand with him. I don't know if this is a friendship, a working relationship, or if we are dancing around a romance." She scrubbed her face with her hands. "I think he got mad at me today because Douglas stopped by, and I've told him I have no interest in my ex."

Charlotte looked understanding. "Can you talk to Luke and ask him where he stands?"

Jenny shuddered. "What if he rejects me?"

Charlotte held up her hands. "So, you feel dumb for misreading him, but what if he says he has feelings for you? You'll never know until you come right out and talk to him."

Jenny chewed her lip and thought about it. "Maybe I can do that."

Charlotte finished her last sip of wine. "I'm the last woman you should be taking relationship advice from, but it seems worth a try."

Jenny ticked off points on her fingers. "I don't know what's going on with Luke. I'm on the ragged edge money-wise. I'm worried we won't be ready on time, or that we will be ready and then fail." She shook her head in wonderment. "But I feel more content and alive than I can ever remember feeling."

Charlotte gave her a knowing look. "And this adventure is all thanks to your daddy."

Jenny thought about it and reluctantly agreed.

Charlotte tilted her head toward the cardboard box from Jax that was still pushed in the corner. "Had a chance to go through that?"

"I started, but didn't get far. I will, though," Jenny promised, thinking about Jax's role in this new life of hers. She had a lot to be grateful to him for.

Charlotte yawned and stretched her arms over her head. "I need to turn in."

"Me, too," Jenny said.

As she rose, Charlotte held up crossed fingers. "I think the Celeste sale will go fast. I feel it in my bones. If you get in a bind here and need help in any way, promise to call me."

The next morning, Charlotte flew out of the cabin at 5:30, clutching a to-go cup of freshly brewed coffee.

Jenny got ready for the day. She was outside building a fire when Luke pulled up, his sister wheeling in right behind him. Alice slumped out of her car. Last night must not have gone well, Jenny thought uneasily. Puffy-eyed and unsmiling, Alice only raised a hand by way of greeting. Sipping coffee, she walked a few yards away and gazed moodily at the lake.

Witnessing the exchange, Luke met Jenny's eyes. "Let's just let her be. I'm not sure what happened with Mike, but she'll talk to us when she's ready."

"Okay," Jenny said, but felt a pang of worry. Alice was not wearing her engagement ring.

Luke held up his phone and frowned. "Got a weather alert on the way out here. A large winter storm could be coming our way."

"Oh, no," Jenny's heart banged as she thought about icy roads and cancelled reservations.

He glanced at another screen and sent Jenny a reassuring look. "Most stations predict it's going to miss us, but we'll keep an eye on it."

Alice walked closer to them and frowned. "Those weather people get all jazzed up about any chance of a storm and make up terms like *bomb cyclone* or *Arctic vortex* just to get the viewers glued to the screen." She waved a hand dismissively. "It's a snow flurry, people. They happen in winter," she said irritably.

That was true. Jenny bobbed her head in agreement. No need in borrowing trouble, she told herself firmly.

The three of them worked quickly but quietly that morning and without their usual good-humored banter. Luke was outside painting porch railings while Jenny and Alice worked inside screwing in mounting brackets for window blinds. Each woman stood on a step-ladder.

Trying to lighten the mood, Jenny had the radio tuned to the classic holiday station, and Frank Sinatra sang *Have Yourself a Merry Little Christmas*. Jenny loved the song but it was poignant. She knew it had been written during the hardest years of World War II, and it made her think of tired and scared soldiers in bleak places, dreaming of their loved ones and hoping for a brighter future. Softly, she hummed along.

Alice crashed her screwdriver down on the metal shelf of the ladder, put her hands over her eyes and burst into tears. "That song always makes me sad," she choked out in a broken voice.

It was more than the song causing that wave of sadness. Jenny stayed on her ladder and simply said, "Me, too." *Let her be*, Luke had said.

"Last night, Mike did not even bring up the date for the wedding," Alice said piteously, tears streaming down her face.

"Oh, dear," Jenny climbed down, pulled a ball of clean tissues from her pocket, and handed them up to Alice.

Alice gave her a grateful look, and blotted her tears.

"Come on down from there and let's take a break," Jenny suggested, eyeing the slim ladder and deciding it wasn't the safest spot for a crying jag. "I have coffee in the thermos."

Alice nodded and the two sat side by side on a wooden storage bench. Her tears slowing, she took the mug Jenny offered. Both were quiet for a long moment, sipping strong, hot coffee.

"Do you want to talk about it?" Jenny asked softly.

Alice swallowed loudly and sniffed, dabbing a tissue at her red nose. "Mike got me a card and roses, which were nice, but what he wanted to talk with me about were ideas for side work he could do to make more money. He's bought a blade for the front of the truck to do snow removal or grading gravel driveways. A *side hustle* he kept calling it." She rolled her eyes. "He must have read that term on the internet."

Yikes. Mike had some ground to recover. "Hmm," Jenny said mildly. "Not knowing when you're going to marry would make planning hard."

"It does." Alice's tears brimmed again. She paused to blot them.

Jenny gazed out the window, thinking what she'd do in

that situation. "You've come right out and asked Mike to pick a date, right?"

"About a hundred times," Alice said with an exasperated huff, and then held up her unadorned left hand. "I gave the ring back until he can commit to a date."

"But you said you two are perfect together. That kind of big love and a good fit don't come along every day," Jenny said, trying to reason with her.

Alice's face grew red and her eyes flashed. "Well what about you and my brother? You two are a perfect fit and I think you have feelings for each other, yet neither one of you is doing one thing about it." Alice stood, and her voice shook as she said, "You and Luke have a chance for big love, and you're both just throwing it away. So don't tell me to go after love when you're too chicken to do it yourself." Clattering down her mug on the bench, she stormed toward the door, and called over her shoulder, "And I'm going outside to tell my brother the exact same thing I've told you."

The rest of the week was awkward. The three of them spoke only about work as they hit the to-do list hard and finished preparing for the arrival of guests.

The rest of the week and the next were like that, though the inspectors from the county returned and, without fanfare, signed off on the final inspections. Luke claimed the event was a true Christmas miracle, and though they should have been wildly celebratory, the mood was flat. They finished all the wood floors and trim work, installed cabinets and supervised contractors who arrived daily. Though they were polite to each other, Jenny and Luke avoided eye contact and tried to choose projects that kept them on opposite sides of the property.

Today, Alice worked with the stone guy, putting the finishing touches on an outdoor fire pit. Jenny gave a quick coat of spray paint to five worn Adirondack chairs she'd found beside the county trash dumpster. Even freshly painted, they were on the shabby side but she'd just not been able to resist, picturing guests sitting in them around a fire, making friends, and sipping a glass of wine or a cup of hot chocolate.

Jenny tried to be subtle as she stole glances at Alice, trying to assess what kind of shape she was in. Somehow fragile looking even in her bulky coat and work boots, Alice carried an air of defeat. Her bare ring finger looked white and as small as a child's as she repositioned pieces of stone.

Jenny's heart went out to her friend, but she also kept re-running Alice's comments. *You and Luke have a chance for big love and you're both throwing it away.* Was it true? Luke had gotten the same blunt feedback. Maybe Alice had it all wrong, and Luke was just finishing work as fast as he could, counting the minutes until he could get away from her. Maybe that was why every time she walked into a cabin where he was working, Luke found an excuse to hurriedly leave and work somewhere else.

As Jenny put the cap on the paint, she thought about it. She missed her closeness to Luke. He was the kindest, smartest, best man she'd met in a long time. He'd encouraged her about the cabin project, worked like a stevedore, and found ways to help her save money. He believed in Jenny, even when she didn't believe in herself. She closed her eyes for a moment, melting a little as she remembered the undeniable pull she had toward him. Luke's tall, broad-shouldered solidness made her feel she could slip right into those arms of his, lean her head against his chest, and feel safe forever.

But when she glanced up and gave a little smile to Luke as he hurried by, he didn't even acknowledge her. As she lifted one of the chairs to place it near the fire pit, Jenny felt like she could cry, realizing she'd kidded herself. The whole attraction was one-sided. He just thought of her as a client. She'd surely miscalculated with Douglas. Friendliness and encouragement could just be part of good client relations for a contractor. Maybe Luke had scoffed when Alice told him he was wasting a chance for love. After Jenny put the chair in place, she tripped over a partially covered root, and stopped to give it a kick.

Luke approached her. "I'm going to find garland and a big

Fraser Fir we can put in the middle of the cabins and string with Christmas lights."

"Good," Jenny said.

"I'm watching the weather," Luke added, frowning in concentration as he studied his phone, then looking relieved. "Both of the big TV stations say that the front that seemed like it was coming through isn't going to happen. Or if it does, it'll be mild and hit west of us."

"Whew." Jenny shuddered at the thought of bad weather ruining their opening.

Luke still looked troubled and glanced down at the phone one more time before shoving it in his pocket. "I'll still keep an eye on it. You know how fast things can change."

Jenny nodded, remembering last year's bum weather predictions. In January, the eight inches they'd predicted, which had caused people to rush to the grocery store and empty the shelves of milk and toilet paper, turned into a dusting. In February, two days after Punxsutawney Phil did not see his shadow, a foot of snow had dropped overnight.

Alice hurried over to Jenny and Luke, holding out a ten-inch-long, thick red-and-white striped candy cane. Cupping her cheek with her hand, she looked pitiful. "I bit into this and I've cracked a tooth or filling." She winced. "It's like a little man with a pickaxe is taking swings at my tooth."

"Oh, no," Jenny said, touching her shoulder.

Luke rubbed his forehead. "You need to get to the dentist today. If the tooth or filling is cracked, it's not going to just mend itself. It'll get worse."

"He's right," Jenny said, trying to appear calm as her thoughts were racing. Unfinished cabins, disappointed guests, one-star reviews, her anxiously sitting at a computer where *no more reservations would ever come in.*

CHAPTER 17 — FIRST STEP'S A DOOZY

ALICE LOOKED MISERABLE. "WE'VE GOT so much left to do. I feel like I'm letting you down."

"You're not." Jenny stood up straighter. "Make an appointment and get back to town. Luke, when you get here, let's talk about how to handle what we have left to do."

Luke nodded. "I'll be back in just over an hour."

Alice looked resigned. "I'm so sorry, Jenny."

"We'll be fine. Get to the dentist." Reaching over, she gave Alice a quick hug.

In her ear, Alice said softly, "I'm sorry for being so snappy with you."

"You were fine," Jenny murmured. "Don't give it another thought."

Luke put his hands on his sister's shoulders and gave her a gentle push toward the driveway. "Get going." Turning to Jenny, he sent her a look of concern. "I can stick around and try to get the tree later."

"No, go. We promised guests an amazing tree." Jenny said firmly. "I can handle things here."

Jenny kept up a brave front as she waved them off, but as soon as they'd pulled away, her smile faded. She had so much to do. Jenny pulled her to-do list from her pocket and skimmed it, moaning out loud. Then she swiped over to her reservation site, and felt even more overwhelmed.

Viv and Hugh, the couple from Southern Pines, were arriving

in four days as were Daniel Wise and his daughters. They'd all be staying through the New Year. The other five cabins were booked almost solidly until January 1st. Now, Jenny was getting bookings for the *Valentine's Day Lakeside Romance Package* she'd rhapsodized about online one night when she'd had a large Wilma Flintstone glass of wine and been so tired she was punchy.

Jenny was fuzzy about how she'd described that package until she re-read it the next morning, but her website promised: Romance, romance, romance! Amour is in the air at The Lakeside Resort! Complimentary strawberries and champagne, winter moonlight hikes, blazing bonfires beside beautiful Heron Lake and a minister available for a renewal of vows. Jenny couldn't believe her own audacity. Moonlight hikes sounded dangerous and she could picture a tipsy couple falling into the frigid lake beside the fire, but the copy she'd written must have sounded alluring.

By tomorrow, she needed towel bars put up, reading lights mounted, shelving installed in the bathrooms, and beds put together and made up with the new linens and down comforters she'd ordered online. Welcome baskets needed to be assembled with boxes of chocolates, bottles of water, lovely lemony scented bars of verbena soap that were locally made, and maps of things to do in the area.

Jenny made herself draw in several slow, deep breaths, and closed her eyes. When she opened them, she saw the crew of painters in white coveralls loading up the van to head home after coating the interior walls of the cabins with that crisp but calming paint color Jenny had picked. Determined and desperate, Jenny hurried over to the crew leader, and gave him a pleading look. "Joe, I need help. Can I pay you and your men double time to work with me for about two hours longer?"

The crew worked hard, and by the time they'd finished, the cabins looked charming, welcoming, and thank heavens, close to complete. Breathing out a whoosh of relief, Jenny thanked the men profusely. She paid them, and Joe and his crew chugged off. When she put up the last towel bar in The Camellia, Jenny's back ached and she was bone weary.

Ready to go to her cabin for a break, Jenny walked outside and stood on the stoop. It had been raining or maybe even sleeting. Hands on hips, she looked at the half arc of the cabins with their chocolate brown logs and dark green roofs and let herself admire how beautiful they looked. They'd painted the doors a cherry red and added green-and-white striped awnings over the porches. Small window boxes stained the same rich brown of the logs hung on the porch railings, and they'd put potted Poinsettias in them before the guests arrived. They'd have fires burning in every wood stove so guests would walk into warmth and coziness.

Jenny's phone rang, and Alice's name came up. "How are you?" she asked, closing the door to the cabin.

"Cracked tooth. I'm numbed up and the dentist is working on it. But have you seen the weather?" Though Alice's speech was muffled, the intensity of her voice cause Jenny's heart to lurch.

"What about the weather?" she asked, peering out at the choppy gray lake. "We've just got rain here."

"It's not rain here. They're saying it's a freak weather event and rain is turning to ice immediately," Alice said in a terse tone. "Cars are sliding all over the roads. Traffic lights are out. I've already seen about eight fender benders. Y'all need to stay put."

Jenny sagged. Maybe the ice was just happening in town. Tentatively stepping a foot on the top stair, she put her weight on it. Relieved, she took another step but her foot slipped out from under her and she fell hard. *Ooomph.* Thank goodness for the bulk of her coat.

"Jenny? Jenny?" Alice's voice called anxiously.

"Ow." Jenny picked herself up from the ground rubbing her elbow. Carefully, she reached for the phone that had skated away and pressed it to her ear. "You're right."

"I know. So, get buttoned up before you lose cell signal or power and ..." Alice's voice stopped. Air. The connection was lost.

Gingerly, Jenny edged back into The Camellia, her hip and elbow feeling sore already. She pulled up the weather on her phone, saw the large red cloud the meteorologists were animatedly pointing toward, and felt a cold dread in her stomach.

The expanding, angry looking blob of red was heading right for Heron Lake.

From the window, Jenny glimpsed Luke's truck in the driveway and felt reassured. The enormous Fir tree that filled the truck bed and extended over the cab was lashed on with straps. Luke must be in her cabin. Jenny had to tell him what was going on. Grabbing a five-foot piece of scrap wood to use as a walking stick, Jenny headed back outside, this time stepping as cautiously as a novice tightrope walker approaching the wire. First, the treacherous stairs. Freezing rain pelted her face and hurt like little cuts. Tucking the stick under her arm, Jenny grasped the railing with both hands and eased down the two steps. Slowly making her way to her cabin, she bent her knees, keeping her center of gravity low. No sudden movements. No strides. For a moment, the sun peeked from behind ominous gray skies, and the cabins and the grounds glittered like diamonds with what Jenny now knew was a coating of treacherous ice.

Every muscle tensed, Jenny approached the stoop of The Dogwood. Dropping the crude walking stick, she grasped the ice-coated railing. Her feet slipped this way and that. She took one step and slid back one, just catching herself before her face hit the railing. Inching forward, she dug each boot into the frozen mess as far as she could before she tried her next step. Encouraged, Jenny realized she was making progress.

The door flew open, and Luke stepped outside at his usual *let's get things done* pace. His eyebrows shot up and he caught Jenny's surprised look as he slid forward, crashed into her and bowled them both down the steps into a heap.

Jenny opened her eyes and saw there was an inch of air between her face and Luke's. She felt the not unpleasant warmth of his body pressing into hers. Wiggling, she tried to see if all limbs were intact. Check. Luke rubbed his head and stared so intently at her that she had a crazy thought that he might kiss her. But he blinked instead and asked slowly, "You okay?"

"I think," she said. "You okay?"

"What happened?" Luke started to disentangle his legs from

hers. "I got back about twenty minutes ago and was looking online trying to locate a few generators in case we lost power. It was a little slick when I got back here, but this is an ice rink."

"It is. Alice called to warn us." Jenny paused to sniff his breath that smelled of peppermint and a hint of coffee. Nice smells.

Luke gave a crooked smile, and gently rolled off her. In their two fat winter coats, Jenny had a crazy thought about colliding walruses. She started to giggle.

He raised a brow but smiled. "You're sure you're good? No blows to the head?"

"I'm fine." Jenny rested on the ground for a moment, missing the unexpected closeness with him. "This is my second fall in five minutes, so I'm getting good at them."

Giving her a ghost of a smile, Luke raised his head and looked around. "Nothing *looks* treacherous."

"And it's already a solid sheet of ice. I just caught part of the weather, but the meteorologists are saying this is just the beginning." Jenny pushed herself to a seated position, feeling a wave of panic. "If the roads are as slick as Alice's saying, and the cell goes out and the power goes out..." she trailed off, shaking her head, a thousand thoughts flying through her brain. How would guests get here? What if they all cancelled?

Luke fixed her with a steely glint of determination in his eyes. "We need a plan. And a contingency plan."

"I agree," Jenny said solemnly, and they helped each other scramble to their feet. Just when she thought she was secure, Jenny's foot shot out from under her and Luke caught her, steadying her. Again, that lovely closeness to him.

Luke may have felt it, too, because he looked away for a moment. "You go inside and get us loaded up on water. Fill up every bucket and all pots and pans you've got. Fill that tiny excuse for a bathtub," he said with a sliver of a smile. "If we lose power, the pump won't work and we've got no way of getting water from the well." He held up his cell and moved it in a circle and then over his head. "Nothing," he said. "First priority, see if we can get a decent, local forecast before we lose communication completely. I can get better reception near the dock."

But Jenny was running a terrifying movie in her head about Luke sliding into Heron Lake, getting hypothermic immediately and sinking like a boulder in the icy water. She handed him her makeshift walking stick. "Promise you won't fall in. I mean it, Luke," she said, the hoarseness in her voice betraying her fear.

"Promise." Luke's eyes caught hers and held them for a moment. "Be safe. I'll see you at your cabin in a few." Giving her a crooked smile, he steadied himself with her makeshift walking stick and skidded off.

Jenny slipped up the stairs, her mind racing. Besides the water, she wanted to get the animals in from their current favorite hangout spot in the Silver Belle and settle them into the warm cabin. She'd also grab her sleeping bag from the Airstream for Luke to sleep in.

Jenny also wanted to write a reassuring post for her guests who had weather alerts on their phones that were dinging like crazy and those who stayed glued to The Weather Channel at the first dusting of snow. She didn't want them to start canceling now. The meteorologists were hyped up, but they were also saying the system may only brush by them. This was North Carolina, not North Dakota. Everything could be back to normal in the morning. If Jenny made the tone of the post chipper and reassuring and if she worded it right, she could tell the truth while reassuring the worriers.

With her teeth, Jenny pulled the gloves off her frozen fingers and warmed them by the wood stove. Thinking about her wording, she sat down at the laptop. Jenny got to work decorating the post with memes of cheerful reindeer, a tree twinkling with Christmas lights, and a jolly Santa sipping cocoa. Flexing her finger for a moment, she tapped out:

Warm greetings from Heron Lake! We are so looking forward to having you be our guests. The holidays are a magical time at Heron Lake and today's dusting of snow – she edited "freakish ice event" – makes the cabins, the woods surrounding them, and the lake look even more like a fairyland. Pack your warm clothes and get ready to relax, get cozy in your cabins, and make family memories in our Winter Wonderland!

Jenny chewed her lip, hoping the family memories didn't involve search and rescue teams, and camping out in their stranded cars on I-40 eating protein bars from the glove compartment while they waited to be rescued by the National Guard. Feeling a pang of conscience, she added a final note:

Over the next few days, we'll keep you posted on the weather conditions here. If travel conditions deteriorate, we'll gladly refund your money or rebook you for another time.

If the Lakeside Resort was still in business.

Muttering *please, please, please*, Jenny held her breath and hit SEND, knowing that the message would either go out now on some thread of storm-buffeted Wi-Fi or catch the next wave of signal whenever that came along.

Quickly, she began pouring water in every vessel she owned. Slipping her coat back on, Jenny shoved a hat on her head and gingerly crab-walked the ten feet to The Silver Belle, where Bear and Buddy were curled up beside each other on the couch and Levi was standing beside them with that contented expression on his face that Jenny read as, *Yup, I'm just hanging with my boys.*

The cabin would be crowded with the boys inside, but the Airstream had little insulation and got cold fast. Letting Levi, Bear and Buddy out to take care of business, Jenny grabbed feed, water bowls and the sleeping bag and headed back to the cabin. The boys trailed behind, Levi mincing as he trod on the icy snow.

Jenny got them settled inside. She turned the stove on low and dumped a frozen brick of turkey chili into a pot. She'd made the chili last week and seasoned it with enough cumin and chipotle to heat her and Luke up from the inside out. Opening drawers, Jenny gathered flashlights and candles. She heard a stomping outside and Luke blew in, propelled by a blast of Arctic air. Ice droplets clung to his lashes, eyebrows and hair, and he carried an armful of firewood that he dropped beside the wood stove.

"Hey, there. Did you have any luck?" Jenny helped him off with his sodden coat, a surprisingly intimate act. She felt the warmth of his body and breathed in Luke's familiar pine, wood-smoke scent. Gracious. She busied herself draping his coat over a chair to dry.

"I had some luck." Luke pointed at the window. "But check out what's happening."

Rubbing a spot in the frosted window, Jenny peeked out and drew in her breath sharply. All she could see was driving white snow coming in sideways and piling up fast. "Mother of pearl."

"Yup." Luke's eyes were lit with worry. "The signal is spottier than ever, but I caught some weather." He had trouble meeting her eyes. "They're predicting a possible eight to ten inches of snow, and that's on top of this ice layer."

Jenny put her hands on her forehead and sat down hard, feeling sick to her stomach.

"No," she said weakly. "Just days from opening. This can't be happening." Closing her eyes, she fought back tears.

"Hey, now," Luke said gently. He put a hand on her shoulder and gave it a squeeze. "Let's not panic here. This could all veer off or blow over. We've just got to wait it out."

Jenny knew he was right. But instead of being reassured by his words, she examined her palms, her mind careening around. How did bankruptcy work? Did you file Chapter 11 or Chapter 9? Did they seize your pets, too?

"Cut it out." Luke snapped his fingers in front of her face. "Stop thinking about catastrophe and let's get a plan going."

Jenny nodded reluctantly. "But if we have to cancel all the reservations because none of our guests can get here, I can't make payments on the loan." She chewed her lower lip. Maybe she could move into that country rental with the older-adult-undergarment-wearing gentleman and learn to bale hay. Or, maybe she could pack up again and move to Wylie, Texas or Olive Branch, Mississippi, both towns with very high ratings for reasons she couldn't remember. She just liked the names.

"Jenny." Luke pulled up a chair and sat in front of her so she had to meet his eyes. "Here's what I think. We can't control the weather. We can't control the bank, although I do think that since you've finished the cabins and got so many reservations before even opening, they could be convinced to work with you a few months. They don't want you to go under any more than you want to go under."

That made sense, but Jenny was afraid to let herself be heartened.

CHAPTER 18 — COMING CLEAN

"WE NEED TO FOCUS ON what we can control." Luke touched her shoulder and gave her a reassuring look. "Let's not borrow trouble."

Jenny slumped, feeling defeated.

"Let's finish off any punch-list work that needs to be done on the cabins before we lose power." Luke looked out the window, which was now becoming encrusted with ice. "That could happen any time, so let's get a move on."

Giving herself a mental pep talk, Jenny slowly rose. She leaned over and gave Luke a quick hug. "I'd be a nervous wreck without you," she said, her voice taut with emotion.

Luke squeezed her shoulder and then pretended to look stern. "I need all hands on deck and a one hundred and fifty percent effort," he said, sounding like the personal attitude coaches on the *Me Booster* YouTube clips.

"Yes, boss." Jenny failed in her attempt to smile gamely and rummaged through a drawer to find a dry hat and gloves. "Here's what I wrote our guests about the weather..." She relayed her spiel about the winter wonderland.

"Wow. Cheery." Luke was still smiling as they stepped out into the wintery blast.

Shocked at how cold it now was, Jenny pulled her scarf down to shield her face.

"We just had the water turned on in the cabins. We can't let pipes freeze," Luke called, raising his voice to be heard above the wind.

The snow blowing in their eyes made it hard to see, but gave them more sure footing than the ice. They made their way to each cabin, turned off the main water valve and drained all the faucets. As they finished the last, Jenny stopped picturing their beautiful wood floors and fresh drywall ruined by broken pipes.

Prioritizing the remaining items on the punch list, the two worked for a solid two hours. The work was hurried and hard, but they made good progress.

The power died just as Luke drove a nail into a piece of barn-wood siding on an accent wall in The Hydrangea.

When the lights flickered and the room fell dark, Luke put down his nail gun. "Well, we almost got to everything," he said.

"I agree," Jenny said. They'd about finished the last of the punch list. "I'm running out of steam anyhow."

"Let's call it a day," Luke said, sounding tired. Turning on the flashlight on his phone, he shone the way to the door.

The wind gusted hard off the lake and whipped around the corner of the cabins. The snow was coming down harder, and Jenny could scarcely see more than two feet in front of her. Taking too big a step, she lurched but caught herself.

Luke grabbed her gloved hand and put it on the back of his coat. "Hang on," he called and plunged forward.

Jenny grasped tightly to the fabric between her fingers, squinting her eyes against the sleety snow that pelted them. The cabins were now blanketed in white. Sliding, she staggered forward, catching Luke's coat with both hands and managing to stay upright.

Luke reached around to pull her up beside him, and put an arm around her shoulders as they walked the last twenty yards to her cabin. Fighting the wind to get inside, Luke closed the door with a thud.

Inside, the air was redolent with the spicy smell of chili. Jenny turned off the now powerless stove and moved the pot to warm on the wood stove. The faint scent of wood smoke added to the heady mix. "Man. That smells like heaven."

Luke pulled off his gloves and rubbed his hands together.

"Homemade turkey chili," Jenny said and turned on all the

165

battery-operated candles. Already missing being under his arm, she busied herself giving the dogs and Levi reassuring pats. The boys watched intently as she stirred the pot of chili. "I know, I know. I'm two minutes late fixing supper." Jenny gave the animals their supper.

Luke added more logs to the wood stove. Outside, the wind was howling. "I better go scrape off the windshield and get the truck cranked up."

Jenny stared at him, slack-jawed. "Tell me you're kidding. You've seen how bad it is out there. Even with four-wheel drive, you'll get no traction on the ice."

He rubbed his head, looking distinctly uncomfortable. "I don't want to intrude. How about I stay next door in the Airstream?"

"We never got the wood stove installed," she reminded him. "That's still on the list. The space heater keeps it cozy for the animals, but without power, you'd freeze."

"I don't know," he said doubtfully and rubbed the back of his head.

Was he so repulsed by her that he'd rather drive through a blinding snow storm than stay one night on her couch? Her old doubts flared up, and Jenny remembered Douglas's excuses for not wanting to be near her once he'd started running. *Let's do dinner or a movie, not both. I'm tired. It's been a long day.* Wondering if Luke was doing the same thing, Jenny stirred the chili too vigorously. Without looking at him, she said stiffly, "You're a grown man, Luke. If you want to drive off an embankment or slide into a telephone pole, go for it. One less paycheck to write," she snapped. Clanging the lid on the pot with unnecessary vigor, Jenny decided she liked being mean.

Luke walked over and gently eased the spoon out of her hand. He put fingers under her chin and made her look at him. "Jenny, I like you more and more every day, and it scares the heck out of me. I love your laugh, your sweetness, your courage, your big brown eyes, your skills with a saw…"

Drawing a shuddering breath, Jenny felt giddy with relief. She said nothing for moment, reviewing each nice thing he'd said and savoring them. He liked her. Luke liked her. Jenny fought the urge to grin so broadly her gum showed. "So, you'll stay on my couch?"

"I will," Luke said, his eyes locked on hers.

"I thought you couldn't wait to get away from me," Jenny admitted.

Luke stared uncomprehendingly and shook his head. "A man would be a fool to want to do that."

"Douglas couldn't get away from me fast enough," Jenny said softly, flushing as she realized she'd let him in on her biggest insecurities.

Leaning against the log pillar, Luke crossed one long leg over the other. "I'd already concluded Douglas was a fool, and I guess I worried that he wanted to get back together with you."

"I'd have zero interest if he did," Jenny said firmly and saw a look of satisfaction flit across his handsome face. This made her like him even more. Nice to have a man be jealous.

"You never told me exactly what happened." Luke tilted his head in interest.

Jenny fought a smile. "And you haven't told me one thing about your late wife, except that she was incredible. I'm picturing a Mother Theresa, Charlize Theron, June Cleaver combination and you two being blissfully happy all the time," she admitted. "A tough act to follow."

"So, I made it all sound perfect?" Luke put his hands in his pockets, looking sheepish.

"Pretty much so," Jenny said lightly, but was ashamed of being jealous of a dead woman.

"No marriage is perfect. Ours wasn't," Luke said flatly. He eyed the wine rack on her counter. "Since I'm not driving, how about I open a bottle of wine and we talk about it?"

"I'd like that." She beckoned him to sit on the couch with her. The two dogs were already sprawled out on the cushions, but with a little gentle shoving, made room for them. Flames from the wood stove and the flickering candles cast a warm, sepia-toned glow on the room.

Luke took a sip of wine and looked at her expectantly. "You first."

Jenny flashed back to Alice's words. You and Luke have a chance for big love, and you're just throwing it away. So don't tell me to go after love when you're too chicken to do it yourself. Her mouth went dry as cotton and her palms were icy. But Jenny knew what she had to do. She'd be brave and tell him the unvarnished truth.

Taking a large swallow of wine for courage, she began. "Just after Douglas and I got engaged, he had back problems and went on a health kick. After he finished physical therapy with the beautiful and talented Aiden, his current fiancée, he joined a running group. A group of guys and gals met and ran together a few times a week."

Luke nodded, stroking Levi's muzzle.

"Then, Douglas and his group began training to run in the Marine Corps Marathon in October." Jenny paused, still stung by how it played out. "After that, all he wanted to talk about was pace and how far he ran. He'd obsess about what to eat before he ran and spend hours online selecting the perfect new pair of running shoes." She felt exasperated just talking about it. "I'd bake cookies, and he'd glance at my waistline and give me a lecture about sugar being poison and that once a woman got fat, there was no going back."

"Whoa. He said that?" Luke shook his head. "The man was a fool with a death wish."

Jenny was relieved at his reaction to the details she'd shared. "So, the runs went from three times a week to five times a week and then twice a day. Douglas started bailing out on dates early because of his training schedule. And then he just stopped calling." Remembering her confusion and sense of being abandoned, Jenny felt the unexpected burn of a lump in her throat. She'd hoped she was past all that anguish. But she made herself go on. "So it turns out his physical therapist, Aiden, was a member of the running group, and Douglas found he had feelings for her. One week before the Save the Date cards were to go out, he broke things off with me. Now Douglas and Aiden, the glamour couple, are getting married on Christmas." Drawing in a deep breath, Jenny managed a smile.

"Very tough. Now I understand your lack of enthusiasm about Christmas," Luke said sympathetically. Taking a swallow of wine, he gave her a speculative look. "Sounds to me like missing that marriage was the best Christmas present you could have ever been given. As much as I really don't like him, Douglas may have done you the biggest favor of your whole life."

Weighing his words, Jenny rose and poked back a log that was coming too close to the front of the fire box. Back in her spot on the couch, she slowly turned the globe of her wine glass so the liquid swirled. "It still hurts a little, but you're right. Absolutely right."

"Are you sure you don't still have feelings for him?" Luke's tone was casual, but his eyes were serious.

"I'm over him completely," Jenny said firmly.

Luke gave a glimmer of a smile and reached his socked foot over to touch hers. "I'm glad all that happened or I never would have met you." With a mischievous twinkle in his eye, he smoothed back an imaginary pompadour. "Of course, when you came into the store like a Christmas Grinch, I swept you off your feet. You had no choice but to fall for me," he said with a smug smile.

Jenny cracked a smile and paused for a moment, looking at the flickering flames and glowing embers of the fire. "You said you'd been dating but were bad at it. How bad?"

Rolling his eyes, Luke leaned back in the couch. "So bad."

Jenny gave him an appraising look. "Come on. You're handsome... in a rough way. You have good teeth and a lot of hair left. And all those women you must have met through work and at the hardware store? You must have had your share of admirers," she said in a teasing tone.

Rubbing the back of his neck, Luke actually blushed. "I could put women off like you wouldn't believe."

After she'd told him stories of her missteps and humiliations, Jenny couldn't wait to hear about him being graceless. She smirked. "How?"

Luke grimaced. "I'd call dates by the wrong name. Doris instead of Diana. Nicole instead of Noelle."

She fought to hide her smile. "You were close on the consonants, thought."

He grinned good-naturedly and held up a hand. "There's more. I'd have a 7:00 date, start working on the computer and suddenly realize it was 8:00. I'd get their professions wrong. I'd talk about what a noble calling nursing was when my date was a bookkeeper."

Jenny was laughing now, not bothering to hide it. "You were bad."

"I was," he said, wincing. "There weren't that many dates, but each was a fiasco."

Jenny shook her head. Luke being inept at something was reassuring to her. "Tell me more."

Luke thought for a moment, the corners of his mouth turning up. "On a first dinner date, I took a woman to a fancy restaurant and forgot my wallet. I never forget my wallet. The woman had to pay and she was steamed." He hesitated. "And then I'd talk about my wife and how great she was."

Jenny's smile faded. "I understand," she said quietly.

His expression grew serious. "I realized I wasn't ready to date, so I found a good counselor. He said I was self-sabotaging with women because I hadn't really worked through my grief. I went and talked to him for two years and joined a widow-and-widower support group. It helped a lot."

The silence spun out and she had to ask. "Are you ready for a relationship now?"

Luke examined her, his eyes as dark and deep navy blue as Heron Lake in the snow. "I am. But I won't take a step in that direction if you're not ready or if I think I could hurt you."

Jenny looked at him and found herself unable to look away. "I think I'm ready, but we need to take it really slowly," she said haltingly.

"Fine by me," Luke said in a throaty voice and moved closer to her. Putting an arm around her shoulder, he pulled her toward him and gave her a slow, ardent kiss.

Jenny leaned her head on his shoulder. And she just sat there, savoring a kiss that was every bit as intense and lovely as she'd imagined it would be. A few moments later, her head fell forward and she jerked upright. "Oh, my," she said, embarrassed that she'd fallen asleep on him. "I'm beat. I've got to get to bed." Rising, Jenny handed Luke a sleeping bag and a pillow.

After carefully clambering up the ladder of death and vowing she'd get Luke to put in some stairs as soon as he could spare the time, Jenny lay in her bed in the loft. Closing her eyes, she tried to sleep but all she could picture was the warm, vulnerable, lovely man sleeping on the couch below her. "Good night, Luke," she called.

"Sweet dreams, Jenny," Luke said, tenderness in his voice.

Jenny slept hard and woke the next morning to the scent of a freshly peeled orange and coffee. Blinking, she glanced over the railing and saw Luke. The two dogs and Levi were standing three across, watching Luke as he sat at the kitchen table peeling oranges and whistling softly. In front of him was the breakfast he'd assembled for them: a plate of orange segments, cut-up apples, and slices of sharp Cheddar cheese. A pot of simmering water was on the wood stove, and he sipped coffee he must have made with the coffee bags. It smelled heavenly.

"Good morning," she said, her voice raspy.

He looked up and broke into a slow smile. "Morning, sleepy girl." He resumed peeling. "I never slept with a horse before last night, but I recommend it. Levi curled up at my feet and was a good foot warmer."

Jenny broke into a smile. "Welcome to my world," she called. Knowing how wild her hair usually looked in the morning, Jenny tried to smooth it and wondered how she'd slither into jeans without him noticing.

Luke dunked a coffee bag in a second mug of hot water. "Here's your coffee. I'm going to shovel a path for the boys so they can go outside, and I'll check out the situation. The snow is slowing, and they say we're going to get warmer weather." Slipping on his jacket, he opened the door and stepped over eight inches of banked snow that was wedged behind it.

The yard piled high with drifts of snow, Jenny couldn't believe the winter scene. Chest tight with worry, Jenny reminded herself of Luke's coaching. *Focus on what you can control.*

Grateful for the privacy, Jenny used the bathroom, tied back her hair, and washed up. Picking up the warm mug, she closed her eyes with pleasure as she took a first sip of coffee. It tasted delicious. Glancing out the window, she saw Luke struggling to power through snow that came up over his knees. The sun was blindingly bright as it glinted off the white stuff.

After a while, Luke stomped the snow off his boots at the door and came back inside. "I got a small path cleared, but it's slow going. There's heavy snow on top of that ice."

Jenny made them both another cup of coffee and worried what havoc a deeper freeze tonight could wreak. Giving herself a mental shake, she helped him round up the dogs. Buddy and Bear knocked over the floor lamp as they wrestled, which usually meant they needed fresh air. With a frosty gust from the open door, Luke and the boys headed outside.

When the four adventurers returned, Jenny helped Luke give the boys a quick towel – off. "What's it like out there?" Jenny tried to sound upbeat while dreading his answer.

"It's warming up," Luke announced. Peeling off his outerwear, he swung into the kitchen chair and popped a segment of orange in his mouth.

Jenny felt a flicker of hope and slipped into a chair beside him. "After the freakishly cold and snowy day, maybe we could get a freakishly warm day to start a big melt."

"Maybe," Luke said noncommittally, but looked troubled. His phone dinged several times. "We got signal," he said. Glancing at his phone, he grimaced and turned it around so she could read the updated forecast.

A snowstorm blankets the state and slippery roads are making travel treacherous. Though road crews are working round the clock to clear the roads, progress has been slowed by ice and freezing temperatures. By tomorrow, most major roads will have been plowed, but with temperatures expected to dip into the teens tomorrow night, those roads will likely refreeze. Downed power lines and fallen trees and branches are adding to the problem. Three hundred thousand Summit Power customers are without power.

CHAPTER 19 — FALLING

J ENNY SHOOK HER HEAD SLOWLY and handed the phone back to him. "Even though the Heron Lake area's thawing, if people check the weather for the general area, no one would know it. Plus, if they made it here to the cabins, we'd have no power." Lacing her fingers together, she rested them on top of her head and slumped in her seat. "What now?"

Luke scratched behind Levi's ear and thought about it. "Today's the 12th. We've got two days for weather conditions to improve. If a few people make it in on the 15th, you've started to generate positive cash flow. If you reschedule them for later this year, you'll have those reservations on the book to show the bank that you're a viable business." He held up a hand. "I'm not saying this will all work out fine and dandy because it probably won't. But in the meantime, no need to panic."

Picking up a segment of orange, Jenny chewed it without tasting. No matter how Luke was trying to put a positive spin on it, she was fairly certain she was sunk.

Luke smiled gently and reached both hands across the table and took her hands in his. "Come on, Jen. We'll work on what we can. Let's start by shoveling the driveways and walkways to the cabins. I also need to wheelbarrow in more firewood to each cabin. I've got a stack of seasoned oak under tarps outside The Azalea."

Jenny scooted her chair over and rested her head on his shoulder, feeling just as discouraged but grateful for his presence.

Luke looked at her, held her face in his hands, and kissed her.

When they separated, Jenny felt momentarily bereft. She breathed out shakily. Studying him unblinking, she felt peace steal over her. He was so handsome and the kindness in his eyes made her heart ache.

Luke gave her a searching look and folded her into his arms.

Grasping her fingers in his hair, Jenny pulled him close and leaned her forehead against his. Her heart was banging its way out of her chest.

After a long moment, he let her go, but his beautiful blue eyes held hers. "I'm falling for you, Jenny Beckett, whether I want to or not," he said in a low voice. "It scares me."

"Terrifies me," she admitted.

Luke broke into a grin that lit the room. "Slow and easy, right?"

"Right." Jenny's emotions were on a roller coaster ride with Luke, thrilling elation one minute, gut-churning terror the next.

That night, Jenny and Luke each wore sweatpants and fleeces as they sat at the kitchen table playing cards by the light of the flameless candles. Buddy and Bear were sprawled underneath the table snoring, and Levi had folded himself into a compact bundle and lay on the rug near the stove. "Gin," Jenny said with a smug grin as she fanned her cards out on the table.

"I should never have taught you how to play this game," Luke groused, but the corners of his mouth turned up. "Do you want to play another hand?"

"No thanks." Jenny stretched and stifled a yawn.

Luke crossed his ankle over his knee. "What do you think it will be like living out here on the lake?"

Jenny took a sip of ice water and set her glass carefully down on the table. "I'll be lonely with you all gone. I've gotten used to you and I'll miss you," she admitted.

"I'll miss you," Luke said with quiet intensity.

"Getting the business going will be a challenge, but I think I'll really enjoy digging into it after I get the hang of things." Jenny tried to sound upbeat while feeling bleak about life without a daily visit from Luke. "I'll get involved some in the community, join the library, and take one of Lily's yoga classes. I'll probably end up making friends with some of the guests. The ones I'm not crazy about will at least be company and help pay the bills." Jenny searched Luke's face. "What about you? What do you think you'll do after you finish this job?"

His eyes met hers. "I'll call off my sabbatical soon. Doing this project reminded me of how much I like working hard and having a challenge. After this job is over, I'm ready to get back to work."

"Does that mean you'll go back to Athens?" Jenny asked in a small voice. An ache filled her chest at the thought of Luke living so far away.

Luke gave a sideways smile and held up his phone. "My old partner sends me five or six texts a week asking me to come back. He's planning a major expansion into Thailand and Korea and wants me to come back on board to head that up."

Jenny's heart sank and she actually felt like she might cry. Luke living two states away was bad enough, but halfway around the world made her feel desolate. "Gosh. I guess I thought you were staying local."

Luke rubbed the bridge of his nose and suddenly looked weary. "I don't know what I'm doing. Mama and Daddy are getting on in years, and I'd like to be around them as much as I can in case they need me. If we ever get Alice married, I've got high hopes about being an uncle."

Jenny heard blood thrumming in her ears. She wanted to take him by the shoulders and shake him and say, *What about me? How do I fit in?* She wanted to remind him of their kisses and the million reasons he should stay in North Carolina. Jenny might even want him to marry her and stay at Heron Lake, but Luke was going to do what he was going to do and acting too clingy would scare him off. Jenny flashed back to Douglas's mealy mouthed exit speech. Men were too crazy. She pretended to yawn. "Trying to hack through glaciers today really wore me out. I think I'll head up to bed."

Luke nodded and rose. "I think I'll do the same." He gave her a brief hug and kissed the top of her head.

Jenny stewed as she called up the dogs, went up to the loft, and shimmied into her nightgown. That kiss was a fatherly one or one you'd give to a frail maiden aunt, not one you'd get from a man who claimed he was falling for you.

Though she was exhausted, Jenny lay in her bed with her eyes wide open, thoughts and emotions racing as she tried to sort things out. Luke was sure giving her mixed signals. He just told her he was ready for a relationship and afraid he was falling for her, but then dropped a bombshell about planning to move back to Georgia. Maybe Luke was just as scared as she was about letting love in.

Jenny thought about Charlotte's advice. Talk to Luke and ask him where he stands. Then came Alice's honest feedback. *Don't tell me to go after love when you're too chicken to do it yourself.*

She sat bolt upright, startling Bear and Buddy, who had curled up beside her. No chickens here, no ma'am. Crawling over the mattress, she leaned over the side of the loft, and saw in the dim glow of the firelight Luke on the couch in his sleeping bag. "Luke," she called, her voice urgent.

Luke propped himself on one elbow and looked up at her. "Everything okay, Jen?"

"No, it's not," Jenny said loudly though her voice shook. "What about me? I don't want you to move away."

Luke sat up. "Maybe you better come down here," he said in a tone gruff with emotion.

Jenny braced herself for another breakup speech like the one Douglas had given her. *Just not ready. The feeling's gone. Maybe our timing's all wrong. I need to find myself.* Blah, blah, blah. Throwing on sweats, she climbed down the ladder feeling like a doomed woman headed for the firing squad.

Luke patted the spot on the couch beside him. "Sit."

Jenny crossed her arms and sat, her eyes not meeting his. But now tears were streaming down her face. "Out of the blue, you announce you might move back to Georgia, but I don't want you to go."

With gentle fingers, Luke brushed away her tears. "Forgive me, Jen. I'm acting like an idiot."

"I think so," Jenny agreed, blotting tears with the sleeve of her sweatshirt.

"I've been thinking about these work decisions but not talking about it, and I might have drifted back to work with my old company if I'd not met you. But that's not what I want." Luke reached an arm around her shoulder and pulled her closer to him.

Jenny tensed, ready for the *not ready, bad timing, find himself* jive talk breakup caveat but none came. Still, she braced for it. "You got scared, right?"

"Yup," Luke said, and took her hands. "I might be halfway in love with you."

"Well, join the club," Jenny said. The tears started again, this time happy ones.

The next morning, Jenny was dreaming a Doctor Zhivago-inspired romance that featured her snuggled under what she hoped were faux furs, riding in a horse-drawn sleigh with Luke, who sported an Omar Sharif style moustache. He was giving her a heavy-lidded smoldering look when the clock radio blared out the Alvin and the Chipmunks classic, *Santa Claus Is Comin' to Town*. Jenny's eyes flew open and her heart pounded. The lights flickered, dimmed and came on again, lighting up the cabin. The clocks flashed. The microwave dinged. Jenny leaned her head over the side of the loft and called excitedly to Luke, "Power, Luke. We've got power."

Luke opened his eyes, blinked, and broke into a grin.

Flopping back down on her bed, Jenny called down to him. "I love every employee at Summit Power. I'm going to write each one a thank you note, or bake cookies for them all, or..." she trailed off, having run out of ideas.

Luke chuckled and called up to her, "I agree but let's get going. There's a good chance we'll lose power again."

Savoring remembrances of her conversation with Luke the night before, Jenny was filled with a heart-fluttering sense of joy. Closing her eyes, she let herself run the whole scene again in slow motion, trying to recall Luke's every word and expression. Jenny couldn't believe it. She was in love with Luke and he was falling in love with her, too. Rousing the sleeping dogs, she threw on her clothes and hurried downstairs.

Hooking his arm around her neck, Luke pulled her in for a scratchy kiss. "Morning, Jen."

"Morning, you," Jenny said, still dazzled with happiness that this beautiful, kind man might be in love with her.

Luke turned on the coffeemaker and, as the smoky scent of dark roast filled the air, leaned against the counter and met her eyes. "Let's assume everything is going to work out and you'll have a full house on Saturday. We need to be ready."

"Right." Jenny grabbed a mug and poured herself a taste of the brew from the still – dripping carafe. "Ah!" she closed her eyes with pleasure. As Jenny offered her mug to Luke for a taste, her phone dinged rapid fire.

"Holy smokes." Luke broke into a grin and shook his head. "Your Wi-Fi's come back strong."

Hurriedly, Jenny grabbed her phone and stared incredulously at the screen as all the messages and texts arrived. Fingers trembling, she listened to her voice-mail messages and held the phone out so Luke could listen.

This is Daniel Wise. Hey there and happy holidays. I managed to reserve the last SUV at the airport for our arrival Saturday. By then, the flights should be coming in and out of Charlotte Douglas with just a few delays. The girls are excited about our adventure. See you soon.

Almost in tears with gratitude, Jenny gave Luke a high five. "One cabin still rented."

"Let's hear the next." Luke pointed at the phone. "I'm feeling lucky."

Knocking on the wood of the table, Jenny tensed, bracing for a cancellation as she played the next message.

"Hey, doll. This is Viv Sanders. Merry two weeks before Christmas. Hugh and I'll be there on the 15th at three. No prob with the driving. We're from up North and we love snow, right? We might slip and slide but Hugh's a great driver and we'll have a marvelous time."

Gripping the phone so tightly that her hand was white, Jenny beamed at Luke as the message went on. In a girlfriend-to-girlfriend tone, Viv added, *"So, Santa got me a fabulous new faux fur coat and hat for Christmas. If you don't think it's over the top, I can't wait to wear them at the cabin. See you soon, doll."*

When the voice-mail finished, Jenny held her hands together and looked up. *Thank you, thank you, thank you.* Next, she hurriedly scrolled through her emails and texts and pumped her fist in the air. "Yes!" Grabbing Luke by the arm, she jumped up and down. "Can you believe it?" she asked exultantly.

Putting his hand on her shoulders to slow her down, Luke grinned. "Believe what? Tell me the rest of the good news."

"The older couple from High Point cancelled, but the two sisters and the bird – watcher texted or emailed this morning saying they hoped we were still on for Christmas," Jenny said wonderingly.

"Good." Luke smiled broadly but paused a moment. "So no word from the guests booked in the other cabins?"

Her mind racing, Jenny felt even more determined. "Not yet. But if the snow melts more tonight, I'm going to call or text them and encourage them to come. Can you get me one of those stunning pics you took of the cabins in the snow? I'll post those as an enticement."

"Good idea." Luke pulled the phone from the pocket of his jeans.

Jenny closed her eyes for a moment, concentrating. Sliding over to her laptop, she tapped out a draft. "How's this?"

The snow is melting fast, and the morning sun makes the view out of every cabin glorious, dazzling, sparkling! We so look forward to seeing you. Get ready for the romance of a crackling bonfire, Canada geese calling as they fly overhead, the sparkling lights of our sixteen-foot Christmas tree, and the serene beauty of a starlit night on Heron Lake. If we're lucky, we'll catch the Geminids Meteor Shower, one of the prettiest events in the heavens.

Luke whistled. "That's good. I'd want to visit and I'm already here." But his smile faded. "One hitch. The roads into the neighborhood are state maintained. Department of Transportation is going to clear all the major roads first, so I'm guessing they won't get to us for days. I'd hate for guests to make it all the way to the main road and get stuck trying to get to the cabins."

Wilting, Jenny sat down hard on the kitchen chair. Crestfallen, she put her elbows on the table, and sank her head in her hands. "You're right," she said. "The road into the cabins is long and shaded. The snow will last for days if not a week." She gave him a beseeching look. "It's not just the money I won't make. I don't want to let people down, Luke. If they worked hard to get here, I don't want them to have to turn around and go home. I want them to be able to stay in those darling cabins."

Luke's look signaled his understanding. He held up his phone. "I can call D.O.T. and see if there's any way they could put us at the top of their lists for secondary roads in the county. Everybody and their brother is probably making the same call, but it's worth a try."

"Good idea." But Jenny wasn't holding out much hope.

CHAPTER 20 — HOMECOMING

ENDING THE CALL, HE DREW in a breath and released it before speaking, "I left a message."

Jenny thought about it and shook her head slowly. "I can't in good conscience send out that message to guests if the road isn't passable. Maybe I should call the guests who have confirmed and cancel."

Luke mulled it over, absently stroking Buddy's head. "Let's try to ride it out and see what kind of shape the roads are in. Then you make your decision." He pulled on his coat.

"Good," Jenny said, bundling up and stepping outside.

"We'll take my truck. The weight in the bed will help with traction," he said tersely, lifting the tarp and gesturing at another load of firewood in the back. The two trudged to the truck, struggling at times just to pull their feet from the deep snow and make the next step. Luke started the engine to warm it up, and the two of them used their arms as brooms to brush snow from the windshield. Slowly, the big truck plowed, crunched and slid around the driveway and out to the road. Luke's jaw tensed as he worked to steer out of a skid, narrowly missing a towering pine tree.

"Some of the snow is over two feet deep." Jenny blew on her gloved hands, fruitlessly trying to warm them. She stared out the window at the sea of white. If the long road in was this bad, guests would never make it to the cabins.

"Should have raised my truck up high like Mike's," Luke said wryly as he turned the defroster to high.

Jenny's shoulders hunched. She was feeling defeated, a feeling she'd had when Jax took off, when Douglas dumped her, and when Odious Earl kicked her out. She didn't like that feeling one bit.

Think. She needed to think. Surely there was a solution to the fix she was in besides crossing her fingers and hoping for the best. Jenny drew in her breath sharply, remembering. A snip of conversation replayed in her mind. Straightening, she touched Luke's arm and when he looked at her questioningly, she flashed a tentative smile. "This is a long shot, but let me use your phone. I want to make one call."

Three hours later, Jenny had defrosted a pot of savory beef stew and left it on the back burner of her stove ready to warm. The timer dinged and she pulled a fresh-baked pan of sweet potato rolls from the oven. Jenny smiled. She loved, loved, loved electricity and would never take it for granted again.

Throwing on her coat and gloves, Jenny took a shovel and resumed the hard work of trying to clear more of the walkways between the cabins that had frozen again last night, while Luke backed the truck in from cabin to cabin, packing down snow to make pathways passable.

Her cell rang, and Jenny scrabbled in her pocket to grab it. "Are you here?" she asked, talking fast.

"Walk on down the road," Alice said in a mischievous tone.

"They're here," Jenny called to Luke, dropping the shovel and hurrying over to him, grinning like a loon.

Luke flashed her a smile as he tossed the last piece of oak on the woodpile outside The Redbud and strode over to her. He reached out a gloved hand, and she took it. Luke started to try to run up the driveway.

Jenny whooped with laughter as she tripped and caught herself. Taking a glove full of snow, she tossed it at him, hitting him square in the back of the head.

Grinning, he hooked an arm around her neck and gave her an exuberant kiss. Both heard the throaty growl of a powerful engine.

"Let's go, slowpoke," Luke said and pulled her along behind him.

Laughing, Jenny clumsily took larger steps as Luke hurried his pace.

The monster truck had the silver blade of a plow attached to the front of it, and roared up the driveway, almost effortlessly scraping aside piles of snow. Wearing a Santa hat and blue reflective sunglasses, a grinning Mike leaned out his window. He gunned the engine and gave them a thumbs up. Alice leaned out the other window, waving both arms and blowing extravagant kisses. "Hello, sweeties," she called.

When they got closer, Alice took off a glove and waved a Queen Elizabeth wave, with the screwing-in-the-lightbulb motion. Jenny threw back her head and laughed at her friend's silliness and started to wave back in the same queenly way. But she put a hand to her mouth and broke into a smile.

Luke looked at her questioningly.

"The ring," she said, choking back tears. "She's wearing her engagement ring again."

"Good." But Luke looked distracted and was gazing at Mike's truck. "That's a 6.8 Turbo Diesel with Super Torque and the 840 Power Thrust," he said in an awed voice.

"Got salt and sand back here," Mike hollered, tipped his head toward the bed of the truck. "Jump in, Luke. Let's get her done."

Alice leaped down gracefully from the passenger seat and skipped toward Jenny, beaming. Luke swung up into Mike's truck, trying to look nonchalant at getting to ride shotgun in the beast of a truck. But a split-second later, he broke into an ear to ear grin.

Jenny pulled Alice into a bear hug. "The engagement is back on. Good, good, good. I want to hear everything. Let's make hot chocolate for the boys and you can tell me all."

Alice nodded happily, linking her arm in Jenny's as the two began the trek back to the cabin. Pausing, she examined Jenny's face. "You're as lit up as a Christmas tree and you've got a sparkle in your eyes. Luke looks like the smiley emoji. I believe you've got news of your own." She linked thumbs and tapped her fingers together, looking like she couldn't wait to hear every word.

In the cabin, Jenny made hot chocolate and she and Alice

talked excitedly, giving each other updates on the latest romantic developments. As they sipped the chocolatey sweetness, they schemed. Jenny picked up her phone and dialed Ella Parr. "Ella, I'm wondering if we could borrow your husband Paul..."

After eating a bone-warming bowl of beef stew and warm rolls, Alice and Mike roared off in the truck. Jenny and Luke finished decorating the cabins and the big Christmas tree, which they'd strung with lights and centered in the middle of the crescent of the cabins. They'd laid the wood and kindling in the new fire pit and checked every item off their to-do list. It was after midnight when they finally finished, and Jenny was filled with such floaty exhilaration that she thought she'd never sleep. But when she finally called down her goodnight to Luke and burrowed in her bed between Buddy and Bear's warm bodies, Jenny fell asleep almost as soon as her head hit the pillow.

When Jenny woke, the inviting scent of brewing coffee wafted up to her. Her eyes flew to her bedside clock, she saw the red digital display of the time, and she blew out a breath. The power had stayed on. Peering out the window, she saw Luke's truck was gone. Jenny missed him already. He'd headed back to Shady Grove early to run errands, but would be back later to help her get ready.

Today was the day. Jenny hummed Christmas carols as she slipped on her flannel robe and padded downstairs. Gathering ingredients, she tied back her hair, put on an apron and started mixing.

After she'd pulled the cakes out of the oven, Jenny took the dogs and Levi out for a walk. Her hand on her forehead to block the glare of the sun, she peered at the driveway. It looked mostly clear, and through the trees, she could see the road into the Lakeside Resort. Though the roads were still snowy, she saw spots of black asphalt. Guests with experience driving in snow could make it in. Thank goodness for Mike's snow blade. Nervously, Jenny pulled out her phone and looked again at the forecast. Sunny, thirty-eight degrees by noon tomorrow. The snow was melting.

All three of the boys sniffed and dawdled down the path,

the snow having amplified the scent of every nighttime visitor, raccoon, deer, fox or possum. The two dogs raced around, clumsily leaping through snowbanks while her cautious guy Levi stayed at her side. Jenny felt a sense of contentment that she hadn't felt in a long while, a feeling that all was right with the world. Maybe that's because it was, she thought with a little smile. Rounding up the boys, she headed home.

Jenny finished wiping down the counters and was drying the heavy skillet when she heard a knock. Throwing open the door, she smiled at Luke, who was clean-shaven, pink – cheeked and smelling of sandalwood soap. Jenny suddenly felt nervous as a girl on her first date.

Luke swept her into a bone crusher of a hug. "How's my girl?"

His girl. Jenny felt a swooning, fluttery joy. "Missed you even though you were only gone a few hours."

"Missed you, too." Luke held her a beat longer, as though reluctant to let her go. "Those look and smell wonderful," he said, eyeing the cakes now cooling on racks on the table. Glancing around the cabin, he gave her a twinkly smile. "I hate to tell you, Ms. Scrooge, but this place looks like you figured out how to love Christmas again."

"I have." With a Vanna White arm movement, Jenny pointed out all the decorating she'd done. A two-foot-high, brightly lit tree sat in the middle of her kitchen table. Though the tree was an artificial one made of tinsel-like silver, it looked warm and cheerful. Jenny had put tea lights around the room, and the garlands of real pine and cedar that were draped on her kitchen counters filled the room with a clean, woodsy scent.

"It looks great," Luke said admiringly.

Jenny couldn't resist giving him one more hug. He lifted her off the ground, kissed the nape of her neck and, with one final smoldering look, set her back down.

Holy moly. Luke Hammond made her heart bang and her face burn. "Everyone will be here soon. We need to get finished up," she said, reluctantly.

"You're almost ready," he said and gave her an encouraging smile.

"*We're* almost ready." Jenny took his hand and squeezed it. "You've been my rock."

"I'm glad I could help," Luke said mildly, but his eyes signaled some potent mixture of longing, happiness and caring.

"I'm staying ten feet away from you, lovely man," Jenny said, wagging a finger. Taking his shoulders, she wheeled him toward the door. "Git. I'll see you soon."

With a grin, he ducked out.

After she finished knifing on the last of the fluffy vanilla buttercream frosting and sprinkling on the toasted coconut, Jenny stopped to admire all four of the tall coconut cakes she'd baked that morning. As she took off her apron and washed pans, she listened for cars. When she heard the crunch of snow and ice at the head of the driveway, Jenny hurriedly slicked on a red lipstick called Holly Berry that she hoped looked festive and went to greet her first arrivals.

Smiling, she walked toward the SUV that eased to a stop, loving the idea of welcoming guests, giving them a haven where they could be closer to nature, reconnect with each other, and shed the day-to-day worries they dragged around. All her guests sounded excited about the prospect of a white Christmas. Each cabin was warm, welcoming and smelled of balsam and fresh cut wood.

The couple from Southern Pines stepped out of their Lincoln SUV. Hugh was a beefy guy with a gruff voice and an endearing smile. Viv chattered about the road conditions, swooned at the view, and burbled. "I know our stay is going to be just so rustic and fabulous. When we get unpacked, I can't wait to meet that precious pony and those dogs that were on the website and give them a cuddle." In bright red lipstick that matched her Christmas red scarf, Viv wore her big faux fur coat and a tall fur Cossack hat that Jenny couldn't decide looked chic or like a possum or raccoon was curled up napping on her head. Liking Viv instantly, she decided to go with chic.

Jenny extended the invitation, and Viv put a hand to her cheek.

"Oh, doll. We'll be there with bells on." Hugh gave his wife an indulgent smile and winked at Jenny.

Daniel Wise and his daughters pulled in next. "What an adventure we've had already," he said. He was pink cheeked and sparkly eyed like he'd enjoyed their snowy driving adventure. The two slouching girls made no eye contact and looked bored as Jenny gave him the rundown on their cabin. Daniel spoke sotto voce. "The girls are mad because I told them no devices. Kiera tried to smuggle her cell here in her boot, and security at the airport found it." He shook his head wryly. "So this could be the disaster trip of a lifetime or the perfect Christmas for us."

"Good luck." A small, enclosed space with two sulky girls could be a nightmare. "One more thing," Jenny said as they turned to go. She extended the invitation.

Daniel broke into a smile. "No kidding! Count us in."

The couple celebrating their third wedding anniversary rolled in next and beamed with pleasure as Jenny handed them their key and a chilled bottle of wine tied with the big red bow. When she invited them, they beamed. "Of course."

Harriet the bird-watcher was a petite brunette wearing tortoise shell glasses. Swimming in a knee-length down coat that was built for a heftier woman, she pulled a notebook and a field guide from her large purse as she rummaged for her wallet. "I'm hoping to add several waterfowl to my life list." She pushed her slipping glasses back up her nose and handed Jenny her debit card.

In her mid-thirties, Harriet was pleasant looking with bright, intelligent eyes. Jenny snuck a glance at her hand. Ah ha. No wedding ring. Making a quick decision, Jenny switched her from The Redbud to The Mimosa, the cabin next door to the Wise's. "The man in the next cabin and his two daughters want to go bird-watching, too," she said casually as she handed her a receipt. "They might be grateful for any tips you could give them."

Harriet's eyes shone. "Such a great sport for young people. I'd be happy to share tips."

"I bet they'd like that," Jenny said and told her the plan.

Peg and Lucy, two sisters with graying pixie cuts and ready

smiles, were from Hollis, North Carolina. "We're hunting widows," Peg, the shorter one explained. Her sister, Lucy, chimed in. "If our husbands' idea of relaxation is freezing their behinds off sitting in a deer stand, they can have at it." The ball was back in Peg's court. "We decided to have a relaxing time of our own." With a puckish grin, she raised a heavy mesh grocery bag that clanked when she lofted it. "We each brought tons of books, wine, great cheeses, nibbles and chocolate. Lots of chocolate. We intend to be total slugs."

"The Lakeside Resort is just right for that," Jenny said. If she'd have let Charlotte post her *Plain Folks Only* designation on the website, these two would have fit the bill. "I have a special event I wanted to invite you to." Jenny gave them the details.

Just before 3:30, Lena and Jason, the couple from Carrboro, North Carolina arrived.

Jason proudly showed Jenny his sled and their snowshoes and asked for advice on hikes. Lena smiled, but when her husband went to unload their car, showed Jenny her canvas tote filled with library books and a tablet. "I'll do some outdoor things with Jason, but I plan on binge reading," she confided with a mischievous smile. When Jenny issued the invitation, Lena looked thrilled.

Just before 5:00 o'clock, the winter sun was already sinking into the waters of Heron Lake. Jenny gathered the boys and put on their dress-up attire. Buddy and Bear looked handsome in jaunty, red-plaid, bow-tie dog collars and Levi seemed comfortable with the red velvet bows secured to his mane. "You look so festive." Jenny gave them each a quick pat.

Peeking out the window, Jenny slipped into her dress, slid up the zipper, and smoothed it. Looking in the mirror, she liked what she saw for once. The sheath had a V neck and fell gracefully to just above her knees. She put on low heels, reminding herself to be careful of any slippery ice or snow remaining on the ground.

The guests trickled out of their cottages looking unsure of themselves, but were drawn to the fire and the decorated tree. Luke recruited Jason to help him pop corks on bottles of Prosecco and open bottles of sparkling nonalcoholic grape juice. The two men poured drinks into plastic flutes and handed them out.

The guests sipped and chatted with one another, slipping into the Adirondack chairs and warming themselves by the fire. All looked spiffy in their hastily put together semblance of finery. Hugh wore a plaid shirt with a bolo tie, and Viv had thrown a dramatic winter white pashmina over her fur and pinned a sprig of mistletoe on the big fur hat. The two sisters, Peg and Lucy, wore velour pantsuits, one in green and the other in red.

Looking outside, Jenny saw Luke add logs to the bonfire and stoke it. The flames danced as they caught and the fronts of the cabins seemed bathed in golden light. Stepping out to her porch, she picked up the orange extension cords, held her breath and plugged them in. The Christmas tree softly lit the sky with its red, yellow and green lights. Against the backdrop of the indigo blue lake, the white of the snow and the blazing yellow and red flames of the fire, the tree looked ethereal.

Jenny felt a squadron of butterflies launch in her stomach. Peeking out the window again, she let her eyes rest on Luke, watching as he greeted guests, brought Bear, Buddy and Levi over to meet the two adolescent girls, and introduced the young married couple to Viv and Hugh. As if he could sense her gaze, Luke paused, looked directly at the window and broke into a smile. Grinning, she formed a circle with her thumb and index finger in an okay sign.

Handel's "Arrival of the Queen of Sheba" began playing. Everyone was ready for a Christmas wedding.

CHAPTER 21 — A CHRISTMAS WEDDING

EARING THE DISTINCTIVE ROAR OF a truck with a huge engine, Jenny stepped outside and walked to the driveway to greet Mike, who pulled up with a flourish and gave her a happy wave. After helping his parents, Nona and Pete, and future in-laws, Caroline and Frank, from the cramped back seat of the crew cab, he hurried around to open the door for Alice. Gently, almost reverently, Mike lifted her down from the truck, her billowing skirts and petticoats almost blocking him from sight.

Alice's hair was twisted in a romantic chignon with draping curls and her face was suffused with joy. She looked like a beatific Christmas angel in the white velvet dress that suited her far better than it ever did Jenny. Alice had a creamy cashmere shawl draped gracefully around her shoulders and she clutched a bouquet of baby's breath and yellow roses

"You look astonishingly lovely," Jenny said, brushing away brimming tears.

Alice gave her a hug. "We'll be forever grateful to you for this, Jen."

Mike pretended to gaze at an imaginary watch and tapped his toe. "Let's get this show on the road."

Alice laughed and hooked her arm in Mike's. "When this guy makes up his mind, he makes up his mind." She dimpled up at him.

"Come on, pumpkin," Mike said, lifting her train so it wouldn't drag in the snow.

Jenny introduced herself to the Hammonds and Mike's folks, chatting with them as they followed the couple on their walk toward the lakeside Christmas tree. Alice took in the beauty of the ceremony site, got misty-eyed, and sent Jenny a grateful look. "It's even more beautiful than I imagined it would be."

When the guests glimpsed the wedding party, they broke into smiles and began to clap. Mike's face turned crimson, flustered at the attention, but then held up Alice's hand like a victorious man who'd finally gotten his girl. A violin and cello rendition of Pachelbel's "Canon in D" began to play softly.

Viv was already dabbing her eyes with a tissue, and Hugh gently rubbed circles on her back. Daniel's teenaged girls had given up the studied ennui and looked rapt. Lena and Jason had their arms around each other's waists, and every guest enraptured.

Resplendent in his blue-and-gold vestments, Ella Parr's husband, Paul, took his place in front of the couple and opened his Bible. A hush fell over the small crowd.

Holding Luke's hand, Jenny's heart swelled as she watched the radiant couple and listened as the clergyman opened the marriage ceremony with familiar words. "Dearly beloved, we have come together in the presence of God to witness and bless the joining together of this man and this woman in holy matrimony." Alice's face was luminous, and Mike looked like he was holding back tears.

Tissue in hand, Viv dabbed at tears that were streaming down her cheeks and Hugh kissed the top of her head. Daniel's daughters stroked Bear and Buddy and watched the ceremony intently, awestruck. The couple celebrating their anniversary leaned into each other, enjoying their own memories.

The clergyman asked Alice, "Will you have this man to be your husband; to live together in the covenant of marriage? Will you love him, comfort him, honor and keep him, in sickness and in health; and, forsaking all others, be faithful to him as long as you both shall live?"

Alice's face was red and she didn't answer, struggling to keep from sobbing. She held up a finger and tried to compose herself. Mike gave her hand a reassuring squeeze and Paul handed her a tissue, but Alice's shoulders heaved and she covered her face with her hands.

Levi casually strolled into the clearing and approached the clergyman and the couple, probably looking for one of the carrots Alice always had for him. Walking up to the bride, he nuzzled her. The guests chuckled and Alice broke into a smile as she took Levi's head in her hands and planted a big smooch on his head. Fixing her eyes on her groom, Alice said in a clear, strong voice, "I will."

Mike boomed out his vows, his eyes never leaving his bride's.

In a sonorous voice, the clergyman announced. "I now pronounce you husband and wife, in the Name of the Father, and of the Son, and of the Holy Spirit. Those whom God has joined together let no one put asunder." Looking delighted, Paul nodded at Mike. "You may kiss the bride."

Mike put a hand on either side of Alice's face and gave her a scorching kiss.

Everyone burst into applause and Hugh stuck two fingers in his mouth and whistled. Looking radiant, Alice held up the bouquet and Mike raised his fists in the air.

For the recessional, the bride and groom had chosen *Forever and Ever, Amen*. Randy Travis's warm, full-bodied baritone filled the air with words about everlasting love. The sentiments of the verses made Jenny's heart squeeze.

The wedding supper was a hastily organized potluck. The men were happy to help. Luke enlisted Daniel the widower to help erect several long tables fireside. Hugh from Southern Pines and the fathers of the bridal couple, Pete and Frank, hiked to the truck and carried in several portable outdoor heaters and went to work setting them up.

The mothers of the bride and groom tried to make a beeline for Jenny but had a few weather-related slowdowns. Nona's wide-brimmed, pink, Kentucky Derby-style hat threatened to blow away on a wind gust, and she paused to take both hands and mash it further down on her head. Caroline's lavender heels, which matched her lavender mother-of-the-bride suit, may not have been the best choice for a mucky, slushy day. She got stuck and put a hand on Nona's arm to steady herself as she paused to extricate a heel from the melting snow. The two linked arms and giggled as they moved determinedly to Jenny's side.

Caroline held her hands together as in prayer. "We are so grateful to you for hosting this beautiful wedding."

Nona chimed in, touching Jenny's shoulder. "And whatever you did to get these two hard-headed children of ours down the aisle, we can never, ever thank you enough."

"They thought of this all by themselves," Jenny said with a smile and gazed fondly at one and the other. She'd had so many conversations with them about the reception over the past day that she felt like she knew the women. "I can't thank *you two* enough. You two were the lifesavers. We could have never pulled this wedding off without you."

"Whew." Nona grinned good-naturedly and passed the back of her hand across her forehead. "It was actually fun. Caroline and I were on the phone the whole evening, and I pulled the last dish out of the oven at 2:00 this morning. It was like a slumber party, staying up late to study for exams, and a cooking extravaganza all in one."

"I haven't been awake that late in who knows when," Caroline said. "But it was also a fun challenge because neither of us could get to the grocery store. We had to use what was in our chest freezers and get creative. The meal will be a bit of a hodge-podge," she explained.

"That's what potlucks are for. I know it will be delicious," Jenny said, beckoning them to follow her to the driveway. "Let's go get the food set up."

"With the amount of baking and cooking we did last night, we could open a catering company," Caroline drawled as she and Nona followed Jenny to Mike's truck to carry in the feast they'd prepared on very short notice.

Jenny watched them as they talked. The mothers of the bridal couple seemed destined to be good friends.

The three of them hauled food storage bags, Tupperware

containers, and tightly wrapped foil platters from the bed of the truck.

Her arms laden with casserole dishes, Jenny's mouth watered as she caught the delicious aroma of fried chicken. "We'll borrow one or two guest's cabins and heat these up in the microwave."

"Perfect," Caroline said. The two women bustled around to set up the feast and Lena and Viv pitched in, pink-cheeked at being part of the impromptu wedding and reception.

The two hunting widows jumped in to help Caroline and Nona heat up the meals. Lena and Harriet corralled Daniel's daughters to help Jenny in her cabin with cake and punch. The girls walked slowly as they carried out two bowls of pink wedding punch while the adult women walked outside, carefully holding the tall, elegant, coconut wedding cakes.

Pulling off an outdoor wedding right after a snowstorm in the middle of nowhere seemed to have bonded all the guests and the wedding party. Faces wreathed in smiles, they laughed and talked convivially like they'd all been longtime friends.

After toasts, Jenny and Luke took their glasses of champagne and wandered down to the water's edge. They looked back at the convivial crowd. "We did it," Jenny said and slipped an arm around Luke.

Luke pulled her closer, took her hand, and kissed it. "I love you, Jenny."

Blinking back tears, Jenny let herself lean into him. Trembling with emotion, she looked up at him. "Love you back, Luke."

On Christmas Eve morning, Jenny kept her eye out the window for Charlotte. Meanwhile, she added fresh sage, crushed garlic cloves, and leaves of thyme to a lemon juice and olive oil mixture that she'd use to coat the small turkey breast she planned on roasting for supper. Her friend had texted her to ask if she could stop by for a quick visit on her way home to Shady Grove. Jenny couldn't wait to see her, especially now that all her guests were settled in and happily enjoying Christmas at the Lakeside Resort.

Smiling when she saw the familiar green sedan pull into the driveway, Jenny hurried out to greet Charlotte. The car looked festive with two plush, fabric-covered antlers poking from each of the front door windows and a big red nose attached to the front bumper. Jenny had missed Charlotte and now that things were running smoothly, she planned on seeing her more. But it was Ashe Long who stepped from the driver's seat and smiled while Charlotte waved wildly from the seat beside him.

Ashe looked so different than he had when she'd first met him at his legal office, all buttoned up, earnest, and professional. Today, he wore a claret-colored fleece, his cheeks were rosy, and he looked boyish and happy. "Hey there, Jenny. Merry Christmas," he said.

"Merry Christmas, Ashe. Good to see you," she said, and impulsively hugged him.

Any man who made Charlotte happy was a friend of hers.

Color stained Ashe's cheeks, and Jenny rounded the car, broke into a smile and embraced Charlotte. "Merry Christmas, sweets. You look amazing." Her friend's lustrous black curls were held back with a red velvet hairband; under her black-and-white windowpane wool coat, she wore a red cashmere turtleneck and blue jeans. Charlotte looked somehow lit from within.

"Merry Christmas. It's so good to see you." Charlotte kissed her on the cheek. "We're on our way to Mama and Daddy's, but I wanted Ashe to see this darling place. We can only stay a half-hour and then we need to skedaddle." From the car, she pulled a large shopping bag overflowing with colorfully wrapped presents and handed it to Jenny.

"You shouldn't have." Jenny said, but took the bag and peeked inside. "But I love presents."

"This is mainly stuff for the cabins, but you need to open this." Grinning, Charlotte pulled a card from the top of the bag and handed it to Jenny.

The glitter covered Christmas card featured Mr. and Mrs. Claus sitting in front of a camp fire beside a shiny gold metallic RV that looked like the Silver Belle. Ms. Claus was knitting busily and Santa had a peppermint stick in his mouth as he examined a Garmin GPS. Rudolph and the rest of the reindeer wore brightly colored Christmas sweaters as they lounged in recliner lawn chairs. Smiling at the whimsy, Jenny opened the card and read the note.

Sweet Jenny,

My Christmas present to you is the gift of adventure. I'm going to fix up the interior of the Silver Belle for you. Luke's agreed to help.

One stipulation, though. Just because we're both finally in love, let's not ever let our men come between our friendship. Promise me that in the spring when we've finished, you and I will take a long road trip in the Silver Belle. And let's plan on doing a girls' getaway every year for the rest of our lives. Love, love, Love. Charlotte PS I want to visit every waterfall and lighthouse in North Carolina.

Jenny brushed away brimming tears and hugged Charlotte. "I love this idea and promise we'll do a yearly getaway."

Charlotte nodded, blinking back her own tears. "We have a deal, then."

Jenny stuck out her hand and they shook on it.

"I brought something for you, too," Ashe said shyly. Reaching into the back of the car, he handed Jenny a newspaper-wrapped bundle of greenery.

Jenny pulled back a corner and smiled. "Fresh Mistletoe. Wherever did you find it?"

Charlotte's eyes danced. "At your daddy's house. Ashe spotted it, and one of my young girlfriend helpers climbed up that tree as nimble as a cat and nabbed the mistletoe. We wanted you to have it for your first Christmas here by the lake."

"I'm going to hang this greenery all around the cabin." Jenny carefully nestled it into the bag of gifts on her arm. "Ashe, Luke is out front, getting the fire pit going for the day. He'd be happy to give you a tour. He's wearing a purple down coat." She pointed toward the lake.

Looking excited the way men do when there's a fire to mess with, Ashe trotted off.

Charlotte's face glowed as she watched him.

Jenny put an arm around Charlotte's shoulder. "How are you, girl?"

"Wonderful, marvelous, fantastico," Charlotte warbled. "Best Christmas ever."

Jenny put a finger on her lip and pretended to look thoughtful. "Let's see. You're walking on air. You're bringing the man home to meet your mama and daddy. Are you by any chance in love?"

"I'm so in love and the best thing is, Ashe is, too!" Charlotte said, wonder in her voice. She grabbed Jenny's hands and squeezed them. "You matchmaking us is the most precious gift I've ever been given." Her eyes sparkled with mischief. "And we did it all *in accordance with the terms of the trust,* too."

"Sorry about that double talk, but it got you to the happy ending." Thrilled at her friend's elation, Jenny tilted her head. "Is this heading where I think its heading?"

CHAPTER 22 — A FOREVER LOVE

"Yup." CHARLOTTE'S FACE SHONE WITH joy. "I think we'll get married, and I'll move to Celeste. We'll live not far from you at the lake. You and Luke and Ashe and I will have grand adventures and lots of laughs. Ashe and I will buy an RV and go on camping adventures with you and Luke. I'll bet Nell and Beau would babysit the cabins. Maybe we'll adopt a child, or just take in rescue dogs or cats or horses." Charlotte slipped an arm around Jenny's waist and they walked toward the cabin. "We'll all live happily ever after."

"I love that idea. I hope it turns out exactly that way," Jenny said.

On the stoop of The Dogwood, Charlotte paused to take in the green roofed cabins with their red doors adorned with wreaths and twinkling white lights. She put a hand on her cheek. "This place looks like a rustic, warm, charming fairyland. You did it, Jenny."

Jenny held up a hand. "Not without a ton of help from Luke and his sister, Alice."

"I need an update on that sitch," Charlotte said.

Jenny smiled and pushed open the door of The Dogwood.

Inside, Charlotte quickly shed her coat and kissed Levi on the nose. "Before we catch up, I have a big, fat happy surprise for you."

Jenny sank on the sofa and looked at her expectantly. "Yes?"

Charlotte plunked down beside her. "I told you the open house went well, but I didn't tell you how well. We had sixty-three people come through. This week, the realtor got multiple offers. Three buyers were duking it out." With a flourish, she pulled an envelope from her purse and handed it to Jenny. "This offer is for ten thousand over the asking price with no repair requests. The realtor and Ashe think this is the best offer. If you agree, sign here." Charlotte produced a pen and pointed to spots where Jenny should sign.

Exhaling with a whoosh of relief, Jenny put both hands over her heart and then took the contract. "You don't even know how marvelous this news is. You really don't." She held an inch of air between her thumb and her forefinger. "I've been this close to broke, and every time I turned around, someone was handing me a bill for two hundred or four hundred or a thousand dollars." Jenny signed the document and looked at her friend intently. "Because of your talent and hard work, you've given me a cushion. I can't thank you enough."

"I'm honored to have helped," Charlotte said proudly. Taking a breath, she swished her hair back over her shoulders and got down to business. "All right. I need the CliffsNotes on Luke and on the cabins, STAT."

And Jenny told her everything.

After she'd waved at Charlotte and Ashe as they drove off, Jenny glanced at the time and walked over to see what Luke was up to. He and Hugh had their heads together and a toolbox at the ready as they problem-solved a malfunctioning smoker Hugh had brought with him from home to cook a special Christmas supper for Viv. Luke warned Jenny that the problem might require a run to the hardware store for a part. The two men looked like they were having a grand time.

Calling the dogs and Levi in for company, Jenny turned on the classic holiday station as she scrubbed new potatoes, rinsed asparagus, and put together pecan pie. She hummed along to carols. *God Rest Ye Merry Gentleman* was followed by *The First Noel* and then her favorite, *The Little Drummer Boy.*

After she'd popped the pie in the oven, she pulled up the travel rating site, and felt proud. The Lakeside Resort had been open since only the fifteenth, and she already had four five-star ratings along with enthusiastic descriptions of the property and pictures of the Christmas tree, the cabins, the reclaimed wood on the cabin walls, the dogs and Levi. Lena had posted a whimsical poem about the wonders of the cabins that included verses about *no bears, no cares* and *views of water everywheres.* No wonder Jenny had already gotten those reservations for March earlier this morning and two bookings for June.

On impulse, Jenny got the box Jax had left for her and put it on the kitchen table. Bracing herself, she opened it. Underneath the un-mailed card she'd already read was a folded piece of cream-colored paper, the heavy kind used for sketching. Carefully, Jenny unfolded it, and saw a colorful, detailed, hand-drawn rendering of the property. Jenny recognized her daddy's handwriting in the printed title, *The Lakeside Resort.* In addition to his drawing of the finished cabins, Jax had included four vintage RV's similar to the Airstream situated prettily on the other side of Jenny's. She shook her head in wonder. Daddy had planned on including RV's like his precious Silver Belle. She looked more closely, and saw details like several red canoes pulled up on the lawn waterside, a rope swing that was hung out over the water, and a power boat zooming by towing two small children on tubes. Jenny smiled. She'd found Daddy's vision for the property, and it was surprisingly similar to her own except for the RV's. She couldn't wait to show the rendering to Luke.

Beneath the drawing were more un-mailed cards. Jenny counted ten cards in total, addressed, stamped, sealed and never mailed. Jenny chewed her bottom lip, feeling confused and then pitying Jax. He'd thought enough to buy them and address them, but didn't have the courage to stick them in the mail. Why? Had he been afraid to mail them, worried she wouldn't want to hear from him? Did he feel he didn't have the right because he'd let her down so often?

Digging underneath the pile of cards, Jenny found more cards, but these were ones she'd given him for his birthday and for Father's Day. At the bottom of the box was every school picture she'd ever taken: her as a skinny girl with a pixie cut and bashful expression; an awkward pre-adolescent with braces; a teen with a defiant look in her eyes; and finally, Jenny as a pretty high school senior. Every photo was mounted in a cheap plastic frame.

That was all that was in the box. Jenny rubbed her eyes with her fingers. Jax had wanted to make sure she got the box because he was sending a message. He wanted her to know that he had loved her and had thought of her often, but, for some reason she'd never know, could never be there for her. She sighed so deeply that Levi walked over and rested his head in her lap. Jenny felt sad. Poor Jax. Poor her. What a waste of love.

Someday soon, she'd go through the box again and read every note he'd written in every card, as well as what she'd written to him. But not today. Today was about the present and the future, and she felt a wave of ebullient joy about them both.

Jenny put the box away and sprawled on the couch, thinking. Buddy leaped on the couch and curled up beside her. Jax's gifts to her had provided her with a brand new life. Inheriting the cabins, and being given the gift of a financial buffer with the sale of his house, had changed her life. Closing her eyes, Jenny sent up her version of a prayer.

Thank you, Daddy. I'm not sure you know exactly how much you've helped me, but I'm forever grateful. You have changed my life and helped me feel more alive and happy than I can ever remember being. I'll bet you still love these cabins and are happy to see we managed to finish your dream. They turned out pretty, didn't they? So here's the deal: I'm going to start talking with you more, and I'll be listening for your voice, too. Merry Christmas, Daddy.

After Jenny and Luke shared their Christmas Eve supper, they went outside. The weather was in the high thirties, balmy after the snowstorm just nine days ago. Jenny had splurged on a Christmas present for her and Luke, a double chaise lounge that she'd positioned between The Dogwood and the Silver Belle. Being a proprietress could mean spending a lot of time with guests, and Jenny needed quiet time and privacy, too. This could be a comfortable haven for Jenny and for the two of them to enjoy looking at the lake.

Luke lit a match to the kindling in the little fire pit just outside her cabin, the one that now felt like home. Small flames caught, flared and began to dance.

Luke and Jenny sat side by side and stretched out in the comfortable new chair. Holding hands, they looked out at the moonlight shining a shimmering path on the water. A V-shaped formation of Canada geese flew over their heads, and they could hear the whirring *ffft, ffft, ffft* of their wings.

When Luke pulled her close, Jenny leaned into him, loving the warmth and comfort of being held by this man.

"I got you three practical Christmas presents," Luke said.

Jenny groaned and covered her face with her hands. "I've only gotten you this joint present," she said, tapping a hand on the wooden arm of the chair. "I would have gotten you a few more small presents but I've been going so fast I haven't even been off the property for weeks."

Luke waved a hand dismissively. "Here's number one." He pointed at the fire. "I'm getting that stone man back to build a real fire pit for you. The sand pit served its purpose, but we need something more permanent."

"I love that idea." Jenny said, touched by his thoughtfulness.

Luke went on. "Here's number two. Be right back." Rising, he stepped into the cabin and returned with a microwave oven box that he laid at her feet.

"Appliances *do* make festive Christmas gifts," Jenny said in a teasing tone.

"I just needed a box and recycled one," Luke said with a sheepish grin. "Open it."

Pulling it open, Jenny pulled out a piece of the old barn wood board and tilted it toward the firelight to read the sapphire blue script etched into the sign. *The Dogwood*. A dogwood flower was carved beside the name. Under that sign were seven more for the other cabins.

Touched, Jenny said, "I can't believe you got someone to make such gorgeous signs."

"Glad you like them," Luke said, looking pleased at her reaction. "Number three, you already know about. Charlotte and I are going to fix up the Airstream." His voice grew animated. "We'll make it very cool. We'd respect the vibe and era of the Airstream, but let's modernize it and add a few luxuries."

"Lovely." Jenny pictured a rambling road trip to Nova Scotia or Niagara Falls. Jenny leaned over and touched his cheek. "Let's not improve it so much that it has to stay in one place. I want to see more of America in it with you."

"Agreed." Luke kissed the top of her head. "We'll do that after we get married."

Jenny stared at him, realizing she'd just been proposed to. "Good. I like that plan," she said simply and rested her head on his chest.

Filled with contentment, Jenny watched the guests. They were gathered around the fire pit talking softly and laughing. Viv Sanders in her faux fur hat was teaching a new young guest how to crochet. Hand in hand, Daniel and Harriet walked out to the dock. From an Adirondack beside the fire pit, Hugh strummed a guitar and, in a fine tenor, began singing *Greensleeves*. The other guests gathered around, and when he moved into *It Came Upon a Midnight Clear*, they sang along.

Jenny looked up at the moon and thought about it. For those who believe, Christmas is about love, grace, hope and miracles. She had all those tonight with this lovely man and the Lakeside Resort.

A SPECIAL INVITATION

Dear Reader,

Thank you so much for reading *Christmas at the Lakeside Resort* and spending time with me at Heron Lake. Hope you loved this book.

I'd like to ask for your help. Reader reviews are the most powerful tool for making my book successful. While the story is fresh on your mind, would you please go to Amazon, Goodreads, or your favorite online retail site and write a review?

As always, I am so grateful for your support.

Susan Schild

ACKNOWLEDGEMENTS

My sincerest thanks to:

My lovely readers who have encouraged me and inspired my writing with their comments, reviews and stories.

My wise, encouraging writer friends, Scarlett Dunn, Susie Haught, Barbara Solomon Josselsohn and Judith Keim. Have a look at their books. I think you'd enjoy them.

Queen Kathy L. Murphy who nurtures talent, promotes reading, and inspires adventuresome women everywhere.

Susan Walters Peterson who is a fabulous supporter of writers and reading, and is unfailingly kind. Her FB page is Sue's Booking Agency.

My walking friends, Barb, Gin, Linda, Carol, Gail, Wendy, Charlyne and her husband, *Love ya, honey* John, for their kindness, humor and fashion tips. (Yes, ma'am, you do cut a hole in your sneaker if your toe rubs)

My husband Bryan, who steadies me, rarely complains about frozen dinners during deadlines, and encourages me to put more car chases in my books.

ABOUT THE AUTHOR

Susan Schild writes heartwarming, feel good Southern novels of love and family featuring women over forty bouncing back from trouble, having adventures, and finding their happily ever afters.

A wife and stepmother, Susan enjoys reading and taking walks with her Labrador retriever mixes, Tucker and Gracie. She and her family live in North Carolina.

Susan has used her professional background as a psychotherapist and management consultant to add authenticity to her characters.

Readers can visit Susan's website at:

www.susanschild.com

and sign up for her quarterly newsletters
at http://www.susanschild.com/newsletter/

Follow Susan on Facebook
at https://www.facebook.com/author.schild/

LOOK FOR MY NEXT BOOK

Summer at the Lakeside Cabins, the next book in The Lakeside Resort series, will be released in June of 2019. Look for newbies taking camping trips, adventures on the open road, a visit from Mama, cabin guests who will make you laugh out loud, inn-keeping mishaps and maybe another *I Do* or two.